It Takes a Nation

It Takes a Nation

A NEW AGENDA

FOR FIGHTING POVERTY

• *REBECCA M. BLANK* •

RUSSELL SAGE FOUNDATION

NEW YORK

PRINCETON UNIVERSITY PRESS

PRINCETON, N. J.

Library of Congress Cataloging-in-Publication Data

Blank, Rebecca M.
It takes a nation : a new agenda for fighting poverty / Rebecca M. Blank.
p.   cm.
Includes bibliographical references (p.   ) and index.
ISBN 0-691-02675-0
ISBN 0-691-00401-3 (pbk.)
1. Public welfare—United States.   2. Poverty—Government policy—United States.
3. United States—Economic conditions—1981–   I. Title.
HV95.B59   1996   362.5′8′0973—dc20   96-8671

This book has been composed in Times Roman

Princeton University Press books are printed on acid-free paper and meet the guidelines for
permanence and durability of the Committee on Production Guidelines for Book
Longevity of the Council on Library Resources

Fifth printing, and first paperback printing, with corrections and a new preface, 1998

http://pup.princeton.edu

Printed in the United States of America

5   7   9   10   8   6

• *TO HANNS* •

THE BEST PART OF MY LIFE

• C O N T E N T S •

LESS THAN TWO years have passed since this book went to press in late 1996. During that time, the fundamental facts about poverty in the United States have not changed. But the policy environment has changed, much more extensively than most observers would have predicted, particularly for single mothers with children. One of the primary points of this book is that "poverty" is not synonymous with "single mothers and their children on welfare"; in fact, the majority of the poor are in other types of households and have traditionally had little access to direct cash assistance. Yet, in light of the extensive public attention given to recent policy changes, this preface describes how traditional welfare policies have evolved in the past two years.

The Personal Responsibility and Work Opportunity Reconciliation Act became law in August 1996. One of its most important provisions was to abolish the Aid to Families with Dependent Children (AFDC) program and replace it with the Temporary Assistance for Needy Families (TANF) block grant. This gives states far more leeway to design and run their own public assistance programs, as TANF simply provides a lump sum of money to states which they can use at their discretion to assist low-income families. (TANF dollars combine the support states used to receive for both AFDC cash assistance and welfare-to-work programs.) The legislation also provides strong incentives for states to strengthen efforts to reduce public assistance caseloads and place more recipients in mandatory job search programs.

This book discusses many of the provisions of this new legislation, but it was written before there was an opportunity to observe how states would respond to this challenge. In general, states have responded faster and changed their public assistance systems more extensively than I would have expected. States are experimenting with a host of alternative ways to provide public assistance, including such diverse policies as strong diversion programs (that attempt to provide short-term assistance to applicants without enrolling them in public assistance), lower benefit reduction rates (allowing persons receiving public cash assistance who go to work to keep more of their earnings), case management (providing more aggressive and coordinated assistance to help applicants move into employment), and strong sanctioning policies (strictly enforcing behavioral requirements for public assistance recipients.)

So far, TANF-funded state programs have lived charmed lives. Just as states were trying to move more public assistance recipients into employment, the United States economy produced the strongest labor market of the past thirty years. As I write this, aggregate unemployment rates have been below 5 percent for almost a full year, and unemployment rates among black and Hispanic adult workers are at thirty-year lows. The last two years have provided a better economic environment in which to implement a work-focused welfare reform than any two years since the 1960s.

Strong economic growth has made it possible for states to concentrate on the design and implementation of their new TANF-funded programs, without needing to worry overmuch about the availability of jobs. The strong labor market not only means welfare reform has been easier to implement than it would otherwise, but also promises greater long-term success. The longer the labor market remains strong, the greater the permanent gains made by welfare recipients who enter work—the longer they have to acquire skills, build job experience, and order their lives around a regular schedule of employment, making them less vulnerable to layoffs in the next recession.

Strong state efforts to expand and enforce work requirements, combined with the booming economy, have produced an unprecedented decline in public assistance caseloads. Since 1994, the number of recipients has declined by one-third, with more than four million people leaving the rolls. Like most other economists, I would have expected caseloads to decline during the current long economic expansion, but I would never have predicted the magnitude of change that has actually occurred. The research on why caseloads are shrinking so rapidly indicates that the strong economy is the primary cause of these declines, but state policy innovations have also been important.

As a result of this unexpectedly large caseload decline, most states in the short run are awash in money to spend on public assistance recipients. This is because a state's TANF block grant allotment depends upon how much was spent on public assistance in the state in the early 1990s, a period of record-high caseloads. As caseloads have fallen, states have far more to spend per case than expected. Many states have used at least some of these extra dollars in innovative ways, to strengthen job placement and training programs, to provide smaller caseloads for case managers, to develop follow-up services that help recipients retain jobs, or to fund diversion activities.

Written two years ago, this book is extremely cautious about states' abilities to utilize their TANF dollars effectively to move people off welfare and into employment. This appears in stark contrast to the current claims of success by many governors and state human service commissioners. While I did not foresee the magnitude of caseload declines that has actually occurred (and hence, the extent to which TANF funds have been adequate for most state programs in the short run), I stand by my long-run concerns about funding levels in the TANF block grant and the ability of states to maintain effective employment programs for public assistance recipients in the long term.

I do not think the past two years of booming economic growth provide a good test of the long-run workability of a system of public assistance block grants. Almost all programs work reasonably well in a very strong macro-economy. The question is whether programs can continue to function effectively during times of slower growth or recession. This is particularly important for public assistance, because economic downturns bring increasing program demands. Rising unemployment and limited job availability will both increase the number of people applying for public assistance and reduce the number of people leaving public assistance through employment. The remarkably low unemployment rates of the last two years, which mean that most persons who seriously seek work will find it, are the exception rather than the rule.

At present, it is simply too early to tell how state TANF-funded programs will operate in the long run, which includes both the upside and the downside of the economic cycle. The biggest uncertainty is the extent to which demand for public assistance will increase when the economy slows down. This depends upon how successful the past two years have been in permanently moving former public assistance recipients into stable employment with incomes above the poverty line. Given how poorly anyone predicted the recent caseload decline, the magnitude of any future caseload increase is simply unclear. While I retain a healthy skepticism about the permanence of current caseload declines, largely because of the labor market problems facing less-skilled workers that this book discusses, I also acknowledge the possibility of fundamental changes in the behavior of recipients and in the structure of public assistance programs that may permanently decrease the use of these programs.

Expanded incentives to work, especially among less-skilled women, provide the best reason to believe that at least some share of the current caseload declines may be permanent. Although wages have not risen among less-skilled workers, policies that subsidize wages for low-wage workers have expanded dramatically over the past decade. Since 1990, the maximum subsidy (after inflation) available through the Earned Income Tax Credit (EITC) has expanded by 212 percent for a mother with two children. In addition, the minimum wage has risen from $3.35 in early 1990 to $5.15 in early 1998. (The EITC and minimum wage are described in more detail in chapters 3 and 4.) In the face of long-term declining or stagnant wages among less-skilled workers (see chapter 2), these policies have worked to "make work pay" and offset recent wage declines. These national policy changes have complemented state welfare-to-work efforts as well as the economic expansion, strengthening the impetus toward increased employment and lower caseloads. Several recent research studies indicate these policy changes have been important causes of rising rates of labor force participation among single mothers. If anything, the past two years have only reinforced one of the key policy conclusions of this book—namely, that maintaining the value of the EITC for low-wage workers is crucial for the success of welfare-to-work programs.

One of the most controversial aspects of the 1996 legislation is the federal time limits that mandate that most public assistance recipients can receive no more than sixty months of TANF-funded assistance. At that point they hit a lifetime time limit and are ineligible for any further assistance paid with federal dollars. As of early 1998, thirty-eight states had enacted time limits on the utilization of state funds as well.

Until a substantial share of the long-term recipients approach the time limit, it is very hard to predict how states will implement this aspect of the law.

States can exempt a limited number of recipients from the federal time limits, and states can always choose to continue assistance out of state dollars. I expect that most states will be willing to impose time limits on families who have resisted efforts to help move them into employment (indeed, many of these families will be sanctioned and face benefit reductions long before they hit time limits). It is less clear how willing states will be to impose time limits on families who have made serious efforts at labor market involvement and for whom the time limits would cause hardship. It is also worth noting that few states have the tracking systems that allow them to determine accurately when an individual who moves on and off assistance multiple times has hit the sixty-month time limit, and that there is no cross-state recipient tracking system. These constraints alone will keep time limits from being strictly enforced in many areas.

Despite the foolhardiness of making a prediction about something that will become apparent in the very near future, I expect that the time limits in the 1996 legislation are more likely to be changed in some substantial way than any other aspect of that legislation. Especially if we face a sluggish macroeconomy and higher unemployment at the time when many families begin to hit their time limits, states and the federal government are likely to search for ways to avoid cutting off families who appear to have followed the rules and tried hard to find and keep jobs.

Having said that, I continue to believe that time limits are a very foolish policy. It is always bad policy to enact rules that encourage states to engage in "creative avoidance." Even though I strongly support efforts to help people get off welfare and back to work as soon as possible, I foresee many circumstances where seemingly deserving families who have been working in low-wage jobs hit time limits, and where it may not be in the public interest to cut them off from all further assistance. For example, preset time limits are quite blind to the state of the economy. Time limits make little sense in a recession such as we experienced in the early 1980s, where aggregate unemployment topped 10 percent in some months. Under these circumstances, many less-skilled workers may have few labor market options and hence few alternatives to public assistance.

Eighteen months after the passage of major welfare reform legislation, more has changed than many (including myself) would have believed possible. The labor market has been stronger than expected and many states have taken full advantage of the opportunities handed to them by this legislation to truly "reinvent" their welfare bureaucracies. This is not the end of the story, however. The long-term effects of this law cannot be known until we observe it under circumstances other than a booming economy. Only then will we know how many of those who have left public assistance will reapply and whether current state welfare-to-work programs operate effectively in a slower job market.

This book is about the challenges that face policymakers as they design and refine their public assistance programs in the years ahead. The recent good economic times have made it relatively easy to ignore some of the hard long-term issues that perpetuate poverty in the United States. New state TANF-funded programs designed to move more public assistance recipients into jobs faster have been able to claim substantial success through caseload reductions. Work effort is easy to talk about when jobs are readily available. In the years ahead, we are likely to face an economy with slower growth rates and state programs whose management and design problems will become more apparent over time. A clear understanding of the causes of poverty as well as the promises and problems of various policy remedies will continue to be important; it is to this understanding that my book is dedicated.

WHILE THIS BOOK was in production, Congress passed and President Clinton signed a major new welfare reform bill. This bill abolishes the existing Aid to Families with Dependent Children program and replaces it with the Temporary Assistance to Needy Families (TANF) block grant, giving states far greater discretion over the design of cash public asistance. While the changes in this bill are not yet fully implemented by the states, the implications of this new legislation are addressed throughout these chapters. The new legislation mandates that recipients of federal block grant money must be employed or involved in a work program after two years of cash assistance, and requires states to have 50 percent of their caseload in work programs by early in the next decade. The legislation limits eligibility for federal cash assistance dollars to five years in a person's lifetime, although 20 percent of a state's caseload may be exempted from this requirement.

State program officials, who now face the responsibility of redesigning their cash assistance programs, are the group at whom this book is most directly aimed. This group should find many parts of the book useful, including the sections that summarize what the research literature says about the effects and the effectiveness of various antipoverty programs that have operated in the recent past; the sections that describe how to run effective targeted programs, particularly effective welfare-to-work programs, and the sections that propose how to set up a viable package of public assistance benefits that promote work but also provide assistance to those who need it. Other sections address some of the potential pitfalls and problems that states will face under this new legislation, problems which I suspect will demand future legislative amendments in order to address.

I had been thinking about writing a book like this for several years, but it was the welfare reform debate starting in 1993 within the Clinton administration that gave me the motivation to actually do it. The Congress elected in November 1994 channeled that debate into a variety of new directions. Listening to the public statements about the poor, and about the nature and history of U.S. antipoverty efforts, I became increasingly angry. I thought the discussants across the political spectrum were focusing on a relatively narrow set of issues. In a number of cases, the information being conveyed was simply wrong—contradicted by years of program experience and social science research. In other cases it was incomplete—discussing one aspect of a problem without giving attention to other, equally important, facts and concerns.

For better or worse, I am a social scientist. For me, this means I believe two things. First, I have always found that the world is more complicated than simple answers and simple solutions typically imply. Hence my frustration with those who think single legislative reforms will "solve poverty" or those who present images of "the poor" that typically do more to stereotype than to explain. Second, I believe that there are useful ways to explore and test hypotheses about people's behavior and about program effects. These research methodologies are hardly foolproof, but there are better and worse ways to investigate the world empirically. Rather than viewing social science as a group of competing studies which all say different things (the view one sometimes receives in the popular media), there are ways to distinguish between good and bad research; one should give serious attention to those results based on the most credible research methodologies, and give less attention to other conclusions. Over the past thirty years, social scientists who study poverty have built up an enormous body of research. I take the conclusions from that work seriously. No one study is typically conclusive (in fact, those who cite a single study as proof of their beliefs should be viewed with skepticism), but multiple studies in many areas now point toward the same general set of conclusions.

This book is my effort to talk as a social scientist about what we know about poverty and about policies to alleviate it, utilizing the research and factual data but presenting it in a way that makes it accessible to those who are not trained in the (often obscure) methodological debates and mysteries that fascinate me and my colleagues. As such, it is a response to the past three years of public rhetoric about the poor that too often ignores this evidence.

I also have to confess that whenever one jumps into a project of this sort, it is necessary to be more than just a social science researcher. The last few chapters of this book are much more about my interpretation of the recent policy debate and my judgments about the appropriate direction for policy, than they are about any impartial presentation of the facts. For this I do not apologize. Readers who want to skip those chapters should do so.

I confess up front that I have always considered myself a pragmatist and a moderate in this debate. This book reflects that. While some of the positions that I take here can be labeled liberal, others will resonate with a more conservative perspective. I am less concerned with fitting into any preconceived ideological positions than I am with trying honestly to weigh the evidence and provide a balanced perspective on the problems of poverty and its related policies.

The author of any book of this length and depth owes thanks to many people. The ideas and conclusions developed in this book are based on many years of research and teaching on issues relating to poverty and the well-being of low-income families. I owe a debt to all of the past students who have been in my Poverty and Public Policy classes, as well as to the many colleagues with whom I have discussed these issues over the years.

Having the time to complete this manuscript was a gift. The Russell Sage Foundation and the Rockefeller Foundation provided me with generous funding to work on the manuscript. The Center for Urban Affairs and Policy Research at Northwestern University gave me additional resources and time.

Leslie Moscow and Rebecca London both did prodigious amounts of work as research assistants and treated this book as seriously as if it had been their own. I owe them an enormous debt. John Williams and Joe Marzo also worked hard on helping me get the facts right and get the manuscript into its final shape. Susan Lloyd and Peter Gottschalk read the entire manuscript in draft form and provided extensive comments. Timothy Bartik, David Card, Janet Currie, Fred Doolittle, Harry Holzer, Larry Katz, Frank Levy, Jane Mansbridge, Robert Moffitt, Richard Nathan, Jane Waldfogel, and Burton Weisbrod read particular chapters where they knew much more than I and were kind enough to correct some of my mistakes. The "Well-being of Children" research group at the National Bureau of Economic Research provided good feedback on chapter 4 of the book, and several groups of colleagues at Northwestern did the same for chapter 6. Irv Garfinkel, John McKnight, Richard Murnane, Alice O'Conner, Ed Pauly, and Jim Rosenbaum all provided useful suggestions on content at an early stage. All of the remaining errors are my fault alone.

A number of organizations let me visit, talk, and observe their operations. I am particularly grateful to Jody Raphael and the staff at the Chicago Commons' ETC program; to Steven Redfield at STRIVE; to the staff of CET in San Jose, including its executive director, Russell Tershey; to the staff at the Riverside, California, GAIN office, particularly director Marilyn Kuhlman; to the staff of the Dudley Street Neighborhood Initiative, particularly its acting director, Al Lovato; and to the staff at the Grand Rapids Parents' Fair Share Program, particularly its program director, Ray Jackson.

Eric Wanner and David Haprof at the Russell Sage Foundation, and my editor at Princeton University Press, Peter Dougherty, have provided both wisdom and encouragement.

Finally, I thank my husband, Johannes Kuttner, the person who has provided the best advice, the most careful comments, and the most love throughout the process of writing this book.

It Takes a Nation

ABOUT twenty-five people were in the room, largely middle class, largely white, and ranging in age from their early twenties to mid-seventies. They were concerned and caring people; who else would attend a three-week discussion series on poverty and public policy at their church? I opened the conversation by asking them what they hoped to learn from me and from the discussion. The gentleman in the front row spoke first. "I read so much about inner city poverty here in Chicago," he said. "The problems seem so enormous—high crime, no jobs, teenage pregnancy. I want to know if there's anything we can really do to make things better."

The woman behind him spoke next. "I really worry about all those mothers out there on their own raising children. People in Washington talk about cutting off welfare, but won't that just make it harder for them? I know that it's popular to be angry at people on welfare right now, but isn't the program necessary? Would they be able to support themselves and their children if they took a fast food job instead?"

The elderly gentleman toward the back leaned forward. "I don't want to strand the poor, but we're spending so much money on welfare and we've got to get the federal deficit under control. What are we really getting for that money? The problem only seems to get worse. I don't see that past welfare reforms have accomplished much. Maybe it's time to get tough."

As the conversation continued, several themes came through that I hear again and again when I lead public discussions about poverty and need: concern about the effects of poverty on the lives of those who are poor, particularly on children and youth; frustration with a problem that won't go away; anger that current policies have seemingly done so little and a new willingness to blame both the policies and the people for the persistence of poverty; desire for a solution to poverty that really works.

About a month after this conversation took place, I was sitting at a lunch table with a group of AFDC recipients involved in a Chicago employment training program, talking with them about their experiences with AFDC and with the labor market. These women used different language and spoke from a very different perspective than the other group. When they talked about problems of "the poor" they knew they were talking about themselves. But as I listened to them I started to hear some familiar themes. They were essentially talking about the same issues and concerns: anger with how the current system operates, frustration with their sense of being "stuck," worry about the effect of their economic problems on their children, and hope that this new program might help them accomplish some permanent changes in their lives.

These feelings of frustration, anger, and the desire for something different in dealing with poverty and policy in the United States are widespread. They raise two core questions for American social policy:

1. Why has poverty been so intractable and persistent in this country?
2. How can we design and implement a more effective system of antipoverty programs for this country?

These are the questions that this book addresses.

LOOKING AT THE FACTS

A great deal of rhetoric has taken place about poverty and welfare reform over the last several years, ranging from charges that the poor are simply lazy to charges that existing antipoverty programs have completely failed. Not much of this has involved discussion of the facts. Many Americans are misinformed about who is poor in America today, why they are poor, and how their poverty has been affected by existing public assistance programs. In this book I analyze what we know and what we don't know about poverty and the efforts to reduce it, using thirty years of social science research and program evaluation. One of the book's primary purposes is to break down some of the public myths about poverty and provide a clearer and more nuanced understanding about why poverty has been so persistent in this country, even in the face of enormous public investment and intervention.

Among the statements that have frequently been heard in recent years are claims such as the following:

- The problem of poverty is largely caused by teen pregnancies.
- Welfare programs encourage unmarried women to have lots of children and spend years on public assistance.
- Today's poor primarily live in urban ghettos, and are African American, Latino, or immigrants.
- Poor people today are less willing to work than ever before.
- Public assistance programs have failed, and may even have been a cause of high rates of poverty in the United States.
- The private sector, particularly private charities, would do a much better job than the government in helping the poor.

Like many stereotypes, there is some truth in each of these statements. Some government efforts to reduce poverty have failed, some of the poor are black families in urban ghettos, some of the poor had children as unmarried teenagers, some of those receiving welfare continue to receive assistance for a long time, and some of the poor do not work.

But all of these statements are more false than they are true. Many public assistance programs have accomplished exactly what they set out to do; most of the poor are white, and the vast majority live in areas of mixed and diverse income; many public assistance recipients are short-term users; and many among the poor do work a substantial amount.

This book presents the facts about poverty and policy in America in chapters 1 through 5. Three primary lessons emerge:

Lesson 1. *In the last decade, we have consistently misunderstood the nature of poverty in America, believing that it is more behavioral, more ghetto-based, and more a problem experienced by people of color. Hence, for many middle-income Americans, the poor have come to seem alien and less "like us" than they actually are.* Chapter 1 explores the question of "Who is poor in America today?" and presents a far more diverse population than most people imagine.

For instance, nightly news stories present frequent images of poverty that emphasize the "dangerous poor" in urban ghetto neighborhoods, with high crime rates, gang violence, dilapidated housing, and few job opportunities. Not coincidentally, this image of poverty is almost entirely a black image. The ongoing discussion of the American "underclass," and the images of ghetto poverty that appear continuously on the front pages of major urban newspapers, have made the poor seem increasingly alien to many Americans. It has been easy—for middle-income Americans of all races and backgrounds—to feel angry, frustrated, and distant from this group among the poor.

In reality, the poor are much more like "us" than like "them." The majority of poor live in mixed-income neighborhoods. A growing number of poor families are headed by women, but this is true of middle-income families as well. These women face real strains balancing the joint demands of family and work. To the extent that single mothers make use of welfare, they tend to use it intermittently, when they can't find work or when their family demands are more intense. Very few are continuously on welfare for long periods of time, although uncertain jobs and changing family demands mean that many women go on and off welfare over time. Among all poor—white, black, Hispanic, and others—a great majority express hopes that are very similar to the hopes of all Americans. They want their children to do well and to avoid trouble; they want to find a stable job and a nice place to live.

Lesson 2. *The primary change in the lives of the poor over the past 20 years has been the deteriorating set of economic opportunities available to less-skilled workers. The favorite solution to poverty among most Americans has always been overall economic growth that creates jobs and helps the poor escape poverty through work and wages. Unfortunately, wage rates have declined steadily on the jobs available to less-skilled workers, which means that employment has become progressively less effective at reducing poverty.* Chapter 2 discusses these major economic changes and the ways in which they interact with the problems of poverty.

The U.S. economy experienced several extended periods of economic expansion in the 1980s and 1990s, when unemployment fell rapidly. In past decades, such expansions have always been associated with sharp declines in poverty. As chapter 2 describes in more detail, this did not happen in the most recent decades. The expansion in jobs available to less-skilled workers was offset by declining wages on these jobs. People worked more, but they earned less for every hour that they worked. The net result was that poverty remained stubbornly high throughout the 1980s and 1990s, despite overall economic growth. The problem wasn't behavior. It was the jobs.

Among men who are high school graduates and work full-time, wage rates have declined more than 10 percent since 1979 after accounting for inflation; among high school dropouts, the decline is more than 20 percent.[1] Perhaps not surprisingly, it is exactly the group of men whose earnings opportunities have fallen the most who have been most likely to leave the mainstream labor market over these years. Wages have not fallen as much for less-skilled women, but these women continue to have wage levels far below those of men. This group has always had access to bad jobs at bad wages (far worse than those available to their brothers with low education levels), and they still do. Despite stereotypes about poor single mothers' work efforts, low-income women who head families are working somewhat more in the mid-1990s than they were twenty years ago, but they are earning no more now than then.

Because of their low earnings levels, combined with family obligations, it is extremely difficult for less-skilled single mothers to escape poverty through their own earnings, even when they work many hours. For this group in particular, the exhortation to "get a job" is simply not sufficient. While employment is an important component in their effort to escape poverty, their earnings are often insufficient to allow them to support their family and pay the rent, put food on the table, and clothe their children. Without additional sources of income, work alone does not provide economic self-sufficiency. These economic facts have been almost entirely ignored in the recent welfare reform discussion.

Such economic changes interact with who the poor are and how they behave. For instance, the increasing number of children who live only with their mothers has made children more vulnerable to poverty since single-mother families have less ability to increase their income through work. Similarly, changes in the economies of our cities over the past thirty years have interacted with other forces to worsen problems in urban ghetto neighborhoods. The groups who are working less in recent years are exactly the same groups who have faced significant declines in their earning power through declining wages in the labor market.

Lesson 3. Out of a frustration with persistent poverty, a nihilistic response has emerged that "nothing works" or, perhaps more appropriately, "nothing the federal government does to fight poverty works." *"Nothing works" seriously misinterprets history and ignores the real successes we have achieved. It also ignores thirty years of knowledge about what works and what does not, accumulated through observation, experience, and program evaluation.* Chapters 3 through 5 present evidence about the impact of government programs for the poor, discussing both their successes and failures. Recent reforms in public assistance programs have dramatically changed the nature of

U.S. antipoverty efforts. Some of these changes are long overdue; some of them are shortsighted and create the potential for very real future problems. Chapter 3 reviews the major public assistance programs and policies in the United States over the past twenty years and describes these recent changes.

Chapter 4 directly addresses the "nothing works" claim and shows that many programs have met their goals. To claim that these programs have failed because they haven't removed people from poverty is to expect something that these programs were never designed to accomplish. Many programs were designed as a *safety net*, to give poor families somewhat higher incomes or better access to food and health care than they would have otherwise. In that they have largely succeeded.

For instance, many of our nutrition assistance programs, such as Food Stamps for low-income households, have improved the health of the poor, as has the availability of Medicaid, which provides public health insurance for many low-income families. These programs were never designed to decrease cash poverty; they were designed to improve nutrition and health among the poor and they have done so.

Similarly, virtually all of the evidence indicates that cash assistance programs *have* made families less poor. While these programs have some undesirable effects, extensive numbers of research studies suggest that these effects are small, relative to their poverty-reduction effect. The payment levels in most cash assistance programs are quite low and were not designed to move families across the poverty line and out of poverty entirely. But they *have* raised family incomes closer to the poverty line and reduced economic need. For a mother with two children, having $8,000 to spend on her family is better than having $6,000, even if she remains poor.

Chapter 5 discusses the reasons why the government must be involved in antipoverty efforts. Both political and economic arguments can be made for the public provision of assistance to the poor. It is not by accident that virtually all societies try in some way to assist their poorest members through government-organized programs. In contrast to public programs, the work of private charities in the United States is quite limited and in many cases complements rather than competes with governmental efforts. While some expansions in private effort might be desirable, the charitable sector could not possibly replace the antipoverty efforts of the government. In a similar vein, there are also reasons for wanting *all* levels of government involved in antipoverty programs. While the particular contribution of the federal government should be different from the contribution of state and local governments, all three levels of government have a role to play and bring particular skills and abilities into the public policy arena. Recent efforts to limit the role of the federal government threaten the ability of other levels of government to do their job properly, forcing them to take up functions that the federal government is better equipped to perform.

These three lessons form the core analysis of the book: a better understanding of who the poor are, a better understanding of how deteriorating economic opportunities for less-skilled workers have shaped today's poverty, and a better understanding of what works and what does not work in public policy efforts to alleviate poverty.

Using this analysis, in chapters 6 and 7 I discuss the future of public policy aimed at helping alleviate poverty. Chapter 6 contains an analysis of the current direction of change in public policies for the poor, away from broad-based redistribution programs and toward more targeted, behaviorally linked programs. These changes will solve some problems but may well create others. I draw on past experience to develop criteria about how to run such programs as effectively as possible. This chapter might be particularly useful for state-level policymakers who are thinking about how to reconfigure their public assistance policies.

In chapter 7 I propose a variety of ways to improve current public assistance policy. There is no one answer to the problem of poverty in America today. The poor are too diverse and the problems are too complex. People who claim they have "the answer" to poverty are deluding themselves and others. No single program or approach can do the job. I present a series of proposals that accomplish what I believe most Americans want from their public assistance programs: incentives for individuals to seek employment and act responsibly within their families while providing important safety-net protections.

To the extent this book has a single message, that message is to avoid simple explanations for poverty and the false promise of simple solutions. There is no single cause of poverty, and there is no easy way to abolish it. The challenge is to build a balanced system which relies on the contributions of many different groups and programs. There is certainly no *cheap* way to fight poverty, despite what some would have you believe. In fact, many of the programs that can be most useful in long-term poverty alleviation, such as employment assistance and job training, may cost *more* than simply writing people monthly checks.

Public assistance programs should emphasize (and in many cases demand) employment and enforce the responsibility of the poor to earn what they can, but they must also be realistic about the economic changes of the past twenty years. We must recognize that many people will not be able to earn enough on their own in the labor market to escape poverty without ongoing supplements to their earnings. Ongoing public support for some families is likely to be necessary. We must also recognize the responsibilities of both mothers and fathers in supporting their children and demand private contributions from absent fathers as a complement to public contributions. Public antipoverty programs should work together with the private and nonprofit sectors, using their knowledge and skills as important inputs into antipoverty efforts. Finally, public assistance programs should make use of the comparative advantages of all levels of government, allowing for state and local flexibility, while also utilizing the more stable funding and greater ability of the federal government to evaluate and monitor programs.

The policy proposals in this book are not theoretical notions but ideas that many existing programs have already successfully implemented. Examples of public assistance programs that have met the challenge of operating effectively in today's complex environment are scattered throughout the book, both in the text as well as in a series of inserts that describe some particularly interesting and effective programs that are currently in existence.

We can do better in our fight against poverty than we have in the recent past; our current programs are not as well designed as they should be, and they rely too heavily on the government alone. Ultimately, the long-term costs of poverty in the United States will not be reduced as long as we assume that this is someone else's job.

The government has a key ongoing role in public assistance to the poor, but government programs must be buttressed by the behavior of individuals and the involvement of civic institutions, from charities to businesses to community organizations. Too often, we have been told that the federal government has the responsibility to alleviate poverty, or that state governments can do this if the federal government would just get out of the way, or that private charities can do this more effectively than the government. Reducing the costs of poverty will take involvement by *all* of these groups, as well as by all of us. We need to teach *our* children about the importance of work and the importance of community; *we* need to demand effective public schools for all Americans and to demand effective policing in all areas of our cities; we need to assure that all adults and teenagers receive the message that having children means eighteen years of financial and emotional support and that parenting and marriage are not to be engaged in casually. The government alone cannot solve the problems of our society that lead to long-term poverty. The government can only alleviate some of those problems, and it can do so most effectively only when private citizens and civic institutions are working with it. It takes a nation—all parts of a nation—to fight poverty.

This book confronts the very real and complex problems of poverty, but it also looks beyond them to discuss the new nexus of policy possibilities that are already emerging to deal with the new economy and the new demography of the poor. The problem of poverty in America is not new, but the nature of the problem is changing over time. We need to understand those changes in order to revise our strategies for fighting poverty and to think in a new way about antipoverty efforts. That is the primary goal of this book.

A NOTE ABOUT THE DEFINITION OF POVERTY

The term "poverty" is used throughout this book, and it is important to understand the definition of this word. In the mid-1960s, the federal government adopted an official definition of the "poverty line," an amount of annual income estimated to be necessary for minimal economic survival and social participation in the United States This has been the basis of the U.S. definition of poverty ever since.[2]

For reasons discussed below, I commonly refer to the poor as those who are below this officially designated line. But recognizing the limits to this measure of poverty, I also discuss a variety of alternative forms of deprivation throughout this book. This includes looking at such diverse issues as the duration of poverty over time, nutritional and health status among the poor, or the availability of jobs for less-skilled workers.

"Poverty" refers to people who live in families with cash income levels below the official U.S. poverty line. In 1994, this was $15,029 for a family with two parents and two children and $11,980 for a family with one parent and two children. All related persons who live together and whose total cash income is below these levels are counted as poor. Using this definition, a total of 38.1 million people lived in poor families in 1994, which represents 14.5 percent of the population.[3]

The poverty line is actually not one number but a series of numbers, designed for families of different sizes. The calculations of poverty lines were based on the minimal amount of money that the U.S. Department of Agriculture estimated a family of a given size needed to spend in order to maintain adequate nutrition, multiplied by a factor of three. Why three? At the time, the average family's total expenditures were three times their food budget. In 1965, this method set $3,500 as the poverty line for a family of four. Since that time, the poverty line has simply been updated each year by multiplying the 1965 line by the increase in the Consumer Price Index to take account of changes in inflation in the economy. No changes have been made that would adjust for changes in patterns of spending over the last three decades.

Poverty is a family-based concept in the United States. An individual is poor if his or her family's income is less than the official poverty line for that size family. The family includes all related persons who live together. Thus, a married couple living with their parents is considered one large family unit, and either all individuals in the family are poor or none is poor. Two sisters who live together with their children are considered one family unit. Two unrelated roommates who live together are two separate family units, and poverty is calculated separately for each of them. This family-based concept of poverty assumes relatives who live together share their income and are a single economic unit, while unrelated persons who live together do not share income and are not an economic unit.

To decide if a family is poor, their cash income is compared to the official poverty line. This creates two major problems. First, since our current definition of poverty was set in the mid-1960s many noncash public assistance programs have grown in size. This includes programs such as Food Stamps, publicly provided medical insurance, and reduced-rent housing assistance. These benefits are not counted in family income and thus are not considered when calculating a family's poverty status. If they were included, the poverty count would be lower among groups that receive substantial noncash assistance.

On the other hand, taxes and unavoidable work expenses are not subtracted from a family's resources. A family that earns $12,000 in cash but has to pay $1,000 in taxes should be counted as having $11,000 to spend. But the current poverty count ignores tax payments. Similar problems occur with regard to out-of-pocket work expenses. If a woman must pay for child care in order to work, her available income is probably best calculated as her earnings minus at least some portion of her child care expenses. But the poverty calculation counts her full earnings. If taxes and unavoidable work expenses were included in the poverty calculation, more low-income working families would be counted as poor.

There is also no adjustment for differences in cost-of-living across regions or between urban and rural areas. The poverty line is a single national number, used for all families regardless of where they live. As it turns out, the main item whose cost differs dramatically between areas is housing, and housing is a significant part of many family budgets. Thus, the poverty definition probably counts too many rural and small-town families as poor (who face relatively low housing costs) and too few urban families as poor (who face relatively high housing costs).

There are many other problems with the current poverty measure, which have been well discussed elsewhere. A recent study by the National Research Council[4] proposed major changes that would correct many of these problems, providing an improved definition of both the poverty line and an improved calculation of household resources, and these changes are under discussion within the U.S. government. The adoption of these recommendations would greatly improve our statistics on economic need and poverty.

While recognizing the limitations to the poverty definition used by the United States, in this book I nonetheless use the officially reported poverty numbers in many places in this book for several reasons. First, they are the numbers which have been broadly used in all research and analyses of the problem of poverty over the past twenty years. Although they have problems, they almost surely get the big picture right: for instance, no one doubts the group comparisons in these numbers that show the poverty rate among African Americans is far higher than among white Americans, or that the poverty rate among single mothers is much higher than among married couples.

Second, it is not clear that there is a consistent bias in the current poverty numbers, making them either too low or too high. Correcting some of the problems with the poverty count would raise the number, while correcting others would lower it. The National Research Council report suggests the problem is less with the overall number than with the relative poverty rate among a few groups: poverty among workers should be a little higher, while poverty among some groups that get substantial government non-cash assistance should be a little lower, as mentioned above.

The biggest problem over time in the official poverty numbers probably occurred in the 1970s, when noncash assistance expanded rapidly for low-income families. None of this was reflected in the poverty count. Indeed, data that compare poor people's income to what they actually buy and consume find that consumption clearly rose over that decade. But since 1980, both the official poverty counts and the consumption data show similar trends, with relatively unchanged levels of poverty and need over the past fifteen years.[5] This suggests that during the last fifteen years of history—the main period with which this book is concerned—the trends in official poverty have been similar to the trends in other measures of need.

One charge often leveled against the U.S. poverty calculations is that they include many people who might not be considered "poor" if one knew more about their circumstances. For instance, a small number of people who own their own businesses may actually report negative cash incomes for the year, making them poor in the official statistics even through they have very high asset levels. As it turns out, this problem is relatively small. Only one percent of the poor actually have negative incomes and/or earnings (this is the group among the poor most likely to report much higher incomes in a subsequent year). Similarly, only 6 percent of the poor are full-time students, people who may be cash-poor in the short-term but for whom this poverty is "self-chosen."[6] In short, while there are disagreements about exactly who is above or below any arbitrary poverty line, the current poverty count does indeed appear to be able to identify those with low incomes and limited economic resources.

Finally, a last concern with the typical poverty numbers is that they merely count people as poor or not poor, without any indication of the depth of poverty. Essentially, they show how many people fall on either side of a relatively arbitrary poverty-line threshold. While this provides some measure of need in a society, it tells us nothing about whether some groups of poor individuals are better or worse off than other groups among the poor. For this reason, in a number of places in this book I will look at measures of poverty that go beyond simple poverty counts. This includes looking at the duration of poverty experienced by different groups, as well as looking at the depth of poverty, by calculating *how far* income falls below the poverty line.

The Changing Face of Poverty

WHICH of the following statements are true and which are false?

• Most of the poor are women or children in single-parent families who receive welfare.
• Most poor families have no working adults.
• The majority of poor are African American or Latino.
• The poor typically live in urban ghettos.
• The poor typically live in isolated rural areas.
• Elderly persons are disproportionately likely to be poor.
• Poor families are larger than nonpoor families.

As it turns out, all of these statements are false. The composition of the poor has been changing rapidly over the past two decades. Things that used to be true in the 1960s—the poor lived in rural areas, had larger families, and were disproportionately elderly—were not true by the 1990s. Images of the poor which we often receive in the media—that the poor are mostly black or Latino, are single mothers, live in urban ghetto areas, and don't work—are not accurate pictures.

Our mental images about who the poor are, where they live, and how they live has lagged behind a changing reality. Extensive media coverage of the very real problems of urban ghetto neighborhoods—the so-called underclass areas—has led many Americans to believe that this is the dominant face of poverty, when in reality only about 12 percent of the poor live in such neighborhoods. Ongoing public discussion about the problems of welfare recipients have led many to believe that most of the poor are never-married single mothers and their children. In reality, less than half of the poor are single parents and their children; less than 20 percent of the poor live in families with never-married mothers.

In short, there is no one "face" of poverty in America. Simplistic images of the poor only lead to a misunderstanding of poverty. Some poor live in extremely dangerous and troubled urban ghetto neighborhoods, but most are in more diverse communities. Some poor engage in crime or gang activity, or use drugs, but most do not. Some poor do not work, but most live in families where at least one person works at least part-time and/or part-year.

Much of the recent discussion about poverty has emphasized certain behavioral problems as defining characteristics for poverty, such as teenage pregnancy, poor work habits, parental desertion, or involvement in drugs and crime. These behavioral images particularly emphasize the "otherness" of the poor, making it easy for middle Americans to feel little sympathy or connection with them. All of these behaviors are major problems in today's society, affecting far too many people, but they do not accurately characterize many low-income families.

The face of the poor *has* changed over time, although many of these changes are mirrored throughout society, among the middle class as well as the poor. There are many more single mothers raising children among the poor, as there are among all income groups; there are fewer elderly poor, as resources among the elderly have improved throughout society; poor families are smaller, as family size has fallen at all income levels.

These changes in the composition of the poor have created new challenges for policymakers and made many of our traditional antipoverty strategies less effective. In particular, the growing share of the poor who are single mothers with children face different problems escaping poverty than do single individuals or married-couple families. Single-mother families typically have only one adult, which means that their earning opportunities are limited to what a single person can earn. In addition, single mothers who work often earn less than adult men in married-couple families because less-skilled women typically have much lower earning levels than less-skilled men, a subject that is the focus of the next chapter. Mothers might also be seriously limited in when and how much they can work by parental responsibilities and child care availability.

Similarly, although only about 12 percent among the poor live in ghetto neighborhoods in our inner cities, the multiple problems faced by these families often make them less responsive to many antipoverty efforts. The people in these neighborhoods must deal with poorly performing public institutions (such as inadequate public schools), the absence of any economic base in their neighborhoods, and serious problems of dilapidated housing and high crime. Too many families in these areas are caught in a downward spiral of problems, with no way to escape. Policies that tend to focus on single specific issues—school reform by itself, or welfare reform by itself, or improved policing efforts alone—rarely address the range of problems that encompass these neighborhoods and are rarely effective as single efforts.

The changing face of poverty in American demands programs and policies that are appropriate to today's problems. This chapter lays the groundwork for understanding who is poor and why they are poor, a necessary first step before we can discuss policy in more detail.

1.1 WHO IS POOR IN AMERICA TODAY?

SUMMARY. *The poor are an extremely heterogenous group of persons. Half are either below the age of 18 or over the age of 65. Although poverty among the elderly is at an all-time low, poverty among children remains distressingly high, and is related to the growth in single-parent families among the poor. But even this trend is often exaggerated. Almost*

40 percent of all poor families with children are still headed by married couples. The poor are both white and black, single and married, young and old.

Different images of the poor evoke very different responses from Americans. Imagine four different pictures of poverty: (1) a group of children playing in an urban park with their mothers watching; (2) an elderly woman sitting at a table in a shabby one-room apartment; (3) three African American young men hanging out on an urban street corner; and (4) a homeless man panhandling on the corner of a downtown city. Most people will respond very differently to each of these pictures, with a different mix of sympathy and judgment. Each of these images is an accurate picture of real poverty in America today, although none of them alone is representative of all poor people. The poor are a very heterogeneous and mixed group in America; one reason our responses to poverty often seem confused and contradictory is because we react differently to different groups among the poor.

There were 38.1 million people in the United States in 1994 whose family income was below the poverty line, representing 14.5 percent of the population. These are not small numbers, and it is not surprising that they encompass a wide range of families and individuals.[1]

The eight pie charts in figure 1.1 show how the poor and the nonpoor were distributed in 1993 by age, race, family type, and education.[2] About 40 percent of the poor are children, while only 9 percent are elderly. The remaining half of all poor individuals are adults between the ages of 18 and 64.

Contrary to many people's perceptions, less than half the poor (48 percent) are African American or Latino. Forty-eight percent are white, and the remaining 4 percent are Native Americans, Asians, and other peoples of color. While blacks and Latinos are much more likely to live in poverty than whites, a much larger share of the population is white, meaning that almost half of the poor are non-Latino white. But a comparison between the poor and nonpoor shows a disproportionate level of poverty among people of color in the United States: they compose 52 percent of the poor and only 22 percent of the nonpoor.

In terms of family structure, single-mother families are the largest (and fastest-growing) family type. About 43 percent of all poor persons live in families headed by a single parent, almost all of them women. Among this group, less than half (about two out of five) are headed by never-married mothers. But many poor families are headed by married couples; another 35 percent of poor persons live in married-couple families. The remaining 22 percent of the poor are single individuals who live alone without other relatives. In the nonpoor population, there are far fewer single people, either living on their own or heading families, and far more married couples. We discuss these different groups among the poor in the rest of this section.

Finally, figure 1.1d shows the differences in educational levels between the

Figure 1.1. Composition of poor and nonpoor families in the United States, 1993, by
(a) age, (b) race and ethnicity, (c) family type, and (d) educational attainment (age 25 and up).
(*Source*: Author's tabulations from 1994 March Current Population Survey)

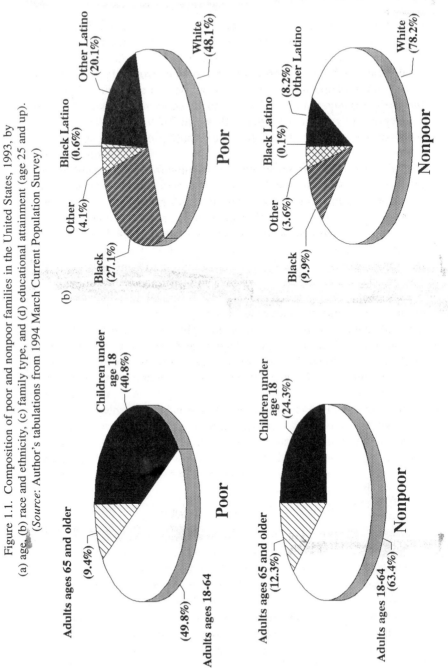

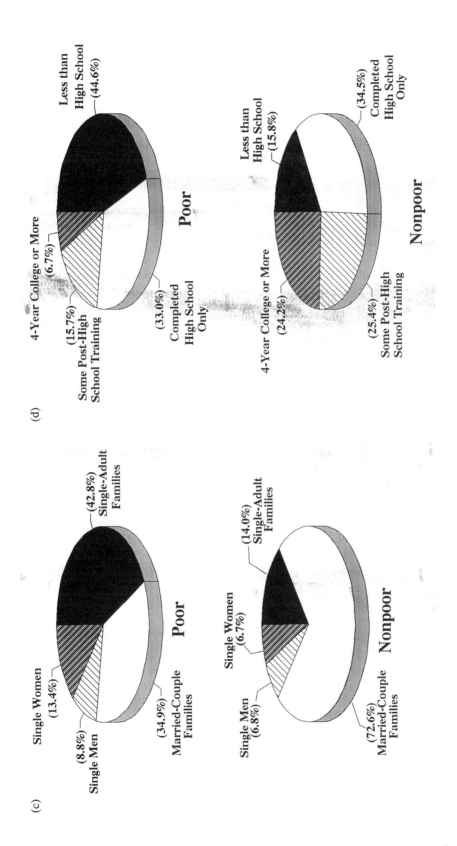

(c)

Single Women
(13.4%)

(42.8%)
Single-Adult
Families

Single Men
(8.8%)

(34.9%)
Married-Couple
Families

Poor

Single Women
(6.7%)

(14.0%)
Single-Adult
Families

Single Men
(6.8%)

(72.6%)
Married-Couple
Families

Nonpoor

(d)

Less than
High School
(44.6%)

4-Year College or More
(6.7%)

Some Post-High
School Training
(15.7%)

(33.0%)
Completed
High School
Only

Poor

(34.5%)
Completed
High School
Only

Less than
High School
(15.8%)

4-Year College or More
(24.2%)

(25.4%)
Some Post-High
School Training

Nonpoor

poor and the nonpoor. These differences will be highly important when we turn to a discussion of wage and earning opportunities among the poor in the next chapter. Among the poor, close to 80 percent have only a high school degree or are high school dropouts. Among the nonpoor, only 50 percent are in this position. Few among the poor hold college degrees.

MOTHERS AND CHILDREN

As the number of single-parent families has grown in this country, single mothers and their children have increased as a share of the poor population. In 1970, 48 percent of poor families with children were headed by single mothers. By 1993, single mothers headed 60 percent of poor families with children. Among all age groups, race groups, and family types in America today, a single mother with children has the highest probability of being poor.

Figure 1.2 looks at poverty rates among single mothers and children and contrasts it to overall poverty rates among whites, blacks, and Hispanics. There is a four in ten chance that a white single mother and her children will be poor, while among black and Latina women who are raising children on their own, six out of ten are poor. These numbers have changed little over time: single mothers have always been extremely poor. What has changed is that there are many more single mothers now than in earlier decades, and as a result, they make up a larger share of the poor. The share of single mothers who have never married is also increasing. In 1983, 27 percent of poor single mothers had never married; by 1994, 39 percent of poor single mothers had never married.[3]

The growth in single-mother families and their very high likelihood of being poor is a primary reason why child poverty rates in America are at appallingly high levels. Well over one-fifth of today's children live in families whose income is below the poverty line, as figure 1.3 indicates. Over half, 57 percent, of these children are in single-mother families. A white child being raised only by a mother has a better than 45 percent probability of being poor. For a black or Latino child in a single-mother household, the probability of being poor is around two-thirds.

Child poverty rates are higher in the United States than in any other industrialized country. In part, this is because the United States has somewhat higher rates of single motherhood. A number of European countries, however, have higher rates of out-of-wedlock births but much lower child poverty rates. The primary difference, as a later chapter will show, is that the United States provides far less public income assistance to single-parent families than do many other industrialized countries.

TWO-PARENT FAMILIES

Although many people have an impression that few poor people are married, this is false. While fewer poor people are living in married-couple families than ever before, this group is still substantial—35 percent of all poor people are children or adults in married-couple families, as figure 1.1c indicates. As

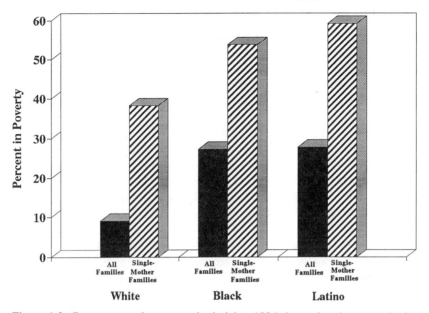

Figure 1.2. Poverty rates by race and ethnicity, 1994, in total and among single-mother families. (*Source*: U.S. Bureau of the Census 1995b)

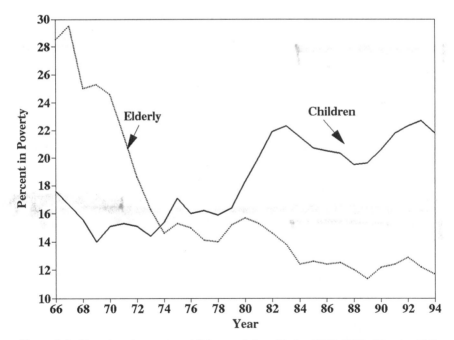

Figure 1.3. Poverty rates among children and the elderly, 1966–1994. (*Source*: U.S. Bureau of the Census 1995a,b)

always, black and Latino couples are much more likely to be poor than white couples. Many people are surprised to learn that many married-couple families are poor because the extensive public discussion about the poor tends to focus on "welfare recipients," who are typically single parents. Married couples typically receive less public assistance and less public attention. Many of these families are among the working poor.

SINGLE PERSONS

Single persons among the poor tend to be either young adults or elderly singles. More poor single persons are women than men, in part because older women are more likely to outlive their husbands and often have more limited income as widows. About 6 percent of the poor are younger adults who report that they are in school full-time.[4] This is one group among the poor about whom we tend not to worry at all. In some sense, their poverty is "self-chosen," and we don't expect it to last very long since most of today's poor students will be making good incomes in a few years.

THE ELDERLY

If children's poverty rates have climbed steadily in recent years, poverty rates among the elderly have fallen. Figure 1.3 plots poverty among these two groups. In 1993, elderly poverty rates were at an all-time low, while children's poverty rates were at their highest level in thirty years. The contrast in poverty trends among these two groups is striking.

The decline in poverty among the elderly is largely due to increases in elderly retirement income. A substantial amount of this is due to increases in Social Security retirement benefits, combined with other assistance programs aimed at the elderly. (As I will discuss in chapter 3, Supplemental Security Income provides cash assistance to poor elderly individuals and couples for whom Social Security does not suffice.) The United States has greatly increased its cash support to elderly families over the years and the result has been a substantial drop in poverty. Thus, the elderly are one of the biggest success stories for public policy; expansion in government benefits to the elderly has resulted in very low poverty rates.

Despite the myth that retirees receive back from Social Security only what they pay in, retirees over the past three decades have made windfall income gains from Social Security. The average person who retired in 1980 received back within the first four years of retirement everything that he or she and his or her employer had paid into Social Security.[5] This is largely due to legislative increases in Social Security benefits, far beyond those expected when these retirees were working and paying Social Security taxes in the 1950s, 1960s, and 1970s. This expansion in Social Security has increased incomes among the elderly at all income levels and reduced poverty among older low-income retirees. In addition, an expansion of private pensions among workers occurred through the early 1980s and has meant that more elderly persons receive private-pension income now than in the past.[6]

The elderly who remain poor are largely older widowed or divorced women who accrued little pension or Social Security income on their own and who have found themselves destitute following a husband's death. The growth in labor force participation among younger women means that this elderly poor female group should shrink in size over time, although continued low earnings among many women means this group will not disappear anytime soon.

RACIAL AND ETHNIC DIFFERENCES AMONG THE POOR

Members of racial and ethnic minority groups in the United States are disproportionately more likely to be poor. As figure 1.2 shows, just under one-third of all African American or Latino individuals live in poor families, much higher than the 12 percent poverty rates among non-Hispanic white persons. Native Americans, particularly those living on reservations, often have extremely high poverty rates. Recent immigrants, like generations of immigrants before them, are also more likely to be poor.

There are many reasons for high poverty among these groups. As will be discussed further below, black Americans have been particularly subject to housing discrimination, which has prevented many black families from following the path pursued by urban white families who moved to the suburbs when jobs started shifting there from the cities. Minority workers still face exclusion and discrimination from many employers, limiting their wages and employment options. Minority workers also have lower levels of formal education on average, a problem that is more acute in the Latino population than in the African American population. More recent immigrants face cultural and language barriers as well as skill barriers when they search for a job.

While this section is designed to provide some sense of the relative presence of different groups among the poor, the bottom line is that the poor are a very mixed group of people: they are white *and* black *and* Hispanic, both single *and* married, both young *and* old. The largest group among the poor is single mothers and their children (if differentiated by race, the largest group in real numbers would be white single mothers and their children). Single-parent families also have higher poverty rates than anyone else. But single parents and their children comprise less than half of all poor individuals.

Single mothers are often a primary focus of policy concern, both because we care about the impact of poverty on the children in these families and because this group receives more public assistance than any group other than the poor elderly and disabled. In fact, one reason that many people have an inaccurate image of poverty is that *poverty* is often assumed to be synonymous with *welfare recipients*. As I will discuss in more detail later, welfare typically refers to the cash assistance program known as Aid to Families with Dependent Children (AFDC), available primarily to single mothers and their children. While 65 percent of single mother families receive AFDC (note that many do not!), only 25 percent of all poor families receive AFDC.[7]

This book will talk more about single parents and their children than about some of the other groups among the poor. But even when we focus on single mothers and their children and on welfare-related policies in more detail, it is important to keep in mind that many poor people are *not* part of this population: the married couples, many of them working but poor; the single men and women among the poor; and the whole mix of poor people who live in different types of neighborhoods.

1.2 MOVING IN AND OUT OF POVERTY

SUMMARY: *We are less concerned with a family that experiences a short spell of poverty than with families who remain poor year after year. The long-term poor often experience the deepest poverty and its most sustained effects. They also use a greater share of public assistance dollars. Only a minority of those currently poor are likely to experience long-term poverty. But among black Americans and among children, the probabilities of long-term poverty are much higher. Long-term poverty among children is particularly worrisome, given its potential to limit children's cognitive and physical development. The majority of poverty spells both begin and end because of economic changes in earnings or other income sources rather than changes in family composition.*

We care not only about *who* is poor and *why* they are poor, but also how long they are poor. People who are poor for only one or two years might be considered less disadvantaged than those who are poor year after year. Those among the poor we worry about the most are those who seem unable to escape poverty. This group may be experiencing the most sustained effects of poverty, through accumulated health problems, long-term inadequate housing, and lack of access to or experience in the mainstream labor market. The long-term poor also use the most government resources and are therefore the most expensive from a taxpayer's point of view.

When we discuss the duration of poverty, we can present the picture in two quite different ways. On the one hand, most people who become poor are not poor for very long. On the other hand, there is a substantial minority of poor persons who seem to be poor for extremely long periods of time. How can both of these statements be true? Let's take a random sample of Americans and follow them over thirteen years to see how many were poor most of those years, some of those years, or none of those years.

Years of Poverty among Americans

Figure 1.4 shows the number of years of poverty experienced among a random sample of Americans whose income was surveyed annually over the years 1979 to 1991.[8] For thirteen recent years, these data indicate how prevalent poverty is and how much it is concentrated in long and short spells.

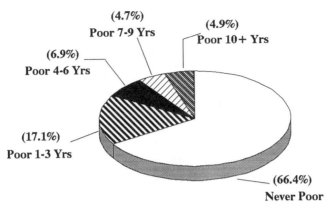

Figure 1.4. Extent of poverty among Americans, 1979–1991. (*Source*: Author's tabulations from the Panel Study of Income Dynamics)

Two-thirds of all persons are never in a poor family during these thirteen years. About half of those who are ever poor are poor for only one to three years. Only 1.5 percent of the population is poor all thirteen years, but 5 percent are poor for ten or more years.

Of course, among different groups, these numbers look quite different. For whites, poverty is much more likely to be short term, while for blacks the duration of poverty is longer. Figure 1.5 shows how the extent of poverty differs among blacks and whites between 1979 and 1991. While only one-fourth of whites ever experience poverty in one of these years, almost two-thirds of all blacks experience at least one year of poverty. Furthermore, among white families who experience poverty, two-thirds are poor for only three years or less; barely 2 percent are poor ten years or more. In sharp contrast, a shocking 17 percent of the black population is poor for ten or more of these thirteen years.

These data suggest that differences in annual poverty rates between African Americans and white Americans *understate* the differences in economic need among these two groups. Black Americans are not only more likely to be poor at any point in time, but they are much more likely to be poor for long periods of time, suffering the cumulative effects of continuing poverty. Continuous, long-term poverty might be a particular concern among children. If we look only at children who were eight or younger in 1980, a tiny proportion of white children (less than 3 percent) is poor for ten or more of the next thirteen years. But over 32 percent of black children are poor for that time.

Perhaps to no one's surprise, those groups most likely to be poor at any point in time are also more likely to be poor over time. One exception to this is the elderly. While overall poverty rates among the elderly are relatively low, when an elderly person becomes poor, he or she typically remains poor for the rest of his or her life.

White

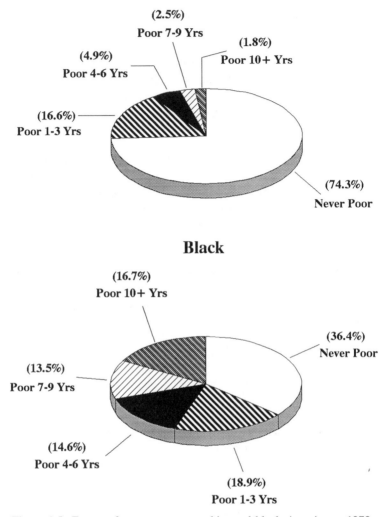

(2.5%)
Poor 7-9 Yrs

(1.8%)
Poor 10+ Yrs

(4.9%)
Poor 4-6 Yrs

(16.6%)
Poor 1-3 Yrs

(74.3%)
Never Poor

Black

(16.7%)
Poor 10+ Yrs

(36.4%)
Never Poor

(13.5%)
Poor 7-9 Yrs

(14.6%)
Poor 4-6 Yrs

(18.9%)
Poor 1-3 Yrs

Figure 1.5. Extent of poverty among white and black Americans, 1979–1991. (*Source*: Author's tabulations from the Panel Study of Income Dynamics)

The long-term poor are more likely to be African American, as we have seen, to have low levels of education, to report health problems, or to be in single-mother families. Those who are least able to support themselves through earnings are also least able to escape poverty.

What Causes Poverty and How Do People Escape?

There is clearly a great deal of fluidity among the poor population. Many people enter and leave poverty each year. How does this happen? By looking at the changing circumstances that lead families to become poor and to escape poverty, we may gain some insight into the problems that poor families face and how they solve them.

We can follow each person in our random sample of the U.S. population over the same thirteen-year period from 1979 to 1991 and identify the family and economic changes that are associated with the beginning of all observed spells of poverty between these years. (Those who never became poor or who were poor in all years obviously do not contribute any information to this calculation.) Similarly, we can also look at the events that occur when people escape poverty for all spells of poverty that end between these years. I assume that changes in marital and family status are of first importance in explaining why a spell of poverty begins or ends. Thus, even though there is often a sharp decline in earnings in families after a divorce when the husband (and his earnings) leaves and the wife becomes the head of the family, I list the cause of poverty in this case as "married couple breaks up." Only in families where the same person is the head of the family for two years in a row can "earnings of head (of family) fell" be the cause of poverty.[9]

Figure 1.6 shows how people enter poverty. In about one-quarter of the cases, a person enters poverty when there is a major change in his or her family composition—either a married couple breaks up, or a child who was living with his or her parents establishes an independent household. In another 10 percent of cases there are changes in family composition other than a change in the family head; for instance, an unmarried sibling who contributed earnings to the family might move out. In 9 percent of the cases, a person is born into a poor family. But in the majority of cases, poverty starts for a person when the economic situation of his or her family changes, with no changes in family composition. Almost half of all poverty spells start when the earnings of either the head or the wife fall, and another 12 percent start when other income sources are lost, such as a decline in child support, public assistance, or pension income.

In short, there are two main reasons why people become poor: either their families change composition in ways that threaten their economic security, or there is a major economic loss (usually in earnings). Most of these are job losses, where family heads experience extended unemployment. Among these two reasons, changes in economics create more poverty than changes in family composition.

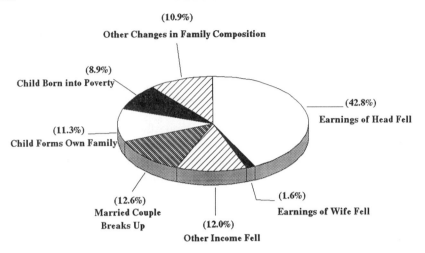

Figure 1.6. Reasons why poverty spells begin. (*Source*: Author's tabulations from the Panel Study of Income Dynamics)

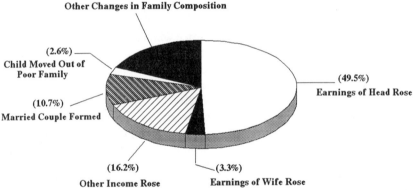

Figure 1.7. Reasons why poverty spells end. (*Source*: Author's tabulations from the Panel Study of Income Dynamics)

Figure 1.7 shows equivalent information on how and why an individual leaves poverty.[10] Over two-thirds of poor people escape poverty when a change occurs in their family's economic resources. In the majority of cases, poverty ends because either the earnings of the head or the wife increase enough to escape poverty, although increases in other income (typically government assistance) ends 16 percent of poverty spells. About 13 percent of poverty spells end with major changes in who heads the family—either a couple gets married, or a child in a poor family leaves and establishes his or her own nonpoor family. Other changes in family composition occur in another 18 percent of cases.

Figure 1.7 again emphasizes the importance of economic opportunities and the ability of poor adults to find and hold jobs. Most people leave poverty when they or the head of their family receives more earnings. Changes in family composition are less important in escaping poverty than they are in beginning a spell of poverty; for example, a woman and her children are more likely to become poor by leaving a marriage than they are likely to escape poverty by remarrying. From the limited evidence available, marriage is declining in its importance as a way to escape poverty.

Changes in earnings and work opportunities are very important in many families, driving them into poverty or helping them to escape. To a lesser extent, changes in family composition are also important in "creating" and "dissolving" poor families. But the discussion in the first part of this section remains relevant. For some substantial minority among the poor—particularly the black poor—poverty is long-term and escape is infrequent.

1.3 The Location of Poverty: It's Closer than You Think

SUMMARY. *The invisibility of modern poverty makes us less aware of its prevalence in many communities. Poverty is most visible in the extremely poor urban ghettos that are frequently depicted in the media. While these may be the worst places to be poor in America, only a small share of poor people live in these neighborhoods. Slightly less than 90 percent of all poor and 75 percent of the black poor live outside urban ghettos, in mixed-income urban or suburban areas or in rural areas. In fact, poverty has grown faster in the suburbs than in central cities in the last decade, particularly in the inner-ring suburbs that are experiencing loss of jobs and population to more distant suburban communities. A substantial number of the poor continue to live in isolated rural areas as well.*

Where do poor people live? If you asked that question thirty years ago, most people would have mentioned rural America: the agricultural South or the isolated mining towns of Appalachia. If you ask that question today, many people will respond with images of urban ghetto poverty: high-rise public housing and abandoned buildings, with an ever-present threat of gang violence. Most Americans have become frighteningly familiar with this image of poverty in recent years, which has dominated the media presentations.

Despite these images, relatively few among the poor live in poor urban ghettos. Most poor live in mixed-income city or suburban neighborhoods. In fact, there are few city neighborhoods, suburbs or midsized towns that do not have a substantial number of low-income families. The best answer to where the poor live: they live among us and with us.

In 1962, Michael Harrington published a book that discussed the "invisibility" of poverty in America.[11] While the location of poverty has changed over the past thirty years, its invisibility has not. Walk through the nearest shopping mall in your neighborhood and try to guess the income levels of the teenagers who are hanging out there. Or try to guess the income levels of the older shoppers. It's not obvious. In most public settings, all Americans dress with similar casualness.

The rising number of single-parent families and their high probability of poverty has also been a force that fosters income mixing within neighborhoods. Divorced women with children often try to stay in the same school district, moving to less expensive apartments. Never-married women often try to live close to parents or sisters. Even the most expensive neighborhoods will contain a few low-rent garage apartments or apartment buildings.

The one exception to the invisibility of poverty occurs in our urban ghettos. Because these are the neighborhoods where poverty is the most visible, we have incorrectly come to assume that these are the neighborhoods where most poverty is located. As typically defined among researchers, urban ghettos are areas where 40 percent or more of the people who live there are poor. These areas are often referred to as "underclass" neighborhoods, and poverty is only one of their many social and economic problems. These areas experience high crime, drug, and gang activity; they often contain tracts of extremely inadequate housing; residents have low levels of education and high rates of nonparticipation in the mainstream economy; a high share of the population receives government assistance; and local institutions like the schools or the police function inadequately. For too many families in these neighborhoods, these are dangerous, desperate places, where children are at risk of dying from random bullets on the street, where apartments have inadequate plumbing and unsafe stairways, and where too many residents live with fear.

Without in any way trying to minimize the problems that families in these areas face, the media images of these neighborhoods in local newspapers or TV news broadcasts have often left the impression that neighborhoods filled with deprivation, danger, and fear are the face of poverty in America. For some families, this is reality. But only a small minority of the poor live in such neighborhoods, and even among those who do, there are many success stories. It is important to remember that in most of these urban ghetto neighborhoods more than half of the population is *not* poor. While the worst of these neighborhoods—the concentrated areas of high-rise public housing—dominate the news in cities like New York and Chicago, many urban ghetto neighborhoods and their residents do not fit the stereotypes. Many of these neighborhoods have strong church and community organizations supported by long-term residents; many of the families in these areas are coping effectively with their lives and raising their children well.

The most recent calculations, using data from the 1990 census, indicate that only about *12 percent* of all poor persons live in urban ghetto neighborhoods with greater than 40 percent poverty rates.[12] Disproportionately, these neighborhoods are likely to have a high share of African American residents. Indeed, the legacy of housing segregation and discrimination has been a major

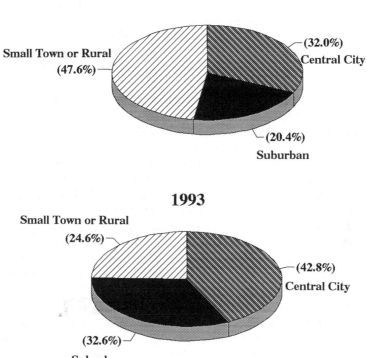

Figure 1.8. Composition of poor persons in the United States, by geographic location, 1970 and 1993. (*Source*: U.S. Bureau of the Census 1971, 1995a)

cause in the creation of these neighborhoods. But even among the African American poor, only around one-quarter live in such neighborhoods. Twenty percent of poor Hispanics are in ghetto neighborhoods. This says that almost 90 percent of the poor do *not* live in such communities. The bad news is that too many poor live in these communities, some of which are worlds where no Americans, and particularly not families with children, should live. The good news is that most poor do *not* live in these areas.

Figure 1.8 indicates the broader geographic composition of the poor in 1970 and 1993.[13] In 1993, 43 percent of the poor lived in the central cities of major metropolitan areas, most of them in mixed-income neighborhoods. Another 33 percent lived in the suburbs of these cities, while one-quarter of the poor still live in small-town or rural America, outside major metropolitan areas. As figure 1.8 indicates, the increase in suburban poverty is greater than the increase in city poverty.

Poverty in rural America, while a shrinking share of the poor, has hardly disappeared. The poorest counties in the United States are rural counties, where many families still live isolated lives. While this book focuses heavily on poverty in more populated areas, because that is where the growth in poverty has been in recent decades, rural poverty is still very present in some parts of the country. Lack of jobs and high unemployment in these areas are often more pressing than in urban ghetto neighborhoods. For people in poor urban neighborhoods, there *are* jobs in nearby suburbs although they may not be readily accessible. In poor rural areas, there often are few jobs anywhere.

Like all Americans, the poor have been moving out of rural areas and into urban areas over the past five decades. But over the last decade, it is not in the central cities where poverty has grown, but in the suburbs. Increasingly, the older inner-ring suburbs are experiencing rising poverty rates, much of it due to the growth of single-parent families in these areas. The growing edge of poverty is single mothers and their children living in suburban areas. This is a very different image than the hard-core urban ghetto poverty often depicted on TV. Those images are not wrong; serious poverty exists in such areas. But this does not represent the experiences of most of the poor. Most poor people live closer than many of the nonpoor realize because often they are not immediately distinguishable from their better-off neighbors.

1.4 WHY DON'T THEY JUST GET JOBS?
WORK BEHAVIOR AMONG THE POOR

SUMMARY. *This section looks at work among adults in poor families. Most poor families contain at least one worker, although the number of work hours among poor adults is much less than among the nonpoor. While work effort has declined among low-income married and single men, among single mothers and married women in low-income families work effort has increased somewhat over the past twenty years.*

Work and poverty are closely linked. Among nonelderly adults who did not work at all in 1993, almost one-third were in poor families. But among nonelderly adults who worked full time year-round, only 3 percent were in poor families.[14] Not surprisingly, full-time employment helps families escape poverty.

The lack of full-time employment among many poor adults raises ongoing questions about their motivation to work: is the lack of full-time work a signal of behavioral problems among the poor, or is it due to constraints imposed by limited labor market opportunities, family demands, or problems of poor health and disability? There is no easy answer to this question, in part because of the heterogeneity among the poor that we have already discussed. Some among the poor could surely work more than they do; others are more constrained by circumstance. We discuss these constraints in the next chapter. As we will see, for many poor families full-time employment is not easy to find. The unemployment rate among less-skilled workers—the share of workers who are actively looking for work but not finding it—is extremely high. Many poor adults, particularly those with young children, find it difficult to work full-time and provide care for their children. In addition, wages among less-skilled workers are low when they do find a job.

Evidence that the employment problems facing at least some of the poor are due to more than their own idle choices is clear from the fact that 20 percent of poor families contain one adult who works full-time year-round. Thus, even full-time work does not always guarantee that a family can escape poverty.

This section discusses work behavior within families, and how it has changed in recent decades. The next chapter discusses the economic forces that have resulted in deteriorating wage rates and continued high unemployment among less-skilled workers. As we shall see, the changes in work behavior discussed in this chapter are closely linked to larger changes in labor market opportunities, particularly among less-skilled men whose earning opportunities have been declining steadily for fifteen years.

Three facts describe poor families and their work behavior: First, the majority of the poor are in families that do receive some income from employment during the year. *Most* (63%) poor families contain at least one worker. Second, the number of work hours among the poor is much less than among the nonpoor. Poor families are much less likely to have a family member who works full-time. Third, married men in poor married-couple families work less now than in earlier decades; this is also the group that has experienced the greatest decline in their earnings opportunities. Adults in poor single-parent families, primarily women, work somewhat more now than they did twenty years ago. We will explore each of these facts in turn.[15]

Most poor families receive employment income. Among all poor families, almost two-thirds (63 percent) contain at least one person who worked during the past year. Not surprisingly, these numbers are greater among families that include adult males. About three-fourths of male-headed poor families include at least one worker, while half of poor female-headed families include a worker. Thus, the majority of the poor live in families where someone is working at least some of the time.

This does not deny the fact that a disproportionately large number of poor people do not work, compared to nonpoor people. These nonworkers are in households with widely varying composition and are both male and female. In fact, over time, low-income men have been dropping out of the workforce, while low-income women continue to work as much or more than they have in the past. Women are still less likely to work than men, however. Among all adult women in poor families, only about 40 percent work (remember that some number of these women are in families with other workers). Among all adult men in poor families, 58 percent work.

Work hours among the working poor are much lower than among the work-ing nonpoor. While many poor families have one family member who works, in relatively few of these families does someone work full-time year-round. Among all poor families, only 20 percent contain a full-time, year-round worker. This is a high number if you think *none* of the poor work. Yet it is a low number in comparison to nonpoor families, where almost 80 percent con-tain at least one full-time, year-round worker.

Given how many poor families include working adults, the problem of low income among poor families is caused at least as much by their not working full-time as by their not working at all. This suggests that the work problem for these families is less one of "won't or can't work" than it is of labor market and family constraints that prevent people from working enough to earn an adequate income. Poor persons who work part-time or part-year, but not full-time, full-year, typically report much higher rates of unemployment and job instability, as well as greater family demands on their time (particularly among single parents). For instance, single mothers in high-crime neighbor-hoods often seek jobs where they can be home when the public schools close at 2:30 or 3 P.M. to insure that their children come home and avoid trouble. These good parenting habits limit their possible work hours.

Declines in work involvement have occurred among men in poor married-couple families. The poor are working somewhat less now than twenty years ago. This fact is often blamed on deteriorating work behavior among single mothers, but that perception is *not* accurate. Poor single parents are as likely to work now as they were twenty years ago. Among those who work, their average weeks of work have actually increased over time. They still work less than the adult men in married-couple families, but they work much more than the wives in married-couple families.

Most of the trend toward declining work among poor adults has occurred in married-couple families. The men in these families were much less likely to work in 1993 than twenty-five years earlier, and the average number of weeks worked over the year among those who do work has declined as well. The underlying causes behind these trends will be explored in more detail in the next chapter: low-skilled men, facing declining wages and no improvement in employment opportunities, are working less than before.

The conclusion drawn from this section is of a both/and nature. On the one hand, many poor families have employment income, with over 60 percent of poor families containing one or more full- or part-time workers. The "working poor" continue to be a substantial group among the poor. On the other hand, poor adults are less likely to work than non-poor adults, and when they do work, they work fewer hours. Work behavior among low-income single par-ents has, if anything, increased over time, but work behavior among poor married couples, particularly among men, has deteriorated. As we shall see in the next chapter, these trends are closely related to the changes in the economy and in wage and employment opportunities.

1.5 Teen Moms and Out-of-Wedlock Births:
Changing Fertility and Marriage Behavior in
the United States

Summary. *The increase in the out-of-wedlock birthrate, particularly among teenagers, has generated enormous attention and concern. About one-third of this increase is the result of married women having fewer children, thereby raising the share born to unmarried women. The probability that an unmarried woman will have a child has increased only slightly over time, but the number of unmarried women in the population has grown rapidly. Thus, it is the decline in marriage, as much as an increase in pregnancies among unmarried women, that is increasing out-of-wedlock birthrates. Changes in economic opportunities among both men and women, as well as declines in social stigma associated with unwed parenting, are the primary reasons behind these changes.*

Few topics generate as much public concern as the rise in births to never-married women. Much of this is tied to a concern about births to teen mothers. The frequently overheated rhetoric around this topic is reflected in a recent column on teen pregnancy written by *Newsweek* columnist Jonathan Alter in which he declares, "The fact remains: every threat to the fabric of this country—from poverty to crime to homelessness—is connected to out-of-wedlock teen pregnancy."[16] This chapter discusses the problems of teen pregnancy and births to unmarried women, but avoids the strident tone that blames these women for all possible social ills. There has been too much heat in our public discussions of unwed motherhood, and not nearly enough of the light of understanding.

The rise in out-of-wedlock births is astonishingly large by any measure. Figure 1.9 shows the percentages of births outside marriage to teenage and nonteenage women by race between 1960 and 1993.[17] In 1990, almost 70 percent of births to teen mothers were out-of-wedlock births, while 25 percent of births to older women were outside marriage. These numbers are particularly high among African Americans, where over two-thirds of all births are to unmarried mothers.

While out-of-wedlock teen births draw particular attention, their numbers are not large. In 1990, just under 350,000 unwed teenagers gave birth, out of a total population of 8.5 million women between the ages of 15 and 19. This is approximately 4 percent of all teen women. These 350,000 births accounted for less than 9 percent of the almost 4 million births in this country. While we should not minimize the problems facing teenage mothers who try to raise children on their own, unwed teenage births remain a relatively small share of total births.

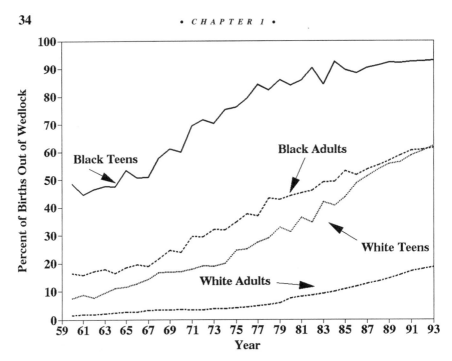

Figure 1.9. Percentage of out-of-wedlock births, by race and age, 1959–1993. (*Sources*: U.S. National Center for Health Statistics 1993b,c,d, 1994, 1995a; U.S. Bureau of the Census 1961–1971, 1972–1990)

To understand the factors behind the huge increase in out-of-wedlock birthrates among women of all ages, it is useful to be clear about definitions. The out-of-wedlock birthrate is the proportion of all births to unmarried women. This is calculated by dividing the number of births to unmarried mothers by the total number of births:

$$\text{out-of-wedlock birthrate} = \frac{\text{births to unmarried women}}{\text{total births,}}$$

where

$$\text{total births} = \text{births to unmarried women} + \text{births to married women}$$
$$\text{births to unmarried women} = (\text{number of unmarried women}) \times (\text{probability an unmarried woman gives birth})$$
$$\text{births to married women} = (\text{number of married women}) \times (\text{probability a married woman gives birth})$$

This simple math means that in order to understand how the out-of-wedlock birthrate is changing, we need to know how its three components are changing: (1) changes in the probability an unmarried woman gives birth;

TABLE 1.1
Birthrates and Number of Births to Single and Married Women, 1960–1990

	Single Women			Married Women			
	Birth-rate per 1,000	No. Single Women in (000s)	No. Births to Single Women	Birth-rate per 1,000	No. Married Women in (000s)	No. Births to Married Women	Illegitimacy Ratio: Share of Births to Single Women
All women, 15–44							
1960	21.6	10,319	222,890	156.6	25,638	4,014,911	5.3%
1990	43.8	26,248	1,149,662	93.2	32,117	2,993,304	27.7%
White adult women, 20–44							
1960	12.4	3,902	48,385	140.4	22,104	3,103,402	1.5%
1990	33.5	13,854	489,299	90.2	27,570	2,486,453	15.7%
Black adult women, 20–44							
1960	115.4	749	86,435	163.2	2,671	435,902	16.5%
1990	83.7	3,632	304,005	77.6	2,867	222,620	57.7%
White teen women, 15–19							
1960	6.6	4,930	32,538	513.0	772	396,036	7.6%
1990	30.6	6,475	198,135	414.4	377	156,229	55.9%
Black teen women, 15–19							
1960	76.5	738	56,457	659.3	91	59,996	48.5%
1990	106.0	1,325	140,450	486.8	26	12,657	91.7%

Source: Population data for 1960 from U.S. Bureau of the Census (1961–1971); population data for 1990 from U.S. Bureau of the Census (1972–1992). Natality data for 1960 and 1990 from U.S. National Center for Health Statistics (1995b).

Note: Comparisons across columns may have small inconsistencies due to rounding.

(2) changes in the probability a married women gives birth; and (3) changes in the relative number of unmarried to married women in the population.

Much of the discussion of rising nonmarital birthrates in the media is misleading. Most discussions of rising out-of-wedlock birthrates assume that single women must be giving birth at much higher rates than ever before (component 1 listed above), and ignore the other two factors that influence this rate. As it turns out, the probability that a single woman will give birth actually declined between 1960 and 1990 among black women and increased only slightly among white women. What *has* changed is that the number of single women relative to the number of married women has grown enormously (component 3), at the same time as the births among married women have declined (component 2). Let me discuss each of these in turn. Table 1.1 provides the actual numbers needed to calculate the out-of-wedlock birth rate in 1960 and 1990 for selected groups.

Fertility among married women has declined as family size has declined. This trend is particularly evident among black women. Married black couples used to have larger families than married white couples; they now have smaller families. When married couples have fewer children, even if there is no increase at all in the number of nonmarital births, the out-of-wedlock birth-rate will go up. Thus, the raw data on the share of out-of-wedlock births over-states the problem. The choice by married couples to limit the size of their families is not a particularly worrisome trend.

About one-third of the rise in out-of-wedlock birthrates has been driven by changes in family size among married couples. Among white women of all ages, the share of nonmarital births has gone from 2 percent in 1960 to 21 percent in 1990. If married white women had continued to have as many chil-dren as in 1960, the out-of-wedlock birthrate would have been only 13 per-cent, or 8 points lower. Among black women, the out-of-wedlock birthrate has gone from 23 percent in 1960 to 65 percent in 1990. If married black women had continued to have as many children as in 1960, the out-of-wedlock birth-rate for blacks would have been 46 percent, or nineteen points lower.

While married women's fertility has declined, single women's fertility has increased somewhat, but not a lot. The probability that a single women will give birth is only slightly higher now than thirty years ago and remains far below the birthrate for married women.

The main factor driving the increase in the number of births to unmarried women is the fact that the number of unmarried women in the population has grown enormously. This pattern is most apparent among single women ages twenty and over; the pattern for teens is different, as discussed below. The probability that an adult white single women will give birth has gone up, but remains relatively low (at 33.5 births per 1,000 single women), while the probability that an adult single black woman will give birth has actually fallen over the past thirty years (see table 1.1). Holding marital fertility constant, virtually all of the increase in out-of-wedlock births among adult women can be accounted for by the rise in the number of single women relative to the number of married women. Women are marrying later (or not at all) and are more likely to be divorced. Thus, the rise in the share of nonmarital births to adult women is occurring not because single women are increasingly likely to have babies, but because more adult women are single and hence more babies are born to single women.

Among teens, the pattern is somewhat different. There have been signifi-cant increases in *both* the probability that a single teenager will give birth and in the number of single teens relative to the number of married teens, so that both effects are important. As the age at which people first marry has risen, there are fewer and fewer teen marriages. Thirty years ago there were many teen births, but most of these were among married teenage women. Today, very few women marry as teens; teenagers who become mothers are not married when they get pregnant, and do not get married before they give birth.

Finally, it is worth emphasizing that the rise in single motherhood is not confined to low-income women. While the more-educated women still have lower rates of unwed births, the percentage increase in unwed births among more-educated women is greater than among less-educated women.[18] The trend toward a rising share of births to unmarried women is also mirrored in virtually all industrialized countries.[19] While the United States has a relatively high share of single-mother families (and the highest rate of teen pregnancy), single motherhood—whether due to divorce or to unwed births—is rising everywhere. Whatever the cause of these changes, they are widespread throughout modern developed societies.

Why Are Out-of-Wedlock Births Rising?

No one factor fully explains why more and more women are choosing to be single mothers. Any trend that is this prevalent must have many overlapping economic and social causes. In chapter 4 we analyze the charge that public assistance programs increase nonmarital births, and find little evidence to support it (not surprisingly, perhaps, given the widespread nature of this trend across countries and across income groups). Three primary factors are most commonly mentioned in the research literature on changing birth patterns.[20]

First, as discussed in more depth in the next chapter, for all but the least-skilled women wage opportunities have risen and occupational choices in the workforce have expanded. This gives women more economic independence. Many women no longer feel they need to marry for economic security. Of course, the high rates of poverty among women with children attests to the fact that too many women have still not achieved economic security in the labor market, either because they cannot or do not work enough, or because their earnings are not high enough.

Second, as the earnings opportunities of young men—particularly less-skilled young men—have declined, their attractiveness as marriage partners has presumably declined as well. As any married person can tell you, there are both costs and benefits to marriage. The topic of the next chapter is the declining wage and work opportunities available to less-skilled workers, particularly men. As men's economic opportunities have shrunk, the women who would have married them in previous times are more likely to stay single.

It has been suggested that the availability of potential marriageable mates has fallen among low-income black women in urban ghettoes even more than among other women. Not only have working men in these neighborhoods experienced declining wage rates, but many do not work at all in the mainstream economy. Some are involved in the dangerous world of drugs, gangs, and urban street life. Many have been incarcerated, and a jail record substantially decreases their future employment and earning possibilities. (We discuss the lives of the single men who are the fathers of these children in a later section.) Given these realities, the fact that many low-income black women choose to remain unmarried is perhaps not surprising.

Third, the social stigma associated with unwed motherhood has declined. As more women choose to be single mothers, the stigma associated with being a never-married mother has fallen dramatically throughout society, and, by most accounts, entirely disappeared in some communities, particularly in the African American community. This means not only that single women are willing to give birth to and raise children, but that single men also feel far less compulsion to marry the mothers of their children.

For teenage mothers in particular, the responsibilities of motherhood may create serious long-term problems, especially if these women drop out of high school to raise their children. The lack of a high school degree limits their earning opportunities and their ability to provide an economically secure life for themselves and their children. If some of these teenagers are also unprepared to be effective parents, teen parenting might limit their children's cognitive and emotional development as well.

A growing research literature is investigating the effect of teen pregnancy on the long-term economic options of teen mothers. The next section discusses the very real problems faced by single-mother families, but it is important to note here that there is increasing evidence that teenage mothers do not face substantially worse situations than other single mothers from similar backgrounds. Teenage mothers disproportionately come from lower-income homes and attend lower-quality schools. They are more likely to be African American or Hispanic. This suggests that their long-term earning power is likely to be limited, even if they did not have children at an early age. Recent studies have compared teen mothers with their sisters—women who come from the same family and neighborhood but who did not have children before age 20. The results indicate that by their mid-twenties, the earnings of teenage mothers are only slightly less than the earnings of their sisters who did not get pregnant as teens. By their mid-twenties, it's hard to tell who was an unwed teen mother and who was not, not because the teen mothers do particularly well, but because their sisters from the same family background do just as poorly.[21]

Other research supports these results, suggesting that teen mothers work less and use more public-assistance income in their early twenties, but they work more and use less public assistance in their late twenties than non-teen mothers from similar backgrounds.[22] In other words, there is evidence that teen parenting changes the timing of work and earnings for these women, but by their late twenties and early thirties, it is hard to say that teen mothers are more disadvantaged than similar women who delayed childbearing. This suggests that the problems of unwed motherhood among young women may be less related to their childbearing per se than to the whole host of factors that limit their opportunities and make motherhood at age 15 or 16 more attractive than school or work.

Finding effective solutions to the problems that result from high rates of teen pregnancy may require less focus on issues of sexual behavior and marriage and more focus on issues of economic opportunity, adult role models, and a sense of possibility in the lives of young women *and* young men.

Women with stronger educational aspirations, with a greater sense of future economic opportunities, and who perceive more choices in their lives are less likely to become teenaged mothers.

1.6 POOR SINGLE MOTHERS: WHAT PROBLEMS DO THEY FACE?

SUMMARY. *The rising number of single mothers—divorced or never married—is one reason that poverty rates have remained high. The fact that many women choose divorce or single parenting over marriage is not necessarily a bad thing. Increasing evidence suggests that poor women experience disproportionately high rates of physical and sexual abuse. Raising their children alone may be preferable to marriage for some segment of single mothers. On the other hand, single parents are the poorest group in society today; their economic problems create social costs and legitimately raise concerns over the growth in single parenting. Because these women are the sole adult earner in their families as well as the only parent, their earning opportunities are often constrained. Children raised in single-parent families are at greater risk of cognitive and behavioral problems.*

Single mothers are constantly working two jobs: they are the primary earners in their household, as well as the primary parents, which puts more constraints on both their parenting time and their work time. Add in the low wages earned by many less-skilled women in the labor market and the bottom line is not surprising: single mothers are one of the poorest groups in American society today. Half of all single-mother families have total annual cash incomes below $12,400, an astonishingly low income.[23]

The number of single-mother families has increased steadily in this society over the past three decades, for two reasons. First, rising divorce rates in the 1960s and 1970s meant more divorced women were raising children alone. Divorce rates stopped rising around 1980, however, and have actually fallen somewhat over the past fifteen years.[24] Second, the recent growth in single-mother families has been fueled by growth in the number of never-married mothers. In 1994, 39 percent of single mothers in poverty had never been married.[25] The previous topical section discussed the question of why the number of out-of-wedlock births are rising. This section focuses on the social and policy implications of growing numbers of women and children living on their own.

There is clearly both a voluntary and an involuntary aspect to the growth in single motherhood. Some number of women *choose* not to marry or to divorce. The advice columnist Ann Landers has long advised women who write her about divorce or marriage situations simply to ask, "Am I better off with him or without him?" The rising number of single mothers suggests that more and more women have decided "I'm better off without him," even if it means being a single parent. The availability of reliable contraceptive techniques, as well as the widespread availability of abortion also make single motherhood appear more voluntary than in the past.

On the other hand, some number of single mothers would surely have preferred to remain married or to get married. Under current divorce laws, if one partner wants a divorce the other cannot stop it, but getting married requires the consent of *both* parties. Some single mothers might have preferred to marry their boyfriends once they became pregnant, but the man refused. The strong right-to-life movement in this country suggests that many women will not choose to terminate an unwelcome pregnancy.

One aspect of the question, "Are these women and their children better or worse off as single-parent families?" deserves much more attention. *There is increasing evidence that many low-income single mothers have experienced substantial physical and sexual abuse in their life.* A random sample of single-mother welfare recipients in the state of Washington found that fully 60 percent reported past sexual or physical abuse. Other studies come up with numbers near the same level. There is some evidence that sexual abuse as a child is particularly prevalent among women who become teen mothers. About half of teen mothers under age 17 are made pregnant by older, non-teenage men.[26]

We need to understand much more about these problems and how they relate to the growing number of single mothers. If these estimates of high rates of sexual and physical abuse are accurate, they put a different light on the "problem" of single motherhood for at least a subset of women. Despite extreme poverty, these women personally may be *much* better off divorcing or not marrying the fathers of their children.

In some ways, it should not be surprising if more women have voluntarily chosen to live apart from their boyfriends or ex-husbands. Throughout our society, more people are choosing to live on their own. Compared to thirty years ago, fewer elderly parents live with their children any more; fewer unmarried adults live with their parents. The growth in single motherhood may reflect similar choices among women. If single parenting makes women happier or better off by their own accounting, why should we care?

We care about the growth in single motherhood because there is evidence that it creates social costs, due to negative effects on children and due to the costs to society of assisting poor single mothers. There are at least three negative effects associated with the rising share of single-mother families in the population.

First, as discussed in the first section of this chapter, single mothers are much more likely to be poor than any other family group. Thus, the more single mothers in the population, the higher overall poverty rates are likely to be. Poverty rates are about three percentage points higher in the 1990s than they would have been had there been no growth in single-parent families in the previous two decades.[27] Similarly, high and rising rates of child poverty are largely due to increases in the number of children in single-parent families. In short, the high and persistent poverty rates of recent decades are at least partially due to the fact that the growth in single-mother families has pushed poverty upward over time.

Second, children growing up in poor single-parent families face a double-negative effect in their lives: living in poverty and living with only one parent. Regardless of family composition, poor children are more likely than nonpoor children to be too short and too thin for their age. They develop academic skills more slowly than nonpoor children, and are at higher risk of educational problems. There is also growing evidence that living with only one parent puts children at risk even when incomes don't differ. Children in single-parent families face greater problems of cognitive and physical development and are at higher risk of dropping out and becoming single parents themselves.[28]

Third, increases in the number of single-parent families have made it harder to bring people out of poverty through employment. It's easier for a two-adult family to escape poverty through work for a variety of reasons. Single-mother families have only one adult available for work, and that adult is also a single parent whose parenting responsibilities may constrain her work effort. Single-mother families often must pay child care when the mother goes to work, requiring higher earnings to reach the same standard of living as a family where child care is provided costlessly by a second parent. Single mothers tend to be less skilled and are likely to be in jobs with low wage levels. Finally, single mothers may also face more constraints on work hours because of concerns about safely getting to and from work late at night. With all of this, employment alone is likely to provide only limited support for single-mother families. Many working single-mother families need to have additional sources of income beyond their earnings in order to escape poverty.

Although there are many negative aspects associated with single motherhood, it is worthwhile to mention some of the positive traits shown by poor single mothers. Unlike the absent fathers (more on them in the next section of this chapter), these women stick with their children and typically work hard to raise them well. These women also work a substantial amount in the labor market, even if they don't earn enough to escape poverty. As discussed in the previous section, work hours among single mothers have risen slowly over time; single mothers work substantially more than married mothers.

The growth in the number of single mothers in our society raises serious questions about the role of marriage and its relationship to the well-being of women and children. Unsurprisingly, this has generated a great deal of heated public debate. Those who argue that single mothers are merely acting in their own best interests and should not be criticized tend to point to the many responsible behaviors these women exhibit as adults and mothers. They also note the evidence that some of these women have experienced abuse from men in the past. Those who argue that stronger incentives should be created to encourage marriage and discourage single parenting tend to point to the high poverty rates experienced by these women and their children and the potential cost to their children as well as to society.

Surely, the truth lies somewhere in the balance between these two arguments. The fact that so many women choose to live extremely poor lives as single mothers suggests that marriage is unattractive to these women, for reasons that we should take seriously. As discussed in the previous topical section, improvements in women's earnings, declines in men's earnings, and declines in the stigma associated with single motherhood have all contributed to this phenomenon. Yet, the negative consequences of single motherhood must also be faced. If we cannot find ways to reduce single motherhood, we must find ways to assure that single mothers are less poor.

1.7 ABSENT FATHERS: WHY DON'T WE EVER TALK ABOUT THE UNMARRIED MEN?

SUMMARY. *The lives of poor single men are much less well understood, since these men typically have less contact with the public and private organizations that serve the poor. By most accounts, poor unmarried men exhibit far more behavioral problems than single mothers, despite the fact that much of the policy discussion focuses on the mothers. A high share of younger men are under the supervision of the judicial system in this country. Child support payments from absent fathers to their children are extremely low, and this lack of parental support is a major factor contributing to the poverty of single mothers and their children. These problems are correlated with the larger economic trends that have affected these men's lives: less-skilled men have faced declines in wages, the changing location of jobs in cities, and high and persistent unemployment rates.*

For every single mother, there is a father who is not living with his children. For every unwed mother, there is a father who did not marry her. The public discussion about growing numbers of divorced and never-married mothers too rarely mentions the missing men in these families. Here we will focus on the absent fathers and their behavior.

We know surprisingly little about the lives of the low-income single men who father the children in low-income single-mother families. This is true for at least two reasons. First, because these men are much less publicly visible than the mothers of their children, they are often ignored in the policy discussion. Because we provide little public assistance to single men, they have less contact with the public and private organizations that serve low-income families. Disproportionately, it is the mothers who show up at schools, who bring their children in for health care, or who apply for public assistance. Thus, these men appear to cost society nothing; it is mothers and children whom we support. Of course, as any economist will tell you, this is a false notion. To the extent that *both* the men and the women choose to divorce or not marry, the resulting social costs are due to the men's behavior as much as the women's.

Second, because none of the data the government collects links absent fathers with their children, they are often ignored in the research literature. The data collected on family and child poverty are based on information about all family members who *live together*, thus we know little about the absent fathers. As noted below, a substantial number of fathers in out-of-wedlock births are not identified on birth certificates. Some of these fathers may not even know they have children. Among those who are known, the fathers typically do not live in the household. It is not possible to study absent fathers without collecting new data that will help identify and contact men who are not living with their children. This is an expensive undertaking.

As a result, we know very little about how absent fathers behave, or even about who they are. At best, we can talk about less-skilled and low-income unmarried men, assuming that many of them are part of the absent-fathers population. In general, this group exhibits more behavioral problems than single mothers.

These men are at greater risk of homelessness, and they are more likely to be involved in crime or illegal drug-related activities. By the mid-1990s, the number of men under the supervision of the judicial system (either in jail or on probation or parole) relative to the male workforce was 7 percent, that is, there was one man under court supervision for every twelve men working; this is higher than the unemployment rate for this group. Among young men between the ages of 18 and 34, 11 percent are under the supervision of the judicial system; among black men between these ages, the share under judicial supervision is an amazing 37 percent.[29] Why are these numbers so high? There is evidence of increasing criminal involvement among younger men, and this interacts with stronger sentencing laws and a growing willingness to incarcerate those involved with drug dealing.

All of this has led to soaring prison populations and large increases in the number of men on probation or parole. These numbers are disturbing not just because of what they signal about current behavioral problems, but also because of the long-term problems they create for these men in finding employment as ex-offenders.[30]

Without excusing these behavioral problems, it is important to recognize that the world has changed for the worse for many less-skilled, low-income men. As discussed in the next chapter, less-skilled men have faced major declines in their earning ability, and high rates of unemployment. These economic changes are strongly correlated with both declines in work effort in the mainstream labor market and increases in criminal activity.

Among African American and Latino men, these problems are greatest and overlap with ongoing problems of discrimination and job access. A number of authors have described the many ways in which young black men are treated hostilely by white society, learn distrust and anger, and develop a responding culture of hostility and violence.[31] The result is a downward cycle, in which problematic behavior and economic and social constraints interact with and reinforce each other.

It is also worth emphasizing that these problems are concentrated among a minority of the poor men. Most poor men are employed at least part-time or part-year or are actively searching for work. Most are not in jail or on probation. Many are married to the mothers of their children. We should not let the real problems of some low-income men shape our image of all low-income men.

Child Support and Absent Fathers

Many less-skilled single mothers find it difficult to escape poverty through their own earnings. One obvious way for these families to obtain more income is through support from absent fathers. Whether divorced or never married, fathers should bear their fair share of the financial responsibility for raising their children.

The growth in never-married mothers has exacerbated the problems of non-support from fathers, although many divorced women also receive little support. Of all children born to unmarried women, less than one-third have paternity established at time of birth.[32] That means that if support from the father is sought at a later stage, he first must be found and identified, not always an easy process.

The level of child support collected among single women in this country is extremely low. Table 1.2 presents the data, showing child support receipt among poor and nonpoor women in 1989.[33] Only 43 percent of poor mothers with children whose father lives outside the household have ever received a child support award by the courts, ordering the father to pay ongoing support. Among never-married women, less than one quarter have such an award. Among women who are divorced or married to a man who is not the father of their children, about 70 percent have an award. While nonpoor women do slightly better, table 1.2 indicates that substantial numbers of nonpoor women are also without child support assistance.

Simply having an award does not guarantee that the father will make regular payments, however. Only 25 percent of poor women actually receive child support payments, and only 14 percent of never-married poor women receive payments. Many women who receive payments do not receive the full amount of their support order, but get only partial amounts. This is reflected in the fact that the amounts of money received are quite low. Among those poor single parents who do receive child support payments, the average payment received for all children is under $2,000 per year.

Teenage men who father children are particularly unlikely to live with the mother of their children, unlikely to pay child support, and have low earnings and employment levels. Thus, the problems of teen fatherhood are closely

TABLE 1.2
Child Support Awards among Women with Children Whose Father Is Not Present
in the Household, 1989

| | *Current Marital Status* | | | |
	All	*Divorced*	*Never Married*	*Married**
Poor Mothers				
Percent with child support award	43.3	70.4	24.5	72.2
Percent with child support award and				
receiving payments	25.4	42.4	14.4	40.4
Average payments among recipients	$1,889	$2,112	$1,553	$2,275
Nonpoor Mothers				
Percent with child support award	64.5	79.1	23.2	79.5
Percent with child support award and				
receiving payments	43.1	57.5	14.5	48.6
Average payments among recipients	$3,304	$3,649	$2,276	$2,972

Source: U.S. Bureau of the Census (1991).

* The "Married" column shows women who are currently married to a man who is not the father of their children.

related to the problems of teen motherhood. Many teen fathers, however, receive higher earnings as they move into their twenties. While they may be able to pay little child support initially, if teen fathers are followed by the child support system, they may be able to contribute more as their children grow older.[34]

The rise in single parenting has not simply led to an increase in the number of children who physically live with and are primarily raised by their mothers. It has also meant massive financial desertion of these children by their fathers. This is a major reason why the women who raise children on their own are so likely to be poor.

One caveat on this statement needs to be noted: at least some financial support from absent fathers to their children goes unreported. For men whose children receive public assistance, the incentives to provide much in the way of financial support are minimal. The first fifty dollars that a man pays in child support each month increases the income of the mother and her children. After that, any additional money goes to offset the cost of public assistance. The result is that child support payments above fifty dollars per month result in absolutely no additional income to the mother and children. This provides a strong incentive for under-the-table payments by men to their girlfriends and children. In-depth interviews with women on welfare in a few selected cities indicate that about one-quarter of welfare recipients in poor urban neighborhoods receive unreported contributions from absent fathers. The average amount of unreported income from children's fathers was relatively small, however, averaging thirty dollars per month.[35]

Of course, many less-skilled women with limited earning ability have children with men of similar economic backgrounds. Thus, the absent fathers of many poor children are themselves poor, suggesting that these men would not be able to pay substantial amounts of child support. Researchers have tried to simulate the effect on poverty among single-parent families of substantially increased enforcement of child support orders, assuming that the absent fathers have the same educational background as the mothers. The results indicate that this would help lessen the depth of poverty among single-mother families but, by itself, would move only some families out of poverty entirely. The amounts that the noncustodial fathers could afford to pay are limited, because many of these fathers are not employed or because they have very low earnings. But these studies also conclude that better child support enforcement would make many single-mother families less poor, raising their income closer to the poverty line. For mothers living on $6,000 per year with their children, an additional $1,000 per year in child support payments provides a substantial increase in income.[36]

Finally, it is worth underscoring the fact that nonpayment of child support awards and nonidentification of fathers among unwed mothers are not problems solely among poor women. A substantial number of single mothers who are well above the poverty line receive little ongoing support from the fathers of their children. Most of the billions of dollars in unpaid child support is owed to nonpoor single women from men who have steady jobs with good incomes. Demanding that fathers accept financial responsibility for their children is not just an antipoverty agenda, but a move that will benefit working women and their children at all income levels.

Lack of financial involvement does not necessarily mean lack of parental involvement. While few men provide much financial support, particularly to low-income mothers, many of them remain in contact with their children. Sociologists Sara McLanahan and Gary Sandefur indicate that two-thirds of all children who live apart from their fathers have contact with them.[37] Surprisingly, this number is only slightly lower among children of unmarried versus divorced women. About one-third of the children who do not live with their father report seeing him once per week.

This information suggests that a substantial number of "absent fathers" are not entirely absent. They are present in their children's lives, even if they do little of the primary parenting and provide only minimal or irregular child support payments. Clearly, many fathers do feel ongoing responsibility and love for their children.

It is worth putting all of this into the context of the larger economic changes that chapter 2 will discuss in more depth. The decline in marriage and the decreased support for children by their fathers are both intimately linked to the economic changes of the last two decades. Less-skilled men—exactly the group most likely to father the children in poor single-mother families—are the group most affected by the changing economy. They have experienced big declines in wages, high and persistent unemployment rates, and (particularly among African American men) a loss of jobs from the changing location of employment in urban areas. Judging their changing parental behavior without these economic trends in mind is to miss an important component of the picture. Demanding that men be more responsible with regard to their children—particularly asking them to provide more financial support—is a harder demand to make when these men are more and more pressed by limited economic opportunities. Though their behavior may not be excusable, ordering them to get a job and/or pay more in child support may not be as easily accomplished as in years past.

Finally, it is important to keep in mind that there is a great deal of variability in the behavior of fathers of poor children. As discussed in the first section of this chapter, in almost 40 percent of all poor families with children *both* parents are present. Many fathers do *not* desert their children. And of those children whose parents are divorced or never married, there are a substantial minority of fathers who stay in their children's lives, spend time with them, and contribute regularly to their financial well-being. While worrying about the missing fathers, we should not forget to appreciate those who are present.

1.8 DRUGS, GANGS, AND ILLEGAL ACTIVITY: CRIME AND POVERTY

SUMMARY. *The correlation between violence and poverty is extremely visible in the urban ghetto neighborhoods of our cities, where random violence has increased and homicide rates have soared, particularly among young black men. The majority of people in these neighborhoods are more likely to be victims than to be participants in this violence, however. Outside these ghetto areas, crime rates in this country have declined over the past two decades. Similarly, while drug problems have intensified among a small population, in most groups they have declined. The share of the poor who participate extensively in illegal activities is small.*

The "dangerous poor" is an image that has often haunted American discussions of poverty. Disproportionately, in an immigrant nation, the poor have always been the most recent immigrant group, which means they have always been "the other"—the strangers who dress differently, talk with strange accents, or follow strange customs. The stranger, the one who is different, has always caused fear. The best example of this, of course, has been African Americans, who are hardly the most recent immigrant group but who bear the scars of racism that defines them as "dangerous strangers" even after centuries of life in America.

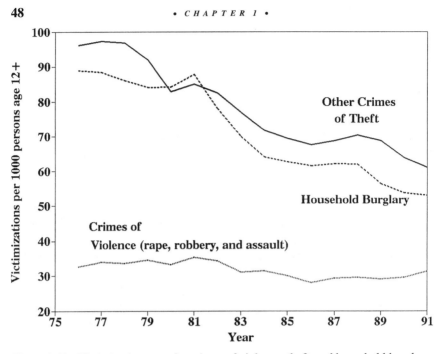

Figure 1.10. Victimization rates for crimes of violence, theft, and household burglary, 1975–1991. (*Source*: Maguire et al. 1993)

Thus, one of the most frequent arguments for revitalizing urban ghettos or preventing child poverty is not to improve the well-being of the poor, but to increase the well-being of the rest of society. As the argument is often presented, poor children must be educated and given a sense of future opportunities to prevent them from turning to crime, to drugs, or to gangs, and thereby threatening the security of the nonpoor. Urban ghettos must be rehabilitated so that their blight does not spread to other neighborhoods.

A discussion of crime and poverty is difficult because many Americans have come to believe "facts" about crime that are not true. Contrary to popular perception, reported victimization rates for most crimes have declined over the last two decades. Figure 1.10 shows the trends over time in the rate (per 1,000 persons age 12 and over) of reported crimes of violence against persons (rape, robbery, and assault), crimes of theft against persons, and household burglary.[38] Since the mid-1970s, crime rates in these aggregate categories and in their subcategories have declined. The only category of crime whose rate has increased is motor vehicle theft. All other forms of crime were occurring at a lower rate in 1991 than they were in 1980. This is true even if the data are disaggregated by city, suburb, and rural area. Crime rates in America have decreased. For most Americans, life is safer now than it was fifteen years ago.

Despite these data, many of us live with a sense of threat. Public discussion of the need for more police and better law enforcement is constant. Polls indicate that over half of all people say that crime has increased in their neighborhood in the early 1990s. In 1993, 71 percent of respondents indicated that "halting the rising crime rate" was a serious problem on which we were spending too little money.[39] Why are we so frightened? There are at least three reasons.

First, our sense of safety is heavily shaped by media reporting of crimes. The national news is dominated by reporting from a few major urban areas, and by the most horrible crimes in those areas. Murder rates rose in Chicago and New York from 1980 to 1993, and soared in Washington, D.C., where the murder rate in 1993 was three times larger than in New York City. But in many other cities (both big cities such as Los Angeles or in smaller-sized cities), murder rates have fallen or remained constant.[40] As long as much of our national news comes from New York and D.C., our sense of reality may be shaped by impressions that do not apply to our own towns.

Local news shows have also increasingly focused on the most gruesome stories. The motto for many local news shows has become, "If it bleeds, it leads." This leaves viewers with an impression that local crime is horrendous and prevalent, without giving them any sense of the actual probability that such crimes will affect them.

Second, many of us regularly watch movies or TV shows that feature murder and threat as their primary plot device. There is accumulating evidence that watching fictional portrayals of crime makes people feel more threatened in their daily life.[41] Regularly viewing stories about conspiracies, stalkings, murders, kidnappings, and assault on a nightly basis persuades too many people that these events are likely occurrences in their neighborhoods.

Third, crime rates are rising among a few groups and in a few neighborhoods, and these crime increases have received an enormous amount of attention. Among young men (particularly young black men) there has been a shocking increase in murder, primarily through increased gun violence. Rates of homicide among young black men between ages 15 and 24 have almost doubled since 1985, and are *eight times* the homicide rate among young white men of the same ages.[42] In urban ghetto neighborhoods, the incidence of handgun possession and use has soared.

People of all ages in these communities live in fear of stray bullets, often shot by teenagers who have little sense of the value of life. A number of shocking incidents in major cities have received prominent attention. For instance, a seven-year-old living in the Cabrini Green housing project in Chicago was shot in the head and killed as he walked across the street to school; a five-year-old boy was killed when several older boys dropped him out of a fourteen-story window while his brother tried to fight them off. We listen to these stories with horror and fear that *our* children may be at risk of equally inexplicable and random death.

Life expectancies for black men have fallen over the last ten years, largely due to an increase in deaths from homicide.[43] Homicides tend to be densely concentrated in urban areas. For instance, a map of the murders in Washington, D.C., shows several tight clusters of dots around several easily identified streets and street corners, and only a slight scattering of dots elsewhere through the city. These deaths are not random, nor are all city dwellers at equal risk.

The picture for drugs is quite similar. Like crime, drug use has fallen over the past fifteen years. This is true of almost all types of illegal drugs, from cocaine to marijuana.[44] On average, Americans are getting high less often. The most commonly used legal drug, alcohol, is also declining in use. Americans who drink are also more likely to drink lower-alcohol drinks (wine or beer) than in the past. Sales of hard liquor have waned.

Yet, like homicide, among some groups drug use is high. We have little data that tabulate drug use by income level, but the statistics indicate that illegal drug use is higher among younger people, men, those with less education, and those who are not working.[45] While the data are admittedly limited, drug use within all of these demographic groups has declined since 1985, although these groups continue to have higher rates of drug use than other demographic groups. Interestingly, people in large metropolitan areas report lower rates of illegal drug use in the 1990s than people in smaller metropolitan areas.

One particular drug that has received a great deal of attention is crack cocaine. While overall cocaine use has declined, the spread of crack cocaine in certain city neighborhoods in the early and mid-1980s made available a drug that was relatively cheap and which produced an intense high. We have little formal data on crack use until the 1990s, when the national drug use surveys started to collect this information. By any measure, crack cocaine is used by a very small proportion of drug users. The share of persons reporting crack use over the past year is one-fifth of those who report overall cocaine use and one-twentieth of those who report marijuana use. Anecdotal evidence suggests that crack users are lower-income persons and concentrated in particular city neighborhoods.

Most troubling, the availability of crack cocaine appears to have led to increased use by women, who typically have had much lower drug usage and addiction rates. The phenomenon of "crack babies" has been a major problem for public hospitals in large urban areas, as babies born with crack addiction (and often with other health problems as well) demand special medical and nursing attention.

Just as the use of crack cocaine is limited to a small share of the population, however, the number of women with children who seriously use and abuse drugs remains relatively small. For instance, Doug Besharov of the American Enterprise Institute has estimated that no more than one or two percent of babies are born to women with crack addictions, approximately 30,000 to 50,000 births per year. Other more recent surveys have found numbers of the same magnitude or smaller.[46] Even if we take the higher number and assume that all of these births were to poor women, this would constitute only about five percent of births to poor women. While I consider this number unacceptably high, it is obviously a problem within a small group of the poor population.

Drug use, gun violence, street crime, gang activities, and other forms of criminal behavior are all more prevalent in poorer areas, and highly prevalent in some of our poorest and most desperate urban neighborhoods. These are not problems to dismiss or to minimize. But there are two generalizations we must be careful not to make.

First, not all poor persons who live in high-crime neighborhoods are part of a culture of crime and violence. In fact, criminal activity and serious drug abuse are, even in the poorest neighborhoods, the activity of a few. Their biggest victims are not those who live outside the neighborhood, but those who live within the neighborhood, trying to protect their children from the gangs, the guns, and the drugs. The primary reason to stop this activity is not because it threatens the middle classes who live 10 miles away, but because it threatens to destroy the lives of those who are trying to live resilient and healthy lives in poor communities. Low-income persons are three times more likely to be victims of violent crimes than are high-income persons. The fear of crime and victimization makes it much harder for mothers to protect their children, for schools to teach well, or for poor families to improve their lives.

Second, we should not ascribe to all poor persons the problems and behaviors of the few. Close to 90 percent of the poor live outside the urban ghetto neighborhoods that are most afflicted with drugs and crime. The visibility of violence and crime among a few groups of the poor should not be taken to indicate that most poor persons engage in this behavior. The steady declines in crime and drug rates among most demographic groups suggests that, if anything, fewer persons are engaged in these behaviors now than they were ten years ago.

While our information on the correlations between poverty, crime, and drug abuse is limited, the images that directly link poverty and crime are often badly overstated. Most people, at all income levels, do not participate in these activities. While concentrated problems of violence, particularly homicide, have increased in our poorest city neighborhoods, even here, the poor are more likely to be the victims than the perpetrators of such crimes. Serious problems of violence—often correlated with drugs—do exist, particularly among younger men in ghetto neighborhoods. These problems deserve serious attention. But the number of poor who participate extensively in these dangerous activities remains small.

A Changing Economy

"It's the economy, stupid."

—Sign posted in the 1992 Clinton campaign headquarters

THE FATE of the poor in America is closely linked to the economy. The Great Depression of the 1930s produced widespread economic destitution and poverty. Similarly, the unparalleled economic expansion of the 1960s produced the strongest and most sustained decline in poverty this country has ever experienced. The rising tide lifted all boats in those years, rich and poor alike. The tide of economic growth rose in the 1980s and 1990s as well, but there was little progress against poverty. What went wrong?

If asked the question, "What change has had the most important effects on poverty and policy in the United States over the past thirty years?" the answer must clearly be, "The changed economic environment for less-skilled workers." This chapter is about how economic growth in America no longer guarantees a decline in poverty. A steady decline in wages among less-skilled workers has offset the improved employment opportunities created by economic growth. From a policy perspective, this is particularly bad news, as it implies that our most popular antipoverty policy—economic growth—no longer works. Economic growth has historically benefited the poor even as it also provided expanded economic opportunities for the nonpoor, making it a classic win-win policy, without the political vulnerability, bureaucratic complexity, or the tax costs of more traditional assistance programs aimed solely at helping the poor.

The changing economy for less-skilled workers has resulted in deteriorating economic opportunities for less-skilled adults in poor families, making it much harder to reduce poverty simply by helping people find employment. The long-time advice to the poor—"Get a job"—is less useful now than twenty years ago. For many less-skilled workers, earnings alone—even from full-time year-round work—are simply not high enough to provide the income that puts a family over the poverty line. These adults must work *and* have access to other sources of economic support (public or private) if their families are to avoid poverty.

Of course, for some number of less-skilled adults, no job is available, however low paid. Unemployment rates have not changed much among less-skilled workers over the past decade. Yet this is not reassuring news, since the share of those who actively seek work but do not find it has always been high among those with less education. Particular problems of job availability and job access occur in isolated rural communities as well as in poor urban neighborhoods, where the economic transformation of our cities has left many families—particularly African Americans—disconnected from the growing suburban job market.

Among less-skilled men in particular, their declining wage opportunities have resulted in declining involvement in mainstream labor markets. A growing share of adult men with limited educational credentials—exactly the group whose earning opportunities have fallen the most—are no longer at work or actively seeking work, although some may be involved in the underground economy that flourishes in certain areas. Bringing these men back into mainstream employment must be a major concern in the near future.

Combined with the growing share of single-adult families among the poor that we discussed in the last chapter, this economic news implies that poverty is becoming doubly hard to address. It is more difficult for single-parent families than for married-couple families to escape poverty through employment, even if their job opportunities were not worsening. But increases in single-adult families are occurring at the same time as the labor market is becoming steadily more hostile for less-skilled workers. Either of these changes alone would have been bad news for those who want to fight poverty. Together, they are devastating. Together, they are the primary reason why we have faced high and sustained poverty rates in this country for over a decade.

2.1 The Death of "Trickle Down Economics": Why Economic Growth No Longer Reduces Poverty

SUMMARY. *Economic growth—long one of the most effective and politically attractive antipoverty tools available—has not been effective in reducing poverty in the United States over the past fifteen years. The economic expansions of the 1980s and 1990s did not produce substantial declines in poverty. Economic booms result in a growing number of jobs, which typically benefit less-skilled workers in poor families more than any other group. When the economy expanded in the 1980s, low-income families worked more and worked harder, just as in earlier decades when job availability grew. Unfortunately, even when overall employment was growing, the wages of less-skilled workers were falling steadily, meaning that increased work effort was offset by declining wages.*

I was working as a senior staff economist for the Council of Economic Advisers in the fall of 1989. One of our responsibilities was to produce short memos for the White House when major economic statistics were released, summarizing the implications of these data. In October, the Census Bureau released its annual report on income and poverty for 1988, which happened to be a year of very strong economic growth and rising average personal incomes. Oddly, however, the poverty rate fell by an insignificant amount that year. I wrote up my summary and brought it to my boss for approval. He read it through, handed it back to me, and said, "Add a paragraph explaining why poverty didn't fall last year." I dutifully went back to my desk, sat down at my computer, stared at it a while, and realized I had no explanation to offer.

Three years earlier, in 1986, I had published an article with my colleague at Princeton, Alan Blinder, in which we documented the effect of economic growth on poverty. Using historical data through the early 1980s, we showed that when jobs expanded and unemployment fell, poverty also declined sharply. We predicted a steep decline in poverty over the 1980s, as the United States economy recovered from the severe recession at the beginning of that decade.[1] I *knew* that economic growth reduced poverty. I didn't have a clue why it hadn't worked in 1988. That puzzle led me and others to the research summarized in this section.

The apparent problem has become worse over the years. In fact, in November 1994, when the government released its official statistics documenting income and poverty changes over the previous year, it showed a historically unprecedented result: in 1993, when the rate of aggregate economic growth (after inflation) was 3 percent—a very healthy growth rate indeed—the proportion of Americans who were poor in that year actually *rose* at the same time as the aggregate economy was expanding. Behind these dry statistics lies one of the most discouraging facts for American social policy: an expanding economy no longer guarantees a decline in poverty.

Rising poverty occurring alongside of economic expansion is particularly troubling because of the long-cherished belief that economic growth is a sure way to reduce need. The experience of the Great Depression stamped in many people's minds the conviction that it is economic hard times that cause poverty, while the economic wonder years following World War II reinforced that belief by producing widespread income gains among rich and poor alike. President John Kennedy frequently used the phrase "a rising tide lifts all boats." Twenty years later Ronald Reagan would invoke this phrase again to argue that economic growth is the best way to help the poor.

Based on the experiences of the first three decades after World War II, Presidents Kennedy and Reagan were right. The longest and strongest expansion in U.S. history occurred between 1961 and 1969; during this time period the economy grew an average of 4.3 percent per year, after inflation. Poverty plummeted. Figure 2.1 graphs both the official U.S. poverty rate and the size of the aggregate economy since 1960, as measured by Gross Domestic Product (GDP) per capita, the total amount of goods and services produced in the United States, divided by the U.S. population.[2] The inverse relationship between per capita GDP (up) and poverty (down) is apparent in this graph, particularly in the 1960s. While 22 percent of the U.S. population lived in families below the official U.S. poverty line in 1960, only 13 percent of the population was poor by 1970. Almost all analysts ascribe most of this steep decline in

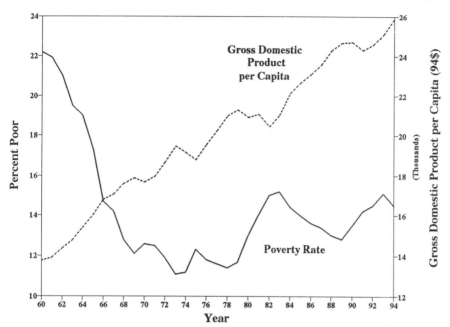

Figure 2.1. U.S. poverty rate versus gross domestic product per capita, 1960–1994. (*Sources*: *Economic Report of the President* 1995; U.S. Bureau of the Census 1995a,b)

poverty to the rapid economic growth that occurred during this period. The war on poverty that occurred in the 1960s was largely fought by the engines of economic growth.

Why does poverty generally decline in times of economic expansion?[3] The primary reason is that the number of available jobs grows. When the demand for workers expands, those who benefit most are unemployed job seekers, the part-time workers who want more hours, and those we call discouraged workers, who are no longer searching for work. People who are already working forty to fifty hours a week can benefit little from the employment expansion in an economic boom. Unemployed, underemployed, and discouraged workers are predominantly less-skilled workers. The poorest 20 percent of all families contain 40 percent of those who report themselves unemployed, an indication of how much more prevalent unemployment is among low-income families.[4] Of course, their low incomes are partially related to their higher unemployment. When the economy expands, low-income families benefit from employment growth much more than higher-income families. The result is a decline in poverty.

In the 1960s, however, another factor was just as important as the employment expansion. Wages rose for workers at all wage levels in the 1960s. Each one percent expansion in the economy over the 1960s was associated with a $2.18 increase in weekly wages after inflation for workers in low-income families. The result was that low-income people in particular had a double-whammy positive effect on their income: they worked more hours *and* they earned more for every hour that they worked. Poverty plummeted.

Now move the scene forward twenty years. Between 1983 and 1989, the U.S. economy experienced its second longest and strongest economic expansion. The economy grew an average of 3.7 percent per year, very similar to the 1960s. But as figure 2.1 shows, poverty fell only modestly during this time period, compared with the 1960s. What went wrong in the 1980s?

It wasn't because of a lack of job expansion. Unemployment fell faster and weeks of work among low-income households expanded at a faster rate in the 1980s expansion than in the 1960s expansion. If we look only at the hours people worked, we would have expected poverty to fall *faster* in the 1980s.

The key to the puzzle is wages. Among workers who were in the poorest 10 percent of the population, which is entirely composed of families below the poverty line, real wages actually *fell* with economic growth. Over the expansion of the 1980s, a one percent expansion in the aggregate economy was correlated with a $.32 *decline* in weekly wages for the poorest 10 percent.

In the 1980s, falling wages offset expanding work opportunities, a sharp contrast to the 1960s when the two effects reinforced each other. The overall result was a decline in poverty, but a much slower decline than earlier.

By the 1990s, things were looking even bleaker. A mild two-year recession in 1990–91 was followed by an economic expansion starting in 1992. Not surprisingly, poverty rose in 1990 and 1991. Very surprisingly, poverty continued to rise in both 1992 and 1993, as figure 2.1 indicates. For the first time in modern economic history, U.S. poverty rates were not falling with economic growth. Not until 1994, the third year of expansion, did poverty rates finally begin to decline. Employment expansion was occurring, as it always does in boom times, but wages continued to fall for less-skilled workers.

The public policy implications of this are discouraging. Economic growth as a means of reducing poverty is a win-win strategy by all accounts. As I will discuss in chapter 6, the alternatives to economic growth involve greater political and economic trade-offs, requiring taxation of nonpoor families in order to pay for redistributive programs provided to the poor. In contrast, economic growth promises to decrease poverty at the same time as economic well-being improves among others in the economy. Everyone becomes better off as poverty also falls. Clearly, this is a preferred strategy. Unfortunately, within the recent past and the foreseeable future, economic growth has not been nor will it be very effective as an antipoverty tool, as increases in the overall economy are offset by falling wages among less-skilled workers. The fact that economic growth no longer means less poverty is a hard blow to those who want to fight poverty. This reality makes policy choices harder, both economically and politically.

The following two sections of this chapter discuss how the labor market has changed in the last several decades. We start by talking about the availability of jobs and then investigate the shifts in wages that are causing serious problems for many of our citizens.

2.2 JOBS: AS AVAILABLE (OR AS UNAVAILABLE) AS EVER

SUMMARY: *Contrary to popular belief, there is little evidence that fewer jobs are available for less-skilled workers now compared to twenty years ago. Workers with lower levels of education, particularly those from minority racial or ethnic backgrounds, have always faced unemployment rates of 10 percent or higher. While this indicates ongoing problems for these workers in locating jobs, these problems seem about as bad (or as good) as they were fifteen years ago.*

How would the American job market respond if the number of people seeking work were to double? That thought experiment is not speculative but describes exactly what happened in the three decades since 1960. The number of American adults seeking work has soared, largely because of the growth in the adult population as the post–World War II baby boomers entered their working years, along with a dramatic increase in the number of adult women who have chosen to work outside the home for pay.

What has been the result? Not massive unemployment, as some might have predicted. Instead, the number of jobs available has expanded along with the number of workers. Employment growth has outstripped population growth in each of the last three decades; most of the growing number of people looking for work have found it. In fact, the group whose work effort has increased the most—adult women—has also experienced a long-term decline in its unemployment rate relative to adult men.[5]

This is in sharp comparison to many other countries. The number of jobs has not grown along with the workforce in many European countries. Nations as different as England, Sweden, and Spain have all seen steep, long-term increases in unemployment over the last fifteen years.

Figure 2.2 graphs unemployment rates among men and women over the past several decades.[6] Only people who are actively searching for work are counted as unemployed; the unemployment rate shows the share of people searching for work among all those at work or searching. Those who do not seek work are not counted. Thus this number does not include people who have become so discouraged about the prospect of finding work that they have stopped looking, or people who report themselves as not working but who are involved with the underground economy. As discussed in section 2.4 a growing number of less-skilled men are neither working nor searching for work.

While unemployment rates trended upward from the late 1960s through the early 1980s, there has been no increase since then. In fact, the average unemployment rate during 1994—6.1 percent—was somewhat below the 1984 rate and at about the same level as the 1974 rate. While unemployment cycles up and down as the economy changes, there is little evidence of long-term deterioration in the labor market in terms of job availability over the past two

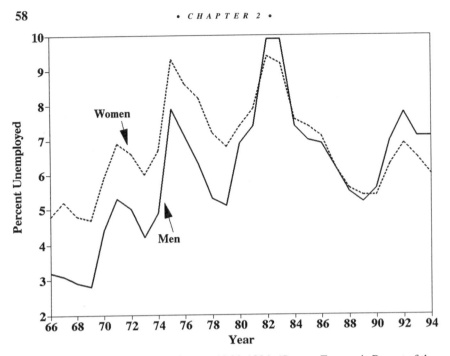

Figure 2.2. Unemployment rates by sex, 1966–1994. (*Source*: Economic Report of the President 1995)

decades. In fact, stable unemployment rates in the face of substantial increases in the labor force are the sign of a very healthy job market.

But before we conclude that job availability is not a problem for workers, we need to look at the differences in the availability of jobs for particular groups of workers. While job availability may not have deteriorated overall, it could still have declined for some.

As it turns out, low-wage workers—the working poor and near-poor—face substantially more problems with job availability than do higher-wage workers. The unemployment rate among workers with less than a high school degree is *five times* what it is for workers with a college degree. Recall that this is the share of the workforce that is actively seeking work but not finding it. Figure 2.3 shows relative unemployment rates by skill level for men and women in 1994.[7] While workers with college degrees have only a 3 percent unemployment rate, the result of what economists call "frictional unemployment"—job switching and job search that would occur in any labor market—high school dropouts have a 15 percent rate. Similar calculations for earlier decades show very similar comparisons.

Not only does job availability differ by skill, but it also continues to differ by race. Black workers, both male and female, have long experienced unemployment rates that were about twice the rate of white workers at the same skill level. Black high school dropouts have an unemployment rate in excess

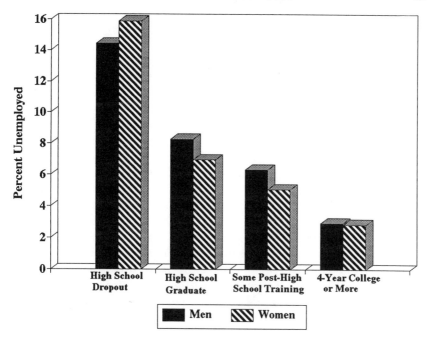

Figure 2.3. Unemployment rates by skill level, 1994. (*Source*: Author's tabulations from 1994 March Current Population Survey)

of 20 percent. Hispanic workers with low educations have high unemployment rates, but below those of blacks.

The ongoing economic shift from manufacturing to service sector jobs in the U.S. economy has affected men more than women. Women's unemployment rates fell below those of men in the early 1980s in part because many more men lost jobs due to steep cutbacks in manufacturing employment during those years. But this decline in manufacturing has not produced a long-term rise in unemployment over the past fifteen years. Men who continue to look for work are finding it at about the same rate now as in the past, although the jobs that they are finding might be much less satisfactory, as discussed in the next section.

The conclusion from this analysis is twofold: On the one hand, the availability of jobs has been relatively stable over the past two decades for those who want to work. While job opportunities rise and fall over the business cycle, the long-term trend over the past twenty years is largely flat. Thus, there is no evidence of deterioration in the overall availability of jobs for those seeking work in this country.

On the other hand, while job availability may not have deteriorated on average, there remains a serious problem with job availability for less-skilled workers. For the working poor, unemployment is as high and job availability is as limited as it has always been. The good news is that unemployment has not gotten worse in recent decades. The bad news is that jobs have never been readily available for many less-skilled workers. At any point, around 15 percent of those who actively seek work remain unemployed, with even greater problems among African American and Latino workers. As we shall see below in the section on the geography of jobs, work is particularly scarce for residents of urban ghetto neighborhoods.

2.3 ONE STEP FORWARD, TWO STEPS BACK:
FIFTEEN YEARS OF FALLING WAGES

SUMMARY. *The nature of the jobs available to less-skilled workers has substantially worsened. Among the least-skilled men, wages have fallen more than 20 percent in the past fifteen years. Fringe benefits and career opportunities have become more limited. Among the least-skilled women, wages have fallen slightly but remain far below those of their male counterparts. More-skilled women and men have experienced substantial wage increases over these years. There is no reason to believe that these trends are likely to reverse themselves in the near future. If anything, wages for less-skilled workers are likely to fall even further.*

In the last section we learned that the overall availability of employment has not changed much during the past twenty years; less-skilled workers continue to face problems finding jobs, but there is little evidence that these problems have become worse. This section goes beyond the question of availability to look at the *nature* of the jobs available. The wage and career opportunities available to many less-skilled workers has deteriorated steadily for the past fifteen years. Employment no longer provides these workers the economic security it once did.

Changes in Wages over the Past Twenty-Five Years

In the 1960s, many men in the U.S. labor force were high school dropouts. In fact, many older men had never started high school but went straight to work in their mid-teens. Thirty-eight percent of the male population between ages 18 to 65 had less than twelve years of schooling in 1968. Adjusted for changes in inflation, the average weekly wage level among these men was $488 per week for those who worked full-time, full-year.

By the 1990s, educational levels in the U.S. workforce had increased dramatically. By 1994, only 17 percent of adult men were high school dropouts, and the average worker had over thirteen years of education. But among men who were high school dropouts and worked full-time, full-year, average weekly wages had fallen to $400 per week.

Figure 2.4 plots weekly wages (after inflation) among full-time, full-year male workers with different levels of skill since the mid-1960s.[8] Figure 2.5 shows the magnitude of what's happened to men's wages since 1979. These graphs include only full-time, full-year workers to avoid any wage changes due to changes in work effort.[9] I use 1979 as the base year because it is a year of strong economic growth, similar to 1993. It was also the year when wages among less-skilled men started to move downward more sharply.

The graph of wage levels over time (fig. 2.4) indicates that wages for high school graduates and high school dropouts peaked around 1970 and have declined since. In contrast, since 1979, wages among college-educated men increased substantially, leading to a substantial widening in the wage distribution between more- and less-skilled workers. As figure 2.5 indicates, the result is that high school dropouts earned *22 percent* less in 1993 than they did in 1979, and high school graduates earned 12 percent less.[10] In sharp contrast, over these years college-educated men experienced a 10 percent wage increase. Though not shown separately on figure 2.5, men with post-college degrees experienced a 22 percent *increase* in their wages since 1979.

It is important to understand that this widening wage distribution is occurring throughout the economy. Less-skilled men in virtually every occupation and industry have faced wage declines, while more-skilled men have experienced increases in earnings. Contrary to popular belief, this phenomenon is not driven by the shift from manufacturing to service sector jobs. Less-skilled men in both manufacturing and service sector jobs have experienced wage declines. This is apparent for workers of all ages, although the trends are steeper among younger workers. Furthermore, declining wage rates are not limited just to high school dropouts but have also occurred among high school graduates. Only college graduates have seen improvements in earning opportunities over the past fifteen years.

The problem of declining wages appears to be affecting men much more than women. Figure 2.6 shows wage trends among full-time, full-year working women at different skill levels, and figure 2.7 indicates how wages have changed since 1979. Overall, for most female workers wages have risen sharply, at least partly because of increased job opportunities for women as gender discrimination has declined. For the least-skilled women (high school dropouts), however, wages have declined by 6 percent since 1979. These women haven't experienced the increases of their higher-skilled sisters, but neither have they experienced the sharp wage declines of their brothers. Weekly wages in 1993 among full-time, full-year female workers who are high school dropouts are a few dollars higher than what the same women would have earned in 1967.

It is important to emphasize that the wages earned by less-skilled women remain far below those of men. Even with declining wages, male high-school dropouts working full-time currently earn $400 per week on average, while equivalent women earn $287. In short, while earning opportunities have declined for less-skilled men, their less-skilled sisters never had access to

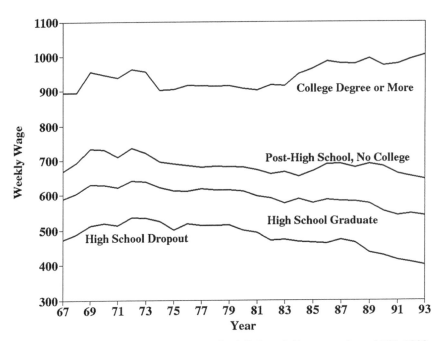

Figure 2.4. Men's average weekly wages, for full-time, full-year workers, 1967–1993, by educational level, in 1993 dollars. (*Source*: Author's tabulations from 1968–1994 March Current Population Surveys)

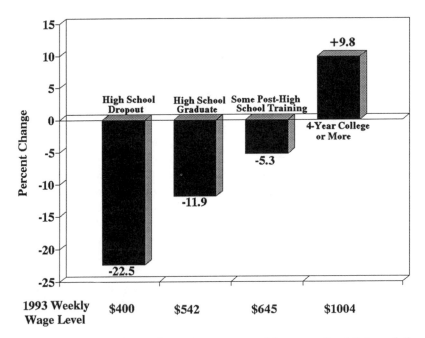

Figure 2.5. Percent change in men's average weekly wages, for full-time, full-year workers, 1979–1993. (*Source*: Author's tabulations from 1980 and 1994 March Current Population Surveys)

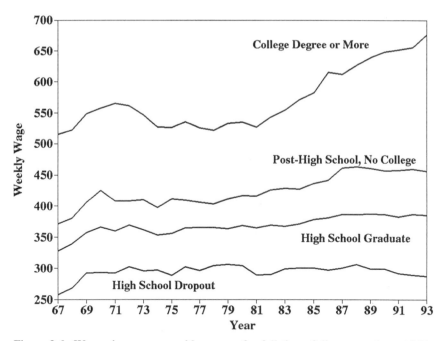

Figure 2.6. Women's average weekly wages, for full-time, full-year workers, 1967–1993, by educational level, in 1993 dollars. (*Source*: Author's tabulations from 1968–1994 March Current Population Surveys)

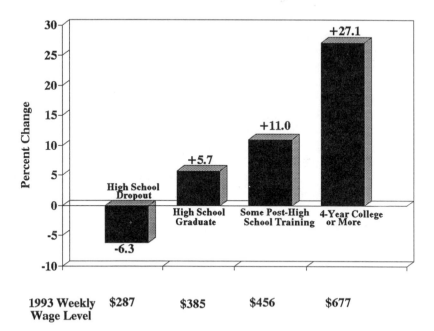

Figure 2.7. Percent change in women's average weekly wages, for full-time, full-year workers, 1979–1993. (*Source*: Author's tabulations from 1980 and 1994 March Current Population Surveys)

better-paying jobs and have faced a largely stagnant set of earning opportunities for twenty-five years. They have always had access to bad jobs at bad wages. Little has changed.

Changes in Nonwage Compensation

Wages are only one aspect of a job, and it is worth asking what has happened to the nonwage aspects of jobs, such as fringe benefits or career and promotional opportunities. Much of the evidence indicates that, like wages, these have also deteriorated for less-skilled workers. The probability that jobs paying below seven dollars an hour (in 1993 dollars) will provide health insurance has declined from 32 percent in 1979 to 25 percent in 1993. Pension benefits show similar trends; 18 percent of jobs paying less than seven dollars an hour included pension benefits in 1979, while only 14 percent did by 1993. Thus, the trends in nonwage compensation have only reinforced the trends in wage compensation.[11]

Long-term career advancement opportunities for less-skilled men have been shrinking for many years. The old success stories about company presidents who started as company stock boys are largely obsolete. Rather than being a long chain of linked upwardly mobile jobs, job ladders between less- and more-skilled positions have disappeared as the entry level positions for management jobs have become open only to college graduates. In fact, top management positions increasingly require MBAs or other post-college degrees.

Ironically, promotional opportunities for women have been less negatively affected than for men. For most women in the past who chose to work, there were never any job ladders that allowed them to move from the pink collar ghetto of low-paid clerical positions into management positions. The "burger flipper" jobs that have been much decried for their low wages and lack of career options are quite similar to the jobs that less-skilled women have always filled. In fact, growing concern about equal opportunity encouraged many businesses to create job ladders between traditional women's positions (often clerical or retail) into entry-level management positions. There has thus been less erosion in women's promotional opportunities. As with wages, the long-term career opportunities for less-skilled women have probably not deteriorated as much as among men. They have always been bad; in some areas of the economy they may even have improved.

What Are the Causes of These Wage Changes?

The causes of these wage shifts are not fully understood. Stated simply, there are two possible reasons for declining wages among less-skilled workers. Either the problem can be on the supply side of the market, with too many less-productive workers driving down wages on these jobs, or the problem can be on the demand side of the labor market, with a declining demand for less-skilled workers on the part of employers. In fact, as average educational levels in the overall workforce rise, the share of the workforce that is low skilled continues to shrink. Virtually all analysts come to the same conclusion: the problem is not on the supply side but on the demand side. Declines in the demand for less-skilled workers are the primary reason for falling real wages.

But this analysis contradicts a few common myths. Before explaining the change in the demand for less-skilled workers, let's talk about two myths that claim the problem is on the supply side.

Myth 1: Today's less skilled workers are less prepared for jobs. Some claim that the reason wages are falling among less-skilled workers is because public schools are failing and traditional family structures are breaking down, producing young people who are less literate and less disciplined. Employers are paying these workers less because they aren't as productive.

There are at least two reasons why this story doesn't work. First, even older less-skilled workers are experiencing wage declines. That means that persons who grew up in the 1940s and 1950s but who dropped out of high school to take jobs in the 1960s and 1970s have been hit with wage declines in the 1980s. This group of workers is presumably just as literate and disciplined as it always was. Second, the gender differences in the results also argue against this story. If the problem is changes in family and school structures, why aren't women (who have grown up in the same families and schools as their brothers) showing the same trends as men?

There is very little evidence that today's less-skilled workers are measurably worse workers than yesterday's. Without denying that America's public schools might be in need of improvement, there is little evidence that they are turning out worse workers now than twenty-five years ago. In fact, regular national assessment tests performed on a random sample of students indicate that average scores on standardized exams of reading and math achievement show no change or slight progress among different age groups since 1970. There is also no evidence that those who perform at the bottom on these tests are performing worse than before.[12] Increases in school achievement are largest among the black population. Literacy proficiency among twenty-one to twenty-five-year-olds showed slight deterioration between 1985 and 1992, but most of this is ascribed to the increase in young immigrants, who did *not* attend U.S. schools during their childhood and who are learning English as a second language.[13]

The problem is not that high school dropouts are less skilled than they used to be; the problem is that the jobs open to these workers are demanding more (or at least different) skills than before. Strong muscles, with limited literacy and numeracy, are not adequate for today's jobs. In short, the job *demands* are changing rather than the worker skills.

Myth 2: Immigrant inflows are pushing down wages. Some claim that the decline in wages is due to the sharp increase in the immigrant population in the United States. These workers are competing for the less-skilled jobs and driving down the wage rate.

It is true that immigration rates to the United States have increased. The share of the population living in the United States who was not born in this country has risen from 4.7 percent to 8.0 percent between 1970 and 1990.[14] After many decades of very low immigration, immigration began to increase sharply in the 1980s due to a change in immigration laws. Immigrants typically have less schooling than native-born workers, largely because education levels in most other countries are below those of the United States.

But there is little evidence that this increase in immigration is a major cause of the wage shifts described above. Immigrants tend to live in a few selected parts of the country upon arrival, so the impact of immigration on some regions (particularly Midwestern inland cities) has been relatively small, while in some of the coastal cities it has been much larger. Yet there is no evidence that cities with larger shares of immigrants have substantially greater wage differentials or higher unemployment among native workers.[15] (Of course, these cities may be facing other problems due to the rapid growth in immigration.) In fact, the widespread nature of these wage trends, in all industries and in all regions of the country, argues that immigration, which tends to be concentrated, cannot be the primary cause. In addition, the time trend of immigration doesn't match well against these wage changes. Wages among less-skilled workers started falling before the big jumps in immigration occurred.

How can a big increase in the number of less-skilled workers due to immigration not affect wages among native-born less-skilled workers? On the margin, if the big immigration inflows continue there undoubtedly will be growing effects. But it is important to realize that new immigrant communities also increase the demand for goods and services, thereby creating new jobs. Many immigrants, particularly those with English-language difficulty, find employment within their own community. Others take jobs (sometimes illegal work) that native-born workers do not want. Immigrants don't displace native workers one-for-one; most estimates show quite small displacement effects of immigrants on native workers.

If both of these myths are false, what *does* explain the decline in wages among less-skilled workers? As noted above, virtually all analysts agree that the problem is due to declining demand by employers, not changes in worker supply or quality. Two primary stories are told to explain the declining demand for less-skilled workers; there is evidence to support both of them.[16]

Explanation 1: The increasing internationalization of the U.S. economy. As America is more and more involved in world trade, our workers compete with workers around the globe. The comparative advantage of the United States in the global labor market is its large share of highly skilled and well-educated workers. The United States has more college graduates than any other country. As U.S. trade expands, these workers' skills are producing products that are in demand around the world.

But less-skilled workers in the United States are at a comparative disadvantage relative to workers in the industrializing world. U.S. wage rates for less-skilled workers are relatively high in the international marketplace, due to higher standards of living in the United States. Less-skilled workers in rapidly industrializing countries such as those in the fast-growing Pacific Rim can be hired at much lower wages than in the United States. In a world where firms are increasingly global and can move their production facilities across country borders, this kind of hiring will disadvantage U.S. workers with fewer skills.

Explanation 2: Technological changes in the U.S. economy that require a more skilled Workforce. There is evidence that the new technologies in the American workplace, particularly the widespread availability of "smart machines" that can do much of the rote work once done by humans, have decreased the demand for less-skilled workers. In manufacturing, almost all industries have retooled their plants in ways that use more smart machines and less human labor. Increasingly, manufacturing employees watch computer screens and feed production programs into large machinery. Persons employed in physical labor and/or repetitive tasks are less and less needed.

In the growing service sector, technologies have also changed. Computers regularly handle a great deal of the accounting and clerical work that was once the domain of an army of clerks. In my own world of the university, the number of secretaries and typists has shrunk substantially, while faculty produce finished versions of letters and papers using word-processing programs on their own personal computers. Readers of this book will be able to think of their own examples where machines do the work that people used to perform—from the of use self-service gas station equipment to the use of ATM machines.

There is evidence to support both the trade and the technology stories, and almost surely both of them are happening at once. These stories explain a variety of other changes in the labor market that are also correlated with declining wages among the less skilled. For instance, union jobs continue to disappear in the United States, in part because of the economic pressures of trade and technology, and this accounts for about one-fifth of the decline in wages among less-skilled workers, since unions typically raise the wages of the least skilled.

The most discouraging aspect of these two explanations is that neither of them is likely to be reversed in the near future. If anything, virtually all economists who have looked at these issues predict that the current trends toward a more internationalized economy with increasing use of "smart" technology will continue into the near future. This suggests that further declines in the earning ability of less-skilled workers are likely.

If the last section indicated that job availability does not seem to be an enormous problem, this section indicates that there is a serious and growing problem with the nature of the jobs available for less-skilled workers. Particularly among men who lack post–high school training, the earnings and career opportunities are much more limited now than fifteen years ago; thus these men's relative position in the labor market has worsened. In contrast, less-skilled women have had much more limited opportunities from the beginning. While they have not seen as large a decline in wages as men, female dropouts today face about the same job opportunities that their mothers did in the late 1960s. Even with the declining male earnings, less-skilled women working full-time and year-round continue to earn substantially less than their male counterparts.

2.4 WORK FOLLOWS WAGES:
CHANGING WORK EFFORT AMONG THE POOR

SUMMARY. *Recent wage trends are highly correlated with changes in work behavior. Men are spending less time at work or searching for work, particularly less-skilled men who face falling wages. Highly skilled women, who have experienced the biggest wage gains, have also shown the biggest increase in employment and hours of work. Although most women are far more likely to work for pay now than in earlier years, this is not true of less-skilled women, whose wages have been stagnant for years and who have shown only small increases in their labor market involvement.*

Given big changes in earnings opportunities among less- and more-skilled workers, it is perhaps not surprising that there have also been dramatic differences in employment behavior between these two groups of workers over the past fifteen years. Most of these mirror the changes in labor demand and wages that we have already explored.

Figure 2.8 shows the share of adult men by skill level who were actively at work or seeking work in 1970 and 1993.[17] Declines in this share indicate the growth of men who are out of the labor market entirely. The difference in trends among these groups is striking.

On average, men's involvement in paid work has decreased steadily over the past twenty-five years. Among all adult men, 86 percent were working or looking for work in 1970, while only 78 percent were active in the labor market in 1993. Some of this change is positive, for it reflects the fact that many men are staying in school longer and becoming more skilled, or that many men have better pension options available and are retiring early. Both of these phenomena reduce the share of adult male workers.

But even among those who are not in school and not retired, there has been a decline in the share who are working or searching for work. Figure 2.8 shows that most of the decline in work behavior is concentrated among less-skilled men. In fact, the lower a man's skill level, the less likely he is to be

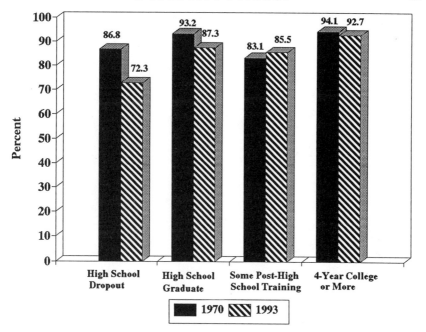

Figure 2.8. Share of adult male population at work or seeking work, 1970 and 1993. (*Source*: Author's tabulations from 1970 and 1993 March Current Population Surveys)

working. Only 72 percent of male high school dropouts are currently in the labor market. Among African American men who have dropped out of high school, only 63 percent are at work or seeking work. This is, of course, exactly the group that has experienced the steepest wage declines.

Economists have long claimed that wages and work behavior are closely correlated, so it may not be surprising to see that men are working less as their earnings opportunities decline. Those who have analyzed the decline in men's labor market behavior indicate that changes in wage rates can explain only some of the decline in men's work behavior over the 1970s. Over the 1980s, however, when wage divergence became more acute, the decline in less-skilled men's labor market behavior can be almost entirely explained by the decline in their wages.[18]

Figure 2.9 shows similar data for women. In sharp contrast with men, women's labor market participation has soared. Even among women at the very lowest skill levels, there have been slight increases in work behavior. Compare figure 2.9 to the wage trends shown in figure 2.7. The women who have experienced sharp increases in wages have also exhibited sharp increases in employment, while the least-skilled women for whom wages have declined are working only slightly more than equivalent women twenty-five years ago. For women without a high school degree, the world has looked

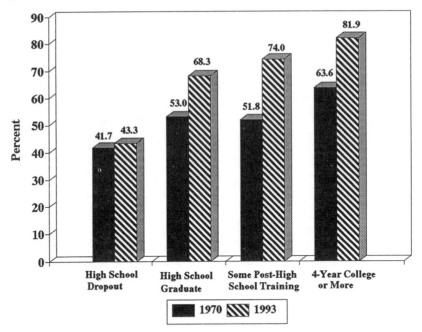

Figure 2.9. Share of adult female population at work or seeking work, 1970 and 1993. (*Source*: Author's tabulations from 1970 and 1993 March Current Population Surveys)

remarkably constant. They've seen small decreases in earnings opportunities, and they have increased their employment only a little. For less-skilled white women, even the occupations in which they work have remained remarkably constant.

This is particularly striking in light of the assumption that virtually everyone makes about working women, that is, that women's labor market involvement and employment opportunities have dramatically expanded in recent decades. While for most groups of women this assumption is accurate, it is not accurate for women who are high school dropouts, and it is less true among high school graduates than among more-educated women. Less-skilled women have seen little growth in their earnings and job opportunities and have had less reason to increase their work effort. As we noted in the last chapter, low-income single mothers are working somewhat more now than twenty years ago. Other low-income women show fewer changes.

This is an important point to keep in mind when reading the next chapters: the overall expansion in women's work opportunities has not affected all women equally. It is often claimed that because women's labor market options have expanded, we can now require less-skilled women to work more than they have in the past. Less-skilled women have not experienced an expansion in their labor market options. These women continue to face a limited set of jobs with low wages and few nonwage benefits, as they always have.

Figure 2.10. Percentage of workers who work part-time, 1968–1993. (*Source*: U.S. Department of Labor 1989, 1990–1993, 1994)

Work effort involves more than *whether* individuals work, it also involves *how much* they work. Figure 2.10 graphs the trends in part-time employment among men and women over the past two decades.[19] Among men, part-time work has increased slowly over time, so that in 1993 over 12 percent of all adult male workers were part-time employees, compared with only 9 percent in 1970. It is worth noting that many part-time men indicate that they are involuntary part-time workers, that is, they want full-time work but can find only part-time work. In general, however, the growing use of part-time work among men reinforces the evidence showing that fewer men are in the labor force; even among those who work, a greater number work part-time.

The share of women in part-time jobs has been largely constant over time, although this clearly cycles with the macro economy. Approximately 27 percent of all women workers are in part-time jobs, and this has been constant for many years. Most of these women indicate they only sought part-time work due to other family demands on their time. Thus, among women who work, their hours of work have remained largely unchanged over time. Combined with the increases in labor market participation among women, this indicates substantially greater work effort among women.

In conclusion, wage opportunities are tightly linked to work behavior. Those who have experienced wage increases in recent years are working more, particularly the more-skilled men and women; those who have experienced stagnant wages show little change in their work effort, particularly less-skilled women; those who have experienced declining wages show declines in work effort, particularly less-skilled men.

This leaves us back where we started: the most attractive goal for U.S. antipoverty policy is to increase work and earnings among adults in poor families, so that they can escape poverty through their own earnings. Unfortunately, the declines in wages experienced by men have induced an increasing number of them to leave the mainstream labor market entirely. Among less-skilled women, stagnant labor market opportunities are reflected in only small increases in labor market involvement. Any policy designed to increase work among these less-skilled adults is going to be fighting against these broad wage trends.

2.5 Cities Down / Suburbs Up: The Changing Geography of Jobs

SUMMARY. *The problems of job availability and adequacy are most acute among less-skilled city residents. Cities have undergone major economic shifts that have removed jobs to suburban locations, and displaced workers from informational networks that inform them about jobs. This has been most true for African American families, who have largely been excluded from suburban housing markets. The most disturbing aspect of this trend has been the growth in high-poverty urban ghetto neighborhoods. The fastest growth in job opportunities for both less and more skilled workers is occurring in suburban, not city areas. Particularly for less-skilled black and Latino city residents, these jobs are often inaccessible.*

In 1950, Chicago was on top of the world. The second largest city in America, Chicago was the Midwestern center of the manufacturing power that placed America first in the world economy. While it was surrounded by a growing ring of bedroom communities that were springing up after World War II (with many houses financed by the housing benefits in the G.I. Bill), the majority of its population lived in the city itself in dozens of well-defined ethnic neighborhoods. Beyond the suburban ring spread the Midwestern plains, dotted by small farming towns. Orchard Field, fifteen miles northwest of downtown Chicago, was being rebuilt and would soon be renamed O'Hare Airport. Its surrounding open fields were just disappearing. Several city leaders worried that it was too far away from the city to grow as an airport.

Forty years later, by 1990, Chicago had changed almost unrecognizably. Former farm towns had disappeared into densely populated suburbs. Gleaming skyscrapers made it clear where the center of the city was located, but the economic base of the city had changed dramatically. Most of the multistory brick manufacturing plants that once dotted the city were closed, either permanently shut down or relocated to suburban sites where new production technologies demanded single-story sprawling facilities. In fact, the majority of the jobs in the area were no longer in the city but had shifted to the suburbs. In 1960, 63 percent of workers in the greater Chicago area worked in the city. By 1990, only 42 percent worked there.[20] Many people lived in one suburb and commuted to work in another, only occasionally venturing into the city.

People who lived in city neighborhoods saw nearby employment opportunities move elsewhere. Increasingly, city neighborhoods, which had once offered a mix of production facilities, retail shops, and residences, were now the new bedroom communities. Except for small local retail outlets, city neighborhoods had few job opportunities and city residents had become the new commuters, sometimes traveling downtown to work but increasingly traveling out to the suburbs.

The demographic and racial mix of the city had changed as well. Its residents were more likely to be single or elderly; married couples with children moved to the suburbs if they could. The one major population group that could not move out was African Americans. Substantial suburban housing discrimination effectively kept African American families in the city.[21] City neighborhoods were also affordable for the growing Latino population, as well as the growing population of immigrants from Asian and Middle Eastern countries.

Many city neighborhoods remained attractive places to live for those who wanted an urban environment, with families from mixed-income, racial, and ethnic backgrounds. A few neighborhoods near the still-thriving downtown remained very exclusive and expensive, and boomed in the 1980s as income among well-educated and high-wage workers soared. But a shockingly large number of once healthy neighborhoods became very poor. In Chicago in 1970 the poorest neighborhood (among seventy-seven defined city areas) had a poverty rate of 38 percent. By 1990, twelve of these seventy-seven neighborhoods had poverty rates over 40 percent, and the worst neighborhood had a poverty rate of 72 percent. These twelve poor neighborhoods included eleven percent of the city's population and they were largely all black.[22]

Along with high poverty went a large number of other economic and social problems in these urban ghetto communities. Many of these neighborhoods included public housing projects built in the 1950s and 1960s that were poorly maintained and poorly policed. Crime was endemic, as were drugs, guns, and gangs. With few jobs, only three out of ten adults were working in some of these high-poverty areas, where holding a regular job became the exception rather than the norm. Increasingly, these neighborhoods looked less like American cities and more like the worst of Third World cities with poor policing, deteriorating housing, and an economy based on public assistance, informal employment, and illegal activities.

Over the 1980s, these extremely poor neighborhoods came to be known as *underclass* areas, urban slums where the problem was not just poverty, but a whole conflux of problems that bred on each other.[23] Badly functioning public institutions, like schools or law enforcement, reinforced problems of violence, family breakdown, and poor education, which in turn overlapped with the loss of connections to jobs and employment. These neighborhoods are the areas most blighted by the economic changes that have hit all big U.S. cities.

Economic shifts in the geographic location of jobs in urban areas are an important caveat on the earlier discussion about the average availability of jobs and the nature of the jobs available. With respect to jobs, for many low-skilled workers in the cities the world is different—and worse—than the average statistics indicate. For instance, a recent study of hiring in fast-food restaurants in Harlem over a five-month period found that there were fourteen applicants for every one person hired.[24] There are at least two reasons why these problems are more acute among less-skilled inner-city workers.

First, the changes in the location and availability of jobs in the cities seriously disrupted the job networks that existed in many urban communities. There are a variety of ways by which workers find jobs, but most jobs—particularly blue-collar jobs—are filled through personal connections. Current employees often recommend people to employers, or encourage friends to apply for job openings. Personal connections provide the worker with information about a job that is often hard to obtain from outside, and they provide the employer with some sense of a worker's ability and background that employers often can't gather easily in a brief job interview. An uncle's report that you're a "good kid" provides information an employer won't know from a written job application. When companies move and jobs shift location, there may still be as many aggregate jobs available for workers to find, but the workers at the old location may be out of the network for the new jobs.[25]

This problem is particularly acute among racial minorities, whose job networks were often more attenuated to begin with. Given extensive exclusion from suburban housing over the past fifty years, many more African Americans and Latinos live in cities than in the suburbs. This means that black and Latino community connections into the growing network of suburban employers and suburban jobs are often tenuous or nonexistent.

The second problem for many less-skilled city workers is that city transportation systems—both roads and public transportation—were largely designed many years ago to help people travel from the suburbs and city neighborhoods into the center city. In many cities, it is difficult to travel by public transportation from a city neighborhood to the suburbs where the job expansion has occurred, without first going into the center city and then heading out to the suburbs. This can significantly add to commuting time and cost. Commute times, whether by car or public transportation, are typically longer for city neighborhood residents who want to work in the suburbs than if they seek work in the city.[26] Commuting time among African American city residents are consistently longer than for other groups, no matter where they work, partly indicating their lower incomes and greater use of (slower) public transportation, and partly signaling the isolation of many poor black neighborhoods.

The result is that many less-skilled workers in the city seek work downtown or nearby rather than in the suburbs. This crowds the city job market with less-skilled workers, further limiting their wage and employment prospects. At the same time, many firms trying to hire less-skilled workers in suburban areas are experiencing labor shortages. Thus, suburban fast-food stores may be advertising for help at a time when youth unemployment in the city is over 30 percent. In addition, the expanding jobs in cities' central business districts tend to be in financial and business services. Particularly for less-skilled men, these areas of the economy have provided fewer low-wage jobs than other sectors of the economy, such as health-care services, that tend to be located outside the central city.

The deep changes in the economy of urban areas in recent decades have resulted in serious problems for the urban poor. Changes in the location and mix of jobs in the city, combined with the nationwide deterioration in the demand for less-skilled workers, have put a double-whammy on many less-skilled urban dwellers. Combined with exclusion from suburban housing, these changes have been particularly devastating for many poor black communities.

Thus, our cities have become the center of seeming economic contractions. While many downtown areas remain economically viable and many city neighborhoods remain pleasant places in which to live and raise children, the worst parts of America's cities have deteriorated. Urban ghettos and their inhabitants have become more isolated from the regional economies that surround them. Within these neighborhoods, job availability has become more limited while the declining demand for less-skilled workers has continued to drive wages down on the jobs that remain available.

2.6 OUTSIDE THE MAINSTREAM:
THE UNDERGROUND ECONOMY AND THE POOR

SUMMARY. *Some poor families are involved in the underground economy, which includes both illegal activities such as drug dealing and crime, as well as legitimate activities that are not reported to tax authorities. Many public assistance recipients have strong incentives not to report their earnings from employment, and there is evidence that many women receive unreported income. This income is typically quite small in absolute terms and rarely enough to actually move them out of poverty, however. Involvement in illegal activities is highly concentrated among young adult men. Most of the income from illegal activities goes to persons with substantial reported income from other (legal) sources, and not to those we would otherwise consider poor. Even when they are engaged in by a small number of people illegal activities can have large negative effects on poor neighborhoods through increased crime and violence.*

As the earnings opportunities for less-skilled workers have declined on many jobs, there has been increasing concern about the rise of the underground economy, particularly in poor urban communities. Sometimes this means involvement in explicitly illegal activities. If working nine to five has shrinking returns, then the relative attraction of making money from crime, drug dealing, or other illicit transactions has presumably risen. But the underground economy also includes income earned in legitimate work that goes unreported to tax and public assistance authorities.

Of course, illegal and unreported economic activity is a notoriously difficult thing to measure. Most measures of underground economic activity are based on ratios of the amount of money in circulation versus the amount of money used in reported transactions. This is a *very* indirect way of measuring illegal activity but may provide some indication of the trends in underground economic activity. Figure 2.11 plots a midrange estimate of the size of the underground economy as a share of the aggregate "above-ground" economy in the United States, based on the available money supply.[27]

For 1990, figure 2.11 indicates that unreported and illegal activity is about 19 percent of overall GDP; in other words, the U.S. economy would be almost one-fifth bigger if we could measure this activity. While there is likely to be a large range of error around this estimate, it suggests that the underground economy is huge. Other estimates done in the early 1980s show illegal activity making up between 6 to 24 percent of GDP. In addition, this estimate (like others) indicates a sharp increase in the size of the underground economy during the 1970s, but little change over the 1980s.

Does it make sense to believe that the underground economy might not have grown over the 1980s? One can only speculate, but there may be reasons why the growth in underground economic activities may have halted. First, more and more states are running public lotteries and licensed gambling to raise revenue, driving similar illegal activities out of business. Revenues from state lotteries increased from $2 billion to $20 billion between 1980 and 1992.[28] Second, increased financial sophistication in monitoring economic transactions may limit the ability to hide income and avoid taxes. Third, there has been a long-term decline in the use of illegal drugs in America, as we discussed in the last chapter, perhaps due to changes in the acceptability or desire to use drugs.

Our concern is the involvement of the poor in the underground economy. There is no good, direct estimate of the extent to which the poor participate in illegal or unreported activities. Those who try to uncover these activities for tax or law enforcement purposes will tell you that the big money makers in these activities are not those we would otherwise count as poor, but people with substantial legitimate reported income who hide their underground

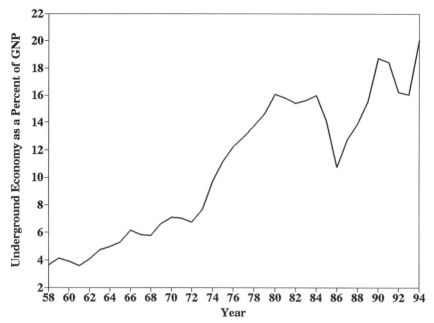

Figure 2.11. Estimated size of underground economy as a percentage of GNP (all reported economic activity), 1958–1994. (*Sources*: Data through 1985 from Fichtenbaum 1989. Formula to calculate later years from Fichtenbaum 1989 and Molefsky 1982, and data from Economic Report of the President 1995)

activities. As we will note below, the income received by the poor from these activities appears to be relatively small, although in some very poor urban communities with limited mainstream employment it could be a significant fraction of income available to the residents. These are also the areas which are most victimized by criminal and illegal activities, and it's not clear that the costs for many low-income families in these neighborhoods are not greater than the benefits.[29]

There is also little evidence that the involvement of the poor in the underground economy has grown. As figure 2.11 indicates, the overall size of the underground economy may not have grown recently. This is consistent with the evidence we discussed in the last chapter showing that drug use and crime have declined slightly over time. On the other hand, the rising number of low-income adult men with little visible support—persons not at work nor looking for work—might suggest growing involvement in unreported activities.

Illegal Income

The Internal Revenue Service estimates that only about 25 percent of the underground economy comes from illegal activities, and a large share of this money involves the illegal drug trade.[30] (The remainder of the underground economy is composed of legal activities not reported to tax authorities.) Young men are particularly likely to be involved in illegal activities. Based on records of arrests, of reported crimes, and other independent information on criminal activity among young men, Harvard economist Richard Freeman estimates that 25 percent of men between the ages of 16 and 34 have participated in at least one criminal activity. Another survey of young men in their late teens and early twenties found that 41 percent admitted to involvement in at least one serious crime.[31] While many of these youths were from middle-income families, those who are involved in serious crime have disproportionately lower education levels and come from poorer neighborhoods.

Young single men—the primary group involved in the illegal underground economy—make up only 7 percent of the poor, however.[32] This suggests that only a very small share of income among poor families comes from the illegal underground economy. This is consistent with other evidence that suggests the big money in organized illegal activity goes to the people and organizations that direct and control these activities, and not to the people on the street who are involved with them.

Even with few among the poor actively engaged in illegal activities, many low-income persons and neighborhoods may be highly affected by illegal economic activities. First, although the total share of underground income going to poor persons is small, this may still be a significant fraction of income in some urban ghetto communities with low levels of legitimate employment. Second, participation among even a relatively small share of persons in the illegal economy may create problems of violence and crime for those who live nearby. Thus, individuals who do not themselves participate in the underground economy may face greater danger of crime and other social problems because of the location of these activities in their neighborhoods. For instance, drug sellers in some communities try to recruit young children as delivery agents, believing they are less likely to be picked up by the police. This puts these children into physical danger and increases their likelihood of becoming drug sellers and drug users in the future.

Organized or illegal underground activities, such as selling drugs or making book, clearly affect the lives of some poor families, particularly those living in poorer urban areas. But this connection between poverty and illegal economic activities is often overstated. Very few poor individuals benefit greatly from illicit activities; many are victims of it.

Unreported Income

The larger share of the underground economy comes not from illegal activities but from legitimate activities that are not reported to tax authorities. Much of this is unreported self-employment or wage and salary income, largely by middle- and upper-income workers. After the tax law revisions in the mid-1980s, virtually no poor families owed federal income taxes (although they still pay social security taxes), so there is less incentive for tax avoidance among poor families than among richer families. But there are strong incentives not to report earnings and other income by those who collect public assistance.

People receiving cash support or Food Stamps from the government have their benefits substantially reduced when they report earnings. This guarantees that benefit payments fall as people's income rises, but it also creates incentives to hide earnings. In fact, for women on welfare for more than a few months, benefits are reduced dollar-for-dollar as their earnings increase. Similarly, if fathers provide over fifty dollars in child support each month to women on AFDC, the mother starts losing a dollar in benefits for each dollar received in child support, so that all child support payments over fifty dollars go to offset AFDC benefit payments. Thus, fathers who want to give their children more money often provide it "under the table."

In many states, payments from public assistance programs are low enough that urban families with few other sources of income cannot cover their expenses by relying only on public assistance. (The design and benefit levels in public assistance programs are described further in the next chapter.) Thus, many mothers necessarily receive small amounts of unreported income on a regular basis.

It is important to quickly underline the word *small* in the above sentence. A study of single mothers on public assistance in poor neighborhoods in four different cities found virtually all of these women supplemented their income in various ways.[33] Few of these women made more than twenty to ninety dollars per month in unreported earnings, and another thirty to fifty dollars in unreported income from other sources. And in many cases this income was necessary to pay the rent and buy food and clothing. Many women earned small amounts of money babysitting or working a few hours for someone. Even more common, women often didn't report gifts they received from family or boyfriends.

Again, all evidence indicates that these are very small amounts of money, so small that they hardly make a bump in the underground economy. But for many women, this unreported support provides the margin of economic survival they need to stay in their apartments and to keep their families intact. Unlike involvement in gambling or drugs, which explicitly promote activities that many observers find socially harmful, unreported earnings among mothers on public assistance often involves employment that we want to encourage and reward. One of the perversities of our welfare system is that we provide incentives for women on welfare to hide their earnings.

2.7 "GET A JOB": HOW FAR OUT OF POVERTY WILL IT TAKE YOU?

SUMMARY. *As a result of recent economic changes, escaping poverty through work alone is increasingly difficult. If earnings are the only source of income available to a family, few less-skilled single mothers earn enough to escape poverty; about three-quarters of less-skilled mar-*

*ried men earn enough to assure that their family escapes poverty through
earnings; and slightly less than two-thirds of single persons earn enough
in the labor market to avoid poverty. These numbers indicate that finding
and holding a job is not an adequate strategy for many of today's poor
families to escape poverty. Their earnings must be supplemented with
other forms of public and private support.*

The conclusion drawn from this chapter is not a promising one: given shifts in
the labor market over time, with declining job opportunities among less-
skilled individuals who are most likely to be the adults in poor families, it is
harder to reduce poverty by encouraging work behavior now than at any point
in the past forty years. Job availability is not improving and wages are deteriorating. Those adult men who seek work with only a high school degree or
less have to work more hours now to do as well as their fathers did, with little
promise of getting ahead by moving up the career ladder over time. Earnings
opportunities among less-skilled adult women have been stagnant over time
and remain substantially below those of men, even with the wage declines that
men have experienced.

Let's consider a few scenarios to see how effective work and earnings are
as a solution to poverty. Table 2.1 shows the earnings that would be necessary
for three different families to escape poverty through employment. These examples assume there is no public assistance available, for instance, no Food
Stamps and no Earned Income Tax Credit (programs we will discuss in the
next chapter). Earnings are the only source of income in these calculations.

Example 1 in table 2.1 takes a single mother with two children, for whom
the official federal poverty line was $11,642 in 1993, the year on which these
tabulations are based. To make this much she has to earn $233 per week. If
she works full-time, $233 per week is equivalent to earning $5.83 per hour,
about $1.50 above the minimum wage. (If she is only able to work part-time,
of course her earnings must be even higher.) Only 31 percent of all single
mothers with high school degrees or less made this much in weekly earnings
in 1993, either because their wages were too low or because they were working only in part-time jobs.[34] This projection ignores the fact that she must also
pay taxes and child care out of her income. (The poverty line was intended as
an after-tax measure, and did not take account of child care expenditures when
it was developed in the early 1960s.) Assuming she owes no federal income
tax but does pay Social Security (FICA) taxes, she must earn $252 for her
take-home pay to equal the poverty line. If one of her children also requires
day care costing $2,000 per year (this is *very* cheap child care for a full-time
worker and probably assumes that she is able to get free care part-time from
relatives and pays for only part-time care), she has to earn $295 per week for
her take-home pay to reach the poverty line. As the last row in Example 1
indicates, in 1993 only 22 percent of less-skilled single mothers had weekly
earnings at this level or higher. Thus, this woman has to earn more each week

TABLE 2.1
Earnings Needed to Escape Poverty for Different Families
(Assuming No Public or Private Assistance to Low-Income Families)

**Example 1: Single Mother with Two Children
Poverty line = $11,642**

	Weekly Earnings	% Less-skilled Single Mothers Currently Earning This Much or More Each Week
Gross earnings equal the poverty line	$233	30.6
Take-home pay equals the poverty line after Social Security taxes	$252	27.4
Take-home pay equals the poverty line after Social Security taxes and $2,000/yr in child care expenses	$295	22.0

**Example 2: Married Couple with Two Children
Poverty line = $14,654**

(Assume the wife works 20 hr/wk at minimum wage, resulting in $85/wk earnings for the family)	Husband's Weekly Earnings	% Less-skilled Married Fathers Currently Earning This Much or More Each Week
Gross earnings equal the poverty line	$208	76.3
Take-home pay equals the poverty line after Social Security taxes	$232	74.9
Take-home pay equals the poverty line after Social Security taxes and $1,000/yr in child care expenses	$254	72.5

**Example 3: Single Adult
Poverty line = $7,518**

	Weekly Earnings	% Less-skilled Single Adults Currently Earning This Much or More Each Week
Gross earnings equal the poverty line	$150	61.8
Take-home pay equals the poverty line after Social Security taxes	$163	59.8

Note: "Less-skilled" in this table includes all adults who hold a high school or a high school equivalency degree but have no further training, or who are high school dropouts.

than do the vast majority of similar single mothers in order to escape poverty through her work effort and earnings alone.

The family in Example 2 is a married couple with two children. I assume the wife works part-time at the minimum wage, bringing in $85 per week to the family. The husband has to earn another $208 per week for their gross earnings to equal the poverty line for a family of four. About 76 percent of current less-skilled married men make at least this much in earnings. Since Social Security taxes are taken out of both the husband and wife's earnings, the husband must earn $232 per week for the family's take-home pay to equal the poverty line. If the family also has to pay $1,000 in child care while the wife works part-time over the year, then the husband must earn $254 for their take-home pay to reach the poverty line. As the last column shows, 73 percent of less-skilled married men report earning this much or more each week.

Our third example is a single adult worker. A single person who earns $150 per week will have gross pay equal to the poverty line for a family of one. For take-home pay (after Social Security taxes) to equal the poverty line, he or she must earn $163 per week. Slightly less than two-thirds (60 percent) of all working less-skilled single adults currently earn this much or more each week.

The bottom line from these scenarios is clear: there must be some additional sources of income available for many workers, since work alone will not provide a route out of poverty. Work by a single low-skilled adult—even full-time work—will leave a family extremely poor, particularly for those families with younger children who must pay for child care while they work. At this point, we do not take up the question of how earnings should be supplemented: multiple adults may live together, adults not in the household (like fathers) may provide additional income, and public assistance may supplement earnings or provide additional income (such as Food Stamps.)

The choice available in today's economy is not between work and other income sources. Both the unavailability of jobs for less-skilled workers and the decreasing returns to work mean that "find a job" is no longer by itself an adequate injunction to many who are poor. Instead, less-skilled workers must both work *and* find other sources of income for their families. The bottom line: given the economic changes of the past two decades, fighting poverty with employment-based strategies is becoming progressively harder.

Changing Policy:

AMERICA'S EFFORTS TO PROVIDE A SOCIAL SAFETY NET

PROPOSALS to reform, expand, or contract antipoverty programs seem to be perpetually on the political agenda. Lyndon Johnson, Richard Nixon, Jimmy Carter, Ronald Reagan, and Bill Clinton all proposed major changes in public assistance programs as part of their legislative agenda. In 1996, the Personal Responsibility and Work Opportunity Reconciliation Act was passed by a Republican Congress and signed by a Democratic administration. This legislation implements fundamental changes in the design and funding of public assistance programs.

This most recent round of Federal legislative changes is at once both less radical and more radical than is often claimed. The changes are less radical in the sense that the criticisms of the existing antipoverty programs they embody are not new and reflect concerns that have long been part of the U.S. debate over helping the poor. Encouraging work, strengthening families, and reducing government costs are not new ideas in the discussion of policy and poverty. On the other hand, these legislative changes will result in more fundamental changes to the federal government's role in antipoverty efforts than any legislation since the Social Security Act of 1935, giving the states much more control over programs and the federal government much less. With this authority, virtually all states have begun to revise their state public assistance programs and many are implementing substantial changes in their cash assistance programs.

Critics of past antipoverty efforts—from both the left and the right—have often charged that existing programs serve the wrong people, serve them ineffectively, encourage the wrong behavior, cost too much, and/or do too little to alleviate poverty. Much of this rhetoric relies on anecdotes or on a few limited (and often inaccurate) images about the poor and their behavior. Like the images of the poor that many Americans hold, many of our ideas about antipoverty programs are often inaccurate.

For instance, a 1995 CBS News/*New York Times* poll indicated that over 50 percent of the population think the federal government spends more than 20 percent of its budget on welfare programs.[1] If Medicaid is excluded, which provides health services for the low-income elderly, disabled, and some low-income families and which is often not listed by the public as a "welfare" program, only 8 percent of federal expenditures go to antipoverty programs, and this has been relatively constant since 1980. If Medicaid is added in, then 14 percent of federal outlays are spent on antipoverty programs. Cash assistance programs to single parents provide *less* support for families now than they did twenty years ago, while the share of the budget spent on non-cash non-medical assistance (such as Food Stamps or housing assistance) has changed little since the 1980s, although it grew rapidly in the 1970s. Medicaid payments, however, have continued to grow. In short, the charge that anti-poverty programs in general are bankrupting the public sector is simply false. It is the cost explosion in health care, which has occurred in private sector as well as public sector health care programs, that is driving the increased spending on antipoverty programs.

This is only one example of the ways in which public perceptions about antipoverty programs are often far from the truth. This chapter and the next two are designed to provide a more balanced view about this country's anti-poverty efforts. In this chapter I will review current programs, how they operate, what they cost, and whom they do and don't serve. In section 3.1 I summarize the major thrust of the legislative changes enacted in the mid-1990s, indicating how the conversation about poverty and policy is changing over time and what the implications of these changes will be. In section 3.2 we will see how the programs in place in the mid-1990s interacted with each other and with family earnings, demonstrating how much of a safety net these programs have provided in the recent past. Sections 3.3 to 3.9 provide brief descriptions of how particular programs work and whom they serve. Readers familiar with this information may want to skip these last sections and move to the next chapter.

Following the review of policy design and structure outlined in this chapter, in chapter 4 I directly take on the question, "Have these programs met their goals?" Finally, chapter 5 moves away from discussing specific programs and asks the big question, "Why should there be any public programs to assist the poor, which levels of government should take on these responsibilities, and why can't private charity do this instead?" Together, these three chapters argue that government programs that assist poor families have been more successful than many want to claim. Though we must be honest about some of the existing problems and failures of these programs, we must also recognize that many of these programs are doing exactly what they were designed to do.

Which Programs Are We Talking About?

Much of the current public discussion is about "welfare reform," a poorly defined term. "Welfare" is occasionally used to refer to the broad set of U.S. public assistance programs, but typically it refers only to the cash assistance program for poor (primarily single-parent) families with children, known as Aid to Families with Dependent Children. Because I want to refer to a broader set of income assistance and service programs to the poor, I will avoid the narrow term "welfare" and use the broader term "public assistance" or "anti-poverty programs," which includes all means-tested cash and non-cash assistance programs, including assistance for food, medical care, and housing, as well as service-oriented programs for the poor, such as the Head Start pre-school enrichment programs for children, job training and placement programs for unemployed adults, programs designed to increase high school performance and graduation rates among the at-risk adolescent population, and economic development efforts aimed at poor neighborhoods and communities. Together, these programs form the social safety net in this country.

While this chapter discusses a broad range of programs, inevitably there will be some programs that provide assistance to the poor that I do not talk about. Most notably, I focus only on those programs that are "means-tested" and hence are only available to families whose income is below a certain level. This excludes such programs as Unemployment Insurance, Social Security and its related health coverage program Medicare, Workers' Compensation, or veterans' benefits. While these programs assist those among the poor who receive them, they were not primarily designed as antipoverty programs and the vast majority of their benefits go to nonpoor families.

In addition, I exclude a number of programs that are almost entirely state, county, or locally run, which are very difficult to summarize since they vary substantially between locations. For instance, this excludes state foster care programs, as well as General Assistance (GA), which is a catch-all term for any cash assistance that states provide to low-income individuals who are not eligible for broader national programs. Finally, out of necessity I say almost nothing about a few federal funding programs that are broadly available to states as block grants. These programs include the child care and development block grant, the maternal and child health block grant, and the social services block grant. Most of these funds provide quite small amounts of money relative to the major programs I talk about here, and their funds are scattered across a wide variety of programs within the states.

The Magnitude of Public Assistance Programs

Before we turn to a detailed look at individual programs, it is useful to get a sense of their comparative size, with respect to each other and government budget items. Table 3.1 shows the comparative size in 1993 of the major public assistance programs discussed in this chapter. The first column compares the number of participants in these programs. The Food Stamp program and Medicaid have the largest number of participants, each with about 28 million beneficiaries. The Aid to Families with Dependent Children (AFDC) and Earned Income Tax Credit (EITC) programs are next in size, followed by much smaller programs.[2]

Dollar costs for these programs are not highly correlated with the number of participants. Medicaid is the most costly program by far, costing nearly $120 billion. As we will learn, the majority of these funds go to the elderly and disabled. Much smaller are AFDC, Food Stamps, and Supplemental Security

TABLE 3.1
Major Public Assistance Programs in the United States

	Year	Parti-cipants (thous)	Total Cost (mil $)	Cost/ Parti-cipant ($)	% Cost Paid by Fed. Govt.	Participants % Child or Youth	% Adult	% Elderly
AFDC[a]	1993	14,144	25,242	1,785	48.6	66.2	33.8	—
SSI[a]	1993	6,011	25,640	4,266	97.7	11.7	52.6	35.7
Food Stamps[a,b]	1993	28,426	26,304	925	94.3	52.0	41.0	7.0
Medicaid[a]	1992	30,926	118,166	3,821	56.9	52.0	37.8	10.3
Housing[a,c] (all programs)	1993	5,625	20,487	3,642	100.0	45.0[c]	na	35.0[c]
JTPA[d], title IIA	1992	955	1,741	1,823	100.0	45.0	49.0	—
EITC[e]	1992	14,097	13,028	924	100.0	na	na	na
Head Start[a]	1993	714	2,776	3,888	100.0	100.0	—	—

Sources:

[a] U.S. House of Representatives (1994).

[b] Heiser and Smolkin (1993) give the percentages by age group.

[c] U.S. Department of Housing and Urban Development (1992) gives the percentages by age group. These numbers show the share of households in rental-assisted units with children and the share of households in rental-assisted units headed by an elderly person.

[d] Data provided by the Office of Employment and Training Programs, U.S. Department of Labor. Percentages by age group are for terminees of the program only.

[e] Data provided by U.S. Internal Revenue Service, Statistics of Income Division.

Income (SSI), each costing about $25 billion. While the EITC is smaller in the year shown here, preliminary cost estimates indicate that the EITC will also cost around $25 billion per year in the mid-1990s.

It is worth noting that the high benefit levels provided by the SSI program for its elderly and disabled recipients make it much more costly per participant than AFDC or Food Stamps. Although public assistance support for the low-income elderly and disabled has generated less controversy, this relatively small group receives the giant's share of public assistance funding. It accounts for all SSI funding, two-thirds of Medicaid expenses, about 20 percent of Food Stamp costs, and about one-third of housing expenses. Roughly, this means that slightly more than 10 percent of the poor (the elderly and seriously disabled) account for close to 40 percent of major public assistance program funding.

The federal government pays all of the costs of the smaller set of targeted programs in table 3.1, as well as all the costs of the EITC. It also pays most of the expenses for SSI and Food Stamps, consistent with the fact that these are national programs whose rules are set at the national level. The programs where the states have much more discretion and control, AFDC and Medicaid, have shared state/federal funding.

While the billions of dollars in spending on the programs shown in table 3.1 are not insignificant, figure 3.1 puts it in context with respect to the federal

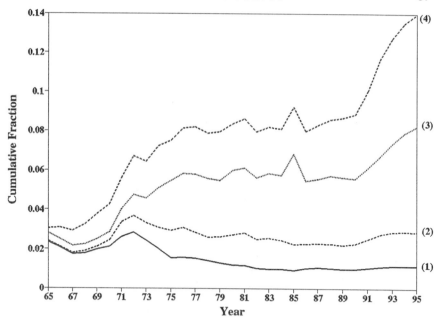

Figure 3.1. Government spending on social programs as a fraction of outlays, 1965–1995. (1) Family Support. (2) Family Support + Food Stamps. (3) Family Support + Food Stamps + All Other Antipoverty. (4) Family Support + Food Stamps + All Other Antipoverty + Medicaid. The category "Family Support" includes payments to states for AFDC benefits, administration, and Child Support Enforcement. The category "All Other Antipoverty" includes Child Nutrition and Special Milk, Supplemental Feeding, Commodity Donation, Legal Services, Day Care Assistance, Low Income Home Energy, Housing Assistance, Supplemental Security Income, and the Earned Income Tax Credit. (*Source*: U.S. Office of Management and Budget 1995)

budget. Looking only at federal expenditures on these programs, figure 3.1 plots the share of federal dollars that have gone to antipoverty programs, including Medicaid, housing assistance, means-tested food and nutrition, SSI, family support (including AFDC and related expenses), EITC, legal services, day care assistance, and other small programs.[3] In 1995, AFDC accounted for 1.1 percent of the federal outlays, while Food Stamps accounted for 1.7 percent. AFDC, Food Stamps, and the host of other in-kind and public assistance programs, *excluding Medicaid*, account for only 8.2 percent of the federal budget. Furthermore, this share has not increased much since the 1980s. Medicaid, a big-ticket program, increases the budget share to 14 percent. As figure 3.1 clearly shows, the one public assistance program whose costs have exploded is Medicaid. This partly mirrors the explosion in all health care plans over the past fifteen years, and it also reflects expansions in eligibility and services provided by Medicaid over these years.[4] The fastest growth in Medicaid costs has been due to the increased cost of long-term care for the seriously ill and disabled.

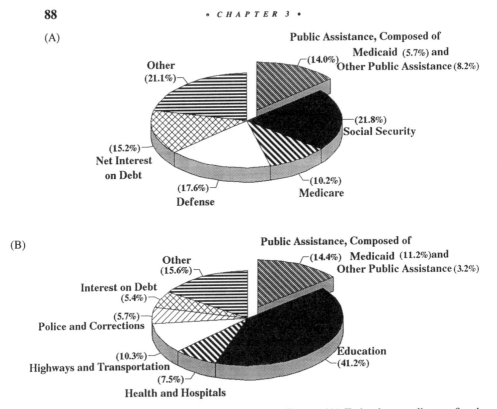

Figure 3.2. Composition of federal and state expenditures. (A) Federal expenditures, fiscal year 1995 (total federal expenditure $1,539 billion). (B) State expenditures, fiscal year 1992 (total state expenditure $453 billion). (*Sources*: A, Office of Management and Budget 1995; B, U.S. Bureau of the Census 1993c)

Figure 3.2A shows how antipoverty programs fit into the total picture of federal government spending. In contrast to the 14 percent of the federal budget spent on antipoverty programs, the Social Security and Medicare programs account for 31 percent of the federal budget, while national defense accounts for 21 percent.

Figure 3.2B shows state spending from state-generated revenues only. (Some of the federal dollars go to the states; these are excluded in our plot of state expenditures, to avoid double-counting.)[5] Figure 3.2 is based on the dollars spent in total by *all* states, so this represents spending patterns in an average state. At the state level, public assistance is the second largest category of spending, making up 14 percent of state budgets. Education spending is much larger at 41 percent. The share of dollars going to public assistance in state budgets has grown over time, but, as at the federal level, this is all due to increases in spending on Medicaid. In fact, state spending on all other public assistance programs has declined, while spending on medical services for low-income people has soared. Medicaid accounts for an even higher share of public assistance spending at the state level than at the federal level.

3.1 NEW DIRECTIONS FOR POLICY

SUMMARY. *In August 1996, Congress enacted significant changes to public assistance programs. While more extensive than other recent reforms, these latest changes are consistent with the general direction of reform over the last fifteen years. Programs have become more* targeted *to particular groups who meet behavioral or other eligibility criteria. States and localities have been given greater* discretion *in the design and administration of certain programs. And all programs are being reevaluated with a critical eye to their effectiveness and even their necessity. Many public assistance programs are under an ongoing threat of* budget cuts.

The configuration of public assistance programs is likely to change substantially in the next few years as a result of major reform legislation. As noted at the beginning of this chapter, in some sense these changes are hardly revolutionary and reflect long-term American political concerns about the design and effectiveness of antipoverty programs. Paying attention to work behavior among the poor or to state discretion in program implementation is not new. On the other hand, the 1996 legislation is likely to have major long-term effects on the operation and availability of U.S. public assistance programs. It moves these programs a giant step in certain directions, whereas earlier legislative changes in the 1980s merely nudged the programs along these directions. The direction of change in these programs since the early 1980s has been markedly different from the reforms pursued in the 1960s and 1970s.

This section provides an overview of the most important aspects of recent legislative changes. The long-term effects of these changes on the design and operation of particular programs are still unclear. Thus, it will be useful to keep this general overview in mind while reading through the discussion of particular programs in the remainder of this chapter. The major thrust of our public assistance system is changing most rapidly along the following three dimensions.

1. *Increasing emphasis on behavioral requirements as part of program eligibility, with particular emphasis on work behavior.* Twenty-five years ago, President Nixon proposed to roll all cash and noncash income assistance programs into one single cash assistance program, available to all families who met the income eligibility requirements. Commonly referred to as a "negative income tax," such a system would minimize administrative expenses by running a single program through the tax system; it would maximize recipients' control over dollars and how they spend them; and it would eliminate both the stigma and the hassle for low-income families of trying to enroll in and use multiple assistance programs with visible identification cards or coupons. Rather than being viewed as a big-government spending program,

support for the negative income tax came from a spectrum of people, including conservative economists like Milton Friedman, who saw it as a more efficient way to help the poor. This proposal did not pass Congress, but it came close.

The pendulum has swung far in the other direction, so that Nixon's not-so-ancient proposal seems almost unbelievable in today's political climate.[6] The current emphasis is very much in the opposite direction: limited programs available for narrowly defined target groups, assuring that large numbers of people are not eligible for substantial amounts of public assistance. Those who do receive assistance must establish their "deservingness" by enrolling in job training and placement programs, limiting their future fertility, ensuring their children are appropriately cared for, or meeting other requirements. I discuss the policy implications of this trend toward more targeted programs in chapter 6 and make only a few comments here.

These more targeted and behaviorally linked public assistance programs will face several major problems that have not yet been fully understood. First, such a proliferation of mandates and behavioral requirements are typically *more* expensive to run (per person) than are cash-assistance programs, because they require much more monitoring. The cheapest and most administratively efficient program is one that simply writes and mails a check each month. The more information case workers need to regularly collect, process, and evaluate, the higher the administrative costs, and the greater the potential for errors, misunderstandings, and management problems.

Second, this trend flies directly in the face of another desire that is often articulated at the same time: to reduce governmental interference in people's lives. Ironically, the conservative promise to get government off people's backs seems to exempt public assistance recipients. By mandating behavioral conformity as well as income eligibility for public assistance programs, government's role in the lives of low-income people becomes much more intrusive.

The effectiveness of these behavioral mandates will depend on exactly what they require, and how easily they can be monitored and enforced. Some behavioral mandates are almost surely a good idea. We should be more willing to evict people from public housing who engage in criminal behavior; more willing to insist that parents who receive public assistance and who can work enter education, job training, and job search programs; and more willing to link job recommendations and placement with high school performance among youth. Other behavioral mandates seem much less sensible and may do more harm than good, such as cutting a family's public assistance benefits if the mother cannot keep a teenager in school, or refusing public assistance to infants born to unmarried mothers.

Deciding which behavioral mandates make sense requires *good judgment* about what can be effectively implemented without vast increases in administrative complexity and cost, what mandates are likely to motivate changes in behavior (rather than being simply punitive), and what actions might produce unacceptable levels of need among mothers and children who could not meet the mandate. Programs with extensive but unmanageable requirements that end up having little effect may only make life harder for the poor and increase public cynicism about the ineffectiveness of government programs.

2. *A return to more local and state discretion in the design of programs.* Public assistance in this country was entirely based at the county or township level 150 years ago. Over time, states took over more and more of the financing and operation of programs, and then, starting in the 1930s, the federal government entered the scene. The role of counties and states has always been important, however. The federal government has never directly administered public assistance programs. The people who actually run programs are all county, local, or state-level employees. The checks received by poor families or by those who run public services for the poor are drawn on state or municipal banks. States continue to provide substantial funding for many public assistance programs, as shown in table 3.1. Over time, however, the federal government has come to fund more programs and has imposed more regulations on how programs could be run. Over the 1980s, states were given the opportunity to apply for waivers to run programs that did not conform to federal rules, but these waivers tended to be limited in scope and often took a great deal of time and effort to negotiate.

With the 1996 changes, a number of programs will be turned over to greater state control through federal block grants. This means that the federal government will continue to provide some (typically reduced) amount of funding to the states, but this funding will not be tied to any particular program structure or design. States can use these funds in any way that relates to the general block grant program category. The biggest program affected by this is AFDC, the program most commonly referred to as "welfare," which will be replaced with a block grant. This allows states to run their own programs (albeit with some ongoing federal constraints), essentially ending the once nationally required AFDC program. While states have always decided how much money AFDC recipients receive in their state, with the block grant they can change the eligibility rules or limit eligibility to particular groups, set time limits on how long a recipient can receive assistance, or impose a variety of behavioral mandates on recipients. These changes would end the "entitlement" status of AFDC, which has meant that anyone eligible for the program must receive it. Instead, if states run short of cash, they can limit payments or even withhold them entirely from some eligible families.

The interest in returning more control to the state or local level grows out of four quite different perspectives. First, some argue that giving more discretion and control back to states will reduce the rigidities and bureaucratic nature of many current public assistance programs. Second, some who believe that we simply don't know enough to design effective nationally run antipoverty programs advocate allowing states to experiment with a variety of programs like job training, education reform, or housing assistance. From this multiple experimentation will come better evidence on what works effectively and what does not. Third, those who are concerned about the growing scope of federal authority want to devolve centralized decision making away from the federal government and back to the states. Fourth, those who worry about the federal deficit and want to reduce federal spending see these changes as a way to cut federal spending on antipoverty programs and induce states to take greater fiscal responsibility for the maintenance of these programs.

Some of these arguments have much to recommend them. Certainly for programs like job training, where there are substantial differences across local areas in the nature of jobs available and the characteristics of the low-income population, running locally designed programs is necessary in order for programs to be effective. Indeed, the federal government has always largely left the specific design of job search and job training programs to state and local discretion. Similarly, in areas where existing programs have been largely ineffective, such as in efforts to engage teenage high school dropouts in employment and training programs, allowing different states to experiment with different programs might result in useful new information.

On the other hand, there are also serious problems with limiting the federal role in public assistance programs to fixed levels of block grant funding. In chapter 5 I discuss in more detail the ways in which federal government involvement in safety net programs can be important. First, states have less ability to finance antipoverty programs than the federal government. The need for public assistance is at its greatest when the economy is the rockiest. Thus, public assistance programs are necessarily *countercyclical*, expanding when the economy is in recession and contracting when it booms. Most states' financial structures are designed so that it is almost impossible for them to run major countercyclical programs. In economic recessions, tax revenue shrinks. Because most states operate under year-to-year balanced budget requirements, this often means they must cut back on spending, at exactly the time when need is increasing. These financial problems, faced by states in the Great Depression of the 1930s, were one of the main reasons the federal government became more involved in financing public assistance programs.

Second, while the federal government has sometimes been inept and sometimes foolish in the way that it has managed and run antipoverty programs, states hardly have a better track record. In fact, much of the impetus toward more centralized regulations and rules in the 1960s occurred because of concern over how these programs were being run by many states, where racist exclusions and arbitrary rule making were all too common. While there are always states that take the lead in implementing new management procedures, the federal government has been a key agent pushing states to reduce waste and fraud by decreasing errors in determining eligibility for assistance, by enforcing regular program usage reports, and by encouraging states to upgrade computer systems.

Third, there continue to be concerns about the equity of state-run public assistance programs. Which programs should be available to all low-income families, and which should be available only to those persons who happen to live in states that have chosen to run them? There is no obvious answer to this question, but any movement to include more state discretion in programs must grapple with it. For instance, if some states choose to dramatically cut all forms of cash assistance and other states maintain their current programs, benefit differences across states could become much larger than they already are. This may not only raise equity concerns, but could also cause substantial migration by low-income families, forcing those states that want to maintain more generous programs to cut them back because of growing low-income populations. This type of competition between states has been referred to as the "race to the bottom," meaning that when states are given complete control over public assistance benefits there are incentives for all states to provide less than they might otherwise choose, out of a fear of being a "magnet" for the poor.[7]

3. *Cutbacks in dollar expenditures and entitlements.* The urge to cut the growth of government programs—all programs, not just public assistance— has been strong in recent years, driven by at least two forces. First, the rapid expansion of the federal deficit that occurred in the 1980s has led some observers to worry about long-term debt commitments. Cutting the deficit can be done by either increasing taxes or decreasing expenditures. While the second is not popular, the first has been political poison. Second, the long-term stagnation in wages among many workers (including actual declines for less-skilled workers) has created economic fears about the cost of more extensive redistributive programs. Ongoing demands for lower taxes mean that there is unlikely to be any more revenue available for public assistance in the near future.

In this debate over government budgets, public assistance programs have more often been a target of cuts than they have been a cause of the problem. In the 1960s and early 1970s, government expenditures on public assistance grew substantially as the Food Stamp program was implemented nationwide and programs like Medicaid and SSI were launched. Since the late 1970s, however, public assistance has been a constant or declining share of the budget of the federal and state governments, with one big caveat: Medicaid expenses have exploded.

This is not surprising, since health care expenses in general have exploded. Almost every state has decreased the share of its budget going to public assistance, excluding Medicaid. But every state has increased the share of its budget going to public assistance when Medicaid is included. In other words, growing health expenses have been crowding out other forms of public assistance. When assistance programs are targeted for cutbacks, few people want to kick folks out of nursing homes, although a primary component of the Medicaid cost explosion in the past fifteen years has been the growing cost of long-term care among the elderly and disabled. Instead, AFDC or Food Stamp benefits and eligibility are cut.

As noted above, the urge to cut program dollars is in direct conflict with the direction of other aspects of reform. Increases in behavioral mandates on program recipients will increase expenses. Job training and placement programs for public assistance recipients, designed to get them into employment and off welfare, *add* to the cost of public assistance in the short run. While one might hope that long-term declines in program usage will ultimately occur, this is in the future and the money for these programs must be available up front. How the conflict between budget cuts and other reforms will resolve itself is still unclear. At present, the contradiction between some of these goals has simply not been well recognized.

Looking at the decade ahead, we are almost certainly in a world where few government programs, and especially public assistance programs, can expect increases in funding. The question is more likely to be "How big will the cuts be?" rather than "What can we afford to do that is new and different (and perhaps more expensive)?" This will be a major constraint on all efforts at welfare reform in the near future. It will almost surely continue to force hard choices on those who want to maintain public assistance programs at current levels of funding, and may particularly constrain states that want to use their expanded control over these policies to experiment with new and redesigned programs. States that want to cut their welfare budget *and* provide expanded job search and training programs for their public assistance recipients to move them into the labor market are going to face these contradictions most directly. Given the problems facing less-skilled workers in the labor market, discussed in the previous chapter, there will be no easy, quick, or cheap way for states to move public assistance recipients into economic self-sufficiency through employment.

For programs to maintain their funding and political support, it will be increasingly important to have evidence demonstrating their effectiveness. This means that reliable research, evaluating programs and their effects, may become increasingly important in the public discussion. It will also be important to build political coalitions that support and protect effective programs in the midst of budget-cutting fervor.

Overall, we are moving farther away from a system that provides direct cash assistance payments to low-income families, toward a system that increasingly conditions its assistance much more closely on particular groups that meet behavioral as well as income qualifications. Dollars are shifting toward work-connected programs, through increases in the EITC, more vigorous child support collection efforts, and subsidized job placement and training efforts (all discussed in more detail in the remainder of this chapter). It is not clear that these reconfigured public assistance programs will provide either a cheaper or a more effective safety net than the one we have at present. It will be different, with a different set of management and incentive problems than are imbedded in the current antipoverty system.

3.2 THE SOCIAL SAFETY NET IN OPERATION

SUMMARY. *This section demonstrates the combined effect of existing social safety net programs on the economic resources available to families.*

The EITC and Food Stamps supplement the incomes of low-income married couples with one or two workers, helping them escape poverty. The examples in this section continue to highlight the problem of escaping poverty among single mothers and their children, however. The combination of employment together with support from the EITC, Food Stamp assistance, and (in higher-benefit states) ongoing AFDC income and child care assistance will raise the income of single-mother families but still leaves many of them poor, unless they have free child care or substantial child support assistance.

The following topical sections in this chapter briefly review the public assistance programs available in the United States designed to reduce poverty and increase skills and earnings among low-income families. This section discusses these programs as a total package. In the last section of chapter 2, we looked at the earnings necessary for different families to reach the poverty line. In that section I concluded that many less-skilled adults would not be able to escape poverty by earnings alone. In contrast, in this section we will look at the entire set of safety net programs available in the current system and ask how effective these programs are at helping families escape poverty. Those unfamiliar with any of the specific programs mentioned in the section can find details in the following topical sections.

Table 3.2 shows the resources available to three different families from the cash, in-kind, and employment subsidy programs available in the present system.[8] I take into account the fact that these earners will owe Social Security (FICA) taxes and federal income taxes on their earnings (beyond a certain level), but I ignore any state or local taxes they will pay. I also assume that the families with children must pay child care expenses for at least one child if the mother works, which can be purchased at two dollars per hour. This is, of course, extremely cheap child care and is below the price for infants or young children.[9] Some mothers will be able to rely on relatives for some of the time (at little or no cost), but must pay at other times.

The first example shows a single mother with two children. (This is the size of the average single-mother family on AFDC.) I assume she lives in Maryland, a state which paid AFDC benefit levels that were about in the middle of state benefits in 1994. If she does not work at all, she will receive AFDC and Food Stamps, leaving her at 61 percent of the poverty line.

Most working mothers with children below age 5 work part-time, whether married or single and whether poor or higher-income. This suggests that few women are able both to work full-time and to provide the care necessary for a preschooler. If our single mother works part-time at the minimum wage, she will earn $5,313 over the year plus receive $1,598 from the EITC in a refund. (In table 3.2, part-time is defined as twenty-five hours per week, or five hours per day, which is how much many part-time employees work.) But her earnings will reduce her AFDC and Food Stamp benefits, and she will have to pay

TABLE 3.2

Effects of Combined Transfer Programs on Take-Home Income

Example 1: Single Mother with Two Children
Poverty line = $11,940

	No Work	Pt-time Work at $4.25	Pt-time Work at $6.50	Full-time Work at $4.25	Full-time Work at $6.50	Pt-time Work at $4.25	Full-time Work at $4.25
Earnings	$ 0	$ 5,313	$ 8,125	$ 8,500	$13,000	$ 5,313	$ 8,500
EITC	0	1,598	2,438	2,528	2,178	1,598	2,528
AFDC	4,392	2,920	107	1,172	0	2,320	572
Food Stamps	2,694	2,581	2,750	2,772	2,044	2,401	2,592
Child support	0	0	0	0	0	1,200	1,200
Gross income	$7,086	$12,412	$13,420	$14,972	$17,222	$12,832	$15,392
−(Soc. Sec. tax)	0	(404)	(618)	(646)	(988)	(404)	(646)
−(Fed. Income tax)	0	0	0	0	(279)	0	0
−(Child care)	0	(2,500)	(2,500)	(4,000)	(4,000)	(2,500)	(4,000)
Take-home income	$7,086	$ 9,508	$10,303	$10,326	$11,955	$9,928	$10,746
Share of poverty	.59	.80	.86	.86	1.00	.83	.90

Example 2: Married Couple with Two Children
Poverty Line = $15,029

Wife: Husband:	No Work Full-time at $4.25	No Work Full-time at $6.50	Pt-time at $4.25 Full-time at $6.50
Earnings	$8,500	$13,000	$18,313
EITC	2,528	2,178	1,232
AFDC	0	0	0
Food Stamps	2,932	1,852	1,297
Child support	0	0	0
Gross income	$13,960	$17,030	$20,842
−(Soc. Sec. tax)	(646)	(988)	(1,392)
−(Fed. Income tax)	0	0	(324)
−(Child care)	0	0	(2,500)
Dependent Care Credit	0	0	484
Take-home income	$13,314	$16,042	$17,110
Share of poverty	.89	1.07	1.14

child care as well.[10] Her part-time work will leave her with total resources from earnings and government assistance of $9,508, still well below the poverty level.

Should she be able to find a part-time job that pays $6.50 per hour, this raises both her earnings and her EITC benefits, but almost eliminates her AFDC benefits. This $2.25 increase in her wages leaves her only $800 better off over the year. She is still below the poverty line.

TABLE 3.2 (cont.)

Example 3: Single Adult
Poverty line = $7,710

	Full-time Work at $4.25	Full-time Work at $6.50
Earnings	$8,500	$13,000
EITC	36	0
AFDC	0	0
Food Stamps	0	0
Child support	0	0
Gross income	$8,536	$13,000
−(Soc. Sec. tax)	(646)	(988)
−(Fed. Income tax)	(339)	(1,016)
−(Child care)	0	0
Take-home income	$7,551	$10,996
Share of poverty	.98	1.43

Source: Author's tabulations.

Women who have extensive family assistance for child care or whose children are older frequently work full-time. If this woman works full-time at the minimum wage, her gross income goes up only about $1,500 over her part-time income at this wage because she loses AFDC and Food Stamp income as her earnings increase. This reflects the steep "tax" on earnings for women receiving public assistance that provides a disincentive to work more. Because her child care expenses have increased, she ends up only $800 better off than when she works part-time. If our single mother can find work full-time for $6.50 per hour, this increase takes her off AFDC entirely. She also starts owing federal income taxes. Her take-home income is now right at the poverty line.

The last two columns show what happens if she is fortunate enough to receive $100 per month in child support for her two children. Because all child support payments above $50 per month are offset dollar-for-dollar with reduced AFDC benefits, she is only slightly better off when she receives child support. *If* she works full-time at a reasonably high wage (for a less-skilled worker), and gets $100 per month in child support, or if she has free child care for all her children, then she and her children can escape poverty with work. Otherwise, in these scenarios the family still remains below the poverty line.

The second example is a married couple with two children. If the husband works full-time at a minimum-wage job, the family receives a substantial payment from the EITC, as well as Food Stamps. The family is still below the poverty line, however. Should the husband be able to earn $6.50 per hour in full-time work, they would receive less in Food Stamps and less from the EITC, but they are now above the poverty line. Most striking, there is only a small gain in take-home income if the wife goes to work part time at the minimum wage in this family. If they must pay child care expenses, the combined reduction in their EITC and Food Stamp income leaves them only about $1,100 more in take-home income when the wife works.

The final example shows a single person. If working full-time at the minimum wage, he or she is not eligible for Food Stamps and receives only a minimal EITC. This person's take-home income is right at the poverty line for a family of one. Increases in wages allow this single person to move well above the poverty line.

Table 3.2 shows how the public assistance programs in this country act in tandem with one another. Because benefits in AFDC and Food Stamps decrease as earnings rise, persons who receive assistance from these programs do not experience as large an increase in their take-home pay as they do in their earnings. But the EITC increases initially as earnings rise, so this offsets the decline in other benefits.

The data in table 3.2 emphasize again how hard it is for a single mother with two children to escape poverty. She must either find a relatively good-paying job, well above the minimum wage, and work full-time and year-round, or she must have someone who will care for her children for free while she works, or she needs substantial child support assistance. Or some combination of the above must occur. If any of these things are not possible, she and her children will not reach the poverty line but will stay below it.

It should also be clear from table 3.2 how important the expanded EITC is in helping these families escape poverty. The approximately $2,000 in subsidy that it provides for low-wage workers typically makes the difference to these families between whether they do or don't get near the poverty line through work. Without this larger EITC, enacted in 1993, most families in these examples would be even poorer.

3.3 Cash Assistance Programs

SUMMARY. *The two cash assistance programs for low-income people in the United States have been* Aid to Families with Dependent Children *(AFDC), available primarily to single mothers with children, and* Supplemental Security Income *(SSI), available to low-income elderly and seriously disabled individuals. AFDC has been an extremely controversial program, largely because of changing views toward its recipient population. Over the last two decades, AFDC benefits as well as eligibility rules have become steadily less generous. Recent changes abolish any national AFDC program and give states discretion to run assistance programs of their own design. SSI is a federal program with national benefit levels. Compared to AFDC, it provides substantially more cash support. The large differences between these two programs underscore our long-term insistence on treating different groups among the poor very differently.*

For most Americans, the word "welfare" is synonymous with a monthly check from the government. In reality, the United States provides less cash assistance (at least to the nonelderly) than most Americans imagine. Cash assistance is available only to persons living in families with particular demographic characteristics and with very limited income and assets. Unlike many other industrialized countries, such as Canada or Germany, there is no overall cash assistance program in the United States available to all poor people.

For those who are eligible, cash assistance has the advantage that it offers recipients maximum flexibility and choice. They can spend the money in any way they want, paying the bills and buying the items they deem most important each month. Of course, this is also the drawback of cash assistance from the point of view of many critics, since at least some recipients will spend the money in ways that the critics deem inappropriate.

The other advantage of cash assistance is that writing checks is typically a less expensive form of public assistance. While recipients' income and eligibility for the program must be verified on an ongoing basis, the cost of processing and sending a monthly check is not large. Cash assistance programs often require less bureaucracy and less management expertise since they do not require that the government operate programs to provide services.

The federal government has historically run only two cash assistance programs, both of which have been considered "entitlements." This means that anyone who met the eligibility criteria for these programs would receive the funds when they apply. Thus, the programs were not "capped" in terms of funding; nobody could be turned away because funding was tight. If the government wanted to limit expenditures on these programs, it had to change the eligibility rules. With the legislative changes enacted in the mid-1990s, however, one of these programs (AFDC) has lost its entitlement status. This means that states can provide (or not provide) cash support to any family they choose, and can skip payments to program participants if the budgeted money for the program runs short by the end of the year.

Aid to Families with Dependent Children

"Welfare" has typically referred to the Aid to Families with Dependent Children (AFDC) program, which provides cash support, primarily to single parents (usually single moms) with children under age 18 living at home whose income and assets were below a specified level.[11] Because this program has been the target of so much criticism, I first describe the way it has operated over the last several decades. I then go on to describe the nature of recent changes.

AFDC was established as part of the Social Security Act of 1935, and it was intended to assist widows left alone to raise children. The likely recipient was seen as a poor widow whose husband had died in an industrial accident and who needed assistance so she could stay home and care for her children. As time passed and the world changed, this program became a major target of criticism for at least three reasons. First, as more and more women entered the labor market, government support that allowed low-income women to stay home with their children became increasingly less acceptable. A series of ongoing reforms since the early 1970s increased work requirements and work incentives for AFDC recipients.

Second, as advances in health and safety have left us with very few young widows, AFDC was predominantly utilized by divorced women and never-married mothers.[12] In particular, as the share of never-married mothers in the population grew, this share also grew among AFDC recipients. This made the program a target of criticism by those who wanted to discourage the formation of single-parent families and who claimed that this assistance encouraged women to have children outside of marriage.

Third, the AFDC program over time evolved into a very bureaucratic, rules-based program that made life difficult for its recipients, often creating barriers that discouraged them from making changes in their life. The next chapter, which discusses the effects of public assistance programs, devotes an entire section to this issue. Both AFDC recipients as well as staff people who work closely with the AFDC program have been very critical of the program's design and how it deals with clients.

AFDC funding and decision making have been shared between the federal government and the states, and this has created many tensions. The federal government has set certain program regulations, enforced quality controls, and collected centralized information on program operation. The states determined benefit levels and therefore also determined the income levels at which women in their state were eligible for AFDC. States, together with counties, operated the program and ran the local offices where people applied for AFDC and where recipients were screened for ongoing eligibility. Costs of the program have been shared between states and the federal government.

The lowest-benefit state, Mississippi, paid $120 per month to a family of three with no other resources in 1994, while the highest-benefit state among the contiguous forty-eight states, Connecticut, paid $680 per month to a similar family. While there is a correlation between cost of living and state benefits, this difference in benefits is much greater than differences in cost of living. States have set benefit levels legislatively and tended not to change them over time. Unlike Social Security or SSI, there was no automatic cost-of-living adjustment to AFDC benefits to keep them up with inflation. As a result, inflation has steadily eroded the dollar value of benefits in almost all states over the past twenty years. Adjusting for inflation, the median state paid $792 per month for a mother with three children in 1970. By 1993, that amount had fallen to $435 per month, as figure 3.3 indicates.[13] Recent benefit levels have been low enough that many poor families did not qualify for AFDC. In 1993, only 61 percent of poor children were in families receiving AFDC.

As with most cash assistance programs, a woman receives maximum AFDC benefits for her family when she doesn't work and has no other income. As she goes to work, her benefits fall as her earnings rise. Figure 3.4 shows this pro-

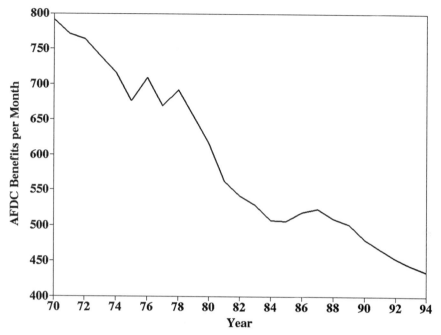

Figure 3.3. Median state AFDC benefits per month, for a family of four, 1970–1994, in 1994 Dollars. (*Sources*: Blank 1994a; U.S. House of Representatives 1994)

cess. At zero hours of work, a woman receives the maximum benefit level, B. As she begins to work, her earnings increase with each hour of work. But benefit dollars are taxed away as earned dollars increase. Thus, her total income, as shown in figure 3.4, rises more slowly than her earnings. At some point, X, her benefits go to zero and the woman has only earned income.

This process creates a work disincentive in AFDC and in all other cash assistance programs. When working, the recipient does not get to keep her entire earnings. Her added income from working is less than her wages, since she loses benefits at the same time as her earnings rise. In fact, under the federal mandates that existed through 1995, a woman who had been on AFDC and working for more than four months faced a dollar loss in benefits for every dollar increase in earnings. This is the equivalent of a 100 percent tax rate, and has resulted in very low work incentives among women on AFDC.

There is also a child support payment disincentive on AFDC. The first fifty dollars in child support payments from an absent father are added to a woman's AFDC check and increase her income. Above that amount, each dollar paid by the father reduces the mother's benefit by one dollar. Thus, only the threat of legal sanctions provides men with an incentive to pay more than fifty dollars per month in child support if their children receive AFDC, since there is no income benefit to the children beyond this level.

These problems are inherent in any cash assistance program. Even though

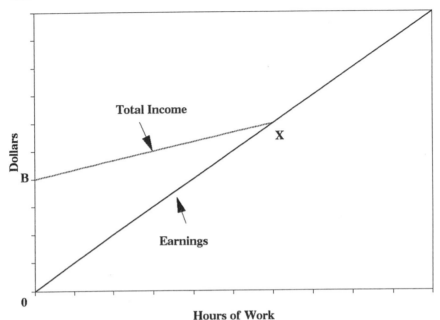

Figure 3.4. AFDC benefit level reduction with increased earnings.

the government wants to promote work effort, it does not want to pay large welfare checks to women who have significant income from earnings or from child support payments. Therefore welfare benefits *must* decline as other income sources rise, although this decline need not be as steep as it has been historically in the AFDC program.

AFDC has often been charged with encouraging negative behaviors: because it pays support to women who don't work and reduces the returns from work, AFDC decreases work effort. Because it provides support to single mothers, it may encourage more single women to have children outside of marriage, or to separate from their husbands. Legislative changes in 1988 forced all states to run at least limited programs for married couples because of this concern. We evaluate the magnitude of these problems in the next chapter. The question is not whether such incentives exist in the AFDC program; they do. The question is their size, and whether they are so large as to offset the positive effects of the program. AFDC does transfer income to low-income mothers and their children, the poorest group in American society. Any reconfigured state-designed cash assistance program will face similar problems of balancing support to children against other program requirements.

Finally, it is worth noting that many women eligible for AFDC have chosen not to receive it. At any time, among those women whose reported income would make them eligible for the program, an estimated one-third were not participating in it.[14] This suggests that there have been significant hassles associated with participation. AFDC offices are often inefficient, hostile, and chaotic places. Many women have always preferred to "stay off the dole."

EXPECTED CHANGES IN THE AFDC PROGRAM

The AFDC program was abolished in 1996 and replaced with the Temporary Assistance to Needy Families (TANF) block grant. This provides states with a fixed amount of federal money, pegged to what they received in the early 1990s. States are expected to replace AFDC with public assistance programs of their own design for low-income families with children. A few important federal mandates will remain, however. For instance, states will have to impose work requirements on more than 50 percent of their caseload by the early part of the next century. In addition, federal funds will be time-limited for many families, with a maximum five years of support.

Even before this legislation passed, a number of states had received approval to experiment with redesigned AFDC programs; TANF only hastens the emergence of a wide variety of unique state-based programs.[15] In the short run, many of these programs are likely to resemble the old AFDC program, simply because this is what the state machinery is set up to run. Over time, however, a number of states are expected to implement at least two types of changes. First, access to AFDC cash benefits will become more limited and more tied to family behaviors. A number of states have already limited benefits for women who have more children while receiving AFDC, or have tied benefit eligibility to older children's school attendance or younger children's immunization. Second, cash assistance is likely to become much more limited. In part, this will be due to time limits, in part it will reflect the fixed federal dollars available. Under block grants states will no longer be required to match federal funds with a high rate of state spending. In the next economic slowdown when state budgets become tight and AFDC applications increase, there is likely to be strong pressure for states to limit AFDC benefits simply to keep their budget balanced, regardless of any concern about work mandates or behavioral mandates. These budget pressures alone suggest that cash assistance for poor families may become unavailable for families in some states while becoming much more limited and difficult to receive in many others.

Supplemental Security Income

Enacted in 1972, Supplemental Security Income (SSI) provides assistance to elderly or disabled persons who are below certain income cutoffs. It supplements Social Security and pension income for those elderly whose retirement income is inadequate, and provides support to those who are medically certified as physically or mentally unable to work. SSI imposes strict certification requirements on disability payments, so that only those with extensive physical or mental disabilities can qualify for the program.

In comparison to AFDC, SSI is a federally designed program with limited state involvement in rule-setting, which means that it provides a standard set of national benefits. A single individual living alone with no other income can receive a maximum of $446 per month. (Support is only $297 per month for those who live with others.) For a couple on their own with no other income, SSI provides $669 per month ($446 if they live with others.) This is substantially more generous than AFDC. In 1994, only thirteen states paid as much to a mother and two children as was available to a single individual on SSI. In addition, twenty-two states supplement SSI checks for elderly recipients by another $5 to $150 dollars per month.

At present, about 40 percent of poor elderly households receive SSI assistance. Many states, facing cutbacks in AFDC and other public assistance programs, are more aggressively advising people with some work disability to apply for federally funded SSI assistance. The SSI program has long fought against broader eligibility definitions for disability, fearing large numbers of applications, although recent changes in allowable disabilities have expanded to include a growing number of children with mental or physical disabilities.

Benefit amounts in SSI are calculated in the same way as AFDC benefits. Those with no other income receive the maximum benefit, while those with other sources of income have their benefits reduced as their other income rises. Perversely, SSI recipients have their benefits taxed away at a lower rate than AFDC recipients as their earnings increase. Thus, those we largely expect not to work have access to a program with greater work incentives than the parents on AFDC whom we increasingly expect to be employed.

The large difference in cash assistance available through SSI versus the AFDC program underscores the diversity of treatment among different types of low-income individuals in the United States. The elderly and those certified as disabled are viewed as "truly needy" and worthy of substantial support for two reasons. By definition, they are judged unable to work. Hence, we have few suspicions about whether they are accepting government support when they could be working. In addition, classification as elderly or disabled is assumed to be outside the individual's control; one cannot prevent aging, nor can an individual be blamed for the accidents or medical conditions that create disability. There is less suspicion that these persons have chosen a lifestyle that allows them to receive government support.

These differences in public support have substantial implications for economic need among these two groups. It is not too far from the truth to suggest that women and children tend to be poor in this country in part because we choose to provide them only limited cash support. The elderly are among the least poor because we choose to provide them with generous cash supplements when they are in need.

Compared to the AFDC program, the SSI program faces few changes in the new legislation. Eligibility for certain immigrant groups is restricted, and recent expansions in SSI eligibility for certain types of disabilities have been rescinded. Some groups whose disabilities are perceived to be more within their control—such as those disabled due to past substance abuse problems—have been removed from eligibility. But the program will remain a relatively generous, nationally available cash support program.

3.4 IN-KIND ASSISTANCE PROGRAMS

SUMMARY. *The in-kind provision of particular goods has typically received greater political support than cash assistance. The* Food Stamp program *is the only national assistance program available to all low-income people, providing vouchers for the purchase of groceries.* Medicaid *is the public health insurance program for low-income families on* AFDC *or* SSI. *Recent expansions in Medicaid have made it available to all poor children as well. Costs of Medicaid have soared in the past fifteen years, and increases in Medicaid expenses—particularly for the elderly and disabled requiring long-term care—have caused major increases in state spending for the poor.* Housing assistance—*either subsidized project-based housing or vouchers that subsidize rent payments—is available only in those areas that have chosen to participate in federal housing programs.*

Rather than providing cash assistance, the vast majority of support for low-income families is provided through programs that subsidize particular types of goods and services. These are typically called "in-kind" programs. Rather than providing cash that individuals can spend, they provide in-kind support for the purchase of certain necessary goods. The federal government spent three times more on in-kind programs in 1995 than it did on cash assistance.

Only Food Stamps and Medicaid are entitlements that must be provided to everyone who is eligible and applies for them. Other in-kind programs are typically available only to people in states or localities that choose to operate them. Alternatively, they may be nationally available but have budget caps so that individuals who meet eligibility requirements can be turned away if the program has spent all its annual program money.

The advantage of in-kind programs is that they subsidize only particular expenditures that taxpayers deem worthy of support—food, medical care, or housing, for instance. Of course, from the recipients' point of view, this may constrain their spending choices and is a disadvantage. For instance, a family that is being threatened with having its electricity turned off for nonpayment cannot pay the bill in food coupons or housing vouchers.

In-kind programs often have more "stigma" associated with them than cash assistance programs. When buying food with dollar bills, no one knows whether those dollars came from a public assistance check or a paycheck. But persons who buy food with Food Stamp coupons are clearly visible as public aid recipients. Similar problems arise for those using housing vouchers, or for children who receive subsidized school lunches. Many recipients complain of being "labeled" and publicly embarrassed by others when they are visibly seen as "poor." Many of those who are eligible for these programs but choose not to participate cite this as a reason. On the other hand, some supporters of these programs believe that it is exactly this "embarrassment" element that makes these programs more effective than cash assistance, since it provides an incentive for people to leave the program.

Food Stamps

Food Stamp benefits are the only public assistance program available to all poor people, including poor families without children or childless single men or women. In 1993, over two-thirds of all poor people received assistance from Food Stamps.[16] Recipients of AFDC or SSI are automatically eligible for Food Stamps since the income levels necessary for AFDC or SSI eligibility also make a family eligible for Food Stamps.

Food Stamp recipients receive coupons that most grocery stores will accept in lieu of cash, and which can be spent on food items only (i.e., no cigarettes, alcohol, or household products). A number of states have recently experimented with replacing the coupons with Food Stamp "credit cards" that can be debited each month by the grocery store cashier, up to the amount of monthly benefits. The Food Stamp program was first established in the early 1960s, as an outgrowth of the surplus agricultural commodity distribution program. Like SSI, the Food Stamp program is nationally run with uniform national benefits. Almost all costs are paid by the federal government.

The maximum Food Stamp payment for a family of three is $295 per month. This provides about $1 per person per meal. As family income increases, Food Stamp benefits decline. Thus, persons in states with very low AFDC benefits receive somewhat more in Food Stamps than persons in states with high AFDC benefits. This means that Food Stamps partially offset the differences in AFDC payments across states.

Figure 3.5 shows the history of how much an extremely poor single-parent family with three children could receive each month in AFDC and Food Stamps.[17] Because different states pay different AFDC benefits, the solid line in figure 3.5 shows payments in the average state and duplicates figure 3-3. The dotted line in figure 3-5 indicates the monthly Food Stamp income available to this family, adding about $275 to the family's monthly income by 1993. The decline in AFDC benefits is somewhat offset by Food Stamp increases over time, but the total assistance available to single-parent families from these two programs has clearly decreased.

EXPECTED LEGISLATIVE CHANGES IN FOOD STAMPS

While several proposals were introduced in the mid-1990s to turn Food Stamps into a block grant and turn the program over to the states along with

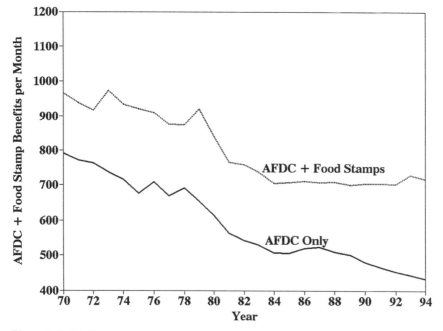

Figure 3.5. Median state AFDC and Food Stamp benefits per month, for family of four, 1970–1994, in 1994 dollars. (*Sources*: Blank 1994a; U.S. House of Representatives 1994)

AFDC, these proposals did not pass. The Food Stamp program remains intact as a nationally provided program with uniform national benefits. Food Stamp availability to immigrants was severely restricted, however, and childless families and individuals are now typically limited to three months of Food Stamps in each three-year period. In addition, cuts in funding and eligibility rules have been proposed that will make the Food Stamp program less generous than in the past.

Other Nutrition-Related Programs

In addition to Food Stamps, a variety of other programs are designed to subsidize nutrition among children. Among these is the Special Supplemental Food Program for Women, Infants and Children, known as WIC. WIC provides special food assistance to low-income pregnant women and preschoolers either by directly providing high-protein, high-vitamin foods like milk, cheese, or fruit juices, or by providing vouchers to buy these items. There are also school lunch and school breakfast programs, which are run at a school's discretion and where children from low-income families can receive free or reduced-price meals.

Medicaid

Medicaid pays health-care expenses for selected groups among the poor. Women and children on AFDC are automatically eligible, as are the elderly and disabled who receive SSI. In addition, all poor children have recently become eligible to receive Medicaid. Medicaid is run by the states, like AFDC, with certain federally imposed constraints; costs are shared between the federal government and the states. (Medicaid should not be confused with Medicare, a publicly run health insurance program for Social Security recipients.)

Like all health insurance, the costs of Medicaid have exploded in the past fifteen years, making it the only public assistance program where costs have substantially increased in recent years. The amount of money spent on the Medicaid program in 1995 was *six times* what was spent in 1980. While much of this increase is due to the overall rise in medical care costs, Medicaid spending still almost doubled in inflation-adjusted dollars.[18] Most of these cost increases have resulted from increasing health costs for the disabled and elderly who are assisted by Medicaid and whose medical bills are large. Thus, even though more than two-thirds of Medicaid recipients are women and children, they account for less than one-third of the cost. Particularly large increases have occurred in the cost of providing long-term nursing home care to the elderly and extremely disabled, who in an earlier era would have lived in large institutions. Many states are continuing to experiment with new ways to control Medicaid costs. For instance, many states are beginning to move the Medicaid population that does not require long-term care into health maintenance organizations (HMOs), which charge a fixed fee to provide care over the year.

In the late 1980s, concern about the lack of health insurance among the working poor and near-poor led to expansions in Medicaid coverage for poor children, which has also pushed costs up. Currently, all grade-school children in families whose income is below the official poverty line are eligible for Medicaid, and over time older children will also be covered.

With these new expansions, publicly provided medical insurance is available to all younger children in poor households. The fact that not all of these children see doctors regularly indicates that expanding eligibility for Medicaid has solved only part of the problem. Having a Medicaid card does not guarantee that a doctor will see you. For many medical procedures, Medicaid pays less than private insurance, and subsequently many medical facilities and physicians prefer not to treat Medicaid clients.

EXPECTED LEGISLATIVE CHANGES IN THE MEDICAID PROGRAM

A wide variety of reform proposals are on the table for Medicaid at the time of this writing, and which ones (if any) will pass is still uncertain. Block grants for Medicaid have been proposed, which would fix federal funding for Medicaid at a set amount. Given recent cost explosions in Medicaid, which have been shared by both the federal and the state governments under matching funding provisions, many states are hesitant about this proposal. In addition, the current extensive list of federal mandates on Medicaid programs is under review and may be modified to give states greater discretion in what medical services they provide and how they provide them. In addition, at both the federal and the state level, there are ongoing discussions about possible ways to better contain costs in the Medicaid program, which will surely result in substantial changes in the way Medicaid-funded services are provided in the years ahead.

Housing Assistance

There is no single program called "housing assistance," but a mix of programs which subsidize rent expenses for low-income families.[19] Large apartment buildings in center cities—"the projects"—may dominate our image of public housing assistance, but most projects are low-rise and located outside the center city. In addition, project-based assistance is a shrinking share of all housing assistance.

The availability of housing assistance programs depends on the willingness of local governments and local developers to participate in them; no programs are nationally available. As a result, low-income housing assistance in some cities is much more extensive than in others. Because available slots are limited, in many cities there are waiting lists of applicants that are years long. Nationally, only 22 percent of all poor families receive housing assistance; 38 percent of women on AFDC receive housing assistance.[20]

For those who make it to the top of the list, housing assistance generally covers all rental expenses over 30 percent of a family's income. For instance, a woman who had only $300 per month in AFDC income would be expected to pay $90 (30 percent of $300) toward her rent, and the government would subsidize all rental costs above that amount.

The two primary types of housing assistance are rent-subsidized units in project-based housing or rent vouchers which families can use in the private rental market. About three-fourths of those with rental assistance are in project-based subsidized housing, and the remaining one-fourth receive vouchers.

Project-based housing comes in all types. For many years, project housing was financed by the federal government and built and operated by local public housing authorities. This included the big high-rise public housing projects built in cities as part of urban renewal projects in the 1950s through 1970s. Many of these projects were located in poor neighborhoods and have been badly maintained over time, making them centers of gang and drug activity. The majority of public housing projects, however, are low-rise units. In the last twenty years, the government has stopped building its own projects and instead funded private developers to build housing projects where some or all of the units are reserved for rent-subsidized low-income tenants. A growing amount of project-based housing assistance is designated for elderly and/or disabled low-income tenants rather than for families. Currently, about

40 percent of project-based housing assistance is given to elderly persons.[21] A high proportion of the remaining units go to single-parent families.

There are also a variety of housing voucher programs, although the most common are known as "Section 8" vouchers, named after the legislation that authorized them. These vouchers provide rent subsidies for tenants in private rental apartments that have been certified as Section 8-eligible, which typically means the building has to meet certain code standards. Landlords have to apply for such certification. Housing vouchers allow low-income families to choose where they will live, unlike the earlier project-based rental assistance, and therefore vouchers distribute low-income renters more broadly through a community. The use of vouchers is typically limited by communities and landlords who do not want rent-subsidized individuals or families nearby. In many higher-income communities it is often difficult to find landlords willing to apply for Section 8 eligibility and therefore hard to find a place that will accept vouchers.

EXPECTED LEGISLATIVE CHANGES IN HOUSING PROGRAMS

The budget for the U.S. Department of Housing and Urban Development (HUD) is facing severe cuts in the years ahead. While it is not entirely clear exactly how HUD will be reconfigured, almost surely there will be less money available for housing programs. Exactly how this will effect specific programs is still unclear.

Other In-Kind Programs for Low-Income Children and Families

A variety of relatively small programs supplement those above but are not available in all communities. Legal Aid services operate clinics where low-income families can receive legal advice relating to civil matters (such as rental disputes). Child health and immunization programs for low-income communities often provide special clinics or fund services within schools or hospitals. Foster care funds supplement state dollars for assistance and services to abused and neglected children. The Low-Income Home Energy Assistance Program (LIHEAP) provides subsidies to poor families to help pay fuel bills, although recent proposals to abolish this program may pass in the near future. In addition, a number of general federal block grants supplement state funding for social services, including day care programs, home care programs, and a wide variety of other services for disadvantaged children and adults.

3.5 EARNINGS SUBSIDY PROGRAMS

SUMMARY. *The* Earned Income Tax Credit *(EITC) is an increasingly large and important part of the U.S. antipoverty strategy, and provides substantial supplemental income for low-wage earners. The* minimum wage *provides a floor on earned income, but may raise unemployment among less-skilled workers. The minimum wage together with the EITC provides many full-time, year-round workers with an assurance that their earnings will come close to the poverty line. An alternative to wage subsidies is* employer tax credits, *typically provided as an initial wage subsidy for employers who hire workers from targeted neighborhoods or disadvantaged groups. Employer tax credits are not much used at present, but may be of interest to states hoping to increase employment among public assistance recipients.*

By themselves, the public assistance programs described in the last two sections do nothing to help families escape poverty; they simply provide a safety net for those who are poor. If we want poor adults to seek employment and replace public assistance with earnings, we need something more than an AFDC program or a Food Stamp program. This section and the next discuss programs that encourage poor people to work.

As we saw in the last chapter, work by itself may not help all poor adults bring themselves and their families out of poverty. Given the declining wages available to less-skilled workers, there may be an ongoing need for earnings subsidies. While this will take public resources, there may be more political support for policies that help the working poor "make it" economically than for general cash and in-kind assistance programs that help the nonworking poor more than the working poor.

The first program discussed in this section, the EITC, has become one of the major antipoverty programs over the 1990s. More than any other program, the EITC directly responds to the economic changes of the past few decades, explicitly supplementing the wages received by low-wage workers. Until recently, the EITC has received broad support from policymakers across the political spectrum. Other earnings subsidy programs have been more controversial. Arguments between those who want to increase the minimum wage and those who want to rescind it continue to rage, as they have for decades. An alternative to the EITC, paid to workers, is employer-based wage subsidies, which give employers tax rebates for employing particular groups of workers. These were used more extensively in the United States in the past than they are now.

The Earned Income Tax Credit

The EITC provides subsidies to low-wage workers through the federal tax system.[22] If you work, have children, and earn low wages, you can get the EITC. If you owe federal taxes, the EITC will either reduce or eliminate that tax liability. If you don't owe taxes, or owe only small amounts, the EITC provides a supplement through your paycheck, which can be received as "reverse withholding" (adding to monthly wages) or as a lump sum amount in April when you file a tax return and claim the subsidy. This means that the EITC is

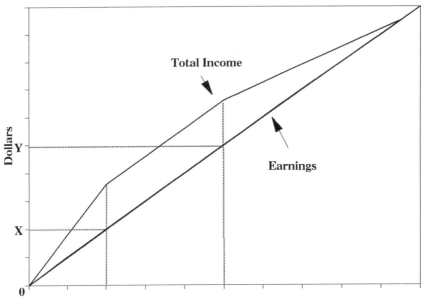

Hours of Work

Figure 3.6. Earned income tax credit with increased earnings.

"refundable," that is, a family whose EITC is greater than its tax obligations will actually receive a check from the government.

The amount you receive depends on how many children you have and your earnings. For a low-wage worker with two children, the EITC can be as large as $3,000.[23] In a world of shrinking wages for less-skilled workers, this is a substantial addition to income and is the major policy response this country has made to the changing economy facing less-skilled workers.

The EITC operates in a way that is almost exactly opposite to the design of cash grants, as figure 3.6 indicates. A cash grant (such as AFDC) is at its maximum when a person earns no other income at all, and declines as earnings increase (compare fig. 3.6 to fig. 3.4.) Thus, imbedded in this grant is a work disincentive: as earnings increase, the benefit dollars decrease, so that a family's total income goes up much more slowly than their earnings. In contrast, the EITC pays nothing if you don't work. As an individual goes to work and earns income, for every dollar earned the EITC provides a thirty cent supplement (twenty-six cents if you have only one child). Thus, income increases faster than earnings as workers at very low earnings increase their hours of work. In figure 3.6 this is apparent because the line of total income increases *faster* than earnings, reflecting the presence of the subsidy. The result is a strong incentive for nonworkers to enter the labor market and earn at least some income. When total earnings reach a particular point (X in fig. 3.6), the EITC grant becomes a constant dollar subsidy that remains unchanged as earnings continue to increase. Finally, at some level of earnings (Y in fig. 3.6), the EITC subsidy starts to decline. Currently, EITC subsidies start to decline once workers earn more than $11,000, and the subsidy phases out entirely for incomes over $24,000.

The EITC began in 1975 and was relatively small until the early 1990s. In 1993, the Clinton administration proposed and passed a major EITC expansion, in part to offset a proposed energy tax increase and in part to give substance to its rhetoric about the need to "make work pay" for low-income families.

Particularly for nonworkers, the EITC increases the incentive to go to work. There are a number of problems with the program, however. First, because it is based on earnings over the entire year, it is difficult to make monthly payouts as the year progresses. Most people who receive funds from the EITC get it as a tax refund at the end of the year. This does little to increase *monthly* income, which is what pays the rent and buys the groceries. On the other hand, many recipients indicate that they prefer a single once-a-year payment, a form of forced savings that guarantees them at least one large lump sum of money during the year. Many people explicitly plan to use their payment to pay off debts, fix their car, go to the dentist, or purchase big-ticket household items.[24]

Second, few low-income families actually understand how the EITC operates, and therefore its value as a *work incentive* is lessened. Very few, even among those who receive it, think of it as a separate program from the general tax system. Partly because it typically arrives in a lump sum at the end of the year, virtually no recipients speak of the EITC as adding to their hourly earnings. Few recipients would describe it in the way I did at the beginning of this section: for every dollar they earn, they get another thirty cents from the government. Given this, while the EITC surely provides an income subsidy and makes low-income working families better off, it may have a smaller effect on work incentives than claimed. On the other hand, studies indicate that the net effect of the EITC on work hours is positive for low-income adults.[25]

Third, when the EITC expanded, a number of persons began to claim it fraudulently. Most notably, the rapid tax refund provisions were used by some ineligible persons to receive the EITC before the IRS could verify their claims. The IRS has since implemented a number of measures to crack down on these fraudulent claims, and these problems are much reduced. It still remains difficult to monitor claims of self-employment income.

Given the long-term economic changes that have led to declining wages among less-skilled workers, discussed in chapter 2, the EITC provides real income protection to working poor families. As such, its expansion may be the most important antipoverty policy implemented during this decade. More than any other public assistance program, the EITC makes persons who work at low wages more economically self-sufficient.

With the recent expansion, the EITC is not a small program. By 1996, it is projected to cost the government $25 billion dollars per year, making it as large as the Food Stamp program. Of course, this money is not as visible as money spent on public assistance programs, because only part of it is actually *paid out* to poor families. The rest of the cost is in taxes *not collected* (economists call this a "tax expenditure"). This reduces government revenue but does not show up on the expenditure side of the federal budget.

EXPECTED LEGISLATIVE CHANGES IN THE EITC

Until recently, the EITC received remarkable political support from policymakers, although not many citizens know much about it, nor think of it as one of the United States' big antipoverty programs. The recent expansions in the cost of the EITC, however, combined with its recent fraud problems, have made it a more visible and, inevitably, a somewhat more controversial program than in the past. In welfare reform debates in Congress during the mid-1990s, a variety of proposals were introduced to significantly reduce the size of the EITC. These proposals were largely defeated, at least in part because a number of legislators recognized the contradiction of sharply cutting cash assistance *and* cutting employment subsidies at the same time. In the end, there are likely to be only limited eligibility and benefit cutbacks in the EITC.

Minimum Wage

The minimum wage is not really a public assistance program, but it interacts with public assistance programs. The minimum wage is a legislated floor enacted by Congress which virtually all employers must obey; as such it is a public mandate funded by employers. In 1995, the minimum wage was $4.25 per hour for adults and slightly lower for teens. Together with the EITC, the minimum wage provides a substantial earnings floor for less-skilled workers.

The minimum wage alone is not nearly high enough to allow persons receiving it to escape poverty. Full-time year-round work at the minimum wage produces $8,500 in gross income, well below the $11,900 poverty line for a family of three or the $15,000 poverty line for a family of 4.

The minimum wage is set legislatively by Congress, and its value has eroded over time. Figure 3.7 plots the inflation-adjusted value of the minimum wage in 1994 dollars.[26] Even with an increase in 1990, from $3.35 to $4.25, the minimum wage is at one of its lowest historical levels.

Changes in the minimum wage do not require government expenditures, but they do impose mandates on business behavior. From a public budgeter's point of view, this is a political advantage, although it is one of the reasons why minimum wage increases typically face sharp opposition from employers. What is the effect of mandating higher wages to less-skilled workers? On the one hand, this encourages businesses to reconfigure jobs and to invest in capital so that even the least-skilled workers produce enough to justify paying them the minimum wage. On the other hand, it raises the cost of hiring less-skilled workers, which encourages business to use fewer such workers and to fire those who may be less productive than their mandatory minimum wage payment. The economic evidence suggests that higher and higher minimum wages gradually reduce employment among less-skilled workers.

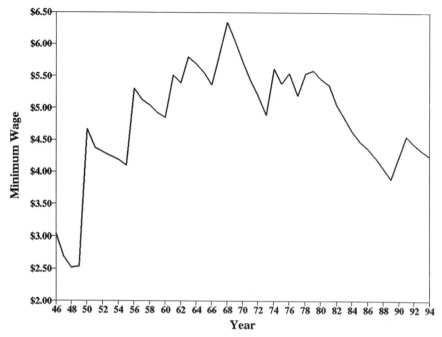

Figure 3.7. Minimum wage levels, 1946–1994, in 1994 dollars. (*Source*: Ehrenberg and Smith 1994)

At the current relatively low level of the minimum wage, however, there is evidence that these disemployment effects may not be very large. A variety of studies have investigated the impact of what happened when the minimum wage last went up in 1990.[27] A substantial number of those studies found only a small decline in the use of minimum wage workers after the minimum wage rose. Of course, the higher the minimum wage goes, the bigger these effects will be. But given that the current minimum wage is quite low, the loss of jobs among less-skilled workers caused by moderate increases in the current minimum are likely to be relatively small.

As an antipoverty device, the minimum wage is not the most attractive policy, primarily because it is not very well targeted. The vast majority of minimum wage workers are second or third earners in middle-income families. Only about one-fifth of minimum wage workers live in poor families.[28] Thus, the benefits of the minimum wage are spread throughout the income distribution. This might create political support for the minimum wage, but it also means that minimum wage increases are a very inefficient way to address poverty.

The minimum wage does provide a strong antipoverty package when it is seen as a complement to the EITC. Alone, however, as noted above, it is not high enough to allow even a full-time worker to come close to the poverty line. While further moderate increases in the minimum may be possible, big increases will produce even greater employment problems among less-skilled

workers than they already face. Similarly, while the EITC has expanded significantly, further increases will probably start costing too much to be politically
feasible. But a combination of the wage floor provided by the minimum wage
along with earnings supplements from the EITC makes full-time, full-year
work much more attractive and moves a worker's family close to the poverty
line. The second section in this chapter showed how the EITC and the minimum wage can reinforce each other.

Employer-Based Wage Subsidies

Rather than subsidizing the income of workers, an alternative is employer-
based subsidies, which typically provide tax breaks or rebates for employers
who hire certain groups of workers. These subsidies often take the form of a
one-time payment or tax break each time an employer hires someone from a
targeted group of disadvantaged workers.[29]

For instance, the Targeted Jobs Tax Credit (TJTC) was available from 1979
through 1994. The TJTC subsidized a share of wages for TJTC-eligible workers
during the first year of employment, through an offset on the employer's tax
payments. Over these years, a changing mix of workers was certified as TJTC-
eligible, including economically disadvantaged youth, public assistance recipients, veterans, ex-convicts, and disabled individuals. At its height in 1985,
all employers combined received credits on the employment of 622,000
workers at a cost of about $500 million to the government.

Other examples of employer-based tax credits include the New Jobs Tax
Credit of the 1970s, which tried to encourage new hiring by subsidizing a
share of wages for employers whose new hires exceeded a minimum limit.
Many states have used job tax credits in enterprise zone developments (discussed later in this chapter), where they reward employers who hire workers
from an economically depressed area. Similarly, as part of their welfare-to-
work programs, some states have experimented with subsidizing earnings for
employers who hire AFDC recipients.

There have been problems with these employer subsidy programs. First, a
surprisingly small share of employers actually uses these programs (typically
no more than 10 percent of those with eligible employees). Many nonparticipating employers claim that it's not worth filing extra paperwork to receive
the subsidy. Second, there is a concern whether such programs actually *increase* overall employment, or whether they simply redistribute employment
from one group of workers to another. Third, these programs have occasionally backfired, particularly when workers are expected to inform employers
about their eligibility for such programs. There is some evidence that such
programs can actually reduce employment probabilities for workers such as
ex-convicts or AFDC recipients if these workers go to a job interview and inform the employer that they are eligible for a tax break because of their background.[30] Such stigma effects seem not to occur when it is up to the employer
to identify eligible workers and claim subsidies, however.

Employer-based subsidies have somewhat faded from the public discussion in recent years. As states struggle with the question of how to design their own public assistance programs, many will be seeking ways to help these adults move into employment. One option is public sector employment programs, which subsidize government-created jobs. An alternative is tax subsidies to employers who initially hire public assistance recipients. Per job created, this may be a cheaper alternative, since the government need only pay the wage subsidy and not the cost of creating the job and matching it with a worker. For these reasons, further discussion of employer tax credits is likely in the future.

3.6 JOB SEARCH AND JOB TRAINING PROGRAMS

SUMMARY. *This section discusses job placement and training programs, including* welfare-to-work programs *aimed at* AFDC *recipients and the* Job Training Partnership Act *for other low-income adults. These programs require substantial resources to implement, although they promise reduced public assistance payments at some later stage as low-income families increase their earnings. An ongoing debate discusses the need to supplement these programs with a* public sector employment *program for workers who have trouble finding work in the private sector.*

If you want to increase employment and earnings among poor adults, what kind of programs help people get jobs or get better jobs? Job search and job training programs try to move low-income adults into the labor market, increase their skills (and hence their employability and earnings), and decrease their need for public assistance. In the last decade, there has been increasing interest in these employment assistance programs and declining support for cash assistance, at least for the nonelderly. In fact, AFDC has not been a simple cash assistance program since 1988, when the federal government passed legislation requiring all states to run job search and training programs for a portion of their AFDC recipients. The employment assistance programs discussed here may be considered complements to the programs discussed in the last section, which increase the wages available to low-wage workers or which encourage employers to hire such workers. Taken together, this group of employment-based policies aims to move more poor adults into the labor force and to improve their earnings while employed.

Although job placement and training programs have received lots of publicity in recent years, no more than 2 to 3 percent of the poor are currently involved in such programs at any time. Like all programs that provide explicit services, employment and training programs require resources to operate effectively. It both costs money and takes management skill to run programs that provide effective job placement and training assistance. Typically, moving from cash assistance to employment assistance costs *more* money at the beginning, because it requires putting together a much more extensive set of services. In fact, in many past cases where localities and states have tried to run employment programs "on the cheap," these have typically involved few participants and had little impact on employment. If effectively run, employment programs *can* increase earnings and decrease public assistance expenditures. But this effect may not occur until several years after a program is in operation.

Job Training Partnership Act

The Job Training Partnership Act (JTPA) is the main program providing job placement and job training assistance to low-income adults.[31] JTPA is run as a public/private partnership. While the federal government provides much of the funding, in each city or region private businesspeople work with local officials to identify labor market needs and set up training opportunities. While in some cases private companies actually run subsidized training programs, in most cases training programs are contracted out to local community colleges or other educational organizations. A potential applicant who walks into the local jobs office will typically sit down with a case evaluator, who will verify his or her eligibility for the program and describe the type of training slots and job programs available. Some places have a wide variety of potential training programs, while in other cities choices may be limited to one or two options.

Most of these training programs are quite short; the average length of enrollment in a JTPA program is around twenty weeks.[32] There are substantial variations between localities in the extent to which training is on-the-job versus in-classroom and the amount of job search assistance that is provided at the end of training.[33] While all localities provide job referrals to JTPA participants, some localities include sessions on "how to look for a job" and mock job interviews as part of the JTPA training.

The JTPA program serves around one million people a year.[34] About half of these are adult men or women, most of whom enter JTPA after an extended period out of work. As we will discuss below, many women use JTPA services as part of welfare-to-work employment programs. (In addition, there are a variety of youth training programs funded under JTPA, such as the Job Corps or summer jobs programs, which we discuss in a later section on youth.)

As it currently operates, the JTPA program provides relatively limited services for a small number of people. This is partly because JTPA services are not widely advertised in many communities, partly because the funding for JTPA is limited and could not accommodate many more participants, and partly because the JTPA program does not have a reputation for effectiveness in all areas of the country. In the next chapter, we will discuss the impact and effectiveness of JTPA and other employment and training programs in more detail.

Work Programs for AFDC Recipients

The hottest question in welfare reform in the last ten years has been how to implement programs that would move AFDC recipients into the labor market and limit their cash benefits. Since 1967, the federal government has encouraged states to experiment with work requirements for at least some of their AFDC recipients. In 1988, the passage of the Family Support Act required all states to run mandatory work placement programs for AFDC recipients who were classified as "work-eligible." The 1996 legislation induced many states to implement even more aggressive welfare-to-work programs.

The underlying philosophy to these programs has become known as *mutual obligations*: women who request assistance from the state in the form of AFDC payments must be willing to take advantage of opportunities provided by the state to move off public assistance and toward economic self-sufficiency. In return, the state has the obligation to provide the services that make employment possible. Thus, in addition to assisting with job search, these programs also subsidize child care or provide transportation assistance in getting to job interviews. They typically try to consolidate and centralize services for clients, so clients are assigned to case managers who are charged with helping to solve the entire range of problems that might prevent their clients from successfully completing the program. Women who are assigned to these programs but do not participate can have their benefits reduced.

As a result of the Family Support Act, every state set up a welfare-to-work program and many have continued to expand their work requirements. These programs vary widely across states. Because of limited funding, most women in these programs primarily receive job-search assistance, along with ongoing child care subsidies for those who find work. All states must require teenage mothers on AFDC to participate in high school completion programs before placing them in job-search assistance. In many states there is also funding for a small group of participants to enter more extensive training programs that allow them to work on completing a high school equivalency degree or post–high school training.

The implementation of the Family Support Act unfortunately coincided with a national recession and budget deficit problems in many states. The result was that most states implemented the minimal programs necessary to meet federal requirements. The federal goal was for states to have 20 percent of AFDC recipients participating in some kind of welfare-to-work activity by 1995. Because of funding problems, many states were having difficulty meeting this goal in the mid-1990s.

EXPECTED LEGISLATIVE CHANGES IN WELFARE-TO-WORK PROGRAMS

The legislation that turns AFDC over to state control through federal block grants includes job programs as well as cash assistance. Thus, the TANF block grant that replaces AFDC also abolished the provisions of the Family Support

Act and left it up to states to establish their own work programs for public assistance recipients. But there is an ongoing federal requirement that states must involve 50 percent of their caseload in work programs by early in the next century. Unfortunately, no additional federal dollars are currently proposed to help states meet this requirement. This means that states will have to meet increased federal requirements on work programs for welfare recipients, but will have no increased federal money to run these programs. While it is still unclear how states will respond to this change, many observers expect to see states *cut back* on their training and education programs for public assistance recipients, simply because of the reduced funds, and focus more on short-term job search assistance. In addition, it is also unclear how the time limits on the use of federal funds will effect job programs for public assistance recipients. Such time limits will provide a strong incentive for states to try to help recipients move into jobs as the time limit approaches. In some states, time limits may also increase the demand for public sector employment or employer wage subsidies for workers who are no longer eligible for cash assistance.

Public Sector Employment

It is also worth noting what is *not* currently available in the United States, namely, public sector employment programs. Public sector employment typically means "creating" subsidized jobs in public or not-for-profit institutions. These are often explicitly short-term jobs, available to low-skilled workers who are having trouble finding work in the private sector. Those who support public sector employment programs believe that these temporary job placements will provide training and work experience to disadvantaged workers, helping them successfully find a job in the private sector when their public sector job ends.

The United States has run major public employment programs at two points in the past. These were large programs for a few years, involving a larger share of the workforce in publicly created jobs than are currently participating in JTPA programs. In response to the Depression of the 1930s, the federal government operated such well-remembered programs as the WPA (Works Progress Administration) and the CCC (Civilian Conservation Corps). During the late 1970s, the United States again expanded public sector employment as part of the Comprehensive Employment and Training Act (CETA), which focused on placing disadvantaged workers into public sector job slots.[35] CETA was abolished and replaced with JTPA in 1983.

There are two primary arguments for public sector employment. First, high unemployment among less-skilled workers means that many simply *will not* find jobs. Subsidizing employment in short-term public sector positions may be better than allowing people to remain unemployed and supporting them through public assistance programs. Second, for someone with few skills and little past work experience, well-designed public sector jobs might provide the job experience and work discipline that will allow them successfully to land a future job in the private sector.

On the other side, public sector job programs can be poorly run. For example, few jobs in the CETA program in the 1970s provided substantial training, and the evidence is mixed on how much these jobs improved participants' long-term labor market prospects. In addition, public sector employment programs have certain inherent political problems. Public employees fear displacement by subsidized employees, simply churning the pool of the unemployed. Running a large public sector employment program also requires substantial management expertise; some localities did a very bad job of job creation, placement, or program oversight in CETA; in a few instances, there was serious misuse of funds. Finally, public sector job programs are not cheap to operate and typically cost more than cash assistance programs.

Although we run virtually no public employment programs right now, a number of states are likely to consider this option as they reconfigure their AFDC programs. Time limits on cash assistance among single parents will generate future proposals to place women who may not be able to find private sector jobs into short-term public sector employment.

3.7 FAMILY-BASED PROGRAMS: CHILD SUPPORT EFFORTS

SUMMARY. *A variety of laws have been enacted over time, designed to make identifying and locating fathers and collecting child support easier. Many states are also working to establish more uniform child support award standards. The federal government has been able to assist and encourage this process, but most of these changes are designed and implemented at the state level.*

As noted in the last chapter, one of the key problems facing single parent families is lack of financial support from absent fathers. Children in married-couple families can count on their fathers contributing to family income; children in single-parent families typically cannot. Over the last twenty years, increasing efforts have been made to identify and locate absent fathers, to impose court-ordered child support awards on fathers, and to enforce the collection of such awards. The federal government became involved starting with the 1975 Child Support Enforcement law that provided federal matching funds to state efforts to enforce child support obligations.[36] Over time, there has been an increase in child support collections and awards, although close to three-quarters of poor single mothers still receive no payments.

Identifying fathers is not a problem for divorced women. Both the father and mother of children born into married-couple families are listed on birth certificates. But paternity is established for only about one-third of births to never-married women. The point at which paternity establishment is easiest is at the birth of the child, and some states have made major efforts to establish paternity for *all* children at birth. For instance, Wisconsin establishes paternity at birth for over 70 percent of children born to unmarried women, but many states still identify paternity in no more than 20 to 30 percent of such births. If a father denies a paternity charge, genetic testing can verify his claim with a high level of accuracy. Women who apply for public assistance are now legally required to cooperate with the state in identifying and locating the fathers of each of their children as a condition of AFDC receipt, although not all states fully enforce this law.

Locating fathers is more of a problem than identifying them in many cases. States are required to cooperate with each other in locating absent parents in other states. The federal government has given states permission to trace fathers through a variety of sources, including Social Security records, tax reports, and Veterans Administration records. But many fathers try hard not to be found.

Even if the father is available, many mothers do not have child support awards. Divorced women are most likely to have such awards, typically worked out as part of the divorce process. As table 1.2 in chapter 1 indicated, 30 percent of poor divorced women and 75 percent of never-married women have no child support award. Awards have historically varied greatly across judges. Since 1988, states have been required to establish child support award guidelines which must be followed by the courts in establishing payment levels for the noncustodial parent. Usually these guidelines involve some combination of dollars needed per child and the ability of the father to pay.

Once a father has been located, and a child support award is in place, many fathers still do not pay regularly or do not pay the award in full. Thus, collecting child support can be difficult. In the past, a woman trying to collect child support typically had to take legal action every time the check failed to arrive, a time-consuming and extremely expensive process which few women were able to use. The federal government now requires states to establish centralized offices that offer services to women who are not receiving their awards regularly, although the responsiveness of these offices and their ability to take on new cases varies enormously. States also have gained the authority to use a wide variety of tools that should make collection easier, including wage withholding, property liens, and withholding from veterans' payments or unemployment compensation.

The child support system in most states has been collecting more dollars, but the number of single mothers who need child support has been growing faster than the system's capacity to help them. Too many fathers remain unidentified, unlocated, or behind in their payments. This is particularly true among women on AFDC, who typically have no personal resources to pursue legal action against fathers and must rely entirely upon the state for any child support collections. Major changes in federal and state laws over the past ten years have given states the authority they need to substantially improve their child support systems, but few states have fully taken advantage of this.

3.8 Targeting Youth: Educational Enrichment Efforts

Summary. *Over the long-term, youth-based programs that increase the skills and employment opportunities for today's children may do more to reduce poverty in the next century than the redesign of public assistance programs. For poor preschool children,* Head Start *provides enriched early childhood learning experiences, involving both children and their parents. For disadvantaged youth, a variety of programs are designed to increase skills and employment experience. These include programs as varied as* Job Corps *and* summer youth job programs. *Increasingly, schools are designing new programs aimed at non-college-bound youth, intended to improve the* school-to-work transition *among young adults.* Pregnancy prevention *programs also work to reduce the chances that young women (and men) will become parents and leave school.*

Demand has declined for unskilled workers who have little to offer besides two hands and a willingness to work. In the modern economy, to earn a wage that places workers and their families above the poverty line often requires formal education or on-the-job experience. Too many of today's poor adults have neither. In 1993, 14 percent of young adults aged 20–24 were high school dropouts, while another 32 percent had only a high school degree.[37] Given wage trends for less-skilled workers, all of these young adults are at risk of low earnings and poverty during their lifetimes.

What can we do about this? In the long run, the most important policy response is to make sure that today's children (tomorrow's adults) start their working lives with the education and skill levels that let them find good jobs in this new economy. Youth-oriented programs may be more important in bringing down poverty levels in the next century than anything else we do to help people in need.

The challenges facing America's schools and families as they teach and train children are complex, and many books have been written about issues ranging from educational reform, to child-rearing practices, to the problems of disadvantaged teens. In addition, many of the issues relating to education are traditionally issues of state and local decision making. The federal government is a small player in the financing of elementary and secondary schools in this country. This means that youth-oriented policies vary enormously across different states and localities. In this section I highlight a few programs that have received national attention or funding and that try to change the behavior or the opportunities available to disadvantaged children and teenagers.

Head Start

Head Start is a nationally available educational-enrichment program for poor preschool children. Begun as part of President Johnson's War on Poverty initiatives in 1965,[38] today it serves about 750,000 children. As psychologists have increasingly come to recognize, the importance of the early childhood years in the cognitive and physical development of children, this has generated concern with both the health care and the learning opportunities available to children in low-income families. If anything, concern with early childhood years has increased since Head Start was founded, giving it a solid base of political support.

Head Start provides funding to preschool programs in which at least 90 percent of the children come from families below the poverty line. Programs which receive Head Start funds must be more than child care centers. They must engage children in a range of educational and learning opportunities. In addition, Head Start encourages parents to be involved as volunteers and teachers and works with them in developing parenting skills that encourage their children's further learning.

Most Head Start enrollees are three- and four-year-olds. The goal of the program is to give children a "head start" before they enter kindergarten, preparing them for the elementary school classroom by providing a mix of social skills and basic knowledge, as well as instilling a belief that learning can be fun. Because Head Start programs are more likely to operate in low-income neighborhoods (in order to meet their 90 percent poor children requirement), they are more heavily used by poor minority children than poor white children.

Head Start works together with the expansion in Medicaid to all poor children, with WIC, and with the wide availability of school lunch and breakfast programs to provide targeted services to younger children. As a package, these programs provide a safety net for the healthy physical and cognitive development of children in their early years.

Youth Employment Programs

Concerned about high dropout rates as well as high unemployment rates among teens from poor families, the federal government has run a number of "second chance" programs. These focus on improving employment opportunities among low-income youth when they are on the verge of quitting school, or soon after they have dropped out.

The training programs of the *Job Training Partnership Act*, which were described in the last section, include many young adult and older teen participants. In fact, around 40 percent of the participants in general JTPA training slots have been under the age of 21. Most of these participants are either male dropouts or young mothers who enter training through AFDC welfare-to-work programs. Also funded through the JTPA are two other programs specifically aimed at youth which have received national attention.

Job Corps offers classroom and on-the-the-job training in a residential setting for disadvantaged youth. It is something of a cross between boot camp
and boarding school. This program began as part of the 1965 War on Poverty
initiatives. Like Head Start, it has survived partly because there has been evidence of its effectiveness, and partly because concern about the problem that
it addresses has continued to grow. Job Corps is designed to move teenagers
off the streets and into a twenty-four-hour-a-day residential program, often far
away from their home neighborhoods. The program emphasizes vocational
training as well as traditional educational skills. The operating theory of Job
Corps is that at-risk teens need high expectations and enforced discipline as
much as they need skill training.

At the other end of the spectrum from Job Corps are a variety of *summer
youth job* programs, primarily available to urban youth. These are relatively
low-cost programs that provide jobs to thousands of teens from low-income
families for one or two months over the summer. Summer job programs subsidize jobs for at-risk youth, often relying on community-based organizations to
identify job opportunities and select participants. While in theory this could
provide youth with job experience and training, these jobs are often hastily
identified and have few formal training components. Their primary effect is
probably to guarantee summer jobs (and earnings) to youth, which reduces
both crime as well as youth unemployment.

Programs Aimed at Teen Mothers

Teen mothers are more likely to leave school without a high school diploma,
limiting their future labor market opportunities, and more likely to make use
of AFDC and other public assistance programs, which is socially costly. A wide
variety of schools and communities run education and health programs designed to reduce the likelihood of teen parenting. Other programs aim at those
who become teen mothers, trying to keep them in school by combining high
school curriculums with parenting classes and child care.

For teenagers who become single mothers and apply for public assistance,
federal mandates since 1990 have required that states provide these women
with special services. Teen mothers who do not have high school degrees
must be placed in degree-completion or high school equivalency courses
(with child care provided while they are in school). In other words, the "work
mandate" that is first imposed on teen moms is to finish high school. Only
after they receive a high school credential are they put into job search and job
placement programs. This mandate, however, has disappeared with the end of
federal oversight over welfare-to-work programs. It is unclear how many
states will continue to provide these services to teen mothers.

Programs That Focus on School-to-Work Transitions

In recent years, U.S. high school training for non-college-bound students
has been compared unfavorably with that provided by many European or

Japanese secondary schools. Other countries often have far more structured programs for these youth that provide direct links between their high school training and post–high school employment. In contrast, U.S. high school performance is rarely linked with future employment opportunities; virtually no employers ever check high school grades or attendance records. Thus, students have little incentive to perform well in school unless they are going on for further schooling (in which case high school grades matter a great deal). A variety of school-to-work programs are being tried on an experimental basis around the country, designed to forge closer links between schooling and jobs. Many of these are funded and run by local school districts, although there is federal seed money available to help start some of these experimental programs. While it is hard to characterize these efforts fully, they generally break down into three types of programs.[39]

Apprenticeship programs match high school students with employers either while they are in high school or immediately upon graduation. Employers make a commitment to train students while they are still in school (often paying relatively low wages), with a promise of hiring them into more skilled and higher wage jobs if they successfully complete the training.

Closer links between schools and employers may be a good idea, but apprenticeship programs face some potential problems. Much of the argument for apprenticeship programs points to their success in Europe. But America is not Europe. Europeans tend to stay in one place, while Americans move around much more. U.S. employers resist training workers who are not likely to stay employed with them. Europeans accept sorting students at ages 12–13 into "vocational tracks" and "college-bound tracks"; Americans resist this. Apprenticeship programs are also relatively expensive, per participant. As a result, the number of slots available in formal apprenticeship programs will probably remain small within the foreseeable future.

A second approach to school-to-work programs is the *career academy*. These are often designed as a "school-within-a-school," admitting students somewhere in their early high school years. The students in these programs take a special set of courses that impose strong expectations and strong disciplinary and attendance requirements. At the same time, they often provide education in a more hands-on context with a strong vocational emphasis. Students who have a history of poor performance in traditional classroom settings may respond much better to special courses that motivate schoolwork differently and that clearly link learning to applied skills. Many of these career academies also develop links to employers in the area and may run internships and/or provide placement in after-school or summer jobs. Many career academy programs use educational models that combine strong discipline and high expectations with innovative learning techniques.

Many forms of "career academies" are emerging in various school districts around the country. The biggest problems they face are often managerial and organizational: running separately delineated programs within larger urban high schools is not always easy. Retaining students and imposing different requirements on them than faced by their peers may be difficult. A number of schools are now running such programs effectively, however, and their success at improving achievement, decreasing school dropout rates, and increasing post–high school employment is being reviewed in a number of evaluation studies.

A third educational approach aimed at the non-college-bound has become known as *tech prep*. While these programs also vary widely across the country, they typically involve a linkage between the high school and local community colleges. Joint curriculum is developed, and students often take academic classes at the high school while also taking more vocationally oriented classes at the community college. Community colleges are typically more connected with local employers and more aware of training needs in the community than are local high schools. Like other programs, most tech prep courses have strict attendance and behavioral standards, similar to job standards that would be imposed on employees in the private sector.

While different analysts might group these programs somewhat differently, all of them involve reforms in school programs aimed at non-college-bound youth. Their intent is to motivate high school students to achieve higher skill levels, stay in school through graduation, and to move more easily into postgraduation employment. All of them, when directed at less advantaged students, are long-term antipoverty programs. If a larger number of disadvantaged teens are able to find skilled jobs soon after they leave high school, there will be fewer poor families in the future.

3.9 IMPROVING NEIGHBORHOODS: ECONOMIC DEVELOPMENT EFFORTS

SUMMARY. *Federal, state, and city governments have tried to reduce poverty by increasing employment, rebuilding slums, and improving housing in neighborhoods with a high proportion of low-income families. Such efforts include* tax incentives *for business entry, loans and capital for physical redevelopment, and special employment programs. More recent programs include the* Enterprise Zones *launched by many state and local governments in the 1980s, the* Community Development Block Grant *program that provides federal funds for locally designated economic development projects, and the recently announced* Empowerment Zone *program.* Public housing *funds have moved away from public construction of projects toward shared public/private partnerships which have generated more small-scale housing redevelopment by community-based organizations. Finally, a number of areas are experimenting with* mobility programs, *which link low-income inner-city residents with suburban jobs.*

All other sections in this chapter discuss programs targeted on families and on people. This section talks about programs targeted on geographical areas, particularly on high-poverty ghetto neighborhoods. Even if these neighborhoods contain a small share of all poor families, these families are often among the poorest of the poor and make heavy use of public assistance. Since the late nineteenth century there has been concern with tenement housing and urban slums. In the years since, a host of programs have been designed to encourage economic development and change in poor neighborhoods.

Underlying these efforts is an assumption that environmental attributes are linked with individual behavior; that improving the neighborhood environment will result in positive changes in the lives of the individuals who live there. At the most basic level this obviously must be true: making available clean water, modern sanitation facilities, and weather-proof housing will necessarily improve the health of residents, assuring that they live longer, healthier, and more productive lives, and raise healthy children. Turn-of-the-century efforts at neighborhood change were often designed to assure that tenements in low-income neighborhoods met such basic standards.

More recent efforts have focused on improving physical structures as well as encouraging broader economic and social changes, such as increasing the availability of nearby jobs, decreasing crime, encouraging commercial development and business investment, or increasing home ownership in the neighborhood. The hope is that such changes will provide opportunities to neighborhood residents in two ways. First, they can improve people's ability to participate in mainstream society, by making it easier to travel to jobs (by lowering crime rates or improving public transportation) or to find jobs (by increasing neighborhood employment). Second, such changes can stimulate attitudinal changes that lead to further behavioral change, providing people with a sense of opportunity and of empowerment by demonstrating that their neighborhood is an important and vital place that people are fighting to preserve and improve.

There are many types of economic development projects that have been tried over the years. This section provides a brief summary of some of the major ones aimed at poor neighborhoods, most designed to improve the physical appearance of neighborhoods and/or to attract employment. The section concludes with a discussion of an alternative type of economic development program, which does not focus on directly changing depressed neighborhoods, but on linking residents in these neighborhoods with jobs and opportunities outside their neighborhood.

Programs to Improve the Physical Structures in Neighborhoods

The first federal housing rehabilitation and renewal act was passed in the 1930s, which signaled the beginning of public housing construction projects.[40] Public housing efforts were supplemented with a variety of slum-clearance and urban renewal funds, culminating in the Model Cities program of the late 1960s, which provided funds for cities to develop and implement plans to demolish older construction and replace it with new housing and commercial developments. Many cities used this money to clear large areas of low-income residences near their downtown areas, often replacing them with municipal structures (like stadiums or civic auditoriums) or with commercial buildings.

In a movement away from federally directed programs and toward more local autonomy during the Nixon administration, a host of federal programs were rolled together into the Community Development Block Grant program (CDBG), which continues to provide lump-sum funding to cities to be used for local community and economic development projects. CDBG block grant money is distributed to cities according to a national formula that determines local need. It is used for a broad range of projects, typically chosen by city development and planning offices.

The federal government also continues to provide dollars for residential construction and housing rehabilitation, but the form of that money has changed significantly over the years. Through the 1970s, virtually all housing funds went to local Public Housing Authorities who built and maintained public housing projects. The most visible of these were the high-rise inner-city public housing projects that have become the focus of so much criticism and controversy. The majority of publicly constructed projects were low-rise, multi-unit buildings, however.

Growing concern with the strategy of publicly built and maintained housing projects led to a shift over the 1970s. One result was substantial growth in the use of Section 8 vouchers and certificates, subsidizing low-income families for rental units in the private housing market. In addition, the federal government halted public construction of housing projects and redirected funding into shared public/private partnership projects. Private organizations and corporations currently build, own, and maintain housing projects, but the federal government agrees to subsidize rents over the long-term in these units, and/or it provides a variety of subsidies for the construction and maintenance of the project (such as mortgage interest subsidies) that keep rents affordable.

As a result of changes in housing funds, a number of local housing developers have sprung up in most major cities. This includes large developers, building multiunit projects in which all or some of the apartments are set aside for subsidies. But this new funding—as well as the tax credits available for low-income housing—has also attracted a number of local community-based organizations into the business of small-scale housing rehabilitation or construction.

The public programs aimed at improving the housing and physical structures in a neighborhood have been very controversial over the years. The urban renewal projects of the 1950s and 1960s often bulldozed entire neighborhoods, displacing many of the residents and markedly changing the character of the area, as will be discussed further in the next chapter.[41] From the point of view of those involved in planning and implementing these projects, this was exactly what they wanted to accomplish. From the point of view of neighborhood residents, many of these projects generated a great deal of anger and resentment. Much of the planning was very "top-down," so that community groups and residents were often not involved in decisions that had major effects on their lives. These urban renewal projects spawned local community-based organizations in a number of neighborhoods and cities, demanding involvement in city planning decisions affecting their neighborhoods.

Even in areas where substantial public housing was built as part of urban renewal, this too has been controversial. The siting of such housing in poor neighborhoods, combined with poor maintenance and incompetent management by many Public Housing Authorities, has meant that these public housing projects—originally designed to help renew neighborhoods—are instead often at the center of crime and gang problems in urban ghettos.

Economic Development Efforts Aimed at Increasing Employment

Changes in the physical appearance and structure of a neighborhood can only go so far. If the services and housing in a neighborhood are permanently to improve, there must be an increase in the income available to residents, which typically means an increase in employment. Bringing more employment opportunities into a neighborhood, through increased industrial and commercial development, can both increase the availability of local jobs for residents as well as extend the tax base available to finance schools and public services. For instance, the Urban Development Action Grant (UDAG) program provided assistance to targeted economic development projects in urban areas between 1974 and 1982. But the UDAG program provides a warning about the difficulty in targeting such programs effectively; UDAGs were discontinued, in part because they funded too many downtown hotel developers and too few improvements in poor neighborhoods.

A series of recent employment-oriented economic development efforts have not been federally funded, but were state initiated. Thirty-seven states launched "enterprise zone" programs over the 1980s.[42] While there was enormous variation in these programs across states, all attempted to increase the attractiveness of poor neighborhoods for employers. This typically meant providing short-term or long-term tax reductions to firms that agreed to locate in targeted neighborhoods and/or employ workers from targeted neighborhoods who qualified as "disadvantaged." While the federal government acted as a clearinghouse for information on these programs, federal dollars were used in these efforts only indirectly, through locally allocated CDBG block grant money.

Recently, there has been greater federal interest in assisting economic development efforts. In 1994, the federal government announced $6 billion in funding for six designated "urban empowerment zones," with much more limited funding for sixty-five urban "enterprise communities."[43] Each of these zones or communities has put together a major development plan for their area. The federal funding to empowerment zones will provide tax breaks to employers who locate in the zone and hire zone residents. The empowerment zones will also receive block grant money to run specially designed social service programs for disadvantaged community residents, such as job training programs or child care centers. Most zones also include plans for some housing reconstruction and rehabilitation. In many cases, the planning process for empowerment zones brought together a wide variety of community and city-based groups, led by the city development office, to create local development plans.

The biggest challenge for economic development efforts aimed at poor neighborhoods is to create noticeable neighborhood change. It is hard to relocate or attract new business into an area, particularly an area whose workers have limited skills and which suffers from problems of crime and physical deterioration.

Mobility Strategies

The alternative to trying to change neighborhoods, by building new housing or attracting outside business, is to improve a neighborhood by helping connect its residents with employment opportunities elsewhere in the city. In short, rather than trying to move jobs into an area, one can try to move people out to jobs. Such efforts are called "mobility programs," and they are being increasingly tried on an experimental basis.[44] A number of entrepreneurial community-based organizations have established mobility programs for poor neighborhood residents. Some experimental state and federal funding has been available for these programs, but they remain primarily local efforts at present.

Mobility programs are a direct response to the problems of changing cities, discussed in chapter 2. As jobs have moved to the suburbs, many urban workers (particularly African Americans and Hispanics) have been left with little information on suburban employment opportunities. They don't have friends who work there, don't know where these jobs are located, don't know whether they have a chance of being hired, and they may consider the suburban location of these jobs "foreign territory."

Mobility programs typically work to improve the public transportation systems that connect inner-city residents to other city and suburban areas where jobs are expanding, often setting up their own private bus and van services as well. But making it possible to reach jobs is only part of the program. Most mobility programs also work at building *networks* between city residents and suburban employers. From the point of view of the employer, this typically means convincing him or her that city residents can provide a stable and productive labor force; from the point of view of the residents, this typically means making them familiar with the jobs available elsewhere and providing the support that enables them to apply for and hold jobs outside their local area. For instance, such programs may take inner-city residents on "tours" of suburban industrial parks, showing them how to get there, how to get around, and introducing them to other workers from the neighborhood who work in these locations.

One quite different "mobility program" is designed to help poor residents move out of inner-city neighborhoods entirely. Interest in this strategy has emerged from the experiences of a pioneering program in Chicago known as the Gautreaux Project, which was the result of a court-ordered settlement in a housing discrimination suit. A limited number of residents in inner-city public housing projects (mostly black single-mother families) were able to volunteer for a relocation assistance program, moving either to other city neighborhoods or to suburban neighborhoods. Participants moved from subsidized public housing projects into private rental units subsidized by Section 8 vouchers. These apartments were identified by those operating the Gautreaux Project in a variety of locations around the Chicago area.[45] As a result of the positive results generated by this program, a number of experimental Gautreaux-like programs have been funded by the federal government in other cities.

Not surprisingly, mobility programs have been criticized by those who think efforts should be made to transform urban neighborhoods through development, rather than to help people escape them. Serious evaluation research on these mobility projects is currently underway in several sites. The evaluations of these mobility programs, still considered highly experimental, will determine how much interest and funding are available for such efforts in the future.

What Do Antipoverty Programs Do?

In 1995, all levels of government spent about $90 billion on public assistance programs providing income and services for low-income families, and another $120 billion on health care for the poor.[1] What did we get for our money? Polls indicate that many Americans feel we spend too much on programs to help the poor. They are frustrated with ongoing high poverty rates and conclude that these programs must be ineffective. We have all heard a great deal in recent years about the problems with public assistance, particularly cash assistance. Who hasn't heard about "welfare dependence" and "incentives for welfare mothers to have more children?" But we have heard far less about the extent to which public assistance programs improve nutrition among poor children or reduce poverty among the elderly. What if none of these programs existed? Would poor families be better or worse off? This chapter is designed to evaluate the effects of America's public assistance programs, both positive and negative.

As we shall see, many public assistance programs have accomplished exactly what they set out to do: food assistance has improved nutrition among the poor, health insurance has increased access to medical care, job training programs for single mothers increase their labor market involvement, and cash transfers seem generally to provide more cash income to families than they would obtain otherwise. The claim that these programs have failed is not based on the evidence. We have talked far too much (and often incorrectly) about the failure of antipoverty programs and not enough about their real successes.

On the other hand, the public assistance system in the United States is far from perfect. Some programs *have* been failures, others have been less effectively administered than they could be, and still others have been designed in ways that create perverse effects, discouraging work among those who should be working more. In this chapter I will discuss these problems as well.

Some critics of antipoverty programs have gone beyond the claim that antipoverty programs are less effective than they should be and have argued that these programs actually made things worse rather than better. Charles Murray in his 1984 book, *Losing Ground*, argued that the net effect of antipoverty programs has been to *increase* poverty rather than decrease it. Summarizing the effects of the government antipoverty programs initiated in the 1960s and 1970s, he claims, "We tried to provide more for the poor and produced more poor instead. We tried to remove the barriers to escape from poverty, and inadvertently built a trap."[2] Murray's argument received a great deal of attention, perhaps because of its shock value. Even in his book, however, there was little evidence to support it. In fact, Murray presented his opinion of how the world would be in the absence of public assistance programs as a "thought experiment."[3]

Two types of mistakes are often made by those who argue that antipoverty programs have been completely ineffective. First, critics (including Murray) often do not look at the full range of effects—both benefits and costs—that such programs generate. Too often, the fact that antipoverty programs have undesirable side effects is used to argue that they therefore should be eliminated. For instance, some have argued that we should abolish cash assistance to never-married mothers because it provides single women with an incentive to have children outside of marriage. Assume the incentives are exactly as claimed: there are more single mothers because of the presence of cash assistance programs. This does not automatically lead to the conclusion "we should not run such programs." To conclude this, one needs to know what the positive effects of the program are as well as the magnitude of the negative effects. Cash assistance does provide additional income to very poor families. If many single women will continue to have children even in the absence of cash assistance, the cost of allowing these children to grow up in extremely poor families may far exceed the benefit of preventing a number of nonmarital births.

In fact, it is striking how frequently the argument "this program has one bad effect and therefore should be abolished" is made, without a recognition that there may be benefits to these programs that offset their costs. This is the equivalent to arguing, "Social Security programs reduce the incentive for younger families to save; therefore Social Security should be eliminated." While it is true that Social Security *does* reduce the private savings rate (which affects the amount of money available for investment and growth), very few people argue that this means the program should be ended. Rather, they recognize that Social Security also provides a number of benefits to the elderly that may be worth the cost of lower savings rates. To judge the effectiveness of public assistance programs, we need to look at *both* their advantages and their disadvantages and weigh them together.

A second major problem with many assessments of antipoverty programs is that they use the wrong yardstick to measure success. Too often we evaluate a program by asking whether it did or did not reduce the number of families below the poverty line. In many cases, this is the wrong question. For instance, nutrition and health insurance programs do not change cash income in families and hence cannot possibly reduce income poverty as we measure it. To evaluate these programs, we must ask whether they improve nutrition and health among their recipients.

Even among cash assistance programs, reductions in the poverty count may be the wrong measure. Most of these programs are quite limited in their benefits. A state that pays a *maximum* of $3,000 per year in income supplements through AFDC, and pays this only to families with virtually no other sources of income, cannot possibly expect this program to move a family of three across the $11,900 poverty line. Thus, we shall see that many cash assistance programs have unambiguously increased income among the poor by making them *less poor* than they would be otherwise. But few of these programs ever make families so well off that they actually move them out of poverty. They were not designed to do so. To criticize them for this failure is simply bad policy analysis.

Finally, a comment on policy and program evaluation is important. Too often programs are labeled successes or failures based only on what appears to happen among their participants. This is *not* the right way to evaluate programs. Serious evaluation requires some sort of *control group*—a group that did not receive the program and which provides a baseline for what would have happened to people in the absence of this policy. For instance, in the midst of an economic downturn, to find that participants in a job training program maintained but did not increase their employment may signal success if those who didn't receive the program faced higher unemployment and fewer hours of work.

The most effective control groups often occur in what are called *randomized evaluations*, where people are randomly assigned into a program group or a control group. If this type of evaluation is done correctly, the only difference between these two groups is that one received the program and the other didn't, which makes it simple to evaluate the program by comparing their outcomes. Other evaluations compare a sample of individuals from before a program is implemented to a group afterwards who received the program's benefits or take a sample from a nearby geographical area where a program is not in place. Sometimes these provide adequate comparisons and sometimes they do not. Those policies that are implemented nationwide as entitlement programs—AFDC or Food Stamps, for instance—can rarely be well evaluated simply because nobody can be excluded from these programs and thus control groups are not available. Thus, the evidence on the success of these programs must be more indirect and deductive. Other programs, such as job training or youth education programs, have a good base of randomized evaluations which provide highly credible statistical evidence on their effectiveness (or lack of it.) Where appropriate, this chapter notes not only the research conclusions, but also the reliability of the methodology upon which those conclusions are based.

This chapter tries to provide a more careful weighing of the positive and negative effects of public assistance programs in the United States over the past decades. The conclusions are not nearly as bleak as many have claimed. There are problems with our public assistance system that can be and should be fixed. But there are also a number of quite striking success stories as well.

4.1 DO CASH TRANSFERS REDUCE POVERTY?

SUMMARY. *This section reviews the evidence on the effect of cash transfers on poverty rates, concluding that transfer programs unambiguously make people less poor. When past legislative changes have eliminated cash assistance for certain groups of recipients, these families have been able only partially to replace public assistance income with earnings and have ended up economically worse off. Estimates of the effect of cash assistance on poverty suggest that while relatively few people are actually moved out of poverty by cash transfers, these programs do result in a big reduction in the level of need among the poor. Comparisons with other countries also indicate that America's high poverty rate is closely related to overall lower cash public assistance benefits in the United States for low-income families.*

Asking if cash transfers reduce poverty may sound a bit like asking if eating reduces starvation. By definition, poverty measures a family's cash income relative to some fixed poverty line. Giving families more income should necessarily reduce the extent of their poverty. These programs provide income support that would not otherwise be available to poor families.

Some recent commentators have suggested that these programs may actually increase poverty if they cause a large decline in work effort and/or a large increase in single-parent families. Certainly, if cash assistance causes some people to be *poorer* than they would otherwise be, this is a very worrisome and perverse effect. In this section, I review the overall evidence behind the question: Do cash transfers decrease poverty? In the following two sections of this chapter, I examine more closely the specific criticisms of cash assistance for single mothers, analyzing the evidence on whether the Aid to Families with Dependent Children (AFDC) program reduces work effort, changes fertility and family composition, or induces people to remain on public assistance longer than is desirable.

There are a variety of ways to analyze the effects of cash transfers on overall income, and I explore four of them in this section. The answer that emerges is clear: cash transfers make people less poor. Their net effect has been to increase the income of recipients. This is not the same as saying there is no reason to reform existing programs; these programs may be less efficient or effective than they should be, or they may have undesirable effects that offset their benefits. But they *have* had an antipoverty effect over time.

Can Poor Families Replace Lost Income When Transfer Payments Are Cut?

If, as critics argue, cash transfers cause substantial behavioral changes that lead people to work less than they would otherwise, then people who are kicked off public assistance should be able to replace assistance income through their own earnings. Current proposals for absolute time limits on cash assistance to single-parent families assume that these parents will be able to find alternative sources of support when public assistance is withdrawn. The best way to investigate this is to look at past situations where eligibility changes have removed low-income families from cash support and study their subsequent behavior and well-being.

In 1981, President Reagan proposed major changes in the rules for AFDC recipients who had jobs. The resulting legislative changes caused about 12 percent of the existing AFDC caseload to lose eligibility for cash benefits in 1981 and 1982.[4] Because of the nature of the legislative changes, those who lost AFDC eligibility were the *least* poor families, primarily those where the parent was both working and also receiving AFDC. Thus, the most "advantaged" among AFDC recipients were forced off the program. Since many were already working, this group should have been able to replace government assistance with earnings more easily than the average AFDC recipient.

A variety of studies were initiated in the early 1980s to track women who were kicked off the AFDC rolls. All of this research came to the same conclusion: women who lost AFDC income worked more and increased their earnings. But on average, their total family income was *lower* several years after these changes than it had been before. They were unable to earn enough to fully replace the AFDC income that they had lost. In a major review of the effect of these changes, the U.S. General Accounting Office concluded that those terminated from the AFDC program typically had 12 to 26 percent lower monthly income eighteen months to two years after the program change than they had before these changes, "even though many worked full-time and increased their earnings during this period."[5] Thus, these women were unambiguously worse off in two ways after these cutbacks. First, they had less family income than before, and second, they were working more, providing them with less time for their children.

This experience strongly supports the claim that cash transfers decrease poverty. When those with the best employment and earnings opportunities were removed from AFDC in the early 1980s, they were still unable to earn enough to replace the cash assistance they lost. Cutting benefits among even more disadvantaged women is likely to produce even larger falls in their income, particularly given the ongoing declines in wage rates that less-skilled women have experienced over the past fifteen years.

Similar studies have been done for a different population in the state of Michigan in the early 1990s. In 1991, Michigan abolished its General Assistance (GA) program. GA was a Michigan-specific program, which provided no more than $160 per month in cash assistance to individuals who did not qualify for AFDC or SSI. In particular, single individuals and married couples received assistance through this program. Many recipients reported health problems, although they were often not receiving disability benefits. Michigan's Governor Engler claimed that most of these persons would find jobs and replace their benefits with earnings once they had no other choice.

Researchers at the University of Michigan tracked a random sample of 426 people cut off from GA benefits as a result of Michigan's action. Most of these people (77 percent) had held a job at some point prior to the termination of benefits, showing that they knew how to find a job.[6] Two years after the end of GA, only 37 percent of former recipients were working. Among those not working, many reported health problems. A large number of these people were actively seeking work but had difficulty finding it. The only group that had as much income after the end of GA as before were those who were able to qualify for assistance through other government programs, replacing GA income with other forms of publicly provided disability income. In other words, persons who lost GA benefits were not able to replace them through employment.

One might argue that the GA program in Michigan served a group with health problems, a group which might have more problems replacing transfer income with earnings than almost anyone else. A portion of GA recipients reported no health concerns after the termination of GA, however. Even among young persons under age 40 without health problems, fewer than half had as much income two years after the termination of GA in Michigan as they received in the last year of the GA program. Only 17 percent of persons over age 40 without health problems were doing as well afterwards as before. This is particularly surprising given the low levels of cash assistance on the GA program; individuals received no more than $160 per month and most received less than this. The inability of ex-GA recipients to find jobs and earn equivalent amounts of money when GA ended (although virtually everyone reported spending some time actively seeking work) suggests serious problems with job availability, low wages, and job-holding behavior.

All of this evidence supports the view that cash transfers generally improve the economic well-being of their recipients. When such programs are abolished, few people are able to fully replace government assistance with earnings or other income sources. They typically end up working more after the end of these programs, but with less total income than before. This brings us immediately back to the discussion in chapter 2 about the problems of high unemployment and low wages among less-skilled workers.

The Effects of Antipoverty Programs on Poverty Rates and Poverty Gaps in the Mid-1990s

One simple measure of the effect of cash assistance programs on poverty is to look at how much these programs add to income. We can look at how much poorer families would be if government cash assistance disappeared tomorrow.

Column 1 of table 4.1 shows the current poverty rate for various families among the poor, while column 2 show the poverty rate that would occur if today's cash assistance programs for low-income families disappeared and no other changes occurred.[7] Column 3 shows what is called the "poverty gap." This indicates how far short the average poor family's income falls from the poverty line. In other words, column 3 shows us *how poor* the average poor family actually is, relative to the poverty line. Column 4 shows what the poverty gap would be if cash assistance programs for low-income families disappeared.

TABLE 4.1

Poverty Rates and Poverty Gaps among Families in 1993,
with and without Cash Public Assistance

	Poverty Rate		Poverty Gap	
	Actual Rate (%)	Without Transfer Income (%)	Actual Gap ($)	Without Transfer Income ($)
All families	14.2	15.3	4,879	6,194
Single adults w/ children	44.3	47.0	6,661	9,231
Single adults w/o children	16.3	17.4	3,930	4,832
Married couples w/ children	9.4	10.0	6,486	7,777
Married couples w/o children	4.6	5.0	5,296	6,025
Elderly adults	14.5	16.0	2,419	3,000

Source: Author's tabulations from the 1994 March Current Population Survey.

Note: This table shows poverty rates among *families* rather than *individuals*. The five family categories are mutually exclusive, based on the marital status of the head of the family, the presence of children under age 18, and age of the head of the family. AFDC, GA, and SSI cash assistance are excluded from income in columns 2 and 4.

Table 4.1 indicates that, perhaps surprisingly, the overall poverty rate among all families would change very little if cash assistance disappeared, increasing only from 14.2 percent to 15.3 percent. Does this suggest that these programs provide little assistance to families? The answer is a resounding no, as columns 3 and 4 indicate. It turns out that relatively few families receive enough in government assistance to move them across the poverty line. But these programs have an enormous effect on the *poverty gap* of families, that is, on how poor these families are. Today's poor families on average have incomes that are $4,900 below the poverty line. Without existing transfer programs, their income would be $6,200 below the poverty line, a $1,300 difference. This is a large boost in income for poor families. About one-fourth of the poverty gap is closed by cash assistance programs.

Understanding that cash assistance programs may make families less poor without necessarily removing them from poverty highlights a problem with how we evaluate these programs. Expansions in cash assistance over time could make many poor families substantially better off, but as long as this does not actually move them above the poverty line, this improvement will not be reflected in reduced poverty rates. Similarly, reductions in cash assistance will have no effect on poverty if they make already-poor families even poorer. Thus, changes in poverty rates may seriously understate the impact of changes in cash transfers on the well-being of poor families.

The effects of cash transfers vary across different family types in table 4.1, although in no case does the absence of cash transfers have a large effect on poverty rates. In all cases, however, cash transfers make families significantly less poor, as measured by the poverty gap. This is particularly true among families headed by single persons with children. Recall from the last chapter that this group is the poorest in our society. In fact, on average their cash income is over $6,600 *below* the poverty line. Without cash transfers the rate of poverty among these families increases only slightly from 44 to 47 percent, but they are much poorer. In the absence of transfer programs, the average single-parent family with children would have income levels over $9,200 below the poverty line.

The alert reader will have realized that there is a big caveat on this discussion of the results in table 4.1. This table assumes that if all income assistance programs were to disappear, nothing else would change in families' income. Almost surely, if families lost all government transfer income, they would offset the decline in transfers through behavioral changes in order to survive economically. Some adults would work more, some families would move in with each other, and some single mothers would have fewer children. Thus, table 4.1 shows the maximum effect of eliminating government assistance.

How big a change in work effort or family configuration can we expect if benefit levels decline? That is the question of the next section. The primary point here is that families would have to increase their income by a significant amount, relative to their current incomes—on average, all families would have to replace $1,300 per year to remain as well off economically as before; single-parent families would have to replace $2,600. These are large amounts for families with current cash incomes below $10,000, requiring substantial increases in work for low-wage workers. So far, the experience with previous benefit cutoffs described above suggests this income cannot be easily replaced through the labor market.

Cross-National Comparisons, Particularly with Canada

Another view of the potential antipoverty effect of cash transfers can be obtained by comparing public assistance programs in different countries. The United States provides less cash assistance to low-income families than most other industrialized nations. Government support to low-income families in other countries often comes through a different mix of programs than in the United States. For instance, many European countries pay high levels of unemployment assistance to people for more than a year after they leave a job, no matter how short their period of employment. Other countries provide "family allowances"—special cash transfers to families with children. A number of Scandinavian countries provide extensive income support for several years to mothers following the birth of a child.

Figure 4.1 provides a comparison between the share of persons in very low income families across selected countries, using a common cross-national measure that counts people as low income if their family income is less than half of their country's median family income.[8] (So this is not confused with the poverty line in the United States, I will use the term "very low income" rather than "poor." In the United States, this establishes a cutoff for very low income families that is slightly above the current poverty line.) In essence,

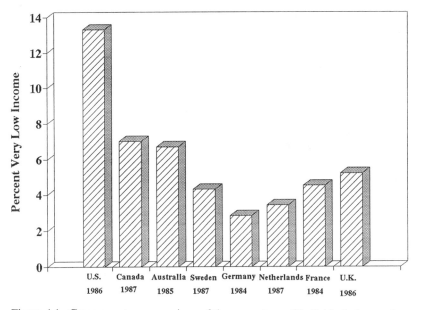

Figure 4.1. Cross-country comparison of the percentage of individuals in very low income families. (*Source*: Smeeding 1992)

figure 4.1 indicates how dispersed income is among lower-income families across countries; those countries with a wider income distribution will have more families far below the middle of the income distribution and thus a high share of very low income families in figure 4.1.

The data in figure 4.1 suggest that the United States has a much higher share of very low income families than is found in most European countries. This is consistent with other evidence showing that the distribution of income is more spread out in the United States than in other industrialized nations. A variety of studies have investigated these differences and uniformly conclude that more families in the United States have very low incomes because the United States provides substantially less in the way of government transfers to poor families.[9] Without their more extensive transfer systems, European countries would also have more very low income families. Of course, the flip side is that there are also more families in the United States with very high incomes, and this is typically considered partially due to the much lower tax rates in the United States. Obviously, the greater amount of transfers to the poor in European countries is integrally linked to higher tax rates on the nonpoor.

I do not want to argue that the European approach to taxes and transfers is better or worse than the U.S. approach. These differences presumably reflect different social choices made from different cultural perspectives. The primary point is that the national choice in the United States to provide relatively less generous transfers to low-income families has meant higher relative poverty rates in this country. While low-income families in the United States work more than in many other countries, they are not able to make up for lower governmental income support relative to their European counterparts. This is consistent with the evidence discussed above, which indicates that persons who lose eligibility for government transfer programs in the United States are usually left with lower incomes. On net, cash transfers have an antipoverty effect.

The clearest cross-national example of this effect can be observed with single-mother families in Canada and the United States.[10] Economically and socially, the United States is more like Canada than any other country. As in the United States, the number of single-mother families has risen substantially in Canada, although the share of families headed by single parents is still somewhat lower. If poverty rates in Canada are calculated using the U.S. definition of poverty, poverty among single-parent families in Canada is about one-third lower than in the United States. This difference is particularly striking given the depth of poverty among this group in the United States. What is Canada doing differently?

The difference is not that low-income Canadian single mothers work more hours or earn more than their American counterparts. Among poor single-mother families in the two countries, work behavior is extremely similar. The amount of earnings among this group (adjusted for differences in the value of the dollar between the two countries) is also similar.

The difference is entirely due to public assistance. In Canada in the mid-1980s, a low-income Canadian single mother received about twice as much in cash transfers as in the United States. The Social Assistance program—Canada's program equivalent to AFDC—has cash benefits that are much more generous in most Canadian provinces than are AFDC benefits in most states. Canada also provided some national transfers for families with children through the tax system. In addition, Canada guarantees health insurance to all families through a national health insurance system, which is not measured in these poverty numbers, but makes Canadian families better off than U.S. families that do not qualify for Medicaid.

This U.S./Canadian comparison provides one more piece of evidence that cash transfers do indeed make single-mother families less poor. And what of fears that more public assistance will result in less work among single women and more families receiving assistance? Canada's more generous system of benefits has not resulted in noticeably less labor market involvement among single mothers, nor has it produced higher rates of single motherhood (quite the opposite). But it *has* reduced poverty for these women and children.

Changes in Public Spending and Changes in Poverty Rates over Time

Poverty rates in America fell in the 1960s, a time when the economy grew rapidly and public assistance spending rose only moderately. Poverty rates went up somewhat during the 1970s, a time when public assistance spending

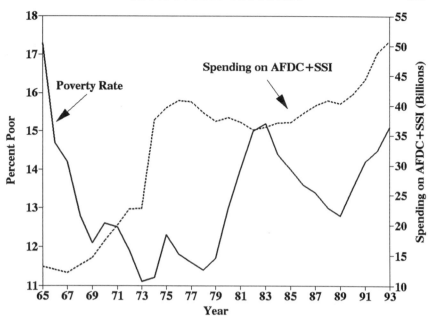

Figure 4.2. Poverty rates versus spending on AFDC and SSI, 1965–1993, in 1993 dollars. (*Sources*: U.S. Bureau of the Census 1995a; U.S. House of Representatives 1994; U.S. Office of Management and Budget 1995)

grew rapidly. Is this evidence that government spending doesn't affect the poverty rate, as some have argued?[11]

Figure 4.2 graphs the official U.S. poverty rate from 1965 through 1993, similar to the graph we looked at in the beginning of chapter 2.[12] The dotted line in the figure graphs U.S. spending on cash transfer programs to low-income families (AFDC and SSI). Recall that the U.S. poverty definition is based only on cash income. Thus, by definition, the expansion of in-kind programs (such as Food Stamps or Medicaid) that are not included in cash income cannot have an effect on the official poverty rate. Only the expansion of *cash* transfer programs, namely AFDC and SSI, should affect official poverty rates, and it is only their expenditures that we explore in this section. Many of those who criticize government spending for not reducing poverty fail to notice that much of this spending is not in a form that actually affects a family's cash income. While this surely indicates a problem with how we measure poverty, it does not indicate that these programs are ineffective.

The data in figure 4.2 suggest that there is some evidence of a simple "eyeball" relationship between poverty rates and U.S. spending on cash assistance: poverty rates typically fall when spending is rising and they rise when spending is falling. But this relationship does not exactly jump off the graph at the observer.

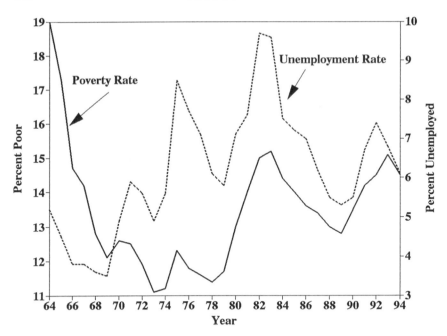

Figure 4.3. Poverty rates versus unemployment rates, 1964–1994. (*Sources*: U.S. Bureau of the Census 1995a, b; Economic Report of the President 1995)

The primary reason is that government spending is only one part of the story. In general, comparing two lines on a graph is a very bad way of doing analysis because it assumes that there is a simple one-to-one relationship between these two items. From the discussion in chapters 1 and 2, we know that changes in the economy as well as changes in family composition have affected poverty rates. Without accounting for these changes over time, simply looking at the two lines in figure 4.2 does not tell us very much about the relationship between government spending and poverty.

For instance, between 1970 and 1977 poverty rates fell only slightly while cash assistance rose sharply. But between 1970 and 1977 the economy also went through a deep recession and a sharp rise in unemployment and inflation. Figure 4.3 graphs the poverty rate and the unemployment rate. These two economic series clearly rise and fall simultaneously, with poverty peaking at about the same time when unemployment is at a peak. This suggests that the mystery is not that poverty was unchanged during the 1970s, but that it did not shoot up sharply, given how rapidly the unemployment rate rose in those years. Expansions in government spending on low-income families over the 1970s prevented the sharp increases in poverty that bad economic times would otherwise have produced; although unemployment rose rapidly in the 1970s, poverty remained relatively unchanged. In other words, over this decade, the economy worked to drive poverty up. Expansions in government programs worked to drive poverty down. The two forces offset each other, and poverty remained relatively unchanged.

This discussion emphasizes how important it is to understand the economic changes that were occurring at the same time as changes in government spending also occurred. The overall health of the economy, changes in family structure and composition, and the extent of government assistance have *all* affected the poverty rate in this country. Analyses of changes in income among low-income families over time that take account of these multiple factors typically find that growth in cash assistance has increased incomes among poor families. But other economic and demographic changes have also occurred over this same time, moving poverty up or down for other reasons. Together, these make it hard to observe any simple visual relationship in figure 4.2 between poverty rates and government spending.

The bottom line is that there is substantial evidence that government transfers reduce poverty and need. All else equal, when transfers are higher, poverty is lower. If our goal is simply to reduce poverty, increasing cash transfers to poor families is a sure way to do this. Why then is there so much opposition to AFDC, a program that gives poor single-parent families more money? In the next few sections, we discuss some of the problems with cash assistance, problems that need to be weighed against the income support that this program provides.

4.2 What Effect Do Cash Transfers Have on Work and Fertility?

SUMMARY. *Probably the most frequent criticism of the AFDC program is that it reduces the incentives for women to work and increases their incentives to have more children. The evidence indicates that the structure of the AFDC program does lead women to work less, but the magnitude of this effect is not large. The expected increase in work if AFDC were cut back would not begin to replace lost transfer income with earnings. In fact, the incentive not to report earnings may be stronger than the incentive to avoid work. With regard to fertility behavior, the evidence suggests that rises in out-of-wedlock births are not closely linked to AFDC benefit levels. The widespread nature of rising out-of-wedlock births suggests that other factors than welfare benefits are driving this behavior. AFDC benefits do appear to have some effect on the likelihood that women will live on their own once they have a child.*

While taking the train downtown to Chicago, I happened to sit behind two business-suited men who were each reading their newspapers and discussing the latest front-page article on proposed welfare changes. One gentleman suggested it was time to get rid of welfare altogether and he hoped the U.S.

government would do it. The other gentleman indicated that he understood the complaints, but was really worried about poverty among children. Could we just abolish these programs? The first gentleman had an immediate response: "If we get rid of welfare, the mothers will go to work and won't have any more children."

Public criticism of cash transfer programs has revolved around two claims: that these programs create a disincentive to work, and that they create an incentive for poor women to have more children. In this section I review the evidence on the magnitude of these effects.

Does Welfare Discourage Work?

Given the high value that most Americans place on paid work, the most damning charge against cash support programs is that they discourage work. The discussion of the AFDC program in chapter 3 noted that benefits are at their highest for someone who does not work at all. When a woman goes to work, her benefits decline rapidly as her earnings increase. This means that her income gains from employment are limited, since she loses close to a dollar in benefits for every dollar she gains from work.[13] Thus, as was discussed in that chapter, there are potentially two work disincentives imbedded in the AFDC program for a single mother: she receives income without working at all, and if she *is* working her incentive to work more hours is reduced because her total income rises much more slowly than her earnings.

A substantial body of research has tried to measure the disincentive effects of the AFDC program on work effort.[14] Differences in benefit levels across states provide a natural experiment for researchers, allowing comparisons between the work behaviors of similar individuals in high versus low benefit states. The results of this research are quite consistent across studies: higher welfare payments discourage work. The higher-range estimate of the size of women's labor market response to benefits suggests that for every $100 gained in monthly benefits, women will work two hours less per month.[15] This suggests that the $200 per month difference in AFDC benefit levels between Indiana and Mississippi leads AFDC recipients in Indiana to work about 48 hours less on average over the year.

Whether this is a big or little effect depends on one's point of view. Those who argue that it is a big effect tend to believe that any work disincentive is too large. Those who argue that it is a small effect tend to emphasize the other gains that welfare provides, relative to this work effect. They point out that these women are also caring for children (many of them preschoolers), and that less time in paid work provides more time to handle the responsibilities of parenting; they also mention the very low earnings opportunities for many of these women, claiming that the problem is not that welfare has a strong work disincentive, but that the labor market provides few good options for these women.

TABLE 4.2
Poverty Rates and Poverty Gaps for Single-Mother Families in 1993,
with and without Cash Public Assistance and Adjusting for
Work Behavior Changes

	Poverty Rate	Poverty Gap
Actual	48.0%	$6,670
Excluding AFDC income	48.7%	$9,277
Excluding AFDC income and increasing work effort based on income loss	48.4%	$8,940

Source: Author's tabulations from the 1994 March Current Population Survey.
Note: Row 2 excludes AFDC income from total income. Row 3 excludes AFDC income but adjusts earnings to reflect the average increase in work hours that this income loss would induce. Work-hour adjustments are based on the average effect estimated in research studies of work disincentives.

One measure of the size of this disincentive can be seen in a simple example. In the previous topical section, we calculated the change in the poverty rate among single-mother families if all government cash transfers were abolished. While this had little effect on whether they were poor or not, it substantially affected the poverty gap, measuring *how poor* they were. Table 4.2 looks at a similar calculation among single-mother families only.[16] Row 1 shows the current poverty rate and poverty gap among these women. Row 2 shows what the poverty rate and poverty gap would look like if all AFDC income disappeared entirely and there were no behavioral changes. Row 3 shows the poverty rate and poverty gap if all AFDC income disappeared *and* if women increased their hours of work by the average amount estimated in the research. In other words, women are assumed to increase their labor market effort in response to the amount of AFDC income they lose.

The results in table 4.2 indicate that women's earnings will increase somewhat in response to the changes in AFDC income, but their net poverty rate is entirely unaffected. Eliminating cash transfers increases the poverty rate only slightly, from 48 to 48.7 percent among this population; adjusting for changes in work behavior has an even slighter effect, bringing poverty down by only 0.3 points to 48.4 percent. The poverty gap, which jumps from $6,700 to $9,300 when AFDC is eliminated, moves back down slightly to $8,900 as women replace some of their lost AFDC income with increased earnings. But the end result is that women's changes in work behavior largely do not make up for the loss of AFDC income.

These results are consistent with the studies cited in the previous section that investigated the effects of past cuts in AFDC assistance: women who lose AFDC income are not able to fully replace it with earnings. AFDC dollars do not reduce work dollars at a rate even close to one-for-one. In fact, the work disincentive effect appears to be relatively small.

Is this surprising? If many of these women are on AFDC because of a variety
of problems and constraints in their life, then this result is not surprising. For
instance, if women have low skills and difficulty finding and keeping jobs or
if preschool children and unavailable child care limit potential work hours,
then employment will be relatively low among the AFDC-eligible population,
even in the absence of welfare.

There is another reason why these results may not be surprising. Increasingly, researchers are coming to believe that one of the most substantial effects of AFDC is not on how many hours women work, but whether or not they
report this work through official channels. The structure of the AFDC program,
with steep declines in benefits as earnings rise, creates a strong *dis*incentive
for women to report their earnings to the public assistance office—or to any
other official government surveyor trying to collect data on income. Recent
research focusing on interviews with women on AFDC in urban areas about
their income and expenditures has found that virtually no woman was able to
live on her public assistance income, and all of them supplemented it in one
way or another.[17] Most of this involved temporary jobs, such as occasional
child care or seasonal work. In most cases, the additional income that women
were able to earn was around $100 per month, not a high level of unreported
earnings, but a substantial supplement to families with only $600 a month or
so in available income from official sources. Even with their unreported
sources of other income, however, all the women interviewed in this research
were still below the poverty line.

What should we conclude about the work disincentive in welfare? There is
clear evidence that the structure of the AFDC program affects both the amount
that women work and the extent to which they report their earnings. These
effects seem relatively small and must be weighed against the antipoverty
effects of these programs. As discussed in the previous section, there is little
evidence that if AFDC payments stopped, these women could replace much of
their lost government assistance with earnings. Women would work more if
benefit levels were substantially smaller, but they would also be poorer. If
large numbers of women were removed from public assistance in a short period of time, there would also be much greater problems with job availability.

Frustration with these facts has led increasingly to a system that combines
both cash support and work requirements for AFDC recipients, continuing to
provide assistance at the same time that it mandates employment. We discuss
the success of welfare-to-work efforts in the section, "Do Job Programs Encourage Work?"

Does Welfare Encourage More Pregnancies among Single Women?

The rising share of never-married mothers in the AFDC program has led many
to speculate about the possible causal link between AFDC payments and out-
of-wedlock births. Many are concerned that AFDC payments provide an incentive for women to have children, since this makes them eligible for AFDC and

Food Stamp benefits. If they already have children, their benefits rise with increases in family size.

A large body of literature explores the causes behind fertility choices.[18] Few studies find much evidence to support the claim that welfare payments are leading to increases in fertility among low-income women. Most of these studies use the differences in AFDC benefit levels across states to control for the effect of different levels of government support on fertility among single mothers. Depending on which study one looks at, the results either indicate that AFDC payments are not related to women's fertility, or that the effect is relatively small. Robert Moffitt, a professor of economics at Johns Hopkins University, was recently asked to write a review of the research in this area for the *Journal of Economic Literature*, published by the American Economic Association. After extensively discussing all the studies, Moffitt concludes: "The failure to find strong benefit effects is the most notable characteristic of this literature."[19]

Since racial differences are often invoked in the public discussion about nonmarital birthrates, it is worth noting that the research literature indicates that the relationship between benefit levels and fertility behavior is slightly stronger among low-income white women than among African American women. Among black women, there is no persuasive evidence that benefit levels and nonmarital births are linked, but there seems to be a weak positive link among white women.

Is this conclusion surprising? It is consistent with several other pieces of evidence that suggest fertility decisions are primarily driven by factors other than welfare support levels. First, the large increases in out-of-wedlock births are very hard to match with trends in AFDC payment levels. As figure 3.5 in chapter 3 indicated, monthly public assistance benefits (adjusted for inflation) have declined over the past two decades, yet the out-of-wedlock birthrate has increased rapidly over this time period. If higher benefits lead to more births, then the decline in monthly public assistance support should have *decreased* this birthrate. If anything, the declining trends in AFDC payments should be discouraging pregnancies to unmarried women, keeping the rate below where it would be otherwise.

Second, as discussed in chapter 1, the rise in births among unwed mothers is not limited to those who rely on AFDC for support. It is a phenomenon spread throughout the income distribution. While higher-income single women still have much lower rates of unwed births, their probability of giving birth has also risen substantially in the past twenty years. Those who claim that out-of-wedlock births are primarily driven by welfare payments, available only to mothers with incomes of $8,000 or less in most states, miss this larger picture entirely.

Third, government assistance to single mothers is much lower in the United States than in most other industrialized countries, as discussed in the previous section. If higher welfare payments lead to higher rates of birth to unwed mothers, then the United States would have lower rates of such births than

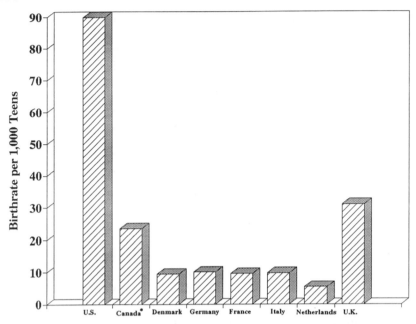

Figure 4.4. Cross-country comparison of birthrates per 1,000 women aged 15–19 in 1987. Canada's figure is for 1986. (*Sources*: Eurostat 1990; Statistics Canada 1988; U.S. National Center for Health Statistics 1991a)

other countries, yet the United States has one of the higher rates of single motherhood and the highest rate of teen pregnancy. Figure 4.4 shows the rate of pregnancy among U.S. adolescents versus adolescents in other countries.[20]

The U.S. teen pregnancy rate is off the chart compared to other countries. (Even if this figure looked only at white U.S. teens, the U.S. rate would be higher than any other country.) For instance, in the mid-1980s Canada's public assistance programs for poor single mothers provided about twice as much support as in the United States. Yet Canada's illegitimacy rate is lower than that of the United States and its teen pregnancy rate is far less. Similarly, if welfare benefits are an important cause of teen births, France or Denmark should have teen pregnancy rates that are well above those of the United States, but instead they are far below.

In chapter 1 I discussed several of the important factors that have driven changes in fertility behavior among women in recent years: expansions in women's economic and labor market opportunities, declines in the labor market opportunities available to less-skilled men, making them less attractive marriage partners, and changes in the social stigma associated with unwed motherhood. These broad social changes have made all single women more likely to bear children without marrying. Those who claim that poverty would have been much lower if out-of-wedlock birthrates had remained stable are correct. Those who claim that this rise was fueled by AFDC payments are incorrect.

While the direct effect of AFDC benefits on fertility might be small, there is some evidence that AFDC benefit levels appear to effect women's propensity to leave their parents' homes and set up their own household once they have a child.[21] More women in high-benefit states live in their own households, rather than with parents, friends, or other relatives. In other words, the "independence effect" of AFDC support seems much greater than the "fertility effect."

Whether we can view greater independence as good or bad requires more information than most current research makes available. As discussed in chapter 1, to the extent that some women live in abusive homes, moving out may be a very good thing for them and for their children. In other cases, particularly among teen mothers with stable home environments, staying in a situation where there is more support and assistance in mothering may be useful. From the point of view of the recipient, the "independence effect" is clearly a good thing; more women voluntarily choose to live on their own when they can afford it. From a social point of view, it is hard to make a blanket statement about whether the "independence effect" is good or bad. For some women it is good, they escape difficult family environments; for others, more isolation may make them worse parents. (It is worth noting that increases in cash support for the elderly have produced exactly the same "independence effect." As elderly incomes have risen in the post–World War II period, fewer and fewer live with their children. Both the elderly and their children appear to view this as a good thing.)

The bottom line of this discussion on both work and fertility behavior is that greater cash support for single mothers has some negative effects on their behavior. On the margin, it makes them less likely to work, less likely to report income, slightly more likely to have a child, and more likely to live independently. Most of the available research suggests that these effects are relatively small, however. Their negative effects must be weighed against the income protection to poor families that AFDC provides. I do not find these particular arguments against AFDC convincing and believe that policies other than AFDC benefit cuts will be more effective if we want to increase work among single mothers and decrease out-of-wedlock birthrates.

4.3 WHAT ABOUT WELFARE DEPENDENCE?

SUMMARY. *About half of those who ever receive AFDC at any time in their life receive assistance for three years or less; another one-quarter receive AFDC for ten years or more. These long-term users tend to be women who are most disadvantaged in terms of their family and labor market situation. There is little evidence that welfare is "addictive," that is, that women who go on welfare lose all motivation to work. In fact, most long-term AFDC users cycle on and off the program, finding jobs but returning to AFDC when these end. Another concern is intergenerational welfare use. Most daughters of AFDC recipients do not use AFDC, but more do become recipients than do daughters whose mothers were never on AFDC. This largely reflects the fact that poor children grow up in an environment that make them more likely to be poor adults, and hence more likely to use AFDC themselves.*

Closely tied to the concern about work disincentives for welfare recipients is the question of welfare dependence. Some women rely on welfare assistance for an extended period of time. Is welfare too easy to receive, inducing women to remain "on the dole" rather than looking for work? State and national proposals to limit the number of years over which a family can receive AFDC cash benefits reflect an effort to limit long-term welfare use.

There are two possible interpretations of the phrase "welfare dependence" that are typically not distinguished in the public debate over this issue. Some who talk about welfare dependence are simply concerned with the fact that some women receive assistance for multiple years. This may be due to many things, from health problems to a lack of skills and job connections. Because of the public cost of long-term welfare recipiency, this creates support for programs that help women move more quickly and permanently back toward self-sufficiency through work in the mainstream economy.

A second group who talk about welfare dependence see welfare in a much more invidious light. For instance, U.S. Representative John Mica (R-FL) stated during the welfare reform debates of 1995, "I submit to you that with our current handout, non-work welfare system, we've upset the natural order. We've created a system of dependency."[22] This group is making a causal argument, claiming that initial receipt of welfare leads to future welfare use. The assumption is that welfare is the easy way out; once women realize they can get a check from the government they stop looking for a job. Thus, welfare must be limited and women must be pushed off it because once they realize it is available they will lose their motivation to work. I will call this the "welfare addiction" argument, to clarify it from the first argument, which is also concerned with long-term welfare use.

In this section we will look at patterns of welfare use over time. The available data largely rebut this second perspective on welfare. There is little evidence that welfare use begets more welfare use. Among those who use welfare, the majority use it only for a limited period of time. Even among long-term welfare recipients, few are permanently on welfare. Rather, they cycle on and off the rolls. They regularly leave AFDC assistance, entering jobs and/or entering relationships with men that give them more income. The primary problem among these long-term welfare users appears to be inadequate work preparation and limited job opportunities rather than inadequate work motivation. The first part of this section looks at patterns of AFDC use over time, the second section directly discusses what these patterns mean for "welfare addiction" arguments, and the last section investigates concerns about intergenerational welfare use.

(A)

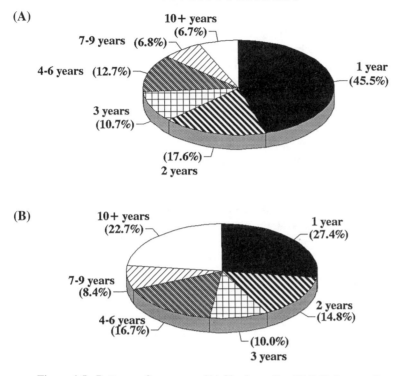

(B)

Figure 4.5. Patterns of AFDC use. (A) Single spells. (B) Lifetime spells. (*Source*: Data provided by LaDonna Pavetti, The Urban Institute)

What Are the Patterns of Welfare Use over Time?

Figure 4.5 summarizes the best data available on AFDC usage over time.[23] The first pie chart shows how long women continuously remain on AFDC. In other words, it looks at the duration of single spells of welfare use. Among all women who apply for welfare and are approved, nearly half—45 percent— will be off AFDC within a year, and nearly two-thirds will be off in two years. Only 7 percent will stay on AFDC ten years or longer.

We have learned, however, that looking only at single spells of AFDC use is somewhat misleading, since a substantial number of women return to use AFDC multiple times during their life. Thus, to understand the extent to which women rely on AFDC income, one has to look at total time on AFDC, not just how long newly approved applicants will stay on the rolls. The second pie chart in figure 4.5 provides an estimate of *total* time on AFDC among those who ever use it. Among those who enter AFDC, 27 percent will use it only for one year over their lifetime, while 52 percent will use it for three years or less. Slightly less than one-quarter of AFDC users will receive AFDC for ten or more years, a much higher percentage than those who *continuously* re- ceive AFDC. (At some point, all women will leave AFDC, since it is not available after one's youngest child passes age 18. Thus, very few older women are recipients.)

From the two pie charts in figure 4.5, we can draw three conclusions that summarize what we know about patterns of AFDC usage. *First, a large number of women who use AFDC use it for only a relatively short period of time.* Over half of all women who use AFDC do not receive it for more than three years over their lifetime. There are lots of short-term AFDC users, who utilize the program when they find themselves in temporary need but get off permanently in a short period of time.

Second, a substantial minority of women rely on AFDC for an extended period of time. The fact that almost a quarter of AFDC recipients will receive income from it for at least ten years during their adult lifetime suggests that there is a valid concern with long-term AFDC usage. These are the women who are most costly to the system. There may be fewer of them than short-time users, but they receive much more in AFDC payments.

Third, most women who use AFDC for a more extended period of time cycle on and off it. The fact that the lifetime usage of AFDC (the second pie chart in fig. 4.5) is different from single-spell usage (the first pie chart) suggests that many women leave AFDC but then return. This is apparent not only in the data shown here but in a variety of other studies.[24] Increasingly, those who work with long-term AFDC recipients are talking about the problems of *cycling*. These women find ways to escape AFDC, but something happens that brings them back on the rolls.

Knowing the characteristics of long-term versus short-term AFDC users is important in understanding the nature of long-term welfare dependence. Perhaps not surprisingly, those who use AFDC long term are the most disadvantaged among recipients.[25] They tend to be the AFDC recipients who have the lowest level of education, who have no recent work experience, who entered the welfare system at a younger age, who have more children, and who have never married. In addition, African-American and Latina women receive welfare for longer time periods, even after taking these other characteristics into account. Interestingly, several studies show that for black women, the more extensive use of AFDC is related to the fact that they are less likely to marry.[26] Black and white women are just as likely to leave AFDC through employment; but poor black women are less likely leave AFDC via marriage. This supports those who argue that the pool of eligible men who might be good marriage partners for low-income black women is limited.

Is There "Welfare Addiction"?

What does all of this evidence on patterns of welfare use suggest about the "welfare addiction" argument? Does welfare use beget further welfare use? There are at least three reasons why this more causal interpretation of welfare dependence is not borne out by the data.

First, there is little evidence that women are becoming permanently "ad-

dicted" to welfare. This obviously is not true for the relatively large number of women who use AFDC for only a few years. But the fact that even long-term users cycle in and out of AFDC receipt suggests that they are not comfortable remaining on welfare continuously. Interviews with women who have used AFDC extensively typically indicate how much they dislike receiving AFDC; they often cite the desire to be self-sufficient and to not put up with the hassles of the welfare system discussed in the next section. Similarly, few women on welfare resist participating in welfare-to-work programs. In fact, the overwhelming majority of participants consider these programs useful and appreciate the help they provide.[27] In short, the problem is not that work motivation has disappeared, but that it is continuously thwarted among long-term AFDC recipients by a labor market that offers few opportunities for women with low skills and by their own complex family and personal problems.

This evidence is further buttressed by the fact that a significant number of persons eligible for welfare elect *not* to receive it.[28] The data suggest that only two-thirds to three-fourths of those eligible for AFDC actually make use of the program. Furthermore, many women who do not use the program are eligible for more than a few dollars. The average welfare payment which eligible nonparticipants would receive is over $250 per month. If government assistance is much more attractive than work, there should be few people who spurn it when eligible.

Second, the characteristics of long-term welfare recipients suggest that many of them would have a great deal of difficulty achieving economic self-sufficiency, regardless of how hard they work. In chapter 2 of this book I discussed the low wages and limited job opportunities for women without high school degrees, the group most likely to be long-term AFDC users. Add the facts that few among this long-term group receive child support, most have two or more children, and a disproportionate share report health problems. This is exactly the group for whom economic self-sufficiency is most difficult. Given that work alone is unlikely to provide enough income to cover family expenses, and that the AFDC system has historically made it quite difficult to both work and receive AFDC at the same time, it may not be surprising that the least work-ready and least skilled group on AFDC tend to rely on public assistance for long periods of time. In short, one need not think in terms of "addiction" to understand why these women are long-term AFDC users.

Third, the reasons that seem to bring women who leave AFDC back into the program also suggest that the problem is not one of AFDC "addiction" but of labor market inadequacy and family problems. A study of women who found work as a result of California's welfare-to-work program but who subsequently left those jobs indicated that almost half reported that they were laid off or their job ended.[29] The short-term and unstable nature of many jobs available for less-skilled workers means that there is no guarantee that women who try to find employment will be able to keep it. Another two-fifths indicated that they had quit. Many of these quits are associated with family issues, including everything from child care problems to problems of domestic abuse.

Another big reason why jobs end is that women have interpersonal problems on the job, including disagreements with their co-workers or supervisors. A study of welfare-to-work participants in a public housing project in Chicago who subsequently lost their jobs concludes that the rules of the workplace are often very different from the neighborhood and family behavior norms learned by women in disadvantaged communities.[30] Without role models or outside counseling and assistance, they quit or are fired when they have difficulty adjusting to a work environment.

While there appears to be little reason to accept the "welfare addiction" hypothesis, there are important reasons to be concerned about the fact that some number of women do use welfare for very long periods of time. Not only is this socially costly, but it is also another signal of the problems faced by some women on welfare who have limited skills, inadequate connections to jobs, and personal and family problems. Providing the assistance these women need to move more permanently into jobs and to deal effectively with their personal problems would be preferable if it can be done.

What About Intergenerational Welfare Use?

Long-term welfare use may not simply occur among women over their adult years, but it may also stretch across generations. If good skills, job connections, and role models are important in escaping welfare permanently, then women who lack these attributes may also pass along these problems to their children.

All research on income mobility across generations concludes that children's economic status is linked to their parents' economic status.[31] Children of parents who are wealthy are very unlikely to be poor. Children of parents who are poor are unlikely to end up at the top of the income distribution. Although there has been more economic mobility across generations in America than in many other countries, a strong correlation remains between the occupational choices and incomes of fathers and the occupational choices and incomes of their sons.[32]

We do know that daughters of mothers who receive AFDC are more likely to receive AFDC themselves than are the daughters of mothers who do not receive AFDC. But it is important immediately to follow this statement by another known fact: *most* daughters whose mothers received AFDC will not themselves receive AFDC. The data suggest that only between one-quarter to one-third of the daughters of AFDC recipients will at some point also receive AFDC. Thus, most daughters do well enough as adults so that they do not need public assistance. But only around 5 percent of the daughters in families that never received AFDC will participate in the program at some point in their life.[33] Thus, the children of poor women are much more likely themselves to be poor and to receive AFDC.

Various studies have tried to investigate how much of these intergenerational correlations are readily explainable.[34] For instance, daughters in poor families are likely to have less education, to have children at a younger age, and to have lower occupational aspirations. All of this is associated with a higher probability of using AFDC. In other words, children in poor families experience many disadvantages that make them more likely to be in need of cash assistance at a later point in life. This may be true whether or not their parents ever received cash assistance. As it turns out, these other variables explain most of the difference in AFDC use between the daughters of poor mothers and the daughters of nonpoor mothers. But even after taking all of these other differences into account, there still remains a small but significant difference in AFDC usage among daughters that is correlated with whether a daughter grew up in a family that received AFDC.

Although most daughters of AFDC recipients do not make use of welfare, poor children are more likely to be poor adults and this means that they are also more likely to use AFDC. This is not surprising. Most of the intergenerational correlation in welfare use can be explained by this correlation in economic status between children and their parents. After controlling for the expected cross-generational immobility, daughters of AFDC recipients have only a slightly higher risk of utilizing AFDC.

4.4 MANAGEMENT MATTERS: THE OPERATING SYSTEM OF AFDC

SUMMARY. *The operating system in most AFDC offices is extremely rigid and rules-driven. It is hard to respond to applicants' particular problems; rather, everyone is forced through a uniform set of program rules. This rule-based system is the result of a past history of arbitrariness and discrimination within AFDC programs, and the proliferation of regulations without attention to problems of their implementation and management. Not only does the system create a sense of helplessness, anger, and frustration in recipients, it strongly discourages them from making changes in their lives that will create more paperwork for AFDC staff workers. In particular, this often discourages work behavior. Though little discussed publicly, these management issues are among the worst problems of the AFDC program.*

> Anyone on public aid, they been treated like dogmeat.
> —*Comment by an ex-AFDC recipient in Chicago*

Perhaps it is not surprising that people who think their taxes are too high dislike public assistance programs. Perhaps it is not surprising that people who have observed self-serving or blatantly fraudulent behavior among certain poor individuals are suspicious of all public assistance recipients. But

why is it that welfare clients themselves dislike AFDC? If this program decreases poverty and economic need among its recipients, then these clients
should be its strongest advocates. Instead, many recipients are very critical of
the AFDC program.

The answer to this puzzle lies in the way that AFDC has been implemented
and in how public assistance offices are run. As the current system is config-
ured, the primary role of most frontline staff is to enforce a set of uniform
rules, designed to police their clients' income reporting and behavioral con-
formance. This is done by ensuring that a standard set of forms is filled out
accurately by applicants and ongoing clients. While this satisfies the requirements of federal and state rules and regulations, it does little to provide anything like real "assistance" to poor women.

David Ellwood, who served as Assistant Secretary of Planning and Evaluation in the Department of Health and Human Services under President Clinton, attended a number of hearings where welfare recipients testified about
their experiences. He frequently describes one woman who had received AFDC
off and on for about ten years. She described her experiences with multiple
AFDC staff and program requirements, and concluded by saying something
like "I always expected the first question to be 'What can we do to help?
What's gone wrong?' Never once did someone ask me this. Instead, whenever
I walked in they immediately started me filling out forms."

I recently interviewed one woman I'll call Sonya, who had successfully
completed a welfare-to-work program in California. In 1988 she had a steady
but low-paying job, but when her husband ran off with another woman and
left her with three small children, she could barely make ends meet. When her
car broke down, she could no longer get to work. Reluctantly she went to the
local welfare office to try and get money to help fix her car so she could get
back to work. The intake worker who took her application told her, "You're
earning too much to get welfare," and suggested she quit her job. Sonya was
still angry when she talked with me seven years later: "I was pissed. I'd paid
into the system for years and I just wanted a little help to fix the car and they
turned me down. They wanted me on welfare entirely and wouldn't help me
with what I needed." Within a month she had lost the job because she had
gotten there late too many times without a car. She looked for another job, but
did not find one and quickly fell behind on her rent. Faced with a landlord
threatening eviction, she had no choice but to go back to the AFDC office.

Public assistance offices, particularly those in large cities that handle large
caseloads, are chaotic. Clients often talk about having to wait half a day to see
a staff member, even when they were told they had an appointment at 1 P.M.,
then find they have to come back the next day and wait again. Many mothers
bring their preschool children, who become impatient during hours in a waiting room.

Not all of this is the fault of those who work in these offices. The average
case worker in an urban AFDC office has hundreds of cases she or he is manag-
ing. They are overworked and the computer systems often function inade-

quately. Staff quickly learn that the best way to keep their jobs is to keep the paperwork filled out properly. Because of the huge caseload, they cannot afford to spend much time with any one client.[35]

How did the U.S. AFDC program get into this situation? There are at least three important reasons. *First, the U.S. welfare system has become entirely rule based.* It allows virtually no discretion on the part of staff who work directly with clients. Indeed, most of the discussions that intake workers have with AFDC applicants involve verifying that applicants bring in all the right information (pay stubs, Social Security card, rent receipt, checkbook, children's birth certificates, etc.) and fill out their eligibility forms correctly. The amount of assistance that an applicant will receive is fully determined by an existing set of rules. The computer provides this information after the intake worker inputs all the forms.

This is in sharp contrast to the system that exists in the public assistance programs in several Canadian provinces. In Ontario, for example, case workers are given guidelines to follow, but they are expected to determine the actual benefit a woman will receive, based on their assessment of the situation. They have substantial discretion to determine assistance levels for different women. Women with differently aged children, with different work histories, or with different housing situations may be approved for different benefit levels determined by the case worker.

There are both good and bad things about discretionary versus rule-based systems. The rule-based system in the United States emerged in part in response to egregious discrimination against black applicants in a number of states.[36] Rather than allowing case worker discretion, which could result in strong racial or ethnic discrimination, a series of lawsuits moved the United States to implement a system where anyone can sit down with a rule book and determine who is eligible and how much they should get. In addition, because they no longer had any decision-making authority, states were able to use less-skilled workers in AFDC offices, lowering their pay scales.

Unfortunately, with a system where everything is calculated on the computer by the rules, it becomes impractical for a case worker to ask a simple question such as "What can we do to help?" This limits the role of AFDC staff—a job where there is high turnover and burnout—and creates a program whose primary goal is seemingly to see that everyone fills out their forms correctly. Someone who walks into a Canadian welfare office needing help to get her car fixed and get back to work may be able to receive just that. In the United States, however, there is no option for a case worker to simply ask, "What's gone wrong? What can we do to help?"

A second reason for the bureaucratic nature of welfare offices is that the proliferation of multiple programs and program requirements creates a difficult management problem. While the existence of multiple programs allows targeted groups of individuals to qualify for assistance, it also makes running these programs an ongoing problem. Because we want to impose behavioral requirements on people, assistance offices must track an enormous amount of detail about people's lives. Women on AFDC who work are required to report monthly and show their paystub so the public assistance office can adjust their benefits accordingly. Not surprisingly, at least some case workers who don't have the time to deal with monthly visits and monthly forms do not encourage their clients to work. People who move must register their new residence and confirm that no household composition changes have occurred to change their benefit eligibility. People on Section 8 housing assistance, when they face a rent increase, must both contact the housing assistance office for an adjustment on their rental assistance, and in turn let AFDC know that their housing assistance level has changed.

All of these program details create serious operational problems for public assistance offices. Many states have consolidated offices, so that AFDC, Food Stamps, and other programs are all available in one location; some have tried to implement combined program eligibility screens; virtually all states have improved their computer tracking and information systems. But working with multiple programs and program requirements is a complex job; inevitably, there are mistakes.

The third reason for these bureaucratic systems is that most legislative discussions of welfare reform focus on program rules, with little attention given to their potential implementation problems. As one welfare reform follows another, the tendency is for regulations to become increasingly complex and detailed. For instance, legislative debates tend to ask "Would it be better if we could require regular school attendance by adolescents in families receiving AFDC?" rather than asking "Is it possible to run a program that checks up on school attendance for thousands of children, communicates with parents when children are not there, and uses this information in writing monthly checks?" One reason many states have been upset with federal mandates on how they run their public assistance programs is that such requirements rarely come with increased appropriations to handle the increased work.

New requirements to impose more behavioral restrictions on public assistance recipients may be useful. But such proposals need to grapple with the management problems they create. For instance, with the expansion of state welfare-to-work programs, more women are required to participate at least twenty hours per week in an acceptable job search or job placement program. This vastly increases the amount of case monitoring that must occur monthly. Similarly, it increases the amount of information that AFDC offices must process accurately and quickly if states condition AFDC benefits on children receiving vaccinations on schedule or attending school regularly. Not surprisingly, this only makes the system more confusing for many women, who often receive notice of potential problems and benefit disqualifications months after a problem occurs.

By many measures, our current AFDC system is virtually unmanageable, particularly in large urban areas with high caseloads. (Small communities with lower caseloads often have much more personal contact.) Or, perhaps more accurately, the system is manageable only as an extremely rigid system that may have as many injurious effects as helpful ones. The rule-bound nature of the system discourages work among recipients because it requires too much paperwork, creates multiple and often counterproductive regulations for both clients and administrators, and adds to the sense of frustration and helplessness experienced by women who are often struggling with other problems in their lives as well.

Though they are little discussed publicly, these management difficulties may be the worst aspect of the AFDC program. My own impression is that the management system of AFDC distorts women's choices and behaviors in a variety of ways. Reforms that ignore these issues are not likely to provide substantial improvements in the public assistance system in the United States.

4.5 HAVE IN-KIND PROGRAMS IMPROVED THE HEALTH AND NUTRITION OF AMERICA'S POOR?

SUMMARY. *Nutrition subsidies and public medical insurance are designed to address problems of hunger, malnutrition, and poor health among the poor. The expansion of Food Stamps has been directly related to the decline in serious malnutrition in this country. Research indicates that Food Stamps increase food purchases. Food Stamps and WIC have been particularly important in reducing low birth weights and improving the health of pregnant women and their children. There is less clear evidence on the effects of school lunch and breakfast programs. The expansion of Medicaid is linked with a substantial increase in access to medical services among the poor, who tend to have greater health problems. In turn, this greater access is linked to improvements in the health of the poor. The recent expansion of Medicaid to poor children who are not receiving AFDC has also decreased low birthweights and improved infant health.*

The first four sections of this chapter have focused on cash welfare assistance, primarily cash assistance to single-parent families. But, as we have learned, cash assistance or "welfare" is only a small share of public assistance in this country, although it continues to be the most controversial form of transfer program. Much more money goes into in-kind programs, particularly Food Stamps and Medicaid.

As was discussed in chapter 3, in-kind assistance receives more public support than cash assistance because it can only be used to fund the purchase of "necessities," which taxpayers are more willing to pay for. By limiting the discretion of the recipient, there is less suspicion that this money might be misspent. But there are criticisms of these programs as well. Some have worried that they may not actually increase the quality or quantity of consumption on the items they subsidize. *If* the purpose of Food Stamps is to increase consumption of food among the poor, then those receiving Food Stamps should buy and eat more food than those without Food Stamps. If each dollar of Food Stamp coupons simply replaces a dollar of cash expenditures on food, families may consume no more food than before. The question, more simply stated, is whether food subsidy programs decrease malnutrition and hunger, and whether medical care subsidies increase the utilization of medical services and improve the health of the poor.

Not all analysts accept this goal, however. Some argue that the purpose of the Food Stamp program is not to *increase* consumption on food, so much as to assure food consumption *and* to free up resources for spending on other necessary items. A family that replaces food dollars with Food Stamp coupons will have more dollars to spend elsewhere, which may improve their ability to find adequate housing or to maintain a car. Thus, there is a difference of opinion about whether we want people consuming *more* of a subsidized good, or whether that subsidy is simply a way to allow low-income families to stretch their resources further. In either case, we investigate the question of whether in-kind subsidies change the quantity or quality of people's consumption.

This first part of this section investigates the effects of food subsidy programs on the food consumption and nutrition of those who receive this assistance; the second part looks at similar questions with regard to medical care. There is strong evidence that these programs have improved the nutrition and the health of America's poor.

Do Subsidized Food Programs Decrease Hunger?

The primary food subsidy program in the United States is the *Food Stamp* program, as discussed in chapter 3. In the 1960s, when Food Stamps were initiated, malnutrition-related diseases could be found in many poor communities in the United States. CBS produced a documentary in the mid-1960s called "Hunger in America" that visited poor communities (many of them rural) and filmed pictures of children suffering from such malnutrition diseases as beriberi (vitamin B deficiency) or kwashiorkor (a protein deficiency). The film, showing children in the United States with the distended stomachs of malnutrition, shocked many Americans.

In 1968 the Field Foundation convened a team of doctors and U.S. senators to report on hunger problems in the United States; their report documented more systematically the presence of serious malnutrition in a number of very poor locations. Ten years later, in 1977, the Field Foundation sent a similar team back to many of the same locations. The report written by the medical team stated that "our first and overwhelming impression is that there are far fewer grossly malnourished people in this country today than there were ten years ago. . . . This change does not appear to be due to an overall improvement in living standards or to a decrease in joblessness in these areas. . . . The Food Stamp program, the nutritional components of Head Start, school lunch and breakfast programs, and to a lesser extent the Women-Infant-Children (WIC) feeding programs have made the difference."[37]

More recent evidence strongly supports the fact that the Food Stamp program has had a significant effect on hunger. A variety of studies have estimated the extent to which persons receiving Food Stamps buy more food than they would otherwise.[38] The evidence indicates that first, most families on Food Stamps spend more on food than they receive in Food Stamps. That is to say, they are not buying food just because they have coupons and need to spend them. Food Stamps operate as a supplement to their food budget. Second, most families buy more food in total as a result of receiving Food Stamps. In other words, Food Stamps do not merely displace other food spending with food coupons, but increase total food purchases.

The best evidence on this comes from some of the "cash-out" experiments. In these experiments, some families received Food Stamps while others received their Food Stamp assistance as cash, through expanded public assistance checks. The most recent review of the results from these studies concludes that families who received cash reduced their food expenditures by between 20 to 25 cents per dollar of Food Stamp benefits that were cashed out.[39] Thus, Food Stamp purchases do not simply displace dollar purchases one-for-one. Replacing Food Stamps with cash assistance would reduce food consumption among low-income families.

What does this tell us about nutrition? This is a harder question to answer. While some research has found a clear correlation between food expenditures and nutrient intake for Food Stamp users, other research shows more mixed results.[40] Studies that directly compare nutrient intake between Food Stamp recipients and nonrecipients (controlling for other differences between these households) find significantly greater nutrient *availability* in Food Stamp households, but it is less clear that this translates into better nutrient consumption among family members.

The evidence on the Food Stamp program indicates that it has had significant effects in reducing hunger and increasing food consumption among low-income families. This does not mean there is no hunger left in America. A 1991 survey of low-income households by the Food Research Action Center indicates that 92 percent say they have run out of money to buy food in the past year, while 33 percent indicate their children went to bed hungry at least once over the past year because of a lack of money to buy food.[41] While this suggests that hunger is still present, evidence of severe malnutrition-related health problems has almost disappeared in this country. The primary reason is Food Stamps.

A more targeted program, the *Supplemental Food Program for Women, Infants, and Children (WIC)*, serves pregnant women and preschoolers. The program either provides actual food items or vouchers for foods containing protein, iron, calcium, and vitamins A and C. Eligibility rules for the program vary across states.

The fact that WIC is not uniformly available to the same population in each state has made it possible to compare similar women with and without access to WIC. This provides information on the effects of WIC on health and nutrition. A major study commissioned by the Department of Agriculture in the late 1980s found that for every dollar spent on prenatal care for mothers in the WIC program, Medicaid savings for mothers and newborns ranged from $1.77 to $3.13.[42] This implies that WIC's targeted services for pregnant women are extremely cost effective. The primary reason for savings was that children born to WIC mothers had higher birth weights, an outcome strongly correlated with better nutrition on the part of the pregnant mother. A large number of other studies of the WIC program have come to similar conclusions, suggesting that both mothers' and infants' health are significantly improved by WIC's nutritional assistance.[43]

The final set of food subsidy programs are the *school lunch* and *school breakfast* programs. These are typically run by school districts for all children who want to participate, but only children in families with low incomes receive subsidized meals. Evidence on the effects of these two programs is more mixed. Most surprisingly, while research suggests that children who eat breakfast are able to perform better in school, recent studies of the School Breakfast Program indicate that children in schools that offer this program are no more likely to eat breakfast than similar children in schools that don't offer it.[44] While there is evidence indicating that those who participate in the School Breakfast Program get more nutrients than those who don't, this is harder to link to school performance.[45]

Evaluations of the school lunch program show that subsidized low-income children are more likely to participate in it, and those who participate consume more food energy over the day. It turns out, however, that those who take school lunches tend to be bigger eaters in general than those who don't, so that much of the difference in food consumption is due to the selection of who takes the program, and not to the program itself.[46] There is also ongoing concern about the nutritional value of many of these meals because of their high fat content. In short, the research evidence on the impact of school lunch and breakfast programs on children's nutritional status is more limited and less compelling than for Food Stamps and for WIC. On the other hand, because these programs provide subsidized meals for children, they lessen the amount of money families have to spend on food and increase their consumption of other items.[47]

Have food subsidy programs reduced hunger in the United States? All of the evidence indicates that these programs have increased food consumption, reduced hunger and serious malnutrition, and improved the nutrient intake of low-income families. The impact of these programs on the health of pregnant women and their children might be particularly important, as in utero and infant nutrition is very important for long-term cognitive development. If a reduction in hunger and malnutrition is the primary goal of these programs, they have met it.

Do Subsidized Health Insurance Programs Improve Medical Care?

In 1965 the United States established the Medicaid program, designed to provide free health care to very poor families. As we discussed in chapter 3, because of recent large increases in health care costs, Medicaid is currently the most expensive public assistance program for low-income families. This is despite the fact that a significant number of poor families have no access to Medicaid. Historically, it has been available only for AFDC and SSI recipients. In recent years, however, Medicaid eligibility for children and pregnant women living in poor families has vastly expanded. Has the large expenditure of money on Medicaid improved the health and the medical care available to the poor?

Most Americans receive health insurance through their employer. Given that low-income persons are more likely to be unemployed, or to work on lower-wage jobs, they are much less likely to have private health insurance coverage. Overall, 29 percent of poor persons had neither public nor private health insurance in 1993, almost twice the rate in the general population, where 15 percent are uninsured.[48] Since most eligible poor elderly persons and children have access to Medicaid, this suggests that prior to the implementation and expansion of Medicaid many of these persons would have been uninsured, leading to even greater differences in the rate of insurance coverage between the poor and the nonpoor. Insurance coverage among poor working-age adults remains extremely low, since few of this group have access to public or private insurance. (The exceptions, of course, are the disabled and the group of poor single mothers who receive AFDC.)

It might seem that the expansion of health insurance should obviously improve access to health care, but critics note that many of the uninsured already receive health care. Most hospitals expect and budget for a certain amount of "uncompensated care," cases that they treat but from whom they cannot collect payment. Virtually all evidence, however, suggests that lack of insurance substantially reduces the use of medical services. Poor families who must seek out free health care services receive less care than those with insurance. This is a particular problem among the poor, who tend to have greater health problems than higher-income families. Those among the poor who report themselves in only fair or poor health see a doctor far less frequently than insured persons who report similar health conditions.[49]

There has been a significant expansion in the last thirty years in the extent to which low-income households receive medical care. At the same time, the health of poor individuals has steadily improved in this country, as measured by a wide variety of variables. Infant mortality rates among poor mothers have declined, life expectancies have grown, and the incidence of a variety of infectious diseases has gone down, although it remains true that poor persons are still at higher risk of medical problems than persons living in higher-income families. A variety of studies have linked these changes directly to the creation and expansion of the Medicaid program.[50] Medicaid clearly increases access to and use of medical services, and the use of medical services is highly correlated with a number of health outcomes. Controlling for other character-istics of the household, evidence indicates that families insured by Medicaid are more likely than similar uninsured families to utilize a range of medical services, although they are less likely to use some of these services than the privately insured.

Further evidence of the value of public insurance for low-income families comes from our nearest neighbor to the north, Canada. Canada implemented a national health insurance plan covering all families in the late 1960s, about the same time the United States implemented Medicaid for selected groups of low-income families. Canada's public insurance was implemented in differ-ent years in different Canadian provinces, however. Maria Hanratty of Prince-ton University has looked at the timing of changes in infant mortality and low birth weights and related this to the timing of publicly available insurance. Her work suggests that widespread availability of health insurance decreased the infant mortality rate by 4 percent and decreased the probability of low birth weight by 3 percent.[51] Since both infant mortality and low birth weight disproportionately occur among poor mothers, Hanratty speculates that the expansion of health insurance particularly benefited the health of the poor.

The recent expansion of Medicaid to all poor and near-poor pregnant women and children provides another measure of the importance of the Medi-caid program on the health of its recipients. Several studies have investigated changes in the health status of newly eligible Medicaid recipients over the late 1980s, as these expansions in the Medicaid program have been phased in. One study estimates that between 1979 and 1990, the fraction of women eligible for Medicaid if they became pregnant expanded from 14 to 34 percent.[52] These changes were associated with a substantial reduction in both infant mortality and low birth weight. There appears to be less of an effect on chil-dren's health, but this is because many of the children who are newly eligible for Medicaid are not enrolled in the program. In other words, for many low-income children there is a problem of information about and availability of services, exclusive of insurance availability.[53]

Does publicly provided health insurance improve health among the poor? The evidence shows that the implementation and expansion of the Medicaid program has increased poor families' access to health care services. While it is easier to link Medicaid with the greater use of medical services than with direct health improvements, some of the significant improvement in the health status among America's poor is surely due to the Medicaid program. (Some would have occurred anyway, as health standards and housing standards have continued to improve nationwide.) Although poor persons are more likely to experience serious health problems, prior to the implementation of Medicaid poor families were far less likely to see a doctor or use other medical services. Since the implementation of Medicaid, its recipients have begun to receive more medical care. While there remain real gaps in the quality and extent of care received by poor and non-poor families, the presence of Medicaid has been important in reducing these differences.

4.6 WASTE, FRAUD, AND ABUSE: ARE THESE COSTS TOO HIGH?

SUMMARY. *Public assistance programs generate constant criticism for "waste, fraud and abuse." Administrative costs for AFDC, Food Stamps, SSI, and Medicaid range from around $100 to $300 per recipient per year. Programs that have extensive turnover cost more per applicant, since certifying initial eligibility is more expensive than ongoing case administration. These costs are similar to those in nonprofit charitable organizations that also provide services to low-income families. Administrative error rates in calculating eligibility and payment levels for public assistance programs have decreased substantially since strict federal guidelines were imposed. The amount of explicit fraud in these programs is not known with much precision. In in-kind programs, much of the fraud results in profits to vendors who provide services to families rather than to poor families themselves.*

Fraud and incompetence in the operation of public assistance programs have always received substantial public attention. Images of fraud are particularly prevalent: "Welfare queens," women who collect multiple public assistance checks and live in luxury; "Food Stamp traffickers," store owners who buy Food Stamps at below face value from poor recipients and redeem them from the government at full value; and "Medicaid mills," clinics that provide low-quality health services but submit large bills to the government for payment.

This section looks at the question of both explicit fraud and administrative incompetence in public assistance programs. In part because so much attention has been focused on this issue, extensive monitoring keeps these problems to relatively low levels. Quality control procedures and the advent of computer-based application and processing systems implemented over the past fifteen years have substantially decreased administrative errors. Although criminal fraud continues to occur and occasional big scandals provide juicy news reports, the extent of fraud is not well known. The first part of this section investigates overall administrative cost levels in public assistance programs, the second part discusses administrative errors, and the final part explicitly addresses questions of fraud.

Administrative Costs on Public Assistance Programs

Any program that distributes benefits must invest in the staff and the equipment necessary to operate effectively. Table 4.3 provides information on the magnitude of administrative expenses in the AFDC, Food Stamp, SSI, and Medicaid programs.[54] As the first row of table 4.3 indicates, about 12 percent of the total AFDC and Food Stamp budget goes to administrative expenses. About 7 percent of the SSI budget goes into administration, compared

TABLE 4.3
Administrative Costs in Public Assistance Programs

Administrative Costs	AFDC	Food Stamps	SSI	MEDICAID
As a share of total costs	11.7%	12.2%	6.7%	4.0%
Per recipient family (annual)	$593	$412	$389	$379
Per recipient (annual)	$209	$107	$276	$129

Source: U.S. House of Representatives (1992, 1993b, 1994).

Note: AFDC data are for 1993, Food Stamp and SSI data are for 1992, and Medicaid data are for 1991.

to 4 percent of the Medicaid budget. These are relatively large differences; do they imply that some programs are much more efficient than others?

Calculating administrative expenses as a share of total budget is a somewhat misleading measure. Programs with exactly the same operating procedure but with higher benefit levels will necessarily show lower administrative costs, even though they may spend as much per household in the program. Row 2 of table 4.3 shows a rough estimate of annual administrative costs per family in each program. For programs that typically certify entire family units, such as AFDC or Food Stamps, a "case" is best represented by a family. For SSI or Medicaid, however, a "case" is less clearly defined. Sometimes it is individuals who are eligible, sometimes it is families. Thus, I also show annual administrative costs per recipient in the third row of table 4.3. The actual administrative cost per "case" probably lies somewhere in between these two estimates. Administrative costs per recipient, the third row in table 4.3, is quite similar across programs, falling between $107 and $276. AFDC and Food Stamps have the lowest cost per recipient but the highest cost per family. This is because they tend to go to larger families than do SSI and Medicaid, which have a large share of single elderly and disabled recipients.

AFDC appears to have relatively high costs per family. Government studies suggest that the largest administrative expenses occur when a recipient applies and is certified as eligible for a program.[55] Ongoing verification of program eligibility is less expensive. Thus, programs that have frequent turnover and people moving on and off the rolls will cost more than programs where people remain eligible for long periods of time. AFDC families are more expensive to service because they stay on the program for a shorter period of time than SSI recipients. A higher share of their costs goes into certifying initial eligibility. Food Stamps' administrative costs per family are also relatively high for the same reason. In contrast, a high share of SSI and Medicaid recipients are elderly or disabled and, once certified for the program, remain on it for the long term. This lowers their administrative costs.

Another reason for cost differences between these programs is that eligibility across programs is often linked. Persons on AFDC or SSI are automatically eligible for Medicaid. Thus, a large number of Medicaid cases are certified for

TABLE 4.4
Administrative Costs among
Large National Charities

Organization	Administrative Cost Share (%)
American Red Cross	4.6
Big Brothers/Big Sisters	17.4
Catholic Charities	11.9
Goodwill Industries	10.8
Habitat for Humanity	10.9
Salvation Army	9.3

Source: Sarver (1994).
Note: Fund-raising costs are excluded from total costs in calculating the administrative cost share.

eligibility through the AFDC system. This makes the cost of AFDC administration higher than the cost of Medicaid administration and is one reason why administrative costs in the Medicaid program are so low. In a similar way, the eligibility certification in many Food Stamp cases is done as an add-on to AFDC certification rather than as an entirely new application.

On the face of it, the administrative costs in these government programs do not seem excessive, given the extensive paperwork requirements that must be completed for every application. But there are large variations in administrative costs across states. For instance, in 1993 Illinois paid only $333 in annual administrative costs per AFDC family, while New Jersey paid $1,160. It would be useful to better understand the mechanisms that result in effective service at a lower price in public assistance programs.

The question of whether administrative costs are low or high must always be asked "relative to what comparison?" Unfortunately, appropriate comparisons are very hard to find. For instance, private insurance companies have much higher overhead costs than Medicaid, but they must also pay for widespread marketing and promotional campaigns which government programs need not do. One comparison for these programs may be large national private charities that also provide services to low-income families. Table 4.4 shows the administrative cost share of a diverse group of such organizations for 1993.[56] The administrative share of costs in table 4.3 of government programs do not appear to be very far out of line with the administrative cost share of the national private charities listed in table 4.4.

Errors and Miscalculations

In the late 1970s, the Carter administration substantially expanded the quality control system in public assistance programs to monitor how accurately staff workers determine who is eligible and what their benefit levels will be. At

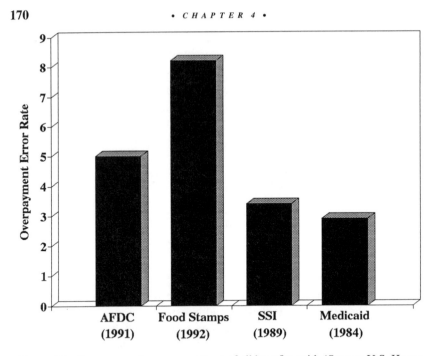

Figure 4.6. Overpayments as a percentage of all benefits paid. (*Source*: U.S. House of Representatives 1993a, 1994)

present, the federal government monitors each state's performance with regard to eligibility and payment errors occurring in the AFDC, Food Stamp, SSI, and Medicaid programs.[57] In particular, they track three types of errors: intentional fraud on the part of applicants, unintentional client errors in the information they provide, and administrative errors in the determination of eligibility and benefits by public assistance staff. For instance, in the Food Stamp program, a little less than half of payment errors appear to be due to misinformation provided by clients, while the rest is due to administrative errors by public assistance offices.[58]

Figure 4.6 provides information on overpayment error rates in four programs: AFDC, Food Stamps, SSI, and Medicaid.[59] This shows overpayments as a percentage of all dollar benefits paid. Overpayments are by far the most common form of error and are most typically cited as a measure of program error. They include both the payment of benefits to persons who should have been ineligible, as well as the payment of greater benefits than should have been allowed. (In the Medicaid program, these are payments to medical-care providers for services delivered rather than to low-income families.)

While the reason for these differences in overpayment rates is only poorly understood, there is evidence that payment accuracy is heavily affected by how much a state monitors accuracy and emphasizes it among caseworkers. Since the Food Stamp program is almost entirely funded by the federal government rather than state governments, states might have less reason to push caseworkers to be careful about costs in this program relative to the AFDC program, which may explain higher overpayment rates in Food Stamps. In addition, Food Stamps is the one program that includes a substantial number of earners among its recipients. The calculation of eligibility and benefit levels is more complex among those who earn income and receive public assistance, and this may also cause higher error rates in the Food Stamp program.[60]

States have come under increasingly strict federal standards regarding their payment error rates. States face strong financial incentives to reduce error rates and keep them low, and may have their federal program dollars reduced if their error rates are above a certain threshold level. As a result of this federal pressure, errors in benefit payments have plummeted in most programs. For example, in the early 1970s, New York State had an overpayment error rate of around 25 percent in AFDC. By the late 1970s, it was down to 10 percent, and it had fallen further by the late 1980s.[61] These changes partly reflect the increased effort at quality control, as well as the widespread implementation of electronic processing for applications. In most states, caseworkers now simply enter information into the computer, which then computes a client's eligibility and benefit levels. As a result of these changes, concern about error rates in public assistance programs has almost entirely disappeared from public discussion.

While these extensive efforts to monitor the processing of applications and benefits have surely lowered administrative and client errors, they have had some significant negative effects as well.[62] The quality control process is one of the major contributors to the paperwork overload facing many staff people. The rule-based, rigid nature of AFDC and other public assistance programs has only been magnified by extensive attention to administrative-processing issues. While accurate processing of applications is clearly important, there are has been a trade-off between greater program oversight and greater program bureaucracy. The current error monitoring system is one reason why welfare offices have become more concerned with filling out forms correctly (as discussed earlier) and less concerned with helping clients.

Fraud and Misuse

The extent of actual fraud in these programs is difficult to determine with any accuracy. Those who intentionally misreport their income, or those who manipulate program rules to their own advantage, are unlikely to admit this to researchers. Quality control data identify certain types of client misinformation but do not provide a good measure of the overall extent of fraudulent claims. Thus, the discussion of fraud in public assistance programs is dominated by anecdotal accounts of the worst scandals. Whether these represent a large amount of the resources of these programs is almost entirely unknown. For instance, estimates of the dollars going into fraud from the Food Stamp program are rarely based on any hard evidence. While many people use

$1 billion as an approximation, this is more of a guess than an estimate.[63] If this number has any validity, it suggests that about 4 percent of Food Stamp dollars involve fraud.

Food Stamps' levels of fraud are probably larger than those of AFDC because they include not only fraudulent claims by clients who are actually not eligible for the program, but also fraudulent behavior by unscrupulous grocers who make illegal profits from Food Stamps through Food Stamp trafficking. Trafficking involves buying Food Stamps at less than their face value and then redeeming them from the government for their full value. People with substance abuse problems appear to be most likely to sell their Food Stamps at the beginning of the month in order to support their habits. Persons who have looked at this issue suggest that recipients who sell their stamps often do so for about 50 cents for every dollar in Food Stamps. This can make a tidy profit for a local grocer willing to make these deals. Estimates of the extent of this problem vary. The Office of the Inspector General in the Department of Agriculture suggests that about one percent of all Food Stamp vendors may be engaged in Food Stamp trafficking.[64]

The movement toward Electronic Benefit Transfer (EBT) is expected to reduce some of these fraud problems. With EBT, recipients receive electronic cards, similar to bank cards, which provide them with access to money in the amount of their monthly benefits. Where this system has been implemented, it appears to be cheaper to administer, as public assistance offices can authorize new payments on these cards monthly, without the cost (and risk) of issuing and mailing monthly checks. It also reduces (although it does not stop) Food Stamp trafficking problems.

One last comment on fraud is important to note: in in-kind programs where providers directly bill the government for services, such as Medicaid and many housing programs, the vast majority of fraud is *not* committed by recipients but by vendors. Those who make big bucks off these programs are not the poor but those who provide the services. For instance, in housing programs it is developers and contractors who have been most effective at defrauding the government, not public housing residents. This does suggest that the biggest money to be saved in these programs by reducing fraud is likely to occur through closer monitoring of vendors rather than program recipients.

Those who propose to save substantial amounts of money in public assistance programs by cutting "waste, fraud, and abuse" typically have little contact with how these programs are actually implemented and run. While there is always room for greater administrative efficiency and greater enforcement of the rules in any program, there is also a cost to this monitoring and enforcement. The extensive funding going into administrative oversight in AFDC or Food Stamps has already brought administrative error rates down far below where they used to be. The lack of knowledge about the actual magnitude of explicit fraud in these programs makes it difficult to predict the effect of greater efforts at reducing fraud. Until we have better evidence about the scope of the "abuse" problem, the primary lesson to be drawn from the presence of visible fraud in these programs is that it provides an easy political tool for their critics.

4.7 DO JOB PROGRAMS ENCOURAGE WORK?

SUMMARY. *Work programs include job search assistance, education and training programs, and public sector employment programs. The effectiveness of these different approaches varies across populations and programs. Welfare-to-work programs, designed to help women on AFDC move into the labor market, have significant and positive effects on employment and earnings and decrease AFDC use among participants. But the magnitude of these effects is not large, with $150 to $1,000 annual increases in participants' earnings, depending on the program. By themselves, these programs do not increase earnings enough to help women escape poverty. Among adult men, JTPA programs and welfare-to-work programs have more limited and weaker effects, a discouraging finding. When used in combination with cash assistance, job programs provide a complementary set of services that encourage work while still recognizing the reality of limited wages in low-income labor markets.*

Americans have long insisted that the best way out of poverty is through employment. The 1964 *Economic Report of the President*, describing the aims of the War on Poverty, stated:

> The majority of the Nation could simply tax themselves enough to provide the necessary income supplements to their less fortunate citizens. . . . But this "solution" would leave untouched most of the roots of poverty. Americans want to *earn* the American standard of living by their own efforts and contributions. It will be far better, even if more difficult, to equip and permit the poor of the Nation to produce and earn the additional [money needed to raise them out of poverty].[65]

As the economic opportunities for less-skilled workers have deteriorated, programs that encourage teens to stay in school, provide additional skills to low-wage adults, or help AFDC women locate jobs have become even more important. The next section will discuss programs aimed at teenagers, while this section discusses the effectiveness of job programs for adult men and women who receive public assistance.

There are three general types of employment-related services that can be subsumed under the rubric of "job programs." First, a program can provide job search and job placement assistance. This is the cheapest—and the only—form of assistance provided by many job programs. Second, a job program can provide training or education. This can include everything from remedial literacy training, to high school equivalency degree classes, to community college certificate programs, to job apprenticeships. Third, a job program may involve soliciting and placing people in "created" jobs. Most commonly, this refers to public sector job creation, although it could also occur through subsidies to private employers. The increasing demand that public assistance recipients go to work has led to growing interest in placing those who cannot find private sector work in short-term subsidized employment.

Because of the variety of meanings that "job program" can embody, it is hard to answer the question, "How effective are these programs?" The answer depends upon which program and which set of clients. There are also serious difficulties with evaluating job programs. Many of them are voluntary, which means that people who enter a program are not a random sample of all those potentially eligible for it. A researcher cannot just compare the employment experiences of program participants and non-participants, since the more work-ready and the more motivated people are more likely to sign up for job programs. This group would often get a job faster or find a better job even in the absence of a program. Many past evaluations were weakened by these problems; more recent (and more credible) evaluations have used randomized control groups that take this selection problem into account.

In this section I will analyze the set of job training programs currently operating in the United States, looking first at AFDC welfare-to-work programs and then at job programs for other adults. The primary question is, "Do these programs increase employment and earnings?" As we shall see, the answer is a definite "yes" for welfare-to-work programs, and a somewhat more muted "sometimes" in job programs for adult men.[66]

Welfare-to-Work Programs for Women on AFDC

As we discussed in the last chapter, over the 1980s a number of states started to experiment with broad welfare-to-work programs. These experiments were successful enough that in 1988 Congress passed the Family Support Act, which required all states to run welfare-to-work programs, called Job Opportunities and Basic Skills (JOBS) programs. While the JOBS requirements are no longer in place since the passage of new legislation in the mid-1990s, these programs provide a good base for evaluation; future state work programs are likely to be quite similar to the programs they started under JOBS. Different states have given these programs different names, ranging from GAIN (Greater Avenues for Independence) in California to Project Independence in Florida.

JOBS programs typically relied heavily on job-search assistance programs for AFDC recipients, with training and education available only to a more limited group of women. States were mandated to provide additional education for teen mothers and those without high school degrees. States were also required to provide child care subsidies and Medicaid eligibility to women for a year after leaving AFDC if they were successful at finding employment. These programs have mandatory participation requirements, meaning that women who are assigned to them must participate, or face the risk of losing public assistance benefits.[67]

Most JOBS programs put participants through a three-step process. First, AFDC applicants are screened to determine if they are "work-eligible." Clients with disabilities or with very young children are typically excluded from the programs altogether, and those eligible for remedial education or training are assigned to them. Second, recipients are required to participate in some sort of work-preparedness program. For those in remedial education or training (for instance, teen mothers), this involves putting in a certain number of hours each week to complete a high school equivalency degree or acquire other skills. For most women, however, work preparedness involves spending from one to three weeks in group training sessions on how to do job search or perform effectively on a job. Sometimes this involves individual job counseling, and sometimes it involves what are called "life skills" classes, which provide discussion and training around issues such as how to budget, how to deal with employers and co-workers, or how to dress and act on a job. Third, after completing the training program, participants are given assistance in locating a job. Clients who do not make an acceptable effort to participate in these activities can be "sanctioned," which means they can have their AFDC benefits reduced or eliminated.

Evaluations of the welfare-to-work programs implemented by states prior to the passage of the Family Support Act are available, and evaluations of states' JOBS programs are just becoming available. The results from these evaluations are complex and vary somewhat from state to state. But at least three points emerge consistently across these studies.[68]

First, even rather minimal efforts at job search assistance seem to produce employment and earnings gains among women on AFDC. These effects persist at least over a three-year period following the program. The group that benefits the most from these programs appears to be women who are neither the most nor the least disadvantaged. Among the least disadvantaged AFDC recipients (for instance, those who have worked recently or who have some post–high school training), many find jobs and leave welfare on their own, so these programs provide little additional help. Among the most disadvantaged AFDC recipients, these programs appear to be too brief and limited to address the multiple problems many of these women face. But the middle group—those with some work experience, with acceptable literacy skills, but who have often been out of the labor market for a while—benefit from the extra support which these programs provide to help them get jobs.

Second, benefit-cost evaluations typically indicate that the returns from these programs are greater than the costs to the government budget. The costs of running the program are more than recovered through decreases in AFDC benefit payments as women work more. In this sense, these programs pay for themselves over the long run, although they may involve more money at the beginning to set up the program.

Third, while the results indicate a clear positive effect on work behavior from these programs, few women escape poverty after participating in them. Women work more and their earnings increase, but their AFDC income decreases, and overall income gains are quite low for most women. While the increase in earnings due to the program is statistically significant in most evaluations, it is on the order of $150 to $600 per year. For instance, the Arkansas welfare-to-work program evaluated in the 1980s resulted in an employment rate among participants that was 6.2 percentage points higher than the 18.3 percent employment rate among nonparticipants; participants' earnings were 31 percent ($337) higher.[69] The highest recorded gains in an evaluation (from the California GAIN program in Riverside County) show an increase of around $1,000 per year in earnings. Almost all gains occur through increases in employment and work hours, rather than in wage rates.[70]

The conclusion from these welfare-to-work programs is clear: they are effective at increasing work effort among women and they more than pay for themselves, but by themselves they are not likely to assist many women out of poverty. Again, we come back to the labor market situation facing these women: their wage rates are low, jobs may not be stable, and their prospects for advancement are limited.

Job Training Programs for Men

The evidence indicates that job training and job placement programs targeted at female AFDC recipients almost always show positive results. Unfortunately, the evidence on job training programs for men is more mixed. Job programs aimed at less-skilled men show smaller effects, and some studies show no significant effects at all. The JTPA program, discussed in chapter 3, is the only job training program generally available to disadvantaged workers, although its funding limits it to a very small number of participants. JTPA underwent a major national evaluation in the late 1980s. The results indicated that adult men who participated in the program experienced less significant and smaller employment and earnings gains than adult women.[71]

This is consistent with a number of other evaluations that investigate the impact of job programs on less-skilled men. Welfare-to-work programs often focus on the men in married-couple families receiving AFDC, who are a very small share of the caseload, but are often more likely to be considered work-eligible than single mothers. While the evaluations for some state programs show employment gains for the men that are of about the same magnitude as for women, other state programs show fewer effects for male participants.[72] Similarly, an intensive experimental program called Supported Work, run in the late 1970s for seriously disadvantaged workers, found few positive labor market benefits for its male participants.[73]

One of the real puzzles among researchers is why job programs aimed at adult men appear less effective than those aimed at women. There are at least two possible reasons. First, men and women come into these programs with very different past labor market backgrounds. Women who enter public job training programs typically have limited labor market experience. With few connections to the labor market, job search assistance and confidence-building exercises about job seeking are useful. In contrast, men who enter these programs have typically been in and out of the labor market, often with negative results. Much more than the women, they are scarred by bad employment experiences, including being fired, arguing with past co-workers and employers, or moving in and out of the underground economy. Programs, lasting a few weeks or months and oriented toward simple skill acquisition or job-search assistance, rarely address the underlying problems that have dogged these men in the past on jobs.

Second, the changing labor market for less-skilled work may increasingly value skills that women are more likely to have than men. Low-skilled service sector jobs value what are often called the "soft skills" much more than low-skilled manufacturing jobs. Fewer jobs are available where physical strength is the most important attribute, and more jobs in the service sector value politeness, customer interaction, and (given that one often works cooperatively with a crew of other workers) acquiescence and team work. Low-income men who have learned to be "streetwise" have often learned a very different set of skills, and are much less prepared for such jobs than their girlfriends or wives. There is also evidence that younger men of color face more discrimination in the labor market than do women of color.[74]

If all of this sounds discouraging for those who want to solve the labor market problems of less-skilled workers by offering them job programs, it is. Despite widespread proposals to increase job training for low-income and less-skilled workers, this is not a simple answer to poverty. For less-skilled men, we have less knowledge about how to run successful job training programs than we should. For less-skilled women, we are able to help them find jobs more readily, but because of the limits on how good a job they can get and their own time constraints (particularly as single parents), the new work typically provides only limited increases in their income.

What is clear is that job search and job training programs are an integral piece of any antipoverty strategy, although they are not a complete solution to poverty.[75] These programs have been successful for public assistance recipients, a group whose work behavior has been the focus of much concern. We should continue to strengthen the links between work programs and welfare receipt for recipients and implement effective welfare-to-work programs. Combining cash assistance and job programs is a good way to address the inherent limits of each type of program alone: cash assistance provides support for those whose earnings are inadequate or who find themselves in unstable jobs that end unpredictably. Job programs keep pushing those receiving cash assistance to get back into the labor market and try again. Together, these two approaches complement and reinforce each other.

4.8 YOUTH EDUCATION AND TRAINING: CAN WE PREVENT PROBLEMS?

SUMMARY. *Public intervention programs for low-income children tend to focus on the preschool years and the teen years. Health and nutrition programs are particularly useful for preschool children. Compensatory preschool education programs, such as Head Start, also generate long-term effects. Participants in these programs are less likely to be held back a grade in elementary school, and less likely to be placed in special education classes. While programs focused on disadvantaged youth who are still in school have had some success, there is a discouraging lack of success in employment and education programs aimed at dropouts. Teen pregnancy prevention programs have had only limited success as well. This suggests that focusing resources on in-school students in the early and middle adolescent years may be the most effective use of funds.*

Today's children are tomorrow's adults. In the long run, the only way to decrease problems of inadequate skills and poor labor market preparation among adults is to make sure that children and youth stay in school and keep learning. Preventive policies targeted at low-income families tend to focus on two age groups: preschool children and teenagers. Preschool children are a target group because of growing evidence that indicates the early childhood years are key years for healthy cognitive and physical development. Young children who experience malnutrition, inadequate health care, or family abuse often show the scars for the rest of their lives. Teenagers are a target group because they are very visible as soon-to-be-adults. As teens move into adolescence they are increasingly at risk of crime, teen pregnancy, or dropping out of high school.

Programs aimed at youth and children are often spoken of as investments rather than as simple antipoverty programs. Indeed, if one can "inoculate" children and youth against certain problems, then the expenditures on these programs may have very large returns over the life of the child. More than for adults, one wants to know if there are any *long-term* effects of government programs on children and youth as they age and enter adulthood, as well as any immediate effects. This is a challenge, since few surveys follow children into adulthood. Increasingly, however, we do have information that links teenage program participation with adult work and family behavior, and which links preschool program participation with later school performance.[76]

Programs Aimed at Preschoolers

We have already discussed the effects of in-kind programs aimed at low-income families that particularly affect young children. One might believe that the initial implementation of Medicaid and Food Stamps thirty years ago had a disproportionate effect on young children since adequate health care and nutrition in these early years is crucial for healthy long-term cognitive and physical development. More recently, expansions in the WIC program and the expansion of Medicaid to young children in poor families has further improved nutrition and health among young children. The effect of these programs on infants' health seems to be particularly significant, through increased birth weights among children born to poor mothers. Since low birth weight is correlated with ongoing developmental problems in children, these health and nutrition improvements among infants will have long-term positive effects on the lives of children. These nutrition and health-related programs have already been discussed above, so this section will focus on educational investments in preschoolers.

DOES COMPENSATORY PRESCHOOL EDUCATION IMPROVE CHILDREN'S SKILLS?

As discussed in chapter 3, Head Start was designed in the mid-1960s to provide an enriched learning environment for young children from poor families, better preparing them for elementary school. Head Start makes special efforts to involve parents as well, so that classroom learning is extended into the home environment. Many compensatory preschool programs other than Head Start have also been developed and implemented by states and communities over the past thirty years.

Advocates of compensatory preschool education talk about the importance of the early childhood years in children's development. Critics suggest that one or two years of enriched preschool programs cannot possibly overcome multiple disadvantages. Early evaluations of a variety of compensatory preschool programs suggested that there was no long-term gain on standardized IQ exams for children who attended enriched preschools.[77] When these results emerged, many interpreted them to mean that these programs had no long-term effects.

More recent evidence suggests that there are long-term gains from compensatory preschool programs, including Head Start, which is the focus of much but not all of the evaluation research. There is evidence that children who participate in Head Start are less likely to be held back a grade during their elementary school years and also less likely to end up in special education classes.[78] In other words, the lack of long-term improvement in IQ scores (which are heavily affected by family and environmental factors which Head Start cannot change) does not mean there are no education-related gains. While studies differ with regard to the magnitude and significance of the measured effects, taken together this research generally shows evidence of gains from Head Start and other compensatory preschool programs that appear to last as long as these studies were able to follow the children (typically through grade school).

The best-known evaluation of preschool compensatory education is based on a group of children who participated in an early 1960s program called the

Perry Preschool Program in Ypsilanti, Michigan. Ongoing evaluations of the effect of this program on participants have shown large benefits as these children were followed into adulthood.[79] The results in the grade school years are generally consistent with those found in other research, although the measured effects are larger. These children have been followed longer, however, and results also show higher high school graduation rates and higher employment and earnings among program participants as adults.

These claims have been viewed skeptically by some critics, since the Ypsilanti program is different from many Head Start settings. From the beginning it was an extremely enriched program, and many of the teachers had graduate-level training in child development. The sample sizes are also quite small. The fact that research on other programs indicates results (at least through grade school) similar to the Perry Preschool Program is reassuring.

One recent study goes beyond the evaluation of a particular group of children in a particular program and uses a national data set to compare youngsters who participated in Head Start to their siblings who did not. This research, by economists Janet Currie and Duncan Thomas, finds persistent test score gains and higher school attainment among white and Hispanic Head Start participants.[80] Participants also had better access to preventive health services than did their nonparticipating brothers and sisters.

In sum, the evidence available on compensatory preschool programs, together with the evidence on the impact of nutrition and health insurance programs for preschoolers, suggests that these programs have improved both the health and the cognitive development of America's poor children.

Programs Aimed at Adolescents

The seeds of tomorrow's poverty are clearly visible in the behavior of today's teens. Young adults who drop out of school, bear children as teenagers, or become involved in gang or criminal activity are likely to work less, earn less, and cost society more through government spending on everything from public assistance to prisons. A wide variety of programs have focused on teens, aiming to prevent problem behaviors or to overcome their negative effects.

Publicly funded youth-focused programs tend to be of three sorts, although there is substantial overlap between the target group of participants in each of these programs. First, some programs focus on at-risk youth who are still in school, hoping to improve graduation rates, long-term employment, and earnings opportunities among their participants. For young women, there is often a desire to prevent pregnancies as well and (among mothers) to improve their parenting skills. Second, some programs focus on dropouts, hoping to help them complete high school equivalency degrees (GEDs), and increase employment and earnings opportunities. Third, some programs focus solely on reducing teen pregnancy and changing sexual behavior.

Most programs have been evaluated by following their participants for (at most) a year or two afterward, to see whether there were any behavioral changes. This seriously limits our knowledge about the effectiveness of youth-focused programs. One might believe that the returns to high school graduation or GED degrees, or to changes in work interests and work discipline, will largely accrue to young workers when they enter their twenties and settle into stable jobs as adults. Thus, some of the apparently disappointing results mentioned below may be the result of follow-up studies that don't last long enough. On the other hand, if a program has no immediate effects on behavior or outcomes, it may be unrealistic to expect that outcomes will emerge years after the program ends.

An enormous range of programs has been implemented in different locations over the last thirty years, designed to improve the life chances of young adults. Rather than providing a comprehensive listing of programs and their evaluation results, this section provides a general sense of what evaluation research has found about what is and is not effective in youth-oriented programs.[81] I pay particular attention to those programs that have received rigorous evaluation of their effects.

First, programs focused on in-school youth have generally larger and more positive effects than programs focused on dropouts. A number of programs implemented inside high schools have been able to increase graduation rates and raise the probability that youth will go on to post–high school training. We often have less information on how much these programs increase future employment and earnings, although high school graduation is strongly correlated with future labor market opportunities.[82]

One program, which followed its participants for five years, is Project Redirection, an experimental program run in eleven different sites around the country and aimed at disadvantaged young teen mothers. Project Redirection showed greater graduation rates *and* significant employment and earnings gains among participants five years after the end of the program.[83] All of these effects were concentrated among women who had been in school when they received services, however, rather than among the dropouts in the program.

But even among in-school youth, not all aspects of these programs are effective. As discussed below, few educational enrichment programs appear to reduce pregnancy among participants. And the overall success of these efforts in keeping young adults in school remains depressingly low. For instance, a program run in a variety of Ohio high schools and aimed at teen mothers was able to raise the high school completion rate from 15.5 to 21.1 percent among participants.[84] While this is a significant and positive increase, these graduation rates hardly signify great success.

Second, programs focused on dropouts have been disappointingly ineffective in improving their employment or earnings. Probably the most discouraging set of results in all of the research literature on government interventions is the apparent ineffectiveness of efforts designed to improve the employment and earnings of high school dropouts. While a few programs have produced gains, most seem to have little effect on this population.

Providing extensive services doesn't guarantee results. In the late 1970s, the Supported Work program provided individual counseling, group support, life-skill training, and formal assistance with job training and job search to disadvantaged young adult dropouts. Although male dropouts showed decreased criminal activity, there was no effect from the program on employment and earnings among participants.[85] More recently, a program called JOB-START was run in thirteen sites around the country, serving seventeen- to twenty-one-year-old dropouts. JOBSTART offered a mix of academic skills, occupational skills, support services (such as child care, counseling, and life skills), as well as job placement assistance to dropouts. While there is evidence that participants had slightly higher earnings by the third and fourth year after this program, these gains were not large and did not offset program costs.[86]

JTPA training programs for young adult dropouts provide short-term limited support for training and job search. Evaluations of JTPA training for teen dropouts show virtually no effects on employment or earnings. In fact, among young adult men, the program appears to result in earning reductions, a perverse and puzzling outcome.[87] The most disadvantaged teenagers (public assistance recipients or those without work experience) show the least response to JTPA programs.

There are two major exceptions to this gloomy news. The Job Corps program takes dropouts, places them in full-time residential centers, and provides an intensive set of academic and occupational skills in a highly disciplined environment. A rigorous evaluation in the late 1970s indicated that Job Corps produced significant improvements in employment and earnings for its participants,[88] enough to recoup its costs through improved earnings and reduced crime. The Job Corps conclusions must be looked at carefully, however. The majority of the benefits came through a reduction in the number of crimes that Job Corps participants committed, which is notoriously hard to value accurately in dollars. A new evaluation is underway that will provide better evidence on Job Corps' effectiveness.

Even if effective, the Job Corps model has its limits. It is a very expensive program, costing around $14,000 per participant. If graduates work a lot more and earn a lot more as a result of the program, then the benefits will outweigh the costs.[89] But high per student costs mean that there are fewer Job Corps slots available. In addition, many teenagers either will not or cannot participate in such a residential program. This is particularly true of teen mothers who are very reluctant to go into residential training programs that limit contact with their children. These problems have resulted in Job Corps' developing nonresidential programs, which teenagers attend during the day only.

The other program which has shown good results for dropouts is a training program started in San Jose, California, and known as CET (Center for Employment Training). CET puts youth (and adults) into intensive hands-on vocational training for selected occupations. CET maintains close contact with employers, both to keep their training up-to-date and to place graduates. Those who complete CET almost always find jobs. Evaluations of the CET program for young dropouts indicate that there are big gains in earnings and employment among those who participate.[90] Because of these positive results, a major replication of CET programs is underway around the country, with rigorous evaluation of their effectiveness.

These two programs indicate that improving employment opportunities for young dropouts is not impossible. While Job Corps and CET are very different in style and approach, both are complex programs that have been carefully designed, they provide training over an extended period of time, and they impose strong disciplinary demands on participants.

It is worth noting that programs aimed at dropouts are able to increase the probability that participants will receive high school equivalency (GED) degrees. In fact, the promise of attaining a GED appears to be an important reason why teen dropouts enroll in these programs. Unfortunately, there is increasing evidence that a GED does not lead to big earnings increases. A major study of a large national sample of GED recipients found that the labor market rewards to a GED are less than those of a high school diploma.[91] This is entirely consistent with evaluation results from specific programs, where more participants receive GEDs but show little evidence of employment or earnings gains.[92]

Third, programs designed to prevent pregnancies have also been disappointingly ineffective. Programs that aim to increase educational attainment and labor market opportunities also often hope to reduce teen pregnancies. Among disadvantaged teens in general, the goal is to reduce first pregnancies. For those who have already become teen mothers, the goal is to reduce second pregnancies. Few of these programs have achieved this goal. In fact, in a few cases program participants appear to have a higher likelihood of second pregnancies than do nonparticipants.[93]

In contrast to broad programs that provide multiple educational services to teenage women, many school districts have experimented with more limited programs focused simply on preventing pregnancies. Initially, many schools tried simple variations on sex education courses, designed to increase teens' knowledge about their own sexuality and about sexual behavior and contraception. While these programs were effective in increasing teens' scores on exams that tested their biological and sexual knowledge, they had no effect on sexual behavior. More recent programs have expanded to provide some mix of education, counseling, contraceptive assistance, and active advocacy with teenagers about the costs of teen childbearing. Of those that have been rigorously studied, the results show mixed effects, with at least some programs appearing to delay sexual activity and produce small decreases in teen pregnancies.[94]

Programs that have positive effects are typically directed at younger adolescents, before they become sexually active. They involve active rather than passive learning. Instead of lectures, readings, or movies about sexual behavior and teen pregnancy, effective courses require teens to present information themselves, to practice concrete "refusal skills," or to be involved in peer and family discussions on sexual issues.[95] (These features are explicitly copied from effective antismoking and antidrug programs, which tend to use similar learning and prevention techniques.) But it is worth underscoring that the positive results shown by these programs are not large. A recent major review of adolescent pregnancy prevention programs concluded, "[I]t is clear from the modest to nil success of most [sex education] programs to date, that these approaches alone are insufficient to produce substantial impacts on teenage childbearing, particularly for adolescents who are most at risk."[96]

All of these results suggest that it might be more effective to put money into dropout prevention programs and school-to-work transition programs to try and retain students in high school rather than to provide training and assistance programs for young men or women after they have dropped out. Substantial evidence indicates that once a teen has actually left high school, there is little that any program can do to increase his or her employment in the next few years. The best prescription is one of waiting: wait until the teenagers are a few years older, when greater maturity makes them more able to utilize what training programs have to offer.

As we discussed in the last chapter, the widespread and growing interest in school-to-work transition programs for disadvantaged youth has led to a growth in apprenticeship programs, career academies, tech-prep programs, and other curriculums that mix occupational and academic skills. Many of these programs are relatively new and none of them has been evaluated in the same rigorous way as the programs discussed above. As a result, we know much less about their overall effectiveness; forthcoming evaluation studies of these programs will be of significant interest. The limited success of programs aimed at strengthening skills and employment opportunities for teen dropouts suggests that programs designed to retain students in school may be the most attractive approach right now.

More than in any other area, we need to experiment with and evaluate the effects of alternative projects aimed at keeping youth in school and linking them with jobs. The discouraging results of some past efforts should not prevent future efforts to find more effective ways to help disadvantaged youth. Improving the motivation and skills of today's teenagers is too important.

4.9 FIGHTING NEIGHBORHOOD POVERTY: DO ECONOMIC DEVELOPMENT PROGRAMS IMPROVE NEIGHBORHOODS?

SUMMARY. *The results of economic redevelopment efforts in poor neighborhoods have been mixed, in part because significant neighborhood change rarely occurs through public policy efforts alone but needs the active involvement of private sector and community-based organizations. Urban renewal reconstruction has had mixed effects, displacing many residents but also leading to new structures that have benefited*

185

cities. Public housing may have contributed to the deterioration of some
of the poorest city neighborhoods, although it has improved housing
quality among some of its recipients. Tax-relief programs designed to
encourage business and job expansion in poor neighborhoods appear to
have small positive effects, but these programs are very expensive. Pro-
grams that relocate individuals out of poor neighborhoods and into sub-
urban neighborhoods are currently generating substantial interest.

For those concerned with urban poverty, the problems that exist in ghetto
poverty neighborhoods are surely the most pressing. Even though only 12
percent of all poor persons live in such neighborhoods, their poverty is often
the most extreme. How can we effectively address the multitude of economic,
social, and behavioral problems that exist in these areas? Of course, efforts to
reform welfare, to improve teenage educational opportunities, or to fight
crime can be important. But major economic changes have to occur for long-
term neighborhood improvement. Economic development is a dynamic process: if more people hold jobs, this creates more local income, which in turn
spawns local resources like grocery stores and retail outlets. This in turn at-
tracts people into the neighborhood, leading to greater local spending, which
creates more income.

Promoting effective economic development is a very uncertain task. There
is no "magic bullet" by which economic development starts or proceeds. Instead, there appear to be a large number of factors that can promote or delay
economic change. A comparative study of several midsized towns faced with
major job losses due to industrial restructuring lists ten broad factors that
contributed to successful economic development in those towns that recovered from their losses.[97] These range from effective local leadership, to the
structure of local institutional connections between public, private, and nonprofit organizations, to the sensitivity of development planners to political and
social culture within an area. In light of this complexity, it is perhaps no surprise that U.S. efforts at renewing and redeveloping poor neighborhoods have
had limited success.

Determining whether economic development efforts funded by federal or
state governments have a positive impact is almost impossible in any overall
sense. The view of the past two decades has been that plans must be developed
and implemented area by area, in ways that match the unique strengths and
problems of each locality. In this situation, understanding which efforts have
been more successful than others requires extensive evaluation across a wide
variety of programs. Unfortunately, few of these efforts have been rigorously
evaluated. Many evaluations are written by the local agencies that headed the
efforts and, not surprisingly, most of these proclaim success.

In addition, even where more impartial evaluations have been attempted,
economic development programs are notoriously difficult to evaluate well.
The question is not "Did jobs increase?" but "Did jobs increase *more than*

they would have in the absence of this effort?"[98] Some sort of comparison group is necessary to predict what would have happened in the absence of the program. For instance, if the evidence shows that slower job growth occurred in a targeted area than elsewhere, this does not mean that the program failed. If the neighborhood was chosen because it had difficult employment problems, one would expect slower job growth. The development program might have been successful, relative to the job growth that would have occurred otherwise.

Because good evaluations are scarce, the comments in this section are based on more limited evidence than in previous sections. The conclusions are more tentative, relying on judgments from a range of evidence rather than from comprehensive evaluations.

The Impact of Urban Renewal and Public Housing Construction

The most well known and longest-running efforts at urban redevelopment have involved clearing "slums," or tearing down deteriorated structures and building anew on these sites. In many cases, this has meant building large city structures in once-deteriorated residential neighborhoods, such as stadiums, municipal auditoriums, or convention centers. Only one-third of urban renewal land, much of it occupied by low-income residents prior to urban renewal programs, have been redeveloped for residential use.[99]

The overall effect of these efforts is difficult to evaluate, in part because they differ from city to city, and in part because they have had both costs and benefits that have been borne by very different groups of people. Many of the new stadiums, convention centers, or office buildings that have gone up on urban renewal sites have been useful additions to cities, attracting tourists and business people and increasing local tax revenues. But this has often done little to improve the lives of those who used to live there. In many cities, urban renewal efforts led to the organization of neighborhood groups, angry about the effects of these projects and demanding greater involvement in any future development efforts.[100]

Many persons displaced due to urban renewal were given slots in newly constructed public housing projects. The effects of expanded public housing have not been well evaluated. Did these projects improve people's lives and the neighborhoods in which they were built?

With regard to high-rise public housing projects, the almost unanimous opinion among policy analysts is that these projects have been disastrous in the long run. In fact, high-rise public housing is sometimes cited as one of the best examples of how good intentions can lead to extremely bad outcomes. Because of political opposition to such buildings in more middle-income neighborhoods, virtually all of them were located in poor neighborhoods.[101] As city economies changed, these poor neighborhoods became even poorer, as discussed in chapter 2. At the same time, most city-based Public Housing Authorities either did not have the money or the competence to maintain these buildings. Elevators stopped working, buildings were not maintained, and units were abandoned as unlivable. These structures have become the center of drug and gang activity in many ghetto neighborhoods, where families are afraid of using the stairways and refuse to let their children play outside.

Over time, high-rise public housing projects in poor neighborhoods have added to the problems of their residents and of the neighborhoods in which they are located.[102] Low-rise projects have fewer problems, but still often suffer from serious deterioration. Congress has not appropriated the funds necessary to keep these buildings maintained, and local housing authorities have often not used available money effectively. Too many public housing projects have vacant units, boarded-up windows, inadequate plumbing, and structural damage such as holes in walls or ceilings. Government estimates indicate that there is an unfunded backlog of repairs in public housing units that would cost $10 billion to $20 billion to eliminate.[103] The movement to Section 8 vouchers and federally subsidized but privately developed and maintained housing projects is an effort to prevent some of these problems in more recent public housing programs.

Poor families tend to live in deteriorated housing even when they are *not* in public housing units, however. A major study from the Urban Institute compared the quality of housing among poor residents in public housing and private rental housing, controlling for other factors that influence housing choices.[104] They find that residents in public housing, on average, have better housing than nonresidents. This is least true among families with children receiving public assistance, the group most likely to be in inner-city high-rise projects. In addition, while the physical structures appeared to be somewhat better among public housing residents, the neighborhood characteristics for families with children were worse. In essence, these families traded off slightly better units than they could get without housing assistance for living in worse neighborhoods. It is not immediately clear whether this has left these families better or worse off.

Overall, it is difficult to draw any final conclusions about whether urban renewal and public housing construction have improved the lives of the poor. Some public housing construction has contributed to neighborhood deterioration over time. Other urban renewal projects caused displacement of poor families. While these efforts may have produced gains for the *city*, eliminating low-rent and deteriorated residential areas and subsidizing the construction of revenue-creating structures, it is unclear whether they had a net positive or negative impact on poor people in their cities.

The Impact of Enterprise Zones and Tax-Based Efforts to Increase Employment

In the 1980s, thirty-seven states developed programs that they called "Enterprise Zones" (EZs), aimed at stimulating economic development in poor neighborhoods. Most of these efforts explicitly identified a set of low-income neighborhoods and targeted tax subsidies and regulatory relief on firms that either moved into or expanded their operations in these neighborhoods. The idea was to provide incentives that would attract more business into poor neighborhoods. A number of these state-specific programs have been evaluated, and the evidence on their effectiveness is mixed.[105]

Most of the firms that received subsidies from the EZs were expanding businesses that already existed in the Zone. There is little evidence that new businesses were attracted into these areas. The cost to the government for each new job created in these areas appeared to be very high, ranging from $4,500 to $13,000 annually. In short, EZs involved relatively high levels of subsidy but produced small numbers of new jobs.[106]

Various evaluations provide mixed evidence on how many of these new jobs are entirely due to the EZ initiatives. A well-known study of the Maryland Enterprise Zone program by the U.S. General Accounting Office found that little employment expansion in the designated zones was attributable to the EZ program.[107] A particularly well done study of Indiana's Enterprise Zones found a small reduction in Unemployment Insurance claims in EZ areas, and an expansion in business size due to the EZ program. There was no evidence, however, that personal income levels within designated Zones increased relative to comparable non-Zone areas.[108] At the far end of the scale, an evaluation of the New Jersey EZ program found that it generated almost two dollars in revenue in Zone areas for every one dollar spent, although this conclusion has also been challenged in more recent research.[109] At best, Enterprise Zone programs appear to have produced small changes in some areas. Given the costs involved, there is little evidence that this program provides a model for effective economic development.

This is consistent with other evidence on the use of state and local tax abatements as a way to generate business activity. One review of fifty-seven major studies of the effects of state and local taxes on economic development finds that lower tax levels appear to have positive effects on a range of business activity measures, implying that tax subsidies in poor neighborhoods will induce business expansion.[110] This effect is smallest in large metropolitan areas, however, and biggest in suburban areas. The annual tax cost per job created also appears to be high, between $2,000 and $11,000.

All of this suggests that economic development strategies for poor neighborhoods that are primarily focused around lower tax rates or tax rebates are unlikely to have large effects, and may be quite expensive. More comprehensive efforts that involve a wider range of simultaneous strategies focused on neighborhood change may have a greater promise of success (although they will also cost more money.)

The six Empowerment Zones recently approved by HUD might be more effective tools of economic development. Recall from the last chapter that Empowerment Zones are designated economically disadvantaged areas for which a city has put together a master development plan. Although many of these Empowerment Zones include state and local tax relief efforts as part of their strategy to attract new businesses to these areas, they also typically include much more, involving everything from housing redevelopment to improved local services and requirements for local hiring on local projects. The more ambitious mix of strategies included in Empowerment Zones is more difficult to coordinate and implement but promises a greater chance of actually having a long-term impact in low-income neighborhoods. The effects of Empowerment Zone plans will be seen only after they are implemented.

The Impact of Mobility Strategies

The previous chapter discussed two types of mobility strategies. The first involved programs that identify jobs in suburban areas and provide transportation and information to link low-income persons in poor city neighborhoods with these jobs. These programs, typically run with a mix of private and public funding, are still relatively scattered and new. Evaluations of the effectiveness of a few of these programs are just being funded; at present, little is known about whether they generate benefits large enough to justify the costs involved.

The second type of mobility strategy is one of permanent relocation. Rather than linking people with jobs, it focuses on helping residents move out of extremely poor neighborhoods and into more mixed neighborhoods. On the one hand, this can lead to further abandonment of ghetto neighborhoods, which might make life even worse for those left behind. On the other hand, if such mobility programs significantly improve the life of those who participate in them, then they should receive serious consideration.

Relocation programs show promise due to the striking results achieved by the Gautreaux project, designed to help families in Chicago inner-city public housing move elsewhere using Section 8 housing vouchers. Participants who volunteered to be part of the program were given only limited choice about where they would be relocated. As a result, some were moved from one city neighborhood to another, while others were moved to the suburbs.

A major evaluation of the Gautreaux project indicated that mothers who moved to suburban locations worked more and spent less time on AFDC. Even more striking, their children had much higher rates of school achievement and high school graduation.[111] Gautreaux children in the suburbs were less likely to have been involved in criminal activities than those who stayed in the city. The results seem to indicate that the surrounding suburban environment and school system changed the behavior of those who moved there much more than those who stayed in the city. As a result of this project, the federal government has funded a variety of Gautreaux-like experimental programs in several cities.

It is worth noting that a major nationally announced Gautreaux project has some inherent limits to it. There is a long history of suburban communities resisting the relocation of low-income families from the city, particularly if those families are from ethnic and racial minority groups. It may be difficult to run a major program that relocates poor mothers and children into the suburbs if those in suburban locations refuse to cooperate. In addition, by definition, such a program will be limited in scope. It can only include volunteers, and many poor families even in very bad neighborhoods may refuse relocation into strange areas where they have no friends. Helping families find housing and resettle in another area is inherently a slow process that can involve only a limited number of people at a time. Even if further evidence on the effectiveness of relocation strategies leads to more such programs, this is likely to remain a route out of ghetto poverty that only a few can take.[112]

Overall, this section suggests that publicly funded urban renewal and economic development programs have achieved only limited success. If we knew more about how to stimulate economic change in poor neighborhoods, we could perhaps have prevented the substantial increase in ghetto poverty that has occurred in our cities over the past twenty years.

Part of the reason why the programs discussed in this section appear to have mixed effects is because we are focusing on the question of "what can the government do to initiate local development in poor neighborhoods?" Many observers of local development suggest that the government is only one player in successful efforts at local development, and not always the most important one. A variety of effective community development efforts have been launched by nonprofit community-based organizations. Typically, these groups bring together many actors, using public funds as well as funds from private sector businesses and nonprofit organizations. This combination of public, private, and community-based involvement is present in most successful neighborhood economic development efforts. While public programs can contribute to these efforts, by themselves they are rarely sufficient to create substantial economic change in poor neighborhoods. Effective economic development initiatives require coordinated efforts involving a broad coalition of actors from all sectors of the community.

Who Should Help the Poor?

ABOUT A YEAR AGO I testified in front of a U.S. Congressional committee working on welfare reform. Following me was a Catholic priest who ran a home for unwed mothers. In his testimony he urged the committee to cancel all their programs and leave social assistance to the churches and the private sector. I chatted with him briefly afterwards, partly because I had never talked with anyone who truly believed there was no role for the government in assisting the poor. I was particularly curious about his perspective since I work with a number of nonprofit and charitable institutions through my church and know that the directors of these programs would never have made such a plea. He claimed that private assistance could easily replace all types of government aid; even when I pushed him about the disparities between the level of charitable assistance and the level of government assistance, he argued that at best there may be a role for a little bit of state or local funding, but no role at all for federal money. Never having been engaged in such a conversation before, I listened more than I talked. This chapter is my response.

Recent proposals to change the structure of public assistance programs have evoked deep disagreement, with passionate arguments among people who hold different views about how to respond appropriately to poverty in this country. Much of this argument has been about the specifics of program design, as discussed in earlier chapters. But some of it is about larger questions relating to the scope and nature of government involvement in public assistance to the poor. Many who propose to cut government assistance argue for two changes in direction: (1) provide more help to the poor through private charities, and less through public funding; and (2) decrease federal involvement in antipoverty programs and let states have more control. This chapter discusses the arguments for a reduced role for government public assistance overall and for a reduced role for the federal government in particular.

This chapter starts with a discussion of the various reasons why public provisions for the poor are present in virtually all societies. Those who want to get government out of the business of helping the poor must recognize that there are many reasons why public sector involvement may be necessary to adequately provide a social safety net. While much of this book is about the presentation of research and factual arguments, the first section of this chapter ventures into the realm of political philosophy, presenting reasons why the government may have certain key responsibilities in creating and maintaining a social safety net, which the private sector operating by itself cannot fulfill.

The second section moves from philosophy back into the realm of research and fact. While there has been an endless public discussion about the size, effectiveness, and appropriate design of government public assistance programs, few people know very much about the scope and nature of charitable assistance in this country. At present, it is inconceivable that the charitable sector could replace significant portions of current government programs, given the difference in size and operating capacity between the two sectors. In addition, private charity often works in *partnership* with the government to provide services. Cuts in government funding typically lead to *cuts* in charitable services, not expansion. Charitable organizations will continue to play an important role in helping low-income families in the United States, but we need to be realistic about what they can and cannot do.

Recent welfare reforms have also thrown open the question of the appropriate responsibilities of different levels of government. The 1996 legislation has brought about a major realignment of responsibility away from the federal level and back to the state level. This has produced new debates on long-standing constitutional questions about the responsibilities of states versus the federal government. Should the federal government simply turn over money to the states to run public assistance programs of their own design, with no strings attached? If not, what is the appropriate ongoing role of the federal government? The third section of this chapter investigates the appropriate roles of the federal, state, and local governments in assisting the poor. As we shall see, there are both philosophical and pragmatic arguments for substantial federal involvement in antipoverty efforts, although clearly there are also functions that state and local governments can perform more effectively. Achieving the appropriate *balance* of responsibility between different levels of government is important for public assistance programs to operate smoothly.

In some ways, the response, "Cut government spending for the poor—especially federal spending—and let states and private charities do it," is a logical outgrowth of all we have discussed in previous chapters. If people have misunderstood the nature of poverty, being too ready to blame the poor, and if people have misunderstood the real successes of past programs and undervalued their contributions, then it may be easy to conclude that "government assistance serves no effective role." The last chapter argued that public assistance programs have been more successful than is typically recognized. This chapter argues that the government—at all levels (federal, state, and local)—should continue to play a key role in ongoing assistance to the poor.

5.1 WHY SHOULD WE OPERATE A PUBLIC SOCIAL SAFETY NET?

SUMMARY. *This section presents eight of the most common arguments for government involvement in assistance to the poor. These include arguments that public assistance is an investment that benefits all persons and that it is a risk-sharing device among citizens, as well as arguments based on the value of human life which claim that government must act to enhance human possibilities, particularly among the most vulnerable. Governments that have the economic and technological capacity to address issues of poverty may face greater moral responsibility. Governments also have administrative and organizational capacities that make them more effective in providing some types of public assistance. Equity arguments suggest that all citizens should have access to equivalent public assistance when in need, while economic rights arguments claim that access to basic economic resources should have the same standing as citizenship rights.*

"We the People of the United States, in Order to form a more perfect
Union, establish Justice, insure domestic Tranquility, provide for the
common defense, promote the general Welfare, and secure the Blessings
of Liberty for ourselves and our Posterity, do ordain and establish this
Constitution for the United States of America."
—*Preamble to the U.S. Constitution*

Reasonable people can honestly disagree over what type of public assistance programs to run and how to run them most effectively. Virtually all nations, however, provide *some* forms of public assistance to their citizens, although this varies from rice subsidies in poor Asian countries to cash assistance in richer nations. This section steps back from the discussion about specific policies to explore a more basic question of political theory: Why is it the responsibility of the government to tax citizens and provide support to those in economic difficulty? The arguments in this section are a reminder of all the reasons why *public* assistance to the poor has been present in one form or another since the founding of this nation.

The role of government in addressing the needs of society's poor is hardly a new topic. One of the first recorded social codes for dealing with poverty is laid out in the biblical book of Deuteronomy. The Hebrew tribes are given explicit rules about how to deal with widows and orphans, those who are likely to be poorest in a patriarchal society where an individual's standing and access to resources is determined by their relationship to the male head of the household. Similarly, rules are laid out to deal with those who become debtors or who are dispossessed from their land. Even in our very different modern economy, we are still arguing over the public rules about how to deal with the poor—today's equivalent of the widows and orphans—among us.

There are many reasons why societies elect to make some public provision to assist the poor, based on a variety of philosophical, moral, and economic arguments. This section highlights eight of the arguments which often arise in the public discussion about government assistance programs. Almost all of the classic arguments about the need for government can be used to support the claim that government should be concerned with the poorest in society. It

194   • CHAPTER 5 •

is worth noting, however, that those who agree with the importance of government involvement in public assistance may still disagree on what type of programs the government should operate, on the amount of assistance, or on the
level of government that should take primary responsibility.

The Investment/Positive Externalities Argument

*Antipoverty programs are investments in the future of a society which benefit
both the poor and the nonpoor and improve the long-term well-being of all
members of society.* Increasing education, health, and employability among
the poor will directly benefit poor families, but it will also benefit the nonpoor through increased productivity, greater citizen participation in democratic decision making, and lower future payments to offset poverty, crime or
social protest. This argument may have particular force with regard to programs that improve child health and education. Investing money in children to
prevent future problems can repay itself many times over if this reduces future
public expenditures and leads to a more productive future workforce.

Underlying this investment argument is a presumption that government assistance to alleviate poverty provides what economists call a *positive externality*. Positive externalities are essentially benefits created by a particular
program and enjoyed by everyone in society and from which no one can be
excluded. This suggests that the government should run antipoverty programs
for essentially the same reason as the government runs defense programs or
public schools, other programs that generate positive externalities. Thus, if I
as a charitable individual adopt a poor family and see that their children are
well educated and that the parents have jobs, I benefit not just myself and that
family, but my fellow citizens if that family and their children become more
productive workers and better citizens as a result of my intervention. My
friends and neighbors are better off—they will live in a nation with higher tax
revenues, a higher standard of living, and where more informed public decisions occur—because of my actions.

Trying to provide a program that creates positive externalities through private markets never works well. Many will refuse to "buy"—i.e., will refuse to
pay for a private defense force, or will refuse to contribute charitably to private philanthropies—but they will still get the benefits from these programs.
If others defend the country's borders, everyone is safe even if they didn't
contribute to that defense. If poverty is reduced, everyone will benefit from
high living standards in the future. Because the benefits of the program can't
be limited just to those who voluntarily support it, programs that generate
positive externalities may be better provided through broad taxation, which
forces everyone to pay fairly for the benefits they receive.

The claim that investments in the poor have long-term positive effects on
the well-being of the nonpoor does not require that antipoverty programs produce direct economic benefits to the nonpoor. Some argue that even if antipoverty programs merely alleviate suffering, say among ill elderly individuals
who will not generate any future economic benefits, this still provides a posi-

tive externality to most people in society. To the extent that citizens feel some national identification with other citizens, it may be painful to see pictures of malnutrition among American children, need among American elderly, or homelessness among American adults. If individuals are better off when they know that other citizens are not in great economic distress, there is a reason for the government to operate antipoverty programs, even if there are no economic returns from these efforts.

The Risk-Sharing Argument

Public assistance programs provide individuals with government insurance against future economic risks. A primary reason to form a government is to share risks—to provide for a common defense, for instance. Another form of shared risk the government can offset is economic risk. The government can pool resources to assure people that they will have protection against future economic bad luck. This may mean anything from providing medical assistance to people who face major health problems due to accidents or disease, short-run assistance to people caught in the midst of catastrophic natural events like hurricanes or floods, or compensatory preschool programs for children born to poor parents to help them "catch up" educationally and developmentally to others with more resources.

These are risks that the private market typically cannot or will not insure against, for a variety of reasons. While this is not the place for an extended discussion of failure in private insurance markets, the primary problem is known as "adverse selection," namely, only those at highest risk will buy private insurance. This often makes it impossible for private insurance companies to function effectively. The government, because it can pool risks across a much larger pool of people, can solve this problem.

The philosopher John Rawls has argued that uncertainty about one's economic placement in society will lead individuals to support programs that assure some redistribution from richer to poorer.[1] A society may form a social safety net via government programs because no individual is certain whether or not he or she will be poor at some point in the future. In a situation of uncertainty, individuals are willing to support programs for the poor as insurance for themselves, their parents, or their children against possible economically disastrous events that could befall them. Many have suggested that this "risk sharing" argument is one reason why elderly assistance programs are more popular than assistance programs for single mothers with children. Virtually everyone hopes one day to be elderly (and hence is willing to support programs that insure against destitution among the elderly), but many are quite sure they will never be a single mother.

These first two arguments are ultimately based on individualistic notions of self-interest. They claim that the nonpoor—acting through the government— should be willing to establish programs that help the poor because it makes them better off, either because of the positive externalities produced by these programs or because of the insurance they provide. Other arguments rely more on ethical notions of community responsibility. For the concept of a "nation" to have meaning, there must be something that all citizens of that political entity share in common. The following arguments suggest that citizens share some common responsibilities for helping the neediest among them, regardless of the effect on their own well-being.[2]

The Human Dignity Argument

Public assistance programs to the poor fulfill the primary role of society, which is to respect human value and avoid wasted human lives. Human beings have a spark of consciousness, creativity, and inner life—the soul in many religions—that gives their existence deep value and meaning. Any morally legitimate government that makes decisions regarding the lives of its citizens must respect the human dignity of all of its citizens. For this reason, nations typically protect human life through a wide variety of legal and regulatory requirements, from prohibitions against murder, to restrictions on child labor, to rules against blatant discrimination in social and economic institutions.

If value is imbedded in human life, a society does active harm when it "wastes" a human life. This can involve sins of commission, such as putting an innocent person to death, as well as sins of omission, such as failing to intervene in situations where human life could have been saved. Thus, just as it is a fundamental responsibility of society to prevent murder, a society is equally responsible to keep children from dying of preventable hunger, or adults from dying of preventable diseases. With only a mild extension of this argument, "wasted" lives can also occur when a society allows children to grow up without learning to read, without receiving adequate nutrition, or without the resources to participate fully in the economy. Providing a safety net of public assistance programs becomes one of the first responsibilities of a society to protect its most precious resource—its living human beings.

There are many nuanced forms of this argument. Some version of it is often invoked in religious writings on the role of the government and the economy. For instance, the Catholic Bishops' Pastoral Letter on the Economy in 1986 stated, "Every economic decision and institution must be judged in light of whether it protects or undermines the dignity of the human person."[3] Other writings have particularly emphasized the issue of *vulnerability*, arguing that a morally legitimate society must care especially for those within it who are most vulnerable. These are the lives that are most in need of formal and publicly acknowledged forms of protection, like the widows and orphans among the Hebrews.

The Capacity to Respond Argument

A fourth argument follows directly from the third: the moral responsibility of a society is much greater when there is the economic and technological capacity to assist the poor. In a society where the vast majority of the population is extremely poor and there are few excess resources (a situation in which too many Third World countries still find themselves), substantial assistance to those who are starving may not be economically possible. But in the United States, such assistance is possible. It is not costless, but neither is it likely to be so costly as to create financial ruin. As we saw earlier, redistribution programs aimed at poor families consume about 14 percent of the federal budget. It is a political and social decision whether that amount goes up to 20 percent or decreases to 10 percent. Each of these choices is *economically* possible, although they both have implications for other spending priorities. Thus, in a wealthy nation with substantial "surplus" resources above the level of income required for minimal survival of the population, there are sharper moral questions about antipoverty efforts than in a poor nation.

One example of this argument is often given with regard to medical assistance to the poor. When smallpox and polio could not be prevented, the government had little responsibility to its citizens with regard to these illnesses other than perhaps to provide the medical facilities in poor neighborhoods to care for those who contracted them. Once there were vaccines for these diseases, however, the human value argument would claim that it became the responsibility of a society, through its government, to assure that all children were immunized. Indeed, the U.S. government launched major immunization campaigns for both diseases. The moral responsibility emerged when the technological capacity for disease prevention became possible.

It is always difficult to decide how much and what sort of public assistance to provide in any society. But if there are problems of great need among some citizens, the government with the capacity to address those problems faces a greater moral obligation to respond in some way than a government without such capacity.

The Administrative Capacity Argument

The government may have a better administrative and programmatic capacity to carry out efficient redistribution than the private sector for some types of programs. The government may be able to gather broad information on need more readily, and may be able to implement programs more efficiently because of its other functions (such as taxation) that collect similar information. For instance, if wage subsidies are provided, linking these into the income tax system as the EITC does is extremely efficient, since workers' wages are already centrally reported to the IRS by employers. In general, the government may be most effective at running large programs that provide simple services (such as monthly checks or Food Stamps coupons) based on similar rules for all participants. It is less clear that government has any comparative advantage in operating programs that provide complex services. Indeed, the operation of many programs, such as Head Start or foster care services, is currently provided by private sector agencies.

The government may also have a comparative advantage in overseeing and coordinating multiple programs. Just as government has a central role to play in regulating and assuring fairness in the banking or insurance industries (places where individuals can come to great economic harm that they often cannot predict or prevent without government oversight), so there may be a role for government in the regulation of public assistance services, assuring that services are available in all areas or that the funds designated for public assistance are used for that purpose.

The more complex the social and economic structure of a nation, the greater the role that exists for the government to provide some overall coordination, direction, and financing to public assistance programs. Just as there is a role for government to demand public disclosure of key private information, forcing companies to provide public information that would be extremely costly for individual consumers to discover on their own, so there is a role for the government to assure a smoothly operating public assistance system, with centralized information and regulation of this system.

The Equity Argument

Those citizens with equivalent problems and needs should have access to similar programs. This equity-based argument relies on the capacity of the government to assure nationally available programs. If a social obligation to help the poor exists, then it may be unjust to provide assistance to some persons and not to others in identical circumstances who happen to live in different communities or who become needy at different times of the year. Yet, in the absence of government involvement, private charitable assistance may vary widely across localities.

Some push this argument beyond "national availability of programs" to include "national availability of uniform programs," so that all citizens with equivalent incomes have access to similar Food Stamp benefits or to cash assistance payments. Obviously, those who believe that state discretion in programs is important would be less likely to agree to this definition of equity. In fact, many would argue that at least for some programs, "equity" demands the running of *different* programs in different locations. For instance, job training efforts should vary as local labor markets vary. In any case, if either uniformity in program rules or national availability of (locally diverse) programs is important, then some form of government involvement in these programs is almost mandatory, to assure their equitable provision.

The Market Failure Argument

Given that the United States has chosen a market-oriented economy, it has a responsibility to those who cannot survive in the market on their own. The market, wherein a person sells his or her labor in exchange for earnings, may not provide opportunities that allow all people to be self-sufficient. For instance, the labor market does not provide good opportunities for the aged, the disabled, the unemployed, the illiterate, or those who have been historically excluded from training, jobs, or housing due to racial segregation or gender discrimination. Even given similar ability, these groups often cannot compete on an equal basis with others. The government can help those who are not fully included in the market either to become more fully involved (through such programs as education, training, search assistance, and antidiscrimination programs) or to survive economically outside the market (through such programs as Food Stamps, medical insurance, or cash supplements to income).

Market economies have often been wonderful engines of growth and productivity. Yet they do not guarantee adequate support for all participants. There is no "floor" of income guaranteed in a market economy. Those who cannot compete adequately in the market will face poverty, a particular concern among children and the elderly, who we typically think should *not* be expected to work in the labor market. As we saw in chapter 2, many workers who are willing to work full time may not earn enough to support their family. If a society is to rely on a market-based economic system, it should also accept responsibility for those for whom the market does not provide adequate support or who cannot compete in it and need alternative sources of assistance and support.

The Economic Rights Argument

Just as individuals have citizenship rights, so they also may have economic rights. In a modern economy, the right of access to education, to food, to medical care, to housing, and to employment are necessary for individuals to participate fully as citizens in society. If one grants this argument for "economic rights" as an important supplement to "citizenship rights" (the right to vote, the right to a fair trial), then the government must be deeply involved in enforcing these rights. Of course, it is unclear exactly what needs to be provided for an economic right to be granted. Does a barracks meet the "right to housing" for the homeless, or must an individual room for each person be available? Most proponents of the economic rights argument expect that establishing economic rights would vastly increase the extent of government funding for public assistance. For instance, it would demand the creation of a large-scale public sector employment program to assure a job to those who cannot find one in the private sector.

The economic rights argument is the most radical argument for government involvement in public assistance, at least from a U.S. perspective. Within the United States, the argument for economic rights has never gained a broad following, in part because it directly contradicts certain market economy arguments that dominate U.S. economic thinking about how to distribute goods and services. Guaranteeing housing or medical care or employment through governmental programs is an apparent threat to the market providers of these goods, as the strong opposition to a government-run national health insurance plan has recently demonstrated. Others argue that implementing economic rights would be far too costly; that even a country with the wealth of the United States does not have the capacity to guarantee some level of economic well-being to all. For these reasons and others, while economic rights arguments continue to surface in the public debate, they do not have the same persuasive power for most Americans as some of the other arguments listed here.

Arguments about whether the society should provide a social safety net say nothing about what the size and nature of that safety net should be. People who strongly agree that the public has an obligation to help the poor differ on whether these obligations should be met through cash assistance programs or job and education programs. Most of the recent discussion about welfare reform has focused on the question of "How do we do it more effectively?" But imbedded in this is the more fundamental question: Is there a public obligation to provide these programs, and what is the nature of that obligation? It should be clear that there are many reasons to provide support to the poor. It is not by chance that virtually every government in the world provides some form of public assistance programs. As Americans, we have obligations to those among us who are less fortunate.

5.2 WHAT CAN WE EXPECT FROM PRIVATE CHARITY?

SUMMARY. *Private charity includes both direct transfers from one family member to another, as well as individual donations to nonprofit organizations that provide assistance to the poor. The extent of both types of private assistance can only be guessed, but each appear to provide roughly $10 billion to $15 billion to low-income families. Increases in government spending on the poor decrease private charitable activity, but by a very small amount—far below a dollar-for-dollar displacement rate. There is no evidence to support the claim that significant decreases in government spending on the poor could be replaced by increases in private charity; the growth that would be required in private donations is beyond the realm of possibility. In fact, many charities rely heavily on government funding and must cut services when public assistance budgets are cut. Currently, private charity provides an important complement to government efforts, but is not a substitute.*

A substantial amount of assistance to the poor is not channeled through the government, but is given from one family member to another, or is donated by individuals to nonprofit charitable organizations that operate everything from homeless shelters to job programs. How important are these sources of income for the poor? Given strong pressure to cut government budgets for public assistance, perhaps low-income families can rely more heavily on personal and charitable support? In this section I argue that private charity plays an important role in the safety net of this country, a role that is too often unrecognized or misunderstood. But as we shall see, private charity is not a feasible alternative to government assistance. In fact, many private charities themselves rely heavily on government funds to provide their services.

Historically, public programs have often been viewed as a "last resort," that is, public assistance should be sought only by those without family or church connections, or those for whom local charitable assistance is inadequate. Over time, however, this conception has changed not just in the United States but in most industrialized countries. In many cases, government assistance is now viewed as the "first resort," while private assistance is left to take care of what public assistance does not. Thus, church soup kitchens and food pantries alleviate hunger among those whose Food Stamps run short at the end of the month, families help out their unemployed relatives whose Unemployment Compensation benefits have ended, and parents help their single-parent daughters and grandchildren when public assistance runs short.

In the first part of this section we investigate the magnitude of private charity for the poor, and in the second part we investigate the effect of government assistance to the needy on private charitable donations. The third part lays out some principles about how charitable assistance and government assistance to the poor might best interact.

Charitable Giving in America

There are two types of charitable giving. The first is money given directly from one family or person to another family or person, often called "direct transfers." Almost all direct transfers occur among family members, as parents assist their adult children, absent fathers provide extra support for their children (beyond their formal child support payments), or brothers and sisters help each other out. The second type of charitable giving is from individuals to nonprofit organizations that provide services to low-income families and individuals.

DIRECT TRANSFERS BETWEEN FAMILIES

Almost all of us regularly give gifts to relatives who are not part of our immediate household. The question in this chapter is the extent to which these family gifts are motivated by need. Do parents give disproportionate help to children who have lower earnings? Are brothers and sisters more likely to give assistance to a poor sibling than to a nonpoor sibling?

Actually, we know surprisingly little about direct transfers among family members. These are not reported on tax forms unless they are very large. All gifts received from another family member of up to $10,000 per year are tax free. Estimates from several surveys that ask about family transfers suggest that higher-income families receive *more* from their relatives than do low-income families, but this is largely because high-income families are likely to have high-income siblings or parents. Controlling for potential donor income, poorer families are somewhat more likely to get family transfers, but the amounts they get are usually small.[4] In short, direct family transfers do little to redistribute income toward low-income families.

A very rough calculation of existing survey data indicates that low-income families who receive public assistance also receive family transfers equal to about one-fifth of their cash transfers from public sources.[5] This means that with every dollar received in cash public assistance, these families receive another twenty cents in support (cash or noncash) from family members. If this calculation is approximately correct, it suggests that low-income families received roughly $15 billion in assistance from other family members in 1995.[6] Even with a large margin of error around this estimate, it suggests that direct transfers to low-income families from relatives are a significant part of the safety net for many people.

CHARITABLE GIVING TO NONPROFIT ORGANIZATIONS

In 1993, philanthropic organizations received $111 billion dollars in gifts from individuals.[7] This includes everything from quarters dropped in Salvation Army kettles to large end-of-the-year gifts to the local symphony orchestra to family contributions to a local church. Only a small share of this money goes to assist low-income families. The largest share of donations (almost 50 percent) went to religious organizations. While some of this was in turn used to provide assistance to low-income people through church-run outreach programs, the vast majority of it went to support religious activities and organizations. Independent Sector estimates that in 1991 religious organizations provided between $2 billion and $6.6 billion in aid to the needy, which averages between 4 and 15 percent of their total budgets.[8]

Other large chunks of charitable giving go to support educational institutions (largely private schools), arts and cultural events, environmental preservation, or medical research. According to *Giving U.S.A.*, an annual report on philanthropic activity, only about 10 percent of charitable contributions have gone to nonprofit human service organizations in recent years.[9] In turn, less than half of the dollars spent by human service organizations pay for services to low-income families, since many of these organizations serve a wide variety of clients.[10] Together with the religious money that is also funneled into human service outreach, this suggests that around $12 billion in private charitable donations were spent to assist low-income families in the early 1990s.[11] While these numbers are very approximate, they indicate that private charities spend approximately the same amount of money assisting low-income families as families themselves provide in direct support of other family members.

In contrast to government spending of $200 billion on programs directed at low-income families, the $10 to $12 billion from private charities is relatively small. It is worth noting, however, that charitable contributions in the United States are larger than in most other countries. In comparison to Britain, Canada, or Germany, U.S. citizens donate more of their income to private charities.[12] Why should Americans give more to charity than people in other nations? While some have interpreted this as greater American generosity, there are other explanations as well. Most obviously, the United States encourages charitable donations through its tax system to a much greater extent than other countries. Economist Burton Weisbrod, who has studied the nonprofit sector in the United States extensively, also suggests that the greater heterogeneity of the U.S. population encourages people to privately support nonprofit organizations and activities.[13] In countries with more homogeneous ethnic and cultural backgrounds, the government provides much greater support to educational, cultural, and social services. In the United States, the government provides less support for these activities (there is less social agreement about what should be done) and individuals privately support those organizations whose work they value.

American citizens are not the only source of income for private charitable organizations, however. When we hear about privately run health clinics for the poor, or when we pass homeless shelters, we tend to think they are supported by individual donations. In reality, a large share of nonprofit funding comes from the government. Among America's one hundred largest charitable organizations in 1993, government support from federal, state, and local sources accounted for 22 percent of all their income. Some human services organizations receive very large fractions of their budget from the government. For instance, Catholic Charities, USA, a group that provides emergency food and shelter services to the poor, received 65 percent of its total income from the government, typically contracting with local governments to provide services.[14] The 1977 Commission on Private Philanthropy and Public Needs concluded that, outside of churches, government is a more important source of revenue for nonprofit service providers than all other forms of private giving combined.[15]

The reliance of charitable human service organizations on government assistance as well as individual donations indicates that many of these groups are not providing alternative and competing services to the public sector. Rather, many of them work in partnership with the government, actually operating Head Start programs, job training programs, or foster care programs. As we will see, this makes it difficult for charitable organizations to provide alternative services that replace government programs when public budgets are cut.

Does Government Assistance Displace Private Charity?

Some have claimed that cuts in government spending on antipoverty programs can be made up by increases in private charity. Behind this claim is the assumption that there is close to a dollar for dollar displacement between government funds and private donations. If the government cuts its spending, so the argument goes, private donations will increase accordingly. Is there evidence for this optimistic forecast?

Certainly one would expect that decreases in government spending for low-income families would have some effect on both direct transfers between families and on individual donations to nonprofit organizations. To the extent that charitable donations are motivated by the need of those who receive them, decreases in government efforts to alleviate hunger, ill health, or poverty will increase the impetus for individuals to respond to these problems through private gifts. On the other hand, there are many reasons for charitable donations other than a pure response to need. Direct transfers between family members are often considered a family obligation, or may be an exchange where economic assistance is given in return for time, attention, and care. Gifts to charitable organizations may be considered a religious or moral obligation, unrelated to the overall level of need in the population.

DIRECT TRANSFERS BETWEEN FAMILIES

A large research literature has focused on why families actually give gifts to each other. Are these expressions of love? Economic assistance to those whose well-being one cares most about? A bribe for attention and concern? I noted above that poorer individuals and families are more likely to get assistance than their richer relatives, which suggests at least some economic motivation behind these gifts. If government spending displaces private spending, then our earlier estimates in chapter 4 of the antipoverty effects of government spending are too high, because they fail to account for the expansion in private family support that would occur if government programs were cut.

In the mid-1930s, in the depth of the Great Depression, direct family transfers were larger than public assistance transfers.[16] Over the following years, government transfers became much larger than private transfers, but this is more because government transfers rose (from 3 percent to over 11 percent of family income) rather than because direct transfers fell (their importance decreased only slightly, from 6.5 percent to 5 percent of family income). One recent study tried to measure the impact of government programs on private family transfers. The results indicate that every dollar increase in AFDC benefits to single mothers and children results in a seventeen cent decrease in family assistance to these women, clearly indicating some displacement between government and family funds, but at a rate of 1 to 0.17 rather than dollar for dollar.[17]

Another study simulates the effect on direct private transfers of cutting all government spending to low-income families, using a variety of estimates of the response of family transfers to changes in government spending. This research also finds that transfers among family members would replace only a small fraction of government programs. The conclusion states, "Studies that implicitly assume no private-transfer response [to cuts in government spending] are likely to be very close to the mark."[18]

CHARITABLE GIVING TO NONPROFIT ORGANIZATIONS

Less has been written about the effect of government spending on donations to charitable service organizations than about direct family transfers. Some researchers have argued that cutting government support for antipoverty programs may not increase private philanthropy at all if government spending and charitable services complement rather than compete with each other. Since many charities provide services that supplement or complement those provided by the government, or act as partners in providing publicly funded services, cuts in government spending which reflect a desire to decrease certain services to the poor may result in declines in charitable contributions as well.[19]

Only one large study has looked at the responsiveness of donations to social service organizations to changes in government social spending. This research found that over the past forty years federal spending did displace charitable gifts to nonprofit organizations, with a loss of about thirty-eight cents for every dollar increase in federal spending.[20] State and local spending, however, had the opposite effect, with an eight-cent *increase* in charitable giving for every dollar increase in state or local spending. This is clearly related to the differing activities supported by state, local, and federal governments. Direct government cash support for the poor has the biggest displacement effect. Other forms of public support have either smaller displacement effects or complementary effects.

Another reason why cuts in government spending may not be easily replaced through increases in private charity is the heavy reliance of many private charities upon government funds for a substantial proportion of their revenues, as was discussed above. Cuts in government spending will reduce the revenue of many charitable organizations, making it hard for them to maintain their preexisting level of services, much less *increase* services for those whose public assistance has been cut.[21]

Overall, no estimate of the discouraging effect of government dollars on private spending comes close to suggesting that decreases in public spending on public assistance programs will be offset by equivalent increases in family-based or voluntary charitable contributions. If government spending on the poor declines, any resulting increase in private support will make up only a small fraction of the loss of government dollars.

A simple comparison of the magnitudes of government spending and private charitable spending indicates the impossibility of charitable contributions to replace cuts in public spending. Assume we eliminated AFDC, SSI, and Food Stamps, on which the government currently spends a total of $77 billion a year. Ignoring issues of service coordination, it seems reasonable to assume that it would cost the private sector approximately the same amount of money to provide these services. The last chapter showed that the share of expenses going into administrative costs was quite similar in public assistance programs and charitable organizations. In fact, private organizations would face fund-raising costs that the government tax system does not confront.

To replace this $77 billion through the religious community requires that every one of the 258,000 religious congregations (Catholic, Protestant, Jewish, Muslim, or otherwise) that exist in this country would have to raise an additional $300,000 per year in all future years. This is far above the average giving currently received by religious congregations, and would require every congregation to *triple* its pledges, and spend all of the increase on services for the poor.[22] Alternatively, if this giving is done through private charitable organizations that serve the poor, it would require those groups to raise over *seven times* more in private donations than they currently receive.

In addition, greater reliance on private giving would raise other concerns. Higher-income families would pay much less than lower-income families if antipoverty contributions were privatized. There are two reasons for this. Poor families are more likely to have low-income relatives, so that family support of the poor would place a heavier burden on lower- to middle-income families than on upper-income families. In addition, private charitable contributions to organizations that serve the poor tend to come more heavily from middle- and lower-income families. Upper-income families provide a larger share of their charitable contributions to private educational institutions or to artistic and cultural organizations, rather than to religious or service-provider organizations. In short, the more that one relies on private sector and voluntary contributions to assist the poor, the more this will result in extremely inequitable burdens that are not well matched with ability to pay.

Integrating Private Charity and Public Assistance

The private safety net in the United States is clearly important, even though it remains much smaller than public assistance, and provides substantial support to low-income families through family assistance and through nonprofit organizations. Given the presence of *both* private charity and large-scale government assistance programs, there are several ways in which these can most effectively work together.

First, as far as possible, government programs should encourage private efforts at support rather than discourage them. With regard to support of nonprofit service organizations, the best government encouragement of these efforts is the continued tax deductibility of charitable contributions.[23] With regard to direct transfers within families, this means that program rules should not penalize family gifts and assistance. For instance, within the AFDC program, if a woman reports assistance from other family members, her AFDC grant is reduced dollar for dollar, with the obvious result that few women tend to report such gifts. This discourages family assistance and encourages AFDC recipients to evade the rules. Treating family assistance differently than other forms of outside income may be one way to avoid this. As discussed in chapter 3, similar problems occur with child support, where fathers' contributions above fifty dollars per month provide no additional income for the children or their mother.[24]

Second, both government and nonprofit service organizations should view each other as allies and partners rather than competitors. On the government side this means designing programs that usefully forge public/nonprofit partnerships to utilize some of the unique advantages of each sector. The government often has a comparative advantage in enforcing overall standards, providing stable financing, and assuring evaluation of public assistance projects. But local organizations often can design specific programs for local clientele more effectively, and may operate them more efficiently as well. Such partnerships are already occurring in many areas, including the operation of homeless shelters in many cities, the rehabilitation of low-income housing by community-based organizations, and the provision of services for foster children.

Nonprofit service organizations, in turn, should strategize about how to complement government programs or provide services that the government cannot effectively provide. Some of this might involve services that fill gaps left by government programs. An example is food pantries or soup kitchens that provide short-term food assistance and that always face greater demands at the end of the month, when Food Stamps run short. Another role for nonprofit organizations is to provide longer-term connections and assistance that more narrowly defined government programs typically cannot. For instance, some organizations work to link people with public services, acting as a clearinghouse of information and assisting families in documenting their eligibility for particular programs. Other nonprofit organizations help to move those using emergency services, such as homeless shelters, into more permanent lodging or linking them with services that assist them in stabilizing their lives by addressing problems of drug or alcohol addiction. Finally, nonprofit organizations may have a particular advantage in contacting, motivating, and changing the lives of families who belong to particular ethnic, religious, or racial groups. Organizations such as immigrant aid societies or inner-city African American churches continue to help poor families, providing role models, information, and assistance to those who are members of their group.

It is appropriate that the public sector remain the primary source of assistance to the poor. But it is important that we recognize the efforts and the generosity of those who want to make additional contributions, providing assistance to other family members or helping to operate local programs that offer services that the government cannot provide as effectively.

5.3 STATES' RIGHTS VERSUS FEDERAL OVERSIGHT: WHAT IS THE APPROPRIATE ROLE FOR EACH LEVEL OF GOVERNMENT?

SUMMARY. *Throughout America's history, there has been an ongoing debate regarding the appropriate role of different levels of government. Those who argue for greater state discretion cite constitutional intention and the need for state and local discretion in program operation. They also claim that states may be more effective in operating programs. Those who argue for substantial federal involvement cite concerns about cross-state equity and an increasingly complex and mobile society that*

*fosters national rather than state identity. They also talk about the com-
parative advantage of the federal government in certain financing, oversight, and evaluation activities. Clearly, an appropriate* balance *among
federal and state governments is needed, and this balance may differ
between programs. The recent debate over block grants provides an example of these issues.*

Until the 1930s, virtually all government antipoverty programs were designed, funded, and operated at the city, county, or state level. In fact, in the
nineteenth century the federal government actively resisted responsibility
for any form of social service provision. In 1853 President Franklin Pierce
vetoed a bill authorizing federal money to buy land on which states could
establish insane asylums, with the firm declaration: "If Congress has the
power to make provisions for the indigent insane . . . it has the same power for
the indigent who are not insane. . . . I cannot find any authority in the Constitution for making the Federal Government the great almoner of public charity throughout the United States."[25] It took the severe economic depression of
the 1930s to break down the resistance to federal involvement in public assistance. When cities, counties, and states ran out of money to address problems
of extreme need, the federal government stepped in with national assistance
programs.

In the decades since the 1930s, the federal government has become increasingly involved in a wide range of public assistance programs, although in
many cases it shares responsibilities with states and localities.[26] Three key
program functions are typically shared across levels of government. These
include financing, policy design (including the design of program eligibility
rules, benefit payment rules, and/or the regulations under which services are
provided), and administration or operation of the program. Table 5.1 lists
some of the major public assistance programs and the extent to which these
three functions were under the control of local, state, or federal officials in the
mid-1990s. (The specific way in which each program operates was discussed
in chapter 3.) As the table indicates, many programs have relied in one way or
another upon all levels of government for their full operation.[27]

As table 5.1 indicates, virtually all public assistance programs are administered at the state or local level. But policy design and financing have been
broadly shared between the federal government and the states for some programs, or handled entirely at the federal level for others. Where there is joint
federal/state involvement, the federal government typically plays an oversight role on policy design, setting broad outlines for a program while states
fill in the details. Shared federal/state financing typically means some federal redistribution, with more federal funds going to those states whose own
revenue-raising capacity is lower (typically states that have larger poor
populations.)

TABLE 5.1
Division of Responsibility within Public Assistance Programs

	Policy Design	*Financing*	*Administration*
AFDC	Federal/state	Federal/state	State/local
SSI	Federal	Primarily federal	State/local
Food Stamps	Federal	Primarily federal	State/local
Medicaid	Federal/state	Federal/state	State
Housing programs	Primarily federal	Federal	Local
Job training	Federal/state/local	Federal/state	State/local
EITC	Federal	Federal	Federal (IRS)
Education	Primarily state/local	Primarily state/local	Local

Proposed legislative changes will shift responsibilities away from the federal government and toward state governments. Most notably, the federal government will lose much of its policy-setting role in the AFDC program with the advent of block grants, which give the states much greater discretion over how they provide income support for nonelderly, nondisabled individuals and families. With block grant funding, the federal government would still retain partial financing responsibility for these programs, however.

In general, there is no right answer to the question of which level of government should run which aspects of public assistance programs. Or, perhaps more accurately, the correct answer is, "It depends." It depends upon the nature of the program, the program's goals and purposes, and the historical setting out of which the program has emerged. Thus, some programs are validly more focused at the state or local level while others are more appropriately focused at the federal level. If one wants to provide national wage subsidies for less-skilled workers, then a program run through the national tax system, like the Earned Income Tax Credit, is likely to work best with federal financing, administration, and policy design. If one wants to run job training and placement programs, the design and the operation of these (though perhaps not their funding) is best done within local labor markets.

The real question is one of *balance*. There are virtually no people who want *all* antipoverty programs to be entirely federalized, and virtually no people who want *all* antipoverty programs entirely funded and operated at the state and local level. The debate should be over the appropriate mix.

This section discusses the appropriate role of the federal government in public assistance programs, laying out the particular advantages and disadvantages of the federal government versus state governments. There are some areas where the federal government has a clear comparative advantage in certain program functions and other areas where it does not. The last part of this section provides an example of these issues by discussing the block grant funding proposals that will expand state discretion over public assistance programs.

While this section focuses on federal/state decision making, it is worth noting that many of the issues discussed here have very close equivalents in a discussion of state versus county/local decision making. At one point in our history, the *county* or the *city* was considered the level of government responsible for public assistance programs. Almost everyone rejects this model today, recognizing the difficulties that counties and cities would have maintaining the funding base they need to run these programs on their own. Yet arguments about the appropriate role for cities and counties, relative to states, will probably intensify in the near future, if legislative changes give states greater control over certain programs and abolish federal mandates requiring that these programs be uniformly available throughout the state. Thus, we may see many of the arguments described here that relate to the appropriate division of responsibility between states and the federal government also emerge in the near future in the discussion about the appropriate division of responsibility between state and local governments.

Arguments for Greater State Discretion in Public Assistance Programs

Since the federal government runs very few programs, its role in program administration is not a point of contention. Conversely, most people agree that the federal government has to be involved in program financing (more on this later). Thus, most of the arguments are over who has primary policy-setting authority in these programs. Those who believe that the balance of power in the design of public assistance programs has tipped too far in the federal direction tend to make four arguments, all of which argue for less federal involvement in policy setting.

First, those who want more state control suggest that the right of states to determine their own programs supersedes that of the federal government. People who use this argument do not necessarily disagree with any of the obligations of the government to provide for the poor; they simply believe that the appropriate political entity within which these decisions should be made is the state and not the nation. Imbedded in this claim is typically a belief that state government is in closer touch with its citizens and that state policy is therefore more democratic and more responsive to citizen concerns. This position argues that the fundamental social contract within the United States—as the very name implies—exists at the state level, not the federal level.

Obviously, this argument has deep roots in U.S. history. The question of the nature of the federal contract versus the authority of the states has interested political theorists since James Madison wrote the *Federalist Papers*, and it was a key issue in America's Civil War. Those who support the more traditional view of the primacy of state authority are opposed by those who argue for an evolving contract between the states and the federal government. Proponents of this newer view claim that the economic and social changes in the United States over the last two hundred years, particularly the growing economic interdependence of states and the growing evolution of a national (rather than a state) identification among the American population, argue for a greater role for the federal government in the 1990s than was necessary one hundred or two hundred years ago.

Second, those who want more state control note that to operate effectively many public assistance programs must operate differently in different environments. Local economies differ, extent of urbanization differs, and cultures differ across regions in the United States. Uniform, federally set rules may be inappropriate when applied to the wide variety of situations and places within the United States. Thus, programs should be both designed and operated at the level closest to those who receive them.[28] (It is worth noting on table 5.1 that many programs allow some discretion in how program delivery and administration is set up at the state and local levels. Thus, even programs with substantial federal policy design and financing are typically administered locally.) This argument may actually create a presumption not for state, but for county and city-run programs, which would differ between urban, suburban, and rural areas.

Third, some argue that the current federal involvement in policy-setting has imposed undue budget costs on the states. In many cases, as table 5.1 indicates, the federal government is often involved in policy-setting that the state governments must actually implement. One result has been a proliferation in so-called unfunded mandates, which are program requirements imposed by the federal government that states must implement and help to fund. In the area of public assistance programs as well as in a number of other areas (such as environmental regulation or transportation policy), this has placed additional burdens on state budgets. If states must administer these programs, perhaps it is only fair that they make the primary policy decisions about how the programs will operate.

Even a quick survey of federal regulations and legislation over the last ten years indicates the validity of this concern. For instance, the Family Support Act imposed a wide variety of mandates on states to run employment programs for AFDC recipients. While the federal government provided matching funds for these programs, many states complained that the federal match was not adequate given the cost of the requirements. Of course, there are two ways to respond to this problem: one is to limit federal policy-setting authority in public assistance programs, the other is to require the federal government to provide funds to implement any requirements that they enact.

Fourth, some proponents of greater state control over public assistance programs argue that the federal government has simply been ineffective in running these programs and state governments can do better. In its boldest form, the argument suggests that existing antipoverty programs have not solved poverty, and the federal government has no good idea of how to make these programs more effective. In contrast, the states have been a laboratory for experiments with welfare-to-work programs, for attempts at more effective child support enforcement, and for innovative educational reform efforts. Out of this history, it is claimed, the states have shown themselves more effective at addressing the problems of poverty and should be given more authority to do so.

This claim validly recognizes the creative efforts of many states to experiment with different public assistance programs in recent years, and the extent to which experimentation with new programs is often best done at a more local or state level and through smaller "trial programs." On the other hand, many who argue this point of view tend to be quite selective in their examples and their memory when they claim that states are more effective in general in providing services.[29] In fact, in the 1960s it was evidence of widespread exclusion and racism in state operations of public assistance programs that created the impetus for expanded federal rule making and control. There are enormous differences between states in the effectiveness with which they operate programs, and it is not at all clear that a thorough review of the past twenty to thirty years would indicate that state-designed programs have been in any way more effective or more efficient in meeting their goals than federally designed programs. As discussed in the last chapter, federal quality control regulations and federal incentives for states to modernize their public assistance procedures have been very important in pushing states to administer these programs in a more accurate and a more coordinated manner.

The Comparative Advantage of the Federal Government

What are the responding arguments by those who believe that the federal government should be integrally involved in designing how public assistance programs work? There are at least four major arguments.

First, the federal government is the only entity that can assure equivalent public assistance programs are available to all citizens regardless of where they live. If one takes seriously the claim that all poor members of a society should have access to similar public assistance programs, this is a strong mandate in favor of federal involvement in program rule-setting. This viewpoint obviously assumes that the appropriate decision-making entity for public assistance programs is the federal government, directly contradicting those who argue that the primary social contract exists at the state level.

The recent debate over changes in the Food Stamp program exemplifies this argument. As discussed earlier, Food Stamps are the only public assistance program that is nationally available to all low-income Americans. There is no other program with standardized, uniform national rules, available to all persons in households below a certain income level regardless of family composition or behavior. This unique role for Food Stamps is one of the primary reasons why proposals to turn it over to the states drew such protests in the recent congressional debate on welfare reform.[30] If policy making authority over Food Stamps were transferred to the states (which means the end of its entitlement status guaranteeing similar assistance to all families below a given income level), there would be no national safety net.

There is substantial disagreement in this country about whether nationally designed programs are desirable. On the one hand, we seem quite willing to run such programs in some areas. For instance, no one has proposed turning SSI back to the states (or for that matter, Social Security) and abolishing its uniform national rules. Other programs are much more controversial; reformers who value the equity provided by nationally designed programs have regularly proposed setting national benefit standards in the AFDC program rather than allowing states to determine benefit standards. Recent legislative proposals to remove many federal requirements on cash assistance payments to single-parent families indicate the depth of opposition to this idea.

A second argument suggests that the move to greater federal involvement simply reflects the changing nature of American society, in which the appropriate level of decision making has broadened over time. It is true that the federal government has become more and more involved in decisions that were once state based, but this growth in federal responsibilities reflects other changes. The technologies that have made instantaneous communication possible have increased people's awareness and involvement in concerns far outside their own local community. The increasingly complex economy in which we live and the ongoing growth in businesses that operate across state and national boundaries has meant that virtually all state economies are closely intertwined with the national and even global economy.

Finally, along with these changes have come fundamental changes in people's connectedness to particular places. While many Americans continue to live close to where they grew up, an increasing number do not. Family mobility across state lines is extremely common in the 1990s, but was relatively uncommon a century ago. All of these changes suggest that our sense of community has enlarged geographically.

In the face of these changes, it may be entirely apt that the level of decision making and resource redistribution has increasingly shifted from a state to a national level. Proponents of this argument believe that more traditional views of states rights have become outmoded over time. This is not a trend limited to antipoverty programs but is visible across a range of issues, from national meat inspection standards to pollution control laws to automobile safety regulations. To return to a world where public assistance programs are viewed as a state rather than a national problem ignores a host of long-term economic and social changes that have created an increasingly interlinked economy and culture in the United States.

Third, the federal government has a comparative advantage in certain program oversight and evaluation functions. Three are typically mentioned.

a. *Compared to fifty separate state jurisdictions, the federal government can enforce the collection of comparable information on how programs are being run.* The federal government has long imposed uniform reporting standards that make it possible to compare state program operations. We would know virtually nothing about AFDC programs if it were left to fifty state reporting systems. Or, perhaps more accurately, we would have little information that was comparable across states. In order to understand how programs operate, whom they serve, and how effectively they serve people, comparable data on program operations must be available. The U.S. federal government has led the way in the collection of usable and timely data on program operations. Our national data collection systems are often used as a model by other countries.

b. *Without necessarily making explicit decisions about how funds should be spent, the federal government can monitor whether larger program goals are being met by state programs.* This need not require detailed federal involvement in program design. A model of this is the involvement of the federal government in the JTPA job training program described in chapter 3. Although each locality decides on the nature of the training and placement programs available in their own JTPA program, the federal government requires that localities meet certain goals relating to the need levels of persons admitted into JTPA programs, the number of people completing such programs, and the number employed after completing the program. Localities can run any program they want, but they have to serve low-income adults, and they have to retain and place a certain share of these clients. Otherwise, federal funding is threatened. These sort of federal mandates enforce program performance without enforcing standardized program design.

c. *Finally, because they don't actually manage most public assistance programs, the federal government plays a key role in encouraging evaluation.* Throughout the past decade, the federal government has approved a wide variety of so-called waivers on federal rules, so states could operate programs somewhat differently from federal requirements. But the federal government required that these innovations tried by the states be seriously and rigorously evaluated, so that their effectiveness was known. The states and localities that actually run the programs often have few incentives to evaluate their own programs; politically, it is dangerous to run the risk that an evaluation may show a program to be ineffective. People who run programs have a strong tendency to give themselves and their programs positive evaluations. Only those who are somewhat distant from the day-to-day operation of the program can enforce honest evaluations.

Some supporters of greater state discretion in the design of public assistance programs claim this is a way to truly experiment with a wide variety of antipoverty programs. This is true *only* if these programs are evaluated in an honest and believable way, so that we can actually learn something about what works and what does not. Good evaluation requires both resources and impartiality. The departments that actually run programs typically see little reason to spend scarce resources on evaluations and often do not have the impartiality to do their own evaluation. The federal government can be crucial in assuring that this happens.

Fourth, the federal government has a comparative advantage in helping finance public assistance programs. In the recent debate over the advantages of devolving more program authority to the state level, it is striking how solid the support for ongoing federal financing remains.

The federal government has widely-recognized advantages in the financing of public assistance programs that states do not have. One of the fundamental aspects of public assistance programs is that they require *greater* funds in bad economic times. This poses financing problems, since rising unemployment and falling incomes typically reduce tax revenue. But these problems also produce growing need levels and a greater demand for public assistance. Thus, public assistance programs are inherently *countercyclical*, that is, they move in the opposite direction from the business cycle. They require more public money to operate at exactly the time when less public money is available.

The federal government can deal with this problem in two ways. At any point in time, the federal government is able to redistribute funds across states, so that states facing economic difficulties receive more federal funds than states with strong economies. Many programs split costs between the federal government and states according to a formula that provides a larger federal share for poorer states and a lower federal share for richer states.

In addition, over the business cycle the federal government has the ability to issue debt and provide countercyclical financing. In contrast, most states operate under balanced budget amendments; in bad economic times, when unemployment rises and personal incomes decline, state tax revenues fall. To balance the budget, states typically have to cut other programs and are in no position to expand public assistance programs as the need expands. Only the federal government can actually run stable public assistance programs, providing more funds in bad economic times (whether or not matched by federal savings in good economic times). As the experience of the Great Depression showed, when city and state budgets run dry and economic need is at its highest, only the federal government has the ability to step in and continue public assistance.

None of these arguments indicate that *only* the federal government should be responsible for public assistance programs, but they suggest that there may be an appropriate mix of federal, state, and local decision-making that involves all of these levels. Indeed, as table 5.1 indicates, this is already true for many programs, although it is quite possible that the current mix of responsibilities in some programs is not well balanced and needs review.

An Example: Block Grant Proposals

The legislative changes in public assistance programs enacted in the mid-1990s provoked a debate over federal/state responsibilities with regard to public assistance. A number of programs with substantial federal involvement in their design have been turned over to state authority, to be redesigned at will. The primary ongoing role of the federal government in these programs is block grant funding, providing a lump sum of money to the states which they can use in any way on programs fitting within the broadly designated area of the block grant. This section discusses two of these block grants, involving quite different programs.

Initially in this discussion, I focus solely on issues of state/federal decision making and avoid the issue of funding levels. However, the financing changes imbedded in these block grants may be even more important than the changes in policy design and authority, and I return to them below.

The Child Care block grant takes the four major child care funding assistance programs, along with a number of smaller programs (costing less than $2 billion in total), abolishes them as separate programs, and establishes a single block grant to the states with this money. The states are required to spend these funds on child care programs for low-income families, but have complete discretion over designing the programs to be funded. The Temporary Assistance to Needy Families (TANF) block grant abolishes the $25 billion AFDC program and turns this money over to the states to use in assisting low-income families. (There are some ongoing federal requirements on states in this block grant).

The child care block grant replaces a number of small programs, some of which provide child care assistance to specific targeted groups (such as mothers on AFDC who find employment) and some of which provide more general child care funds that can be applied for by organizations serving low-income families. For years, those involved in local child care issues have complained about the intricate knowledge needed by providers and parents to identify programs and funds for which they might be eligible, and the different eligibility requirements across programs. Many of the specific child care programs currently run by the federal government almost surely have too many detailed allocation rules written at a national level, without enough discretion to let them be easily used by a diverse set of local child care programs. In this case, the block grant approach which allows states to provide more unified and simplified programs may better meet the need for child care subsidies among poor families.

Of course, the child care block grant assumes that states will be able to design and operate more streamlined programs, an assumption that remains to be tested. Indeed, the special interests that created a plethora of separate child care funding programs at the federal level might be just as effective in duplicating this system at the state level. For instance, the abolishment of child care programs targeted at particular groups means that these groups will no longer have a guarantee of funds, unless states choose to continue federal allocation schemes. This is likely to produce state-level lobbying by representatives of these groups to continue their priority status for child care funds.

The replacement of AFDC by the TANF block grant raises far more serious questions, many of them relating to the comparative advantages of the federal versus state and local governments. Eliminating significant federal involvement and oversight by abolishing the national AFDC program, which is received by a high share of poor single mothers in this country, may create a number of problems. First, the freedom of states, at their discretion, to run (or not run) a cash support program for single mothers with children raises serious equity issues. Do we as a nation want to refuse cash assistance to some mothers and children simply because they live in a state that has decided it does not want or cannot afford such a program? At least to some, the possibility of seriously limited cash support in some states (as opposed to allowing state variations in these programs) raises serious concerns about social justice.

Second, if the differences in public assistance programs become larger across states, as many expect, this could cause cross-state responses. Fearing in-migration of poor families, states which initially wanted to maintain existing levels of support might feel forced to lower their support if the states around them cut assistance, a phenomenon that has been referred to as a "race to the bottom."[31] Indeed, it is a standard result in economic theory that when public services are provided at a subnational level, there is often a tendency to "underprovide" because of interstate competition and cross-state migration problems.[32]

Third, abolishing federal oversight of AFDC programs will not necessarily promise more efficient or effective state programs. Validly, many states argue that federal regulations in AFDC have multiplied and that a major review of these regulations is long overdue. This is different, however, from eliminating federal oversight of the program. While the states could be given much more discretion over determining and enforcing eligibility rules for AFDC, over the years federal insistence on consistent treatment of all applicants, administrative efficiency, and work requirements for work-ready recipients has pushed many states to run more effective programs than they would on their own. More than many other programs, the AFDC program provides examples of the *usefulness* of certain forms of federal oversight. Eliminating most federal oversight because of dissatisfaction with some of it is akin to throwing the baby out with the bathwater.

In short, turning the complex, large, and cyclical AFDC program over to states through a block grant may create more difficult problems than combining the large number of relatively small child care funding programs into a block grant and giving states discretion over this money. As long as the federal government continues to fund programs, it has the right and responsibility to assure that these programs are well run. While in many cases there has been too much hands-on micro-management by the federal government, the solution to this problem is not to eliminate all federal oversight, but to be more balanced about the division of responsibilities between federal and state governments. *Both* have useful roles to play in the provision of public assistance.

The shifts these block grants would produce in federal and state program authority is an important part of their expected impact. But their funding changes would also be very important and cannot be divorced from the expected impact of block grant legislation. There are two major funding changes imbedded in most block grant proposals: First, they provide a fixed amount of federal money to the states, as opposed to the current system of matching funds that increase when state expenditures increase. Existing programs require that the states match the federal contribution at a certain level in order to receive it. Greater state contributions elicit more federal dollars. The block grants provide no incentives for states to put their own money into these programs, and they provide the same amount of federal money regardless of what the states spend. This means that if need in a state increases (through migration or demographic changes), the states must bear the entire brunt of increased costs by either expanding their expenditures or cutting the program.

In addition, these fixed levels of federal funding in the TANF block grant to replace AFDC may cause serious financial problems for states over the economic cycle. The number of people eligible for AFDC varies with the economic cycle, as unemployment rates rise and fall. More unemployment means more people need assistance. Faced with fixed levels of federal block grant money, states may have to cut eligibility or benefits in cash assistance programs during economic downturns in order to maintain their balanced budgets—just the time when need for the program is the greatest.

Second, in addition to fixed federal funding, in most cases the new block grants would also involve *less* federal funding than was previously available. This reduction in federal funds means states that want to simply continue their existing programs would be unable to do so without increased state allocations. To continue existing programs, money would have to be redirected from other state programs into public assistance, or additional state revenues must be raised. Given the tightness of most state budgets and the resistance to tax increases among voters, virtually all observers expect that such block grants would lead to deep cuts over time in the programs that become block granted. Some critics have suggested that the argument that block grants will increase state authority is a smokescreen for the real agenda of those proposing these block grants at the national level, namely, they want to deeply cut these programs and this is an effective way to indirectly make that happen.

As TANF replaces AFDC, state budget officers may face particular difficulties funding work programs for single parents receiving cash assistance. While cutting federal oversight in many areas, the proposed federal legislation strengthens federal mandates in this area, requiring that states have at least 50 percent of their cash assistance caseload in work-related activities by the beginning of the century. Running work programs is not cheap; in fact, it is generally more expensive to run job placement programs and to monitor work behavior among recipients than to simply provide monthly checks. This new 50 percent mandate demands a level of state commitment to job programs that is far beyond past requirements (the JOBS program required that 20 percent of the caseload be in work-related programs in 1995). It will take more money and more effort on the part of states to meet expanded mandates. The TANF block grant dollars from the federal government, however, provide no additional funds to help states meet this requirement.

My own sense is that the potential budget problems that these block grants would create for the states, given their reduced level of federal funding and the abolishment of the matching provisions, will be far more important in shaping future program design than the fact that policy-setting authority has shifted to the state level. A few of the larger states with stable budgets would use their new authority in creative and potentially useful ways to improve the design of public assistance programs. But for most states, the budget cuts will mean that the key question facing them is not "How can we run these programs more effectively?" but "How can we cut existing programs enough to avoid having to put additional state resources into them?" Should this occur, then the move to block grants and greater state authority has the potential for long-term disastrous consequences among many low-income families whose current budgets are already stretched too tightly.

The Movement toward Targeted Programs

PRESIDENT Bill Clinton's famous pledge to "end welfare as we know it" initiated a convulsion of legislative reform efforts. After the midyear elections in the fall of 1994, when both houses of Congress shifted to Republican control, the discussion of welfare reform exploded in a variety of directions. Not only did the congressional Republicans propose a large number of changes in public assistance programs, but the growing group of Republican governors also became increasingly involved in these proposals.

The changes to public assistance programs that were finally enacted in 1996 promise to move these programs in three directions. First, these changes would continue the movement away from broad-based programs toward more targeted programs that link public assistance with behavioral mandates or that limit services to more narrowly defined population groups. Second, a substantial reduction in federal oversight and involvement would occur in many programs. Third, federal support for public assistance programs would be cut disproportionately more than support for other federal programs. This is partly a response to the perceived ineffectiveness of these programs and partly a reflection of the fact that they have had less political support than other potential targets for deficit reduction.

The first three chapters of this book described the changes of the past several decades—demographic changes, economic changes, and policy changes—that lie behind current discussions of welfare reform. The fourth and fifth chapters provided evidence on the effects of existing public assistance programs and discuss the key role played by the public sector in assisting low-income families.

Chapters 6 and 7 move from analysis to an explicit discussion of current policy recommendations. This chapter uses the economic, demographic, and political changes of the past decade to understand the current direction of policy change. The next chapter provides concrete suggestions for policy design and implementation.

The current thrust of policy reform is to target existing programs more narrowly, limiting whom they serve, emphasizing services and noncash support over cash assistance, and demanding that recipients satisfy particular behavioral requirements. Thus, cash support for single parents becomes time limited and is strongly linked to work behavior. Job training programs provide different services to people who fit different demographic categories. Immigrant eligibility for a host of programs is restricted.

The implications of this movement toward more targeted and behaviorally linked programs are not well understood. There is much more discussion in the academic literature about the impact of broad-based cash support programs, or even about the impact of universal income assistance programs (provided to *all* citizens rather than just low-income citizens) than there is discussion of targeted programs. This chapter attempts to fill this gap. In the first section I discuss why policy has evolved in this direction in the United States; in the second section I indicate the advantages, disadvantages, and implications of more targeted programs; and in the third section I show how to effectively operate such programs using a variety of recent examples. The latter section should be particularly useful to state policymakers who are in the midst of revising their own mix of public assistance programs.

Overall, this chapter concludes with the opinion that targeted programs have some real advantages. We have clear evidence that many of these programs produce measurable gains for their participants. The last twenty years of experience has provided useful information on how to run such programs effectively. On the other hand, by their very nature, such programs tend to be limited and, while their benefits are real, the gains they generate for individuals are typically modest. Not one of these programs by itself is going to "solve poverty" among its recipients. Such programs also increase the demands on the public sector for coordinated and effective public sector management, and will not cost any less than more broad-based programs.

In short, we should not expect that the movement toward targeted programs is going to produce more dramatic declines in poverty than we have seen in the past. But neither is an increased emphasis on more targeted programs necessarily the disaster that some critics predict. Much depends on the mix of programs that are provided, how effectively they operate, and how many people they serve. In general, given the modest potential of targeted programs, their expansion (no matter how well run) is not likely to offset the higher long-run poverty rates that are caused by continuing deterioration of labor-market opportunities for less-skilled workers.

6.1 POLICY LESSONS

SUMMARY. *This section presents four lessons about the direction of reform in public assistance programs. First, economic growth is not likely to be effective in the near future in reducing poverty. Second, broad cash transfers are even less popular now than in the recent past. Third, over time, this has resulted in greater and greater emphasis on the use of targeted programs as our primary antipoverty device. This includes both a narrowing of broad-based public assistance programs to include more behavioral requirements and a growing emphasis on programs designed to provide specific goods or services to limited groups among the poor. Fourth, the probability that broad-based redistribution or universalistic programs will reemerge in the near future is very low. Discussions of targeted programs have dominated welfare reform debates over the past fifteen years and this emphasis is likely to continue into the near future.*

This section presents four lessons that emerge from the preceding five chapters of the book. These lessons describe where we are now in the conversation about poverty and policy, and how we got there. The main conclusion is that large-scale redistributive programs are not likely to be on the political agenda within the foreseeable future. Instead, the focus is on more narrowly based programs that provide services to particular groups, or that tie economic support to specific behaviors.

Lesson 1. *Poverty is harder to address through broad-based economic growth policies now than thirty years ago.* Economic growth, which in the past particularly helped low-income families, has recently been a less effective tool for bringing people out of poverty. While it used to be true that a rising (economic) tide lifted all boats, this has not been true for the past 15 years. This is not because economic growth no longer produces more jobs; indeed, the overall expansion in employment and jobs has been as strong as ever during recent periods of economic growth, leading to substantial increases in work among low-income families as unemployment falls. Growing employment has become less effective in bringing down poverty rates, however, for two reasons. First, changes in the jobs available to low-skilled workers have made those jobs less effective in helping people escape poverty. Second, the growth in the single-parent population limits the effectiveness of employment as an antipoverty strategy. Let us explore each of these reasons, in turn.

Changes in the jobs available to less-skilled workers have made those jobs less effective in helping people escape poverty. While economic growth continues to create jobs and employment opportunities, the wages that come with those jobs aren't what they used to be. As discussed in chapter 2, wages for less-skilled men (men with a high school degree or less) have declined substantially over the past fifteen years. Wages for less-skilled women have declined less, but remain at extremely low levels. Possibilities for wage advancement, as well as the availability of nonwage benefits (like pensions and health insurance) on these jobs have also declined. Because of this, employment growth alone has not been sufficient to bring down the poverty rate. Expansions in jobs and employment in recent years have been offset by declines in wages.

The rising share of single parents among the poor means that employment alone will not be as effective in reducing poverty. Single parents face more constraints in their lives: they must assume substantial child raising and child care responsibilities that may limit their available energy and time for paid work; even when they work, they often must pay child care expenses that decrease their take-home pay; because most single parents are less-skilled women, they are likely to get jobs with lower wages than equivalent men, and few opportunities for promotion. Full-time work is thus both more difficult for many single mothers, and the rewards of full-time work are less. They cannot do what many married couples do, and spread the risk of unemployment and low earnings as well as the responsibilities of child raising between two adults. In a single-parent family, when that parent loses her job, family earnings go to zero; in a two-parent family, even if one parent becomes unemployed, the other parent can still bring in income. Even if the economic opportunities for less-skilled workers had not changed over the last thirty years, the growth in single-parent families would have made economic growth and increased employment a less effective strategy to fight poverty.

The decline in the effectiveness of economic growth as a tool to combat poverty creates serious political problems for those who want to reduce poverty in the United States. Economic growth is a win/win solution, since both the poor and the nonpoor gain from overall economic expansion. Poverty falls *and* incomes rise among the nonpoor as well. All other antipoverty efforts require up-front government spending and redistributive taxation from upper and middle-income to poor families. In an era where budgets are being cut and tax increases are considered political suicide, pursuing these alternatives is increasingly hard.

The loss of economic growth as a viable antipoverty solution in the recent past and the foreseeable future has added to the frustration about the persistence of poverty. In part, because things *have* gotten better in recent economic expansions for many better-educated workers (particularly those with professional degrees), this group often does not fully understand the realities of the low-wage labor market and why the decline in unemployment during recent spurts of economic growth hasn't decreased poverty. The tendency is to interpret the problem as one of individual behavior—the poor are simply not working or not working enough—without understanding that the advice to "Get a job" isn't as useful as it once was. All of this creates difficult political challenges for those who argue for increased spending on antipoverty programs to offset these economic changes.

Lesson 2. *An alternative broad-based policy, namely, widespread cash transfer programs, has never been generally supported in the United States (except for limited groups) and is under increasing attack.* An alternative way to address poverty problems on a broad scale is to provide cash transfers to low-income families. We could do like the countries shown in figure 4.1, where few families have very low incomes relative to the average family income level. Countries that provide more extensive transfer programs have lower poverty counts than countries that don't. Even within the United States, the steady decline in poverty among the elderly is largely the result of our willingness to provide cash assistance for that population if not for any other. From an implementation point of view, the government has a great deal of experience and is generally effective at implementing and administering a program that writes checks, based on well-defined and verifiable eligibility criteria.

Broad-based cash redistribution requires broad-based social consensus about its necessity, however. And that social consensus in this country has eroded, as indicated by steady declines in AFDC benefits, and increasing criticism of cash assistance as having undesirable behavioral side effects. There are many reasons for the erosion of this social consensus.

First, support for cash transfers to the poor has never been very strong in this country. We never have had extensive cash assistance programs for any group, except the current elderly. A wide variety of writers have speculated on why Americans, unlike Europeans, have always resisted a more expansive welfare state.[1] Among the possible reasons: the immigrant history of the United States has created a collective memory in which many families escape poverty without public assistance; this is reinforced by the enormous geographic and economic expansion experienced in the United States over the two hundred years of its history, leading to much more economic mobility than in other countries; the changing ethnic and racial diversity in the United States has led to an underlying dynamic of suspicion in American political life about "the other" in American society, typically those who look, dress, or speak differently (often the most recent immigrant group and always African Americans); in addition, corruption in government's use of veterans payments in the last century, at both the national and local level, created an aura of fraud around government-run cash assistance programs that has continued even as the memories of that particular incident have faded.

Second, twenty years of a more cyclical economy and more uncertain and stagnant incomes have made middle-income Americans less willing to accept the tax costs of broad-based redistribution. The historical economic transition that dominates our thinking is that which brought the United States from the Great Depression, through World War II, and into the boom years of the 1950s and 1960s. This enormous economic expansion created expectations about future growth that were unreasonable, but which nonetheless produced a sense of profound economic disappointment in Americans when they were not met in the 1970s and 1980s. There is a recent "golden era" to which we long to return. Most evidence suggests that the 1950s and 1960s were atypical economic times, when a large number of U.S. manufacturing firms had monopoly control over world markets following World War II. As we move into a more competitive global economy, our expectations have yet to adjust to reality. But the economic disappointment and frustration felt by many Americans shapes our political landscape, so that promises of lower taxes, higher growth, and greater competitiveness—however ill-conceived or unrealistic—have a political saliency for many voters. Calls for higher taxes and greater redistributive spending must fight against the sense that "times are hard" compared to what many middle-income families expected.

Third, in recent years the poor have been more easily stigmatized as the "other"—another race, another group, those who behave differently. The rising share of immigrants in the country over the last decade contributes to this. As in all past periods, recent immigrant groups are disproportionately blamed for social problems. It is not by chance that recent legislative changes limit eligibility for public assistance among legal immigrants.

Most important, the enormous attention and media visibility given to urban ghetto poverty has created an image of poverty in many American minds that equates "poor" with unmarried, not working, and/or violent. Given our racial history, it is also not surprising that this dominant image of poverty typically has a black face, as well. As discussed above, this image does not describe the majority of the poor (nor the majority of black poor). By focusing on the small numbers of the poor who are cocaine addicted, or violent, or regularly involved in crime, the impression left by many media articles in the mind of middle America is that those who are poor are morally and behaviorally deficient. Most Americans are surprised to learn that poor single mothers receive *less* cash assistance than twenty years ago, and work more. Given these inaccurate images, the political success of efforts to cut cash assistance and increase work requirements is not surprising.

Fourth, growing economic divisions (that overlap with growing racial and ethnic divisions) between upper and lower income workers also add to this tension. Those who benefited from economic stability and growth during the expansions of the 1980s and 1990s don't understand the frustration of those whose economic experiences were the opposite. In the 1992 presidential election, Bill Clinton won in part because he clearly spoke to this difference and persuaded those who felt they had "lost out" that he understood their situation better than his opponent. As economic realities diverge among different groups in the economy, there is less sympathy and less understanding of the problems facing low-income families by those in decision-making positions.

For these reasons and for others, cash assistance has fallen in political acceptability. We are less willing to provide broad-based income support that can be spent at the discretion of recipients. Rightly or wrongly, our suspicions of the poor have increased, and our willingness to provide assistance with no strings attached has shrunk.

An example of the unpopularity of cash redistribution programs can be seen in the failure of recent efforts to put Child Support Assurance (CSA) on the national agenda. CSA is a proposal to assure that children in single-parent families receive child support by guaranteeing $2,000 to $2,500 per child per year. Monthly checks would be sent to all single-parent families by the government, which in turn would collect the money back from absent fathers through a centralized child support system. If fathers could not be located or could not pay this much per child, the government would pay the difference. This program would essentially provide a guaranteed income support level to low-income single-parent families, with some of the money coming from private funds (from noncustodial parents) and some from government funds.

Proposals to enact a national csa system have received a great deal of attention in the research community, largely due to extensive efforts to design and investigate the potential effects of such a system by social scientist Irwin Garfinkel and other colleagues.[2] David Ellwood's popular book from the mid-1980s, *Poor Support*, called for the implementation of csa and a variety of child and policy-advocacy groups have promoted its feasibility.[3] In the recent round of welfare reform legislation, however, this program did not appear in any of the major proposals. Even within the Clinton administration, where several key advisers had a strong interest in children's poverty issues, the supporters of csa lost the debate. Not only did csa appear to be too much of a "big money" welfare program, but there was no political support for it among any of the key political groups in Congress or among the governors. A broad-based cash transfer program—even when linked with child support payments—was not viable.

Lesson 3. *If economic growth is no longer an effective antipoverty strategy, and if broad-based cash redistribution programs are less politically acceptable than ever, the remaining set of policy options involve targeted programs, aimed at particular groups among the poor and/or focused on particular behaviors.* Since the election of Ronald Reagan as president, the political debate over public assistance programs has focused on questions like "Who should we include and exclude from this program?" "How do we link this assistance more closely with work or other forms of appropriate behavior?" or "How do we provide this group of services most efficiently?" All of these are policy questions about targeted programs, not questions about broad-based support programs. This is in sharp contrast to the 1960s and 1970s, when the idea of a guaranteed minimum income (provided through general cash transfers) received a great deal of attention as a replacement for the plethora of existing smaller and more targeted programs. This proposal came close to becoming national policy during the Nixon administration.

Targeted programs are of two types, as we discuss more extensively in the next section. They include programs that provide general economic support but link that support to specific behavioral requirements (behaviorally linked support programs). For instance, the eitc provides earnings supplements, but the amount received depends upon work effort. In-kind programs limit assistance to approved forms of consumption, such as buying food or housing. Other types of targeted programs provide specific services (targeted service programs), such as job training, compensatory education, or immunization. If broad-based cash transfers provide general income support to low-income families, with eligibility based largely on total income levels, targeted assistance programs provide either a targeted set of services or link general support to behavior as well as income.

One could argue that the afdc program by the mid-1990s was no longer a broad-based cash assistance program for poor families with children, and had essentially become a behaviorally linked support program. It was increasingly tied to specific behavioral objectives. A growing number of states were discussing or had already enacted provisions to reduce AFDC benefits to families if children are not immunized, teenagers are not in school, or unmarried mothers become pregnant. Most obviously, AFDC receipt had been increasingly tied to participation in job search and training programs, so that cash support was received only in conjunction with work or training. New requirements to increase the share of cash assistance recipients in work-related activities will only increase these restrictions.

The next section of this chapter discusses the advantages and disadvantages of targeted programs, and the last section discusses how to run such programs most effectively. Per person served, these targeted programs are typically more expensive to run than cash transfers both because they require more oversight (one has to observe behavior as well as income eligibility) and because they often require the explicit provision of services to participants (one must actually *operate* preschool programs or homeless shelters and pay wages to doctors, teachers, counselors, etc). Higher expenses occur both via higher monetary costs as well as through the need for more extensive and careful public management and program administration skills. Of course, if such policies are effective, their promise is that they will reduce the problem on which they are targeted. In addition, the total cost of targeted programs is often less because they are typically not available to all who qualify (i.e., they are not entitlements), and usually serve much smaller groups among the poor.

There is a temptation to claim for targeted programs what has often been claimed for broader-based programs, namely, that they will address the root causes of poverty among a substantial group of the poor. So the arguments go: if we expand job placement programs for AFDC women, we will substantially reduce single-parent poverty; if we make sure all at-risk children are in Head Start programs, we will reduce basic literacy problems among teenagers; if we expand medical insurance, all children will receive adequate medical care. But each of these programs is designed to affect only a narrow set of problems; alone, none of these programs is likely to make a major dent in the aggregate poverty problem, although each may have useful effects for its recipients. While some programs are more broadly useful than others, the very nature of more targeted efforts is that they focus on particular problems among particular populations. Hence, multiple targeted programs are necessary to produce a broad-based attack on poverty.

Lesson 4. *The near-term prospects for the enactment of new broad-based antipoverty programs or universalist programs of social assistance are virtually zero. While such programs have been the focus of many academic discussions of antipoverty efforts over the past three decades, far too little attention has been paid to the policy implications of expanding narrower, more targeted programs.* Most of the past three decades of intellectual discussion about how to solve poverty has focused on *expanded* and more broad-based public assistance programs. Fewer commentators have discussed the implications of a narrower and more targeted system of antipoverty programs (the biggest exception to this is the last decade of conversation about the effects of welfare-to-work programs). As a result, the implications of the current direction in policy are not well understood.

Throughout the decades of the 1960s and 1970s, the "cutting edge" reform proposal was the Negative Income Tax, which would give cash assistance through the tax system to all low-income families, with a sliding scale that provided more support for those with lower incomes. Other proposals advocated uniform national AFDC benefit levels, or guaranteed child care subsidies (or the construction of public child care centers) for working poor families. All of these proposals supported national programs with uniform standards of assistance (usually cash) for large groups of eligible individuals. In contrast, the standard academic analysis of in-kind or targeted programs has typically been very critical. These sort of programs, it is claimed, limit the choices of recipients, are inefficient to run compared to general cash transfers, are more inequitable, and are less effective in providing a safety net.

Some went even further and called not for broad-based antipoverty programs, but for *universalist* public transfer programs, modeled on Social Security.[4] Such programs provide assistance to all citizens, regardless of income. Examples of universalist programs that have been proposed include nationalized or universally available health insurance, guaranteeing some level of health insurance for all Americans, and (not coincidentally) assuring that the working poor are no longer uninsured. Another frequent proposal is a family allowance plan, whereby each family with children receives a check from the government for a certain amount per child. For low-income families, this establishes a minimum available income. (A number of European countries have family allowances.) Child Support Assurance is also a universalist program, guaranteeing a minimal level of child support to all single mothers (paid by the government if the father is unable or unwilling to pay), regardless of the mother's own earnings and income.

The advantage claimed for universalist programs is that they generate broad-based political support among families at all income levels, since everyone receives benefits from them. At the same time, even though only a small share of their expenditures may be received by the poor, this can still make a significant difference to the total income available to low-income families. For instance, although only 5 percent of Social Security benefits go to poor elderly persons, the expansions in Social Security over the past three decades have been crucial in reducing elderly poverty.[5] Universalist programs attack poverty only indirectly. Because they provide benefits to all citizens, this keeps them from being thought of as "welfare programs." Their supporters claim this guarantees political support for high benefit levels that, at the end of the day, do much to help the poor.

Universalist assistance programs require large public expenditures, typically at the federal level. In many cases, this means higher federal tax rates. This is supportable, argue their proponents, because such programs would visibly return income or services to most families. While broad-based anti-poverty programs involve much lower expenditures than universalist programs, they still require a large and visible budget allocation at the federal level, but only a limited number of taxpayers receive their benefits.

Within the foreseeable future, neither broad-based cash transfer programs nor universalist programs are on the U.S. political agenda, for at least three reasons. *First, the strong concern with the federal deficit and the resulting demand to contain federal spending to address this problem, make it almost impossible to believe that political support can be generated for new big-budget social spending programs in the near future.* The failure of Child Support Assurance to emerge as part of the current welfare reform debate is but one example. The recent largely failed debate over health care reform provides further evidence: the large federal costs involved in President Clinton's proposed health care system, involving substantial public funding in conjunction with an ongoing privately provided health care system, was one of (admittedly many) reasons why this plan ultimately failed.

Those who point to Food Stamps (as model of a nationally provided broad-based antipoverty program) or to Social Security (as a model of a successful universalist program) typically forget that these programs started very small. When enacted, there was little expectation that they would grow to anything like their current size. When Social Security was enacted in 1935, it covered only some workers and provided quite limited benefits. As late as 1955, twenty years after Social Security was established, it accounted for only 6 percent of all federal expenditures, a sharp contrast to its current role as the single biggest federal expenditure item at 22 percent of total federal outlays. Similarly, Food Stamps was enacted as a way to expand a surplus commodity distribution program. In its first six years, it never exceeded three-tenths of one percent of the federal budget. (Even now, it accounts for only 1.7 percent of the budget, although it is the largest federal antipoverty program except Medicaid.)

Broad-based programs that start as small expenditures, but grow over time, provide a very different model than is typically advocated by those who want to enact large-budget programs in one legislative stroke. In fact, there are very few examples (except in wartime) where Congress has knowingly approved new programs with large initial expenditures. This suggests that those who support more broad-based or universalist programs might be well advised to start by thinking *small*, and trying to expand existing programs down the road rather than trying to enact big programs in the immediate future.

Second, the current dissatisfaction with federally run programs and the movement to greater state control make nationally focused programs less likely to get on the political agenda. This dissatisfaction is visible across a broad range of programs, and is not unique to public assistance. Since the early 1980s, there have been a series of initiatives aimed at reducing the size of federal government (President Clinton's "reinventing government" initiative is the latest) and at simplifying or reducing federal regulations on private industry and on state and local governments. The move to reduce federal control over public assistance programs is of a piece with these other efforts.

We are clearly in a time of backlash against the expansions of federal authority that occurred steadily throughout the 1960s and 1970s. In part, this is a reaction against some federal regulations and mandates that went too far and caused more problems than they solved. In part, this may reflect the fact that there are limits to the effectiveness of any level of government. Some states are experiencing similar backlash against the expansion in state government regulations on localities. In part, the dissatisfaction with federal actions is heightened by a host of recent scandals involving federal officials in both the executive and congressional branches.

In part, this backlash reflects popular rhetoric about the federal government that is not well grounded in facts. The number of federal employees has actually shrunk over the past fifteen years, while state government employment surpassed federal employment in the early 1970s and continues to grow.[6] This suggests that the current backlash against federal programs may be repeated in the near future at the state level. For instance, many local school districts are trying to get exemptions from state regulations as part of their school reform efforts.

Whether the current antifederal backlash will take us too far in the opposite direction remains to be seen. Almost surely, at some point in the future, the pendulum will swing the other way. As long as the current climate lasts, however, the enactment of big new federal programs is not likely.

Third, as we have discussed before, there is a perception that existing antipoverty efforts have failed—that we have spent money to no good purpose. The effort to substantially cut the budgets of current public assistance programs, combined with efforts to reduce federal control, all reflect an attitude of "we've failed and need to try something entirely different." In this atmosphere, the idea of new big federally run programs is hardly likely to generate much political interest.

As chapter 4 showed, the nihilistic argument that "nothing works, let's just give up on federal programs" is a very bad misreading of history. There are real successes that have been far too little recognized in the public discussion. Chapter 5 indicated some of the reasons why governmentally based programs (and yes, even federally based programs) are an important component of any social safety net. Had the economic opportunities of less-skilled workers not deteriorated sharply over the past fifteen years (for reasons quite unrelated to the presence or absence of antipoverty programs) and had family characteristics not changed so much (changes which occurred among middle-income as well as low-income families), poverty would be much lower now. The problem is not that programs were ineffective, but that the problems they were designed to address kept changing.

The one federally based program that has expanded dramatically over the past ten years is the Earned Income Tax Credit (EITC). This expansion occurred precisely because the EITC was very different from other federal antipoverty programs. Rather than providing general income assistance to low-income families, receipt of the EITC is linked to work behavior. EITC subsidies *increase* as work increases, exactly the opposite of most cash and in-kind transfer programs, which are at their height when earnings are lowest. (Compare again figs. 3.4 and 3.6 in chapter 3.) This makes the EITC a much more behaviorally targeted program than other large federally funded programs. It is precisely the behavioral link between EITC payments and work behavior that has given it political viability.

In addition, the particular way in which the EITC pays subsidies makes it less visible in the policy debate over public assistance. The EITC is operated by the Department of the Treasury, and its budget is not listed in the usual places where people look for antipoverty subsidies. Furthermore, part of the assistance provided by the EITC comes from the absence of taxes paid in (a so-called tax expenditure in economics jargon) rather than from explicit subsidies paid out. For many low-income workers, the EITC offsets what they owe in income taxes, which means the government receives less income. (Of course, others receive refunds from the government, which is a direct expenditure.) This makes the budget implications of EITC less visible than in programs where all of the benefits are direct government expenditures.

For these reasons, the EITC has received far greater and more diverse political support than many other federally sponsored antipoverty programs in recent years, with major legislative expansions in 1993. Yet, even the EITC came under attack in the welfare reform discussion in the mid-1990s, partly because it had grown to a large enough program that it could no longer be ignored. Proposed changes would target the EITC more narrowly (subsidies to workers without children would be eliminated) and roll back some recent increases in benefit levels. Thus, the changes propsed to the EITC were similar to those occurring in other programs, limiting and targeting its benefits to an even greater extent.

As the social safety net in this country moves away from general income support programs and toward more targeted programs, we need to understand much more about the political and policy implications of a system that relies heavily on targeted programs rather than broad-based programs of support. The next section takes up the implications of this shift in more detail.

For those whose preference is for more broad-based programs, the prognosis in this chapter is not an optimistic one. What are the circumstances that could result in a swing of the pendulum away from targeted programs and back toward more general cash support? One possibility is that the current reforms go too far, leaving a large and visible population without resources. This is particularly possible in a world of strictly enforced time limits, with no job guarantees or assistance at the point when cash support ends. In these circumstances, the current reforms could contain the seeds of their own destruction, generating a political backlash among concerned middle-income voters and renewed sympathy for families who are left destitute despite serious efforts to find employment. Opposition to such outcomes could spawn a new political movement, uniting angry low-income and concerned middle-income voters, and demanding the reenactment of federal programs and increases in public assistance. But these changes at present appear far from the present political reality. Much will depend upon the ways in which recently enacted changes actually get implemented at the state level, the overall health of the macro economy (and the health of state budgets), the ongoing availability of low-wage jobs, and the extent to which low-income families' well-being and behavior are affected by these changes in the public assistance system.

6.2 TARGETED PROGRAMS: PROBLEMS AND PROMISES

SUMMARY. *Targeted programs include* behaviorally linked support *programs that supplement the resources available to particular groups among the poor, but tie this assistance to particular behaviors. They also include targeted* service *programs that provide specific services for particular groups among the poor, with the goal of either changing the environment or changing the behavior of the poor (through such programs as job search assistance or compensatory education). In this section I discuss the political and operational advantages of such programs, as well as their disadvantages. In particular, they often cost more per participant, require greater effort and skill to manage and operate effectively, and may have less overall effect on economic poverty than more broad-based transfer programs.*

The previous section described the movement away from reliance on broad-based antipoverty efforts toward targeted programs. Essentially all of the public welfare reform discussion at both the state and the federal level over the past fifteen years has been focused on such issues as which groups to target, which behavioral requirements to impose, and how to efficiently provide these services to their targeted recipients. What challenges do we face as our public assistance system relies increasingly on such programs?

There are two general types of targeted programs. *Behaviorally linked support* programs include those programs that supplement the resources available to particular groups among the poor, but tie these resource supplements to particular behaviors. This includes many of the in-kind programs, such as Food Stamps, Section 8 Housing Vouchers, or Medicaid, which provide support only for approved expenditures (food or housing or medicine). It also includes the EITC, which ties earnings supplements to work effort, or area-based economic development programs that provide tax incentives or general funding for privately planned initiatives that meet specific requirements. All of these programs redistribute resources, but in a more constrained way than general cash redistribution. As noted in the last section, cash support for single parents is increasingly moving away from general support to behaviorally linked support as well, as work requirements and other behavioral restrictions become more common.

Targeted *service* programs include those programs that provide specific services for particular groups among the poor, with the goal of either changing the environment or changing the behavior of the poor. This includes a wide variety of antipoverty programs designed to offer services to the poor. For instance, job search and training programs provide explicit services focused on employment. Pregnancy prevention programs for teens, Head Start for preschool children, immunization campaigns in poor neighborhoods, school reforms aimed at at-risk adolescents, school breakfast programs, and homeless shelters all provide services for targeted populations, designed to address specific and identifiable problems. In order to operate, they must have a *program*; their purpose is to deliver services of some sort, not to put cash in the pockets of the poor. In some cases the public sector may operate these programs, in other cases the public sector may contract with private agencies to operate them.

The Advantages

The movement toward behaviorally linked support programs and targeted service programs suggests that such programs are successful in garnering support in the current political environment. What are the advantages of these programs?

First, targeted programs respond to the suspicion that high poverty rates are linked to the behavior of the poor by imposing greater constraints on who is helped and how they are helped. As discussed above, the high visibility of inner-city ghetto poverty, the growing presence of recent immigrants among the poor, and the diverging labor market experiences of more- and less-skilled workers have raised the sense of "otherness" that many Americans feel toward the poor and fueled their mistrust of how low-income families use general cash assistance. Many Americans believe (incorrectly) that the work behavior of many persons eligible for public assistance has seriously deteriorated.

Targeted programs address these suspicions by limiting the discretion of poor families in how they use public assistance. By limiting funding only to certain targeted resources, such as food or health care, there is less chance that money will be spent in ways that middle-class taxpayers would not approve. By limiting funding only to certain services that provide "a hand up, not a hand-out," such as compensatory education programs or employment programs, legislators believe they have prevented undesirable behavior.

Second, targeted service programs also have the financial advantage that their total costs are often relatively small. Many of these programs aim to provide specific services to limited populations, thus they are small-ticket items in the budget. This is true of programs ranging from Head Start to JTPA to child immunization efforts. This does not mean that they are cheap programs to run. *Per participant served*, they might be quite costly, as noted below. But because they are not entitlements, they typically serve only some among their target population. The response to budget limits is typically to restrict the number of people who have access to the service by limiting the number of sites where it is available or by limiting the number of people served each month. This means that small targeted programs are not apparent "budget busters" and therefore it is easier to garner support for them. In this sense, a plethora of smaller targeted programs providing specific services to specific populations may be more supportable than one or two big-income support programs. Of course, as we will note below, limitations on the provision of services also create limits on their overall impact on the problems they are designed to address.

Third, increasing interest in rigorous evaluation of public programs has resulted in widely believable evaluations indicating that a number of targeted programs have been effective in meeting their goals. Much of this evidence was discussed in chapter 4, such as improvements in nutrition due to food programs, and improvements in work behavior due to employment programs. When it comes time to review and cut programs, those which show evidence of effectiveness are more likely to stay in the budget.

This is in marked contrast to our evidence on the antipoverty effects of cash assistance. While there is a substantial literature on the behavioral incentives imbedded in cash assistance programs, investigating whether they reduce work support or increase out-of-wedlock births, there is astonishingly little evidence on the aggregate effects of these programs on the well-being of families that receive them. Much less attention has been given to questions such as "Do cash support programs improve physical and cognitive development among children in the families that receive them?" In short, we know a lot about the costs and very little about the benefits of these programs.

In part, this is because broad-based programs that are widely received by many persons are hard to evaluate effectively. The best form of evaluation occurs when one randomly chosen group of people is provided with assistance while another is not. If the groups are truly randomly selected, then the difference in their outcomes should be due to the program. This type of evaluation is relatively straightforward (if not necessarily easy) to perform for a job training program, which has only a limited number of slots available. It is much more politically difficult to exclude someone from a widely available cash support program simply to see how much they are hurt. The growing evidence on the effectiveness of a host of more targeted programs has pushed people to focus more on these programs.

Fourth, a final advantage of targeted programs is that they often have natural constituencies that care about the particular goods or services they provide. Thus, Head Start and adolescent schooling programs have the support of the educational establishment. Medicaid has the support of the medical community. Food Stamps and other nutritional programs have the support of the agricultural lobby. Job training and employment programs often have the support of various business coalitions. In contrast, there are few obvious constituencies for cash transfer programs (other than the poor themselves), since their benefits are diffuse and not easily tracked in the economy.

The Disadvantages

While the value of targeted programs has been much discussed in the public debate, less attention has been paid to some of their disadvantages. There are some fundamental problems associated with increased reliance on targeted programs, both behaviorally linked support programs and service programs.

First, targeted programs tend to cost more per participant than cash redistribution programs, because they require more inputs per person served. Targeted support programs have to verify more than income eligibility. If they provide support for the purchase of particular goods, they must monitor participants' expenditures. If they are linked to approved behaviors, they must monitor participants' actions and compliance with these requirements.

Targeted service programs have to operate and provide a service as well as determine participant eligibility. Thus, their operating expenses per participant served can be quite high. For instance, the GAIN job training program for AFDC recipients in California costs between $3,000 and $6,500 per participant across counties.[7] JOBSTART, a program aimed at helping young dropouts increase their job skills, costs around $4,500 per participant.[8]

This cost problem is particularly clear with regard to welfare-to-work programs. All else being equal, a system where we monitor job search and work behavior and link job seeking with eligibility for cash transfers will cost more than a system that simply provides cash transfers based on income eligibility. If welfare-to-work programs also train workers in job search and work skills, the cost will be even higher. These costs are higher still when employment is linked with support for child care expenditures, health insurance, and other subsidiary services that are necessary for single mothers to be able to support their families on a job. Thus, those who want to link assistance for single mothers with mandates requiring that they either work thirty hours per week or spend thirty hours per week attending a job search assistance or training program are necessarily *adding* to the budget needed to run the assistance program in the short run.

Second, in addition to their actual monetary costs, the effective operation of these programs requires first-rate management and program administration skills. Both behaviorally linked support programs and service programs require good record keeping and effective administrative oversight, but the provision of services requires even greater management and program implementation skills. Even when services are contracted out to private or nonprofit agencies rather than provided by public agencies, an oversight and monitoring staff must verify that contractors are complying with the program rules.

This is one reason why some people are hesitant about the positive evaluation results for targeted service programs, such as employment and training programs for AFDC women. The program sites participating in evaluations have often been either pioneer efforts undertaken in states with great enthusiasm for the program, or they were sites that volunteered for evaluation. When such programs are adopted more broadly, many sites may view these programs as "extra work" and a waste of effort. Lack of management and staff enthusiasm for a program can render it ineffective much more surely than budget limitations. At best, the effects of targeted service programs can vary greatly across locations, depending upon staff and management behavior.

Third, even when targeted programs are cost-effective, there may be problems when the agency that spends the money is not the agency whose budget benefits. If the behavioral changes induced by targeted programs are effective, then the program may pay for itself in reduced public assistance, increased taxes, or decreased crime. In fact, at least with regard to employment programs for AFDC mothers, most evidence indicates that states recoup a good part of the high expenses of these programs via reduced AFDC payments and other government benefits. But the gains are not large. For every dollar spent in the GAIN welfare-to-work program in California, the resulting decline in government spending on AFDC and other services varied between forty-one cents and $2.84.[9]

But for many of these programs, future gains do not accrue to the same agency that spends the money. For instance, when the federal government funds Head Start programs, it is the local and state education budget that benefits if these students need less special education in elementary school. When the federal government funds a crime-reduction program for adolescents, it is the city police and county jail budgets that benefit. This means that there may be difficulty generating political support for program budgets, even when there are net benefits to the government, if one agency is funding the program while another agency is reaping the gains.

People who expect that targeted programs will produce lower future government budgets for antipoverty programs will probably be disappointed. Whether targeted programs reduce government spending depends on both the level of program effectiveness as well as on the nature of the benefits generated. The government may have to run a large number of narrowly targeted programs to address a wide variety of specific problems. In addition, the greater per person cost of operating these programs means that if they are expanded to larger populations or if they start including an extended array of services, they can have very high up-front costs. Even when they reduce long-term government expenditures, this may or may not produce long-term savings in the budget of the agency funding the program.

The declining use of cash assistance and the increasing reliance on targeted programs changes the nature of the U.S. public support system in fundamental ways, giving program administrators and legislative rule makers much more control over the behavior of public assistance recipients. This has clear political advantages in today's climate, but it is not obviously better nor worse than a public assistance system that relies more on broad-based income transfers.

If the primary goal is to achieve large reductions in income poverty as cheaply as possible, cash transfers are probably more efficient than targeted programs. Similarly, if one fears that government management and oversight are often inefficient or inept, then increased reliance on these more highly regulated programs might be viewed as creating an unmanageable system that promises on paper what it cannot deliver. It is possible that expansions of targeted programs will set up their own backlash some years down the road, as taxpayers respond to problems of public management and limited effectiveness in many of these programs.

One last attribute about targeted programs is important to keep in mind, an attribute that might be considered under both the list of advantages as well as disadvantages: *targeted programs are likely to produce relatively modest long-term effects for their recipients.* The good news is that there is substantial evidence that many targeted programs, from job training programs to compensatory preschool programs, do indeed have positive effects on their recipients.

The bad news is that none of these effects are strikingly large. Job programs produce modest increases in employment and even smaller increases in total income (if other cash support falls when earnings rise). Programs aimed at disadvantaged teens can increase graduation and employment rates by modest amounts, but hardly solve the problem of high school dropouts. Programs designed to improve nutrition among mothers and children have positive, but relatively small effects. It is also true that many of these programs serve only a small fraction of the poor due to their limited budgets. Only a small number of slots exist in job placement programs. Many eligible children are not in Head Start programs.

Those who claim that cutting back cash transfers and increasing behaviorally based support programs will make significant inroads against poverty in the United States are being overly optimistic. I read the evidence on these programs to imply that they are typically a good idea. There are a number of targeted programs—particularly those aimed at improving school outcomes among children and teens and those aimed at increasing employment among adults—that should be key parts of our social safety net system. But the availability of these programs, when coincident with steep declines in other forms of cash assistance (which would occur if cash benefits are sharply time limited in the near future) and with a worsening set of economic opportunities for less-skilled adults, should not be expected to produce any net improvement in economic well-being among low-income families.

The appropriate response is to utilize the growing interest in targeted programs to implement those where good evaluation research suggests we can produce real improvements in people's lives. The last section of this chapter discusses how to run such programs as effectively as possible. But some ongoing forms of income support will still remain necessary in this country, for those who cannot work, for those whose work skills are limited, and for those who must deal with extended spells of unemployment.

6.3 FIVE "EFFECTIVENESS CRITERIA" FOR TARGETED PROGRAMS

SUMMARY. *Given some of the operational challenges of more targeted programs, this section establishes a set of five criteria that can be used to evaluate whether future proposed programs or policy changes are likely to be effective. These include the* management *criterion, assuring that such programs have the resources and program design necessary to be effectively implemented; the* sophistication *criterion, assuring that programs are designed to recognize the range of other forces that will impact the lives of participants and limit the effectiveness of the program; the* linkage *criterion, assuring that programs are designed to use the private and nonprofit sectors as partners with the public sector whenever appropriate; the* federalism *criterion, assuring that the program achieves an appropriate balance between federal, state, and local involvement in the program; and the* coordination *criterion, which requires that public programs complement one another and utilize the services and support that other programs provide, rather than duplicating or competing with each other.*

For those who want to provide assistance to people caught in poverty, the issues laid out in the previous section of this chapter pose some difficult questions. If we are reconfiguring our public assistance programs away from broad-based redistribution and toward multiple targeted programs, how do we deal with the cost, management, and effectiveness challenges such programs will pose? Fortunately, this is a question to which there are answers. A wide variety of programs in various states and localities have faced these questions and answered them in effective ways.

While there is no single program that will "solve poverty" in today's world, there are criteria that will make it more likely that a particular program will work well. I propose the following five *effectiveness criteria* for targeted programs. While these criteria can apply to behaviorally linked support programs, they may be more useful for targeted service programs aimed at providing particular services to particular populations. As fifty states debate the appropriate design of their public assistance programs in the years ahead, these criteria can provide important touchstones to help decide whether a new or reconfigured program is likely to be successful.

These criteria emerge directly out of the analysis of the previous chapters, and out of conversations and visits to a variety of existing programs. They are designed in recognition of the changes and challenges facing antipoverty efforts in today's economic environment. The various descriptions of specific programs that are scattered throughout this chapter are all examples of programs that meet these effectiveness criteria.

Criterion 1. THE MANAGEMENT CRITERION. *Does the design of the program allow for effective management and implementation? Is the funding adequate for this? Do the staff and agency assigned to operate this program have the necessary skills?*

A major problem with many welfare reforms passed by federal and state legislatures is that they pay too much attention to a set of program rules and too little attention to the management problems involved in implementing those rules. This is often particularly true of program mandates that enact utopian requirements that legislators would like to see in place, without any attention given to the cost and difficulties of carrying out these mandates on the ground.

During the Bush administration, there was a proposal to mandate that public housing inhabitants must engage in regular job search. The original proposal from the Department of Housing and Urban Development requested no new funds for this mandate, assuming that participants could participate in available JTPA job training and job placement programs or utilize welfare-to-work programs. This mandate ignored a number of key management problems; for instance, public housing authorities would have to become involved in linking housing assistance to labor market involvement, an area in which they had no knowledge or expertise. It ignored the fact that providing information to public housing participants about this new mandate was likely to take a substantial amount of time and money. Nor did it recognize that existing job search and training programs would require more funding if they faced a substantial increase in demand for services from public housing occupants. The mandate was dropped from the proposed legislation after protests by various agencies that it could not be imposed without additional funding, although local housing authorities were encouraged to design their own programs that linked work and public housing receipt.

This is a classic example of the problems that arise when those who draft laws do not consider the management problems and costs that their good ideas might engender. Other examples are readily available, particularly in the increased work requirements that states have been asked to place on welfare recipients. Too many AFDC offices are already underfunded and overstaffed, with individual caseworkers handling caseloads of three hundred to five hundred persons at any one time. In this situation, requirements mandating that a high percentage of recipients must receive job search assistance and career counseling are meaningless unless there is enough funding to increase the staff and operate these mandatory new programs in an effective way. Frustrations with unfunded mandates and unrealistic program requirements are driving state demands for greater discretion over program design.

In contrast, Riverside County, California, has paid a great deal of attention to management issues in implementing the state welfare-to-work program, GAIN. GAIN offices are located in a different place from the AFDC offices, so participants do not think they are coming to another welfare program. While

PROGRAM MODELS:
RIVERSIDE COUNTY'S GAIN PROGRAM

Riverside County has achieved national recognition by running one the nation's most successful welfare-to-work training programs, Greater Avenues for Independence (GAIN). Their clients have consistently shown some of the greatest employment and earnings gains achieved by employment programs for AFDC recipients.

The first thing that strikes you when you enter the main office is that this place is *well managed.* I arrived along with about ten new clients—AFDC recipients who had been told to report at 9 A.M. to enroll in GAIN or face the cutoff of their AFDC benefits. At 9 o'clock sharp, case managers started meeting with people for short introductory conversations about the program. By 9:15, there was no one left in the waiting room; by 9:30 all the clients were participating in a general orientation session. Over the morning, I watched the people and their paperwork progress steadily. Case managers who sat down with the new clients knew the answers to their questions; clerical staff processed information efficiently; people with valid reasons for exemption from the program were quickly identified and dealt with.

GAIN emphasizes finding a job. Many clients go straight into the "fast track" program. They spend one week in classes, developing employment goals, talking about the personal barriers that have kept them out of work, and building self-confidence. The next two weeks involve assisted job search. In the words of the program director, Marilyn Kuhlman, all staff are trained to "Focus, focus, focus on jobs" in everything they do. This is not a training program; it is an employment program. Clients can return as often as necessary. They are considered permanently assigned to a case manager, who is responsible for checking in with them once employed. If they lose a job, they are expected to return to job search.

I spent part of that afternoon at a Job Club meeting. Each person in a group of clients sat at a carrel with a phone, calling employers he or she had identified through newspaper ads, or making cold calls to businesses listed in the Yellow Pages and asking if they were hiring. At the beginning of the hour, everyone applauded when the supervisor announced two people from the group would not be returning since they had been hired yesterday afternoon. Some clients called steadily, clearly determined to make this work; others were more unsure, and the supervisor circulated among them, giving advice and suggestions.

Many GAIN clients start with minimum wage jobs. Case managers work hard to develop realistic expectations about the wages and jobs people are likely to get. The philosophy of the program is that any type of employment is a success, even if a client doesn't earn enough to get off public assistance and still needs government subsidies for child care. Jobs are located both by clients and by an aggressive effort of GAIN job developers to contact local employers and to sell the program (and its clients) in the community.

What are some of the elements that have made this program so successful?

- Good management and clear direction to staff about their job goals.
- A well-formed sense of what the program is about and what it can and can't do. Persons who need other forms of help are quickly referred elsewhere.
- Enthusiasm from staff that is communicated to clients, saying, "This program can work for you!"
- Marketing flair: clients are taught how to market themselves to potential employers, just as job developers market the program to local businesses.

many staff people are hired from jobs as AFDC case workers, staff are given training when they arrive; there is no assumption that welfare staff can automatically run job placement programs. Staff are required to fill a much wider range of functions than the typical AFDC employee, providing career counseling, following up on attendance at job search assistance classes, knowing about the range of public and private employment-related programs their clients can make use of, as well as handling all of the paperwork to verify eligibility and ongoing compliance with the rules. Thus, the welfare-to-work staff receive higher pay and have substantially lower caseloads. To emphasize their position, they are required to dress professionally—suits for men and professional work clothing for women—as are all of the affiliated clerical staff, so the office *looks* very different from the typical welfare office. It looks like a place that knows how to find and place clients in real-world jobs. In short, this is a well-managed program that has paid attention to the details of how to effectively organize a welfare-to-work program.

Legislators who want to add restrictions on program eligibility or create new program requirements targeted on certain behaviors need specifically to ask whether these additional requirements can be effectively met by those who operate the program. If these requirements are workable, legislators need to inform themselves about what it will cost to implement them effectively. Serious and constant consideration to the management and implementation challenges of targeted programs must occur if these programs are going to operate effectively.

Criterion 2. THE SOPHISTICATION CRITERION. *Does this program recognize and deal with the range of problems facing its target population, or is it so narrowly focused on one goal that its participants will be overwhelmed by other issues?*

A danger for many targeted programs is that they focus too narrowly, so that even if they meet their own goals, there may be little long-term effect on the lives of their participants. Programs need to pay attention to the larger context in which they are operating. Many programs that have difficulties achieving results are guilty of ignoring the larger environment in which their participants live.

One example is teen pregnancy-prevention programs that focus solely on providing contraceptive information to adolescent girls. These are relatively inexpensive programs to run, can be easily added onto other classroom requirements, and do seem to improve teens' knowledge about contraception and reproduction. They have been largely ineffective, however, because changes in girls' technical sexual knowledge appears to have little effect on their behavior. Programs with a more complex set of goals are more effective. For instance, programs that work best are those that target both adolescent boys and girls, that involve parents, and that require participants to actively simulate potential situations where they might feel pressed to become sexually active, voicing arguments about birth control with their assigned partners. These "active learning" and behavioral simulation techniques, combined with more knowledge, are more effective in changing behavior.

Another program that ignored potential problems by focusing its attention too narrowly was a tax credit designed to increase employment among minority youth from high-unemployment areas. This program provided lump-sum payments of a few hundred dollars to employers who hired such workers, and then provided the employers with another payment if the worker was still employed a few months later. Some number of employers increased their hiring of the target group, kept them at work long enough to collect their two payments, then fired them and hired another group for long enough to collect another set of payments. While the program was successful in increasing the number hired from its target group, it produced little in the way of long-term job experience while allowing employers to collect government subsidies.

Long experience with welfare-to-work programs has substantially increased the sophistication with which we run such programs. For instance, we have learned that employment assistance programs for AFDC recipients must contain more than job search assistance. These programs must be concerned with child care expenses and availability; in fact, a number of earlier job programs for AFDC recipients were not able to meet their participation goals because they did not include funding for or pay attention to child care. These programs must recognize that transportation constraints and safety concerns among women living in dangerous neighborhoods will affect the location and the timing of acceptable jobs. As health costs have soared, these programs increasingly provide medical insurance for recipients who take low-wage jobs and lose Medicaid eligibility. In short, a "simple" employment assistance program for welfare recipients must contain a substantial number of components, and is neither easy nor inexpensive to operate. If some of these components are missing, the program is less likely to succeed.

Another dimension of program sophistication involves programs' ability to follow up with participants after an initial set of services is provided. Employment programs that push people into jobs but provide no follow-up assistance when a first job ends are likely to produce few long-term effects. In fact, among women who enter job search assistance programs with little past job

PROGRAM MODELS:
THE CHICAGO COMMONS' ETC PROGRAM

The Employment Training Center (ETC) is located in an old manufacturing building in a low-income black and Hispanic neighborhood on the west side of Chicago. Its goal is to create a "bridge program"—to bring women with long-term histories of welfare use, low skills, and limited labor market experience to the point where they could find stable employment. The organizers planned a program that would emphasize basic education, life skills training, and employment planning. But soon after opening in 1991, Jody Raphael, the founding director, realized that a large share of the clients faced a more fundamental problem: many of them were either currently involved in abusive relationships or had been past victims of domestic violence.

For instance, "Gwen" was a high school dropout who tested at the fifth-grade reading level when she came into the program. She had two small children and for five years had been living with a man who physically abused her. While coming daily to ETC, she was making little progress on any of her educational skills. A suicide attempt put her into the county hospital, which started her on drug therapy for depression. Over the next year, her literacy skills improved and she started making plans to leave welfare. Her boyfriend, threatened by her new skills and plans, increased his abuse. ETC helped her and her children move to a battered women's shelter, and then to their own living situation. Soon afterwards she found a job as a bilingual receptionist where she is still employed.

The combination of depression and domestic violence is not unusual and often keeps women from being able to make changes in their lives. One of the biggest problems is that as women make progress in ETC, the men in their lives work to undermine them, threatened by the women's growing independence and often wanting them to stay on welfare for its steady guaranteed income. ETC has had clients who were beaten the night before they were to take their GED exams or go to a job interview. Many of the women are very isolated and have few sources of support to call on, outside their connections at ETC. Their families often urge them to stay with the men. They typically cannot afford to leave the relationship until they have a job, and their lack of basic skills or knowledge about the labor market makes employment difficult.

Raphael and her staff had to start from scratch to put together a curriculum that directly addressed these problems while also providing education and job-related skills. She estimates that it takes one and a half to three years for many women to reach a point where they have the skills and the self-confidence to hold a job and find greater independence. At the end of the ETC program, typically when the women complete their GED, some enter short-term job placement programs; others move directly into employment.

What do ETC's statistics show? About 50–60 percent of their clients from three to four years ago are off welfare and employed. That is a high success rate, but it
continued

comes at a cost. Most women spend between one and three years involved with ETC while still on public assistance. The program remains very small because of limited funding, with about one hundred participants each year.

As a model for how to deal with welfare recipients from severely disadvantaged backgrounds, ETC provides some advice for policymakers:

- Don't assume this population can be quickly prepared to find stable employment.
- Realize that lack of educational skills is only one reason (maybe only a small piece) why some women end up as long-term welfare users.
- Design programs that will address the range of life problems facing clients.

experience, first jobs often last no more than a few months. A program that is available to provide job search assistance for second, third, and future jobs for those whose first job doesn't work out is much more likely to keep people employed in the future.

CET, a highly successful job training agency that serves low-income adults in multiple locations around the country, guarantees participants who successfully complete the program that they can use its job listings and its career counselors whenever they need to in the future. The staff of the program considers this guarantee vital to the success of the program in permanently increasing employment among their graduates. Indeed, the evidence suggests that many first jobs end relatively quickly following job training or job search assistance. People who (on their own or with assistance) find second jobs are likely to stick with these jobs longer. Third jobs are even more likely to result in employment that lasts for workers. The need for a participant to re-access job assistance will decline over time. But if there is no follow-up assistance at all, the effect of the initial program could be lost entirely at the end of the first job.

"Sophistication" has its own definition in each program. In adolescent training programs, it means recognizing and dealing with the mix of peer effects, family problems, and adolescent behaviors that interfere with participation. In programs for the homeless, it means understanding how to deal with substance abuse, street violence, mental illness, and the limited low-cost housing market. In programs for children, it means recognizing the potential problems created by learning disabilities, family abuse, neighborhood violence, and parental stress, and designing a program that can operate even in the face of these problems. In job training for adults, it means dealing with problems of child care, work discipline, unstable and short-term jobs, and abusive spouses. Not all participants will have all these problems; perhaps they will affect just a minority. But a program is much more likely to be effective when its staff recognizes the many forces that influence participants' behavior and designs a program to deal with the barriers these other forces create.

PROGRAM MODELS:
THE CET PROGRAM

The Center for Employment Training (CET) may have started in San Jose, California, but its approach has been replicated around the country. Evaluations indicate that it produces long-term employment gains for its participants, both adults and youth. In one study of thirteen different programs for high school dropouts, only CET showed positive effects.

CET's San Jose program is in an old elementary school, serving a heavily Hispanic population. The walls of the school were covered with exhortations to students, such as "Use English! It's the language of work." Students train for a particular job—from medical assistant to sheet metal fabricator to account clerk to commercial food services worker. While students are given basic math and literacy training, everything is done in the context of job skills. Account clerk trainees learn math by working on accounting problems; medical assistants improve their literacy skills while reading about hospital procedures and filling out patient care forms. Many students are working toward their GED, and know exactly how they will use their skills on the job. The curriculum in each classroom is typically developed by its teachers, who, given a list of the skills their students need to have, put together a set of exercises to provide them. The teaching staff are also responsible for staying in constant contact with the employers in their job area, making sure that the skills they are teaching are those needed by local employers. As local employers switch to new computer systems, procedures, or updated equipment, the training program is expected to change as well.

I visited the medical-assistant training program. This was not a "class" as much as a group of students, all at different stages of training, learning together (and often learning from one another). Students enter the program continuously and progress at their own rate through a series of competency-based exercises over the weeks. The teaching staff were amazingly good. Teachers moved between students, giving them feedback or starting them on a new piece of work.

Students face strict attendance and punctuality requirements and are expected to dress as if coming to work. They are given lots of rewards and feedback as they move through their programs, receiving certificates every time they complete a segment. Finishing a program means a graduation ceremony, with much applause and celebration by staff, family, and friends.

Because CET's program is closely tied to local employer needs, students who complete training are virtually guaranteed jobs. Job loss rates are very low, considering the past employment histories of many of these students. One of the selling points of the program is that new clients are considered "clients for life." If one job does not work out, students can come back and use the placement services of CET as often as they wish.

Russell Tershey, one of CET's founders in 1967, is still executive director. Thirty years later he continues to show enormous enthusiasm for this pro-

continued

gram. What are some of the lessons from CET about effective employment programs?

- Believe in your students, reward them, and encourage them.
- Make it obvious why basic literacy and math skills are necessary for the jobs that students are preparing to take. Tie together training, education, and life skills.
- Keep all training programs closely linked to available jobs and to employer needs.

Criterion 3. THE LINKAGE CRITERION. *Does this program draw effective links outside the public sector, utilizing the expertise and comparative advantage of private sector and nonprofit organizations?*

Targeted programs require management skill, both in monitoring their more extensive eligibility rules and in providing specific services. The government may have a comparative advantage in monitoring eligibility, because of its ability to collect and process information from a variety of sources, including employers, schools, tax authorities, and health care organizations. But it is not at all clear that the government has a comparative advantage in the actual provision of services. In fact, a substantial number of existing programs involve public/private partnerships. Head Start programs are typically run by private nonprofit agencies, with oversight and monitoring from the federal funders; homeless shelters are often run by local nonprofit organizations, but are funded and regulated by the city; job training services are often provided by community colleges, which contract with the local group that oversees the JTPA program.

There have been a number of program disasters in the past, when the public sector tried to operate programs for which it had little preparation or expertise. For instance, adult job training programs have sometimes been run by public sector agencies using donated equipment from private sector firms—equipment that was donated because it was obsolete and no longer in use. Workers who completed the program had few skills employers wanted in the labor market. Public job placement programs in the late 1970s often placed workers in public agency offices. While some of these placements worked well, in other cases unionized city employees felt threatened by these workers and let them know they were unwelcome, or overworked agency staff simply ignored them. Cities that funded more job slots in nonprofit agencies, which typically took their job training responsibilities more seriously, rather than relying only on slots in public sector agencies, often provided better services for their program participants.

Of course, requiring that the private sector operate programs for which they are not prepared may also create problems. Private companies have often found it difficult to provide the initial training on-site for disadvantaged workers who need special attention before they can work side by side with regular employees. Sometimes these workers need help learning how to conform to the discipline of the workplace—how to dress, how to treat other workers, or even learning the importance of always appearing on time when the job starts. Programs that put increasing requirements on these workers over time can often bring them up to speed and ready to work in a standard job environment. But most private employers have little patience with this and are reluctant to treat these trainees differently from other new hires. Thus, training programs for persons who need to learn a range of work and behavioral skills in order to become productive workers are often best run separately, with these workers placed in private sector jobs only after they have received some basic life skills and work skills training.

Programs often work best when a good balance is struck between public and private operations. Schools that try to prepare non-college-bound students for jobs after high school need to include ways to connect students with local businesses, both providing them with job experience and giving them a sense of the skills wanted by employers. Those who run job search programs for AFDC women need to have a close working knowledge of the local labor market. Nonprofit agencies often run lower-cost and better-managed services, whether for foster children or for homeless adult men, in part because they can draw on a pool of skilled, caring employees who may not desire to take public sector jobs. Greater attention to the possibilities for public/private partnerships will improve the effectiveness of public assistance programs.

Criterion 4. THE FEDERALISM CRITERION. *Does this program effectively use the comparative advantages of different governmental levels? Are the financing responsibilities, program design and implementation responsibilities, and the oversight and evaluation responsibilities assigned to the agency and level of government that will be most effective in seeing that these responsibilities are carried out?*

Just as some things are better done by the private or the nonprofit sector and a well-designed program uses the best parts of both, so are there also comparative advantages to different levels of government. An effective program will seek to balance local and state control over design and program operation with state and federal coordination and funding.

In the last chapter I discussed the comparative advantages of the federal, state, and local levels of government in depth. The federal government has particular advantages in funding, since it can redistribute funds from richer to poorer areas of the country (where there may be more program participants) and because it can fund programs at higher levels in economic recessions (when the demand for services often increases). States and localities are much more constrained by annual budget limitations.

The federal government can also provide incentives for states to learn from one another and to use "best-practice" operating and record-keeping

PROGRAM MODELS:
THE PFS PROGRAM IN GRAND RAPIDS

With all the attention focused on getting single mothers from welfare into the labor market, too little attention has gone toward helping the absent fathers find employment and pay steady child support. The Parents Fair Share (PFS) program is designed to do just that. Operating as an experimental program with locations in nine states, PFS provides judges with an alternative for men who are brought to court for nonpayment of child support, many of whom are unemployed. Rather than being jailed or fined (not a particularly effective way to increase their child support payments), they are mandated to participate in PFS.

I visited PFS in Grand Rapids, Michigan, where an enthusiastic and committed staff are working hard to make this program succeed. Men ordered to participate in PFS are expected to be involved in two major activities: Job Club and peer support sessions. Job Club works with clients to assess their employment strengths and weaknesses, provides training on how to look for—and keep—a job, and it gets them engaged in active job search. Many of the men want to find a job immediately and get certified as having satisfactorily completed the program. Because these men often have unstable employment histories, the program staff first help them assess why in the past they have often been unsuccessful at keeping jobs or receiving raises. The biggest challenge for the staff is the high number of men with drug problems and criminal records.

The more unusual part of PFS is the peer support component, whereby the men in the program are brought together to talk about their relationships with their children and their children's mother, their problems in the labor market, and the barriers that have kept them from making regular child support payments. One of the surprise revelations of PFS in all locations has been the importance of such peer support. Many of these men have never engaged in such conversations before. They often arrive at the first session sullen and angry about being required to attend any part of the program. But before long, many of them start to talk. In the session I attended, one man talked at length about his upcoming trial on a felony charge; another was worried that his fifteen-year-old son's mother was unable to control him any more. PFS has developed a curriculum on fathering that is used in these sessions, getting men to think explicitly about their role as fathers.

In the words of Grant Rapids PFS program director, Ray Jackson, the program "will do anything that's reasonable to help." The program is not designed to punish its clients but to help them get their lives stabilized—and put them on the path of regular child support payments in the process. Few program entrants really understand the child support system, and many view it as a punishment heaped on them by their ex-wives or girlfriends, with the help of the state. PFS tries to help them know their rights with regard to child visits as well as their responsibilities with regard to child support.

The long-term effects of PFS on employment and child support payments are unknown, as the evaluation studies are still under way. But some messages come through:

- Threatening nonpayers of child support with jail and fines may accomplish little for men whose employment prospects are limited and whose employment history is spotty.
- Programs for men often face different problems than those for women who have been out of the labor market. The men have often worked, but they have frequently lost or quit their jobs. Involvement with crime and drugs is an ongoing problem.

techniques. Some federal oversight and quality control are often useful, as are federal requirements for program evaluation. Agencies that are running programs directly are often the most resistant to serious evaluation of their programs. Federal oversight need not involve the details of program operation, however, but may focus on whether states are meeting the broad program goals. Can the states show that participants in job training programs are able to find jobs afterwards? Can they show that dropouts in compensatory education programs receive a high school equivalency degree or improve their literacy skills? Can they show that a significant proportion of their AFDC caseload is participating in welfare-to-work programs? While reporting requirements can too easily become overly detailed, some form of federal oversight of those state programs with shared federal/state funding assures that these funds are being spent effectively.

States and localities also need to sort out their respective roles. Employment programs often require a knowledge of local labor markets that is only available at the city or county level. Education programs also often require the involvement of parents and should leave discretion in program design and implementation to local school boards and parent/teacher associations. But just as federal oversight on the states is sometimes useful, so is state oversight on local expenditures of funds and program operations.

As with public/private decisions, there is no one "right" way to balance federal, state, and local involvement in public assistance programs. Policy decisions about programs with more uniform standards which serve broader populations probably are more efficiently made at the state and federal level. Programs whose operating details vary significantly across locations require more local discretion, with state and/or federal monitoring to see whether broad program goals are being met, but without micro-management.

Criterion 5. THE COORDINATION CRITERION. *Is the program set up to work with and complement other efforts and programs that might be operating in the same neighborhood or with the same population? Rather than competing with or duplicating other services and programs, is it designed to be easily coordinated with other programs?*

Given the existence of multiple targeted programs, the target population for one program often overlaps with the target population for another. Single mothers are the target of work programs, nutrition programs, medical assistance programs, and they are involved as parents in programs targeted on their children. Some families that receive Food Stamps will also be eligible for Medicaid. Teen mothers in high school completion programs may also be eligible for WIC programs with their children.

Such overlapping programs create serious problems for both program managers as well as program participants. When the offices that run these programs are in different locations, when participants are required to meet different eligibility requirements for different programs, and when program benefits vary depending upon participation in other programs, it can make eligibility and benefit determination a nightmare for both caseworkers as well as recipients. Too often, new program requirements are imposed, or new programs are designed that pay little attention to the programs and requirements that already exist.

A number of states have made major strides in coordinating services for AFDC women, by siting their AFDC, Food Stamp, and employment offices in the same location. Many states are also using similar forms for eligibility certification for related programs. But the differences in program rules keep this from happening easily. For instance, women who apply for AFDC must have less than $1,000 in cash or noncash assets (excluding housing), and the equity value of any car must be less than $4,500, while women who apply for Food Stamps must have less than $2,000 in cash or noncash assets (excluding housing) and must own a car whose resale value is no more than $1,500. This means that different documentation may be needed to apply for each program. Despite ongoing calls to synchronize the rules for Food Stamps and AFDC, this has not happened and continues to create problems for local public assistance offices.

One problem in the implementation of welfare-to-work programs is that the publicly run job training programs are often under the authority of state employment agencies, while the welfare side is run by state human service agencies. And these two agencies have little history of cooperation or communication in most states. Over time, most states have developed program designs that allow these agencies to work cooperatively, but there were many tensions in earlier programs. One of the reasons why Massachusetts was able to quickly implement an early model of welfare-to-work programs in the 1980s is that the heads of these two agencies were married to each other, a unique way to break down some of the traditional cross-agency barriers!

Another example of useful coordination occurs between Head Start programs and elementary schools. If Head Start teachers meet with kindergarten teachers, they can often provide useful beginning-of-the-year information on children's developmental problems and progress to the new teacher who will be working with these students. Unfortunately, because Head Start is typically not run through school districts but operates as a separate program, often public schools have little contact with Head Start programs, and useful information on children's backgrounds and needs is lost when they enter the public schools.

One aspect of program coordination involves writing consistent eligibility rules and improving communication across multiple programs and agencies. Another involves resisting the spread of a plethora of very small programs targeted at very limited populations. When this happens, it sometimes requires extra staff for local agencies to simply keep track of what programs are and aren't available. For instance, local child care providers for low-income families regularly complain about the existence of multiple child care subsidy programs, each with somewhat different eligibility and payment rules. Recent reforms have aimed at consolidating the federal money for these programs and turning it over to the states as a lump-sum block grant.

Coordination is an ongoing problem in the face of multiple targeted programs. It is a problem that program designers need to be acutely aware of when they implement changes in existing programs or design new ones. Few programs exist in a vacuum; programs that are designed to operate by themselves may create substantial problems when their rules conflict with the rules of other programs available to their target population. It is necessary to pay greater attention to these problems to ensure that targeted programs operate effectively.

Experience suggests that programs that meet the above criteria are more likely to be successful in today's environment. States which are designing new programs and federal legislators who are reforming existing programs need to keep asking some of the above questions as they put program rules in place and write new legislation. We need to learn from past mistakes if we want to make current targeted programs more effective.

• C H A P T E R 7 •

Where Should We Go from Here?

ANY AUTHOR who extensively criticizes and critiques the existing set of anti-poverty programs cannot avoid being asked the question, "Well, what would you do differently?" In this chapter I answer that question, describing the additions or reconfigurations of the present system that I think would best address the current problems of poverty.

It is important to note that the perspective of this chapter is one of *pragmatism*. While it is always interesting to ask, "If anything were possible, what would I do?" this is rarely a fruitful public policy exercise. We live in a world with a particular configuration of programs that cannot be easily abolished or dramatically changed overnight, as well as a set of political beliefs and attitudes which have shaped that system. It is not by chance that the United States has less cash assistance and more targeted programs than most other industrialized countries, and the historical and political realities that underlie the current system cannot be ignored as changes are proposed.

This chapter is about changes that are workable within the context of our existing set of antipoverty programs. They take the current system of public assistance, with the reforms of the mid-1990s, as the starting point from which to build. Yet the changes suggested below are not timid, nor, if fully implemented, would they have a minor effect.

The basis for the recommendations in this chapter is the analysis of the previous six chapters in the book. More precisely, with these recommendations, I try to balance the following concerns:

1. Does this policy recognize both the strong American insistence on the value of work *and* the economic changes of the past fifteen years, creating incentives to work as well as assuring that those who work are able to support a family?

2. Does this policy work to strengthen the incentives for responsible behavior within families and among individuals, particularly encouraging parents to support their children, and for young people to acquire skills and stay in school?

3. Is this a policy that could be administratively and politically implemented in the near future?

4. Is this policy consistent with the five "effectiveness criteria" outlined in the last chapter? Does it build on programs and approaches that have been shown to be effective in the past?

I propose an interlocking system of programs that balances the concerns raised in this book: balancing work incentives with adequate income support, balancing targeted programs with general support programs where necessary, balancing the appropriate contributions of federal, state, and local governments, balancing contributions of both the public and private sectors, and so on. The arguments laid out in this book strongly reject the notion that there is a single program that will solve poverty. Rather, we need a series of programs, aimed at different groups among a population of heterogeneous and geographically dispersed poor families. Taken in combination, these programs *can* both provide the incentives for individuals to act responsibly while they also provide an important set of safety net protections.

I should also note that this chapter is not about the details of how to design and run programs. While the first three sections propose specific policy changes, the last three sections describe the attributes of effective job training, youth, and urban development programs that have been successful in meeting their goals. It is particularly important in these areas to leave wide latitude to individual states, schools, or local authorities to design the specific programs that best suit their own populations.

Finally, it is worth noting that there are a plethora of public assistance programs which I do not discuss in this section. The most notable omission is the Medicaid program, which is under sharp scrutiny because of its soaring costs and (in many locations) inadequate provision of health services to the poor. I omit any extended discussion of Medicaid reforms, not because this is an unimportant topic but because Medicaid reform issues require a rather detailed understanding of the rapidly changing structure of the American health care industry. This would take us too far afield.

I also say little about the Food Stamp program, largely because I believe that the existing program serves a very important function as it is, and believe it should remain intact as it is. A base for all of the programs proposed here is a nationally defined Food Stamp program, broadly available (on a sliding scale related to income) to all families with low incomes. In a world where there are virtually no other forms of general assistance available to all poor, Food Stamps play an important safety-net role. It avoids some of the political problems of pure cash assistance by tying its assistance to expenditures on a necessary commodity. It also provides temporary assistance to many families who find themselves—through bad luck or bad management— in short-term economic need and without employment. If we as Americans want any form of a national safety net—and I happen to believe this is an important role for the public sector, as shown in chapter 5—the Food Stamp program provides it, and, as we saw in chapter 4, provides it relatively effectively.

Overall, these proposals to change and reorient the present system must work in a difficult environment. As wages continue to deteriorate, large numbers of families may successfully work more and still not escape poverty with only their earnings. It will be necessary to maintain a public and private set of programs that supplement wages. In the long run, to permanently lower poverty rates we must focus on the solutions that raise the skill level of young adults over time and decrease the number of less-skilled workers in the labor market.

As a number of the sections in this chapter emphasize, the success of the agenda that is laid out here will require much more than good governmentally run programs. If we are serious about reducing such behaviors as nonpayment of child support by absent fathers, teen pregnancy, and early school leaving, this will require a serious commitment on the part of communities and individuals as well as government. Throughout the culture, for both the poor and the non-poor, we need to reinforce a new set of expectations, behaviors, and goals for our families and our youth. Mentoring programs, youth organizations, churches, community-based action groups, and private sector companies all have an important role to play. Government efforts to change behavior tend to work only when they are reinforced by the behavior and support of families and social institutions.

7.1 A THREE-TIER SYSTEM OF FAMILY ASSISTANCE

SUMMARY. *To replace the AFDC program, a three-tiered Family Assistance program is proposed. A case evaluator meets with applicants and has the authority to provide small amounts of short-term assistance to those who need only temporary help to get back to work as part of the Tier 1 program. Those needing job search and training assistance are assigned to Tier 2, which mandates work in conjunction with cash supplements. Tier 3 is reserved for those who need cash assistance and, at least in the short run, are unemployable. Such a system would provide the states with substantial flexibility to run the programs they believe to be most useful, as well as placing the initial emphasis in the system on "What do you need to get back on your feet?"*

The new TANF block grant leaves the structure of welfare programs largely in the hands of the states, creating both potential opportunities and potential problems. On the one hand, it gives states a greater opportunity to redesign public assistance programs than they have had at any point in the recent past. On the other hand, it creates great uncertainty about how economic need and poverty among America's poor families might change as the structure of public assistance programs is changed. In times of tight budgets it may be hard for states to maintain a stable program structure. In this section we put aside concerns of financing, however, and talk about program structure. Financing issues are dealt with in the section on money.

This section proposes a new way to provide support for low-income families, which I will refer to as *Family Assistance*. I do this not only to emphasize the fact that this is not the same program as the old AFDC program, but also because I think a new name has political advantages. Each state is currently in the midst of constructing its own version of what was once the AFDC program.

If we are reconfiguring the support available to poor families, it is valuable to start with a new name, free from the overtones associated with the label "AFDC."

The Family Assistance program I present here replaces the AFDC system but would operate along with the other existing public assistance programs, namely, Food Stamps, Medicaid, and the EITC. It tries more effectively to fill the gaps which AFDC was designed to address.

One important aspect of Family Assistance needs to be emphasized from the beginning: *This program should not be limited to single parents.* As we have seen in earlier chapters of this book, single parents are often the poorest group but they are hardly the only ones who are poor. Just as AFDC was extended to all low-income families with children in 1988, Family Assistance should also be available to married parents when the need arises. When assistance is primarily available to single mothers, the pressure is greater among poor families not to marry or to break up. As I discuss below, states may want to provide more limited Family Assistance to married couples, but the program should serve a broader group than the AFDC program has traditionally targeted. In fact, Family Assistance is designed so that states that also run General Assistance programs for single or childless people can merge these two programs.

The Family Assistance program that I envision is three tiered, aimed at three different groups among the poor. Tier 1 is available for those with specific short-term needs and provides only limited one-time assistance, pushing its recipients immediately back into self-sufficiency. It also operates as a gateway into the other two tiers for those who need additional assistance. Tier 2 provides cash assistance in conjunction with mandated participation in job training and employment programs. Tier 3 is available to those for whom employment is not a near-term possibility, and provides long-term cash assistance. Let me discuss each of these in turn.

Tier 1: Evaluation and Short-Term Assistance

The old AFDC system included components that look somewhat like Tiers 2 and 3. The real innovation in the Family Assistance program is the addition of Tier 1.

Anyone who enters a public assistance office will deal first with a Tier 1 case evaluator. This person must be among the *most* skilled and experienced in the system (as opposed to the current AFDC program, where the intake workers are typically the least-skilled staff people.) The case evaluator would have three responsibilities:

1. *To determine whether this family should be immediately sent into either Tier 2 or Tier 3 programs.* Both of these programs will provide monthly cash income support, although in Tier 2, this is linked with work and job search requirements.
2. *To connect this family with other programs for which they are eligible.* This

includes publicly run programs such as Food Stamps or SSI, but also involves linking families with local nonprofit programs that may be available to help with health issues or family counseling.

3. *Most importantly, to use discretion to serve persons in the short-run as a Tier 1 recipient.* This means that eligible low-income applicants can receive limited amounts of short-term assistance, provided to meet specific short-term needs. A person who lost a job because of transportation difficulties may get assistance to fix his or her car. A person whose elderly mother is ill and who had to quit her job may be directed to services that will help her to provide care for her mother and still work. Someone who has been evicted may get assistance finding affordable housing. In some cases the case evaluator will provide the funds necessary to meet these short-term needs; in other cases, the case evaluator will simply link the person with already-existing programs.

This Tier 1 level of assistance reintroduces some amount of discretion back into the public assistance program.[1] The goal is to be more responsive to the immediate circumstances that have brought an applicant into the public assistance office. This tier tries to help some applicants avoid entry into Tiers 2 and 3, particularly focusing on those whose needs are more limited. Tier 1 may be particularly useful as a way to deal with married-couple families who find themselves in economic difficulty, but to whom the state does not want to provide ongoing support. The initial response will be, "What can we do to help you get back to work?" rather than "Please fill out these forms so we can see if you are eligible for monthly cash assistance."

Of course, there are also very real potential problems with introducing this sort of discretion. By definition, such a system recognizes that identical treatment for everyone is sometimes less fair than differential treatment based on circumstance; and some applicants will feel mistreated in this system. Oversight procedures have to be in place to assure that some offices do not misuse their discretion to exclude certain racial or ethnic groups from assistance. Rather than giving the case evaluator complete discretion, in most cases Tier 1 will have to work within a flexible set of guidelines that allow for a much wider set of public assistance responses than the current system. It will take some experimentation to set up the regulations and the procedures under which this system can function most effectively.

The role of case evaluator is particularly important in Tier 1, requiring better pay and more training and experience than current intake workers receive. Many states will need to hire and train people for this position. Case evaluators must have knowledge of the entire array of public and privately available programs, allowing them to work effectively as a clearinghouse of information and referrals to clients. In addition, they need to have the experience and authority to exercise some discretionary power over the resources that applicants receive. The case evaluator is not just administering a rigid set of program rules, but has the ability to judge when different needs should lead to different responses by the Family Assistance system. It will cost more to staff

Tier 1 than we currently pay for AFDC intake workers. But the reduced use of assistance should offset those costs.

In order to keep Tier 1 from dealing with an unending cycle of requests by the same applicants, Tier 1 benefits have to be limited. Once a client has been turned down for eligibility to Tier 2 or 3, states will have to establish guidelines about how much financial assistance someone can receive in Tier 1 and how frequently they can reapply.

Tier 2: Job Search and Training Assistance

Many of those who apply for Family Assistance will be unemployed but potentially employable. This is the group that has been targeted in current job search and training programs among AFDC recipients, and it is the group that should be immediately assigned to Tier 2. Most people participating in the Family Assistance program will be in this second tier.

In most situations, Tier 2 will offer three different levels of services. First, for most applicants, short-term job search and employment assistance will be required as a condition of monthly cash support. All that we know about how to run good job search programs should be put to use in designing these programs, as described in the fourth section of this chapter. Second, some applicants may benefit from additional education or training programs, and may be assigned to these programs prior to entering job search assistance. For instance, teen mothers should be encouraged to finish high school or a high school equivalency degree before going to work. People with drug or alcohol problems may need help addressing those problems before job search is useful. Third, there will be a need for some people to receive limited-time job placements. Women who are unsuccessful in their job search or young adults who need work experience before the private sector will hire them may need a public sector job placement or a subsidized private sector job before they can successfully locate an unsubsidized private sector job.

Obviously, different states may decide to write the rules for Tier 2 somewhat differently. Some states may use public sector job placements more readily, others may subsidize private employers to hire short-term "trainees" who are having difficulty landing a job on their own. Some states may want to provide greater training options. What is important is that *all* states have some serious employment assistance program available, for single mothers as well as for other adults who might benefit from them.

Tier 3: Cash Support

Despite the brave assertions by many political figures that welfare recipients need to be cut off from support, the evidence in this book shows how inadequate such advice is in today's labor market. Without some additional support, many women with younger children who can only find part-time, minimum-wage employment will be left desperately poor. Others among the poor are sure to experience extended spells of job search and unemployment. Unpopular as it may be to say so, there *is* a need for ongoing cash support for some groups in the population.

This cash support should be aimed at two populations. First, there are the workers for whom earnings are not sufficient to cover their family expenses. In the next section, I propose a set of policies that will supplement earnings for these families. As that section will show, if such policies are fully enacted, there will be virtually no need for any employed parent to receive additional Tier 3 assistance. If the proposals in the next section are not fully enacted, however, there will be a need to provide ongoing cash support, *even for some low-wage workers*, whose wages alone are not enough to support a family. Certainly, providing cash supplements to low-wage workers has broader political acceptability than providing them to nonworkers.

Second, for a small group among the poor, steady work is not a likely option in the near future. In one way or another, these are people who cannot cope with the labor market, given other problems in their lives. Some may be fighting drug and alcohol addictions; some face problems of mental incapacity; some have become so involved in a set of antisocial or counterproductive behaviors that they are not employable; some face health problems of their own or have young children or relatives that require attention and time. As we have discussed in this book, this is a minority among the poor, but they do exist. Some form of support for them is necessary: it is necessary because their children need the assistance; it is necessary because we are not a society that wants an increase in homeless and destitute beggars; it is necessary because it will lower crime and other social problems.

The level of cash support available to different groups will differ both within and across states. Within a state, the level of support available to single mothers with infants may be higher than that available to single mothers with older children who are engaged in job search programs. As with AFDC, different states will surely choose different levels of support even for very similar populations. The level of cash support that a state chooses to provide as a supplement to other programs will reflect their own state budget and political concerns, although an important ongoing role for federal funding is to provide some redistribution to states facing greater economic problems or coping with larger poor populations.

It is also worth commenting on what this section does *not* propose: time limits on Family Assistance. Rigid time limits do not recognize the diversity in the Family Assistance population. Some parents should receive assistance for no more than a few months before they find employment; others with limited education and several preschool children will take longer. For instance, if one imposed a rigid "two years and off" requirement for public assistance, evidence from existing state welfare-to-work programs indicates that while many AFDC recipients are working two years after receiving some job search assistance, a substantial minority are not, due to reasonable family and health limitations. In addition, even among those who are working, frequent work disruptions due to illness or family emergencies are common.[2] Trying to enforce a "two years and out" system (or any other number of years you want to pick) simply puts recipients back into the one-size-fits all program that has created so many problems in the past; it will provide too much assistance for some and too little for others. The Family Assistance program should do everything it can to encourage employment. But any policymaker who believes that setting rigid time limits will guarantee that current clients find jobs and become self-sufficient is badly misinformed and has not faced up to the new set of social problems and costs that such a policy will create.

How Do These Tiers Fit Together?

There will necessarily be fluidity between these tiers. Some persons who receive short-term assistance under Tier 1 may return and be assigned to job search programs under Tier 2. There may not be enough funds to run job search programs for everyone assigned to Tier 2, so that some persons may be temporarily placed in Tier 3, before their mandated involvement in job programs begins. Some persons in Tier 3 will be moved into Tier 2 as their life circumstances change. Some persons in Tier 2 who do not participate in good faith in employment programs may be removed from support and have access to no assistance or only to limited Tier 1 assistance.

States will need to establish guidelines about who is eligible for different levels of assistance. Certainly, no case evaluator should have complete discretion about who receives long-term cash assistance and who receives only short-term aid. Some appeals process needs to be available for those who believe themselves wrongly refused access into job training (Tier 2) or long-term cash assistance (Tier 3), and such a process can work only if there are general "eligibility criteria" for entry into each tier. These rules may differ for different family types based on their overall needs. For instance, states may want to be much more stringent about allowing married-couple families to participate in long-term cash assistance than single-parent families. Work mandates may vary for married couples versus single parents, whose minimum level of mandated job search or employment hours may be lower.

The point of this chapter is not to provide a detailed plan which every state can follow, but to lay out a framework within which states can work to establish the Family Assistance program that matches their budget. Some states will be more inclusive about who receives different support packages; some states will provide higher benefit levels; some states will be more insistent on differentiating between different family types. The important concept is that Family Assistance be flexible; that it recognize different individuals are at different points along the spectrum of need and job readiness. Rather than a one-size-fits-all cash assistance program, the Family Assistance program works to push those with short-term and limited problems immediately back to self-sufficiency, to encourage those who can work but have been out of the labor market to actively seek employment, and to support those with longer-term needs. There will never be a fool-proof system of differentiating which families belong in exactly which tier. But the fact that it can't be done perfectly should not stop us. Moving closer to this type of flexible system will move us in the right direction on welfare reform.

7.2 Supplementing Income and Making Work Pay: The EITC, Child Care Tax Credits, and Assured Child Support

Summary. *This section suggests a set of programs that supplement earnings and make work—even at low wages—a viable option for families. First, maintaining the current level of support within the EITC is important in order to maintain the rewards from working and to offset the declining wages received by less-skilled workers in today's economy. Second, the Dependent Care Tax Credit should be refundable, so that poor as well as near-poor working families receive child care assistance when the parents work. Third, assured child support payments for low-income single parents is important. Assured child support provides incentives for the government to identify paternity and enforce financial responsibility on parents, it substantially reduces the need to run other forms of cash assistance programs, it splits the costs of support for poor children between parents and the government, and it provides an opportunity to bring noncustodial parents into job search and job training programs.*

Cash assistance in this country has always been relatively limited, has become more limited over time, and is likely to shrink in size even further in the years ahead. With the federal government providing less support for cash assistance, it is unlikely that states will be able to maintain existing levels of assistance. While the last section emphasized the need for some remaining cash assistance, identified as Tier 3 of a Family Assistance program, all of the recent changes continue to move us farther away from reliance on this type of support for the poor.

The public rhetoric has increasingly focused on moving nonworking low-income families into the labor market. As we have seen in the earlier chapters of this book, however, at least among single mothers it is not a decline in labor market involvement that has led to high poverty rates. In fact, these women are working as much or more now as they did twenty years ago. Unfortunately, this is a group whose ability to work full-time has often been limited (particularly for those with preschoolers), and whose wage opportunities have gone from low to even lower.

The recent expansions of the Earned Income Tax Credit (EITC) have helped to supplement the incomes of low-wage workers. But as we saw in chapter 3, when we simulated the income of a mother with two children, she had to work full time at $6.50 per hour (a very high wage rate for many less-skilled women) with the EITC supplement before she escaped poverty. Since many low-wage women cannot work full time and/or earn much less than $6.50 per hour, they are even less able to provide for their family's expenses through earnings.

In this section I discuss three public assistance programs that would insure that employment gets families out of poverty. In fact, it would assure that virtually all families with a working parent will have sufficient income, without relying on the Family Assistance system described in the last section. First, the chapter reiterates the importance of the EITC in making work pay. Second, I propose making the current dependent care tax credit refundable to help offset child care costs among both married and unmarried working mothers. The third proposal is more controversial, namely, assured child support for low-income single parents. This would guarantee child support to children of poor single parents through a joint public/private child support program. This proposal has been lost in the dust sent up by those running to "end welfare as we know it," but it deserves reconsideration.

Maintaining the Benefits of the EITC

As we discussed at length in chapter 3, the Earned Income Tax Credit is the best and most effective response this country has made to the changing economic situation for less-skilled workers. If we want people to work, and if we also want parents to be able to care for and support their children, then the best choice is to supplement the low wages earned by many less-skilled workers. The examples at the end of chapter 3 indicated that both single parents and married couples gain between $1,200 and $2,500 in income from the EITC at reasonable levels of work. Without this income, work would have been a much less worthwhile activity.

The EITC came under attack for the first time in its history in 1995. In part, this occurred because of monitoring and enforcement problems with the EITC in the early 1990s that led to fraud among its claimants. Recent changes in the way that the IRS processes EITC requests has largely eliminated these problems. In part, the EITC has become more visible as its expenditures have grown substantially since benefit increases were enacted in 1993. Between 1993 and 1996, the total benefits received through the EITC (both in refund checks as well as in tax offsets) almost doubled, from $13 billion to $25 billion. This makes the EITC program about the same size as Food Stamps or AFDC, validly raising the concern that this money be spent wisely.

In a world where cash assistance is shrinking, however, and more and more previous aid recipients are being required to work, an expansion in wage subsidies is an excellent way to offset the steady decline in wages among less-skilled workers, as discussed in chapter 2. If we want people to work *and* we want them to be economically responsible for their families, some low-wage workers will need to receive wage subsidies. The EITC allows us to pursue both goals at once. Continued support for this program and maintenance of its current benefit levels are a vital part of the safety net in a time when traditional cash transfer programs are being cut.

A Refundable Dependent Care Tax Credit

A primary reason why women with small children see little economic gain from employment is that their child care costs are often high relative to their wages. While some low-wage women receive free child care from a relative, family-provided free child care is becoming increasingly less available as mothers, aunts, and sisters are also likely to be at work.

If child care costs are high relative to wages, some will argue that these women may be better off staying at home with their own children rather than paying someone else to look after them. I have a great deal of sympathy with such a viewpoint, but it is a less and less viable economic option for single mothers who need cash income, particularly as cash public assistance continues to be cut. Ignoring the issue of child care costs will not make this problem go away, however. A public assistance policy that cuts cash transfers, mandates work, and then expects a woman with two preschool children to be economically self-supporting while earning the minimum wage of $4.25 per hour—when most child care facilities will require at least that much in payment per hour to care for two young children—is a ludicrous and unworkable approach.

This means that many low-income women will need child care subsidies in order to benefit economically from employment. There are a number of child care subsidy programs run by federal and state governments, but these are not broadly available. Only 18 percent of working poor women receive any sort of direct subsidy for child care costs.[3]

At present, we provide a child care subsidy through the tax system, known as the Dependent Care Tax Credit. Low-income families claim a credit against their income tax liability for up to 30 percent of their child care expenses per year for all expenses up to $2,400, with a maximum credit of $4,800, if their income is below $10,000. The credit decreases from 30 percent to 20 percent (maximum credit of $480) for people with incomes between $10,000 and $30,000, and remains at 20 percent for families with higher incomes.

Perversely, however, the poorest women cannot take advantage of this child care subsidy, since it is only available as a federal income tax deduction. Families near or below the poverty level who pay no federal income taxes receive no subsidy. In fact, the expansion of the EITC has reduced the number of low-income families who owe federal income taxes. While this has increased families' take-home pay, it has also meant that fewer families were able to benefit from the Dependent Care Tax Credit.

The obvious solution to this problem is to make the Dependent Care Tax Credit refundable, like the EITC. This would mean that those persons who owed no taxes (or whose taxes were less than the amount of the credit) would get a check back in the mail for the value of the credit. This provides poor women with the same child care credit available to low- and middle-income women.[4]

Ultimately, it makes little sense to provide child care subsidies to working low- and middle-income families who pay taxes, but refuse them to poor families who are below the federal income tax level. If we want to encourage work among the poor, child care subsidies are an important piece of the strategy. Making the Dependent Care Tax Credit refundable is a logical way to help both poor single mothers and poor married women alike.

Assured Child Support for Low-Income Families

Parents have a responsibility to their children, whether they live with them or not. Only recently has extensive attention been paid to child support enforcement. As chapter 1 demonstrated, large numbers of children—both poor and middle-income—still receive limited support from their noncustodial parents (typically fathers).

A number of authors have proposed that the states accept responsibility for collecting child support from absent fathers, rather than leaving the monitoring and enforcement of this up to each woman. Many fathers are effectively able to avoid payments as long as it is the woman's responsibility to go back to court whenever checks don't arrive or are too small. The judicial review process is typically slow and expensive, and is particularly inaccessible to poor single mothers. In the 1950s, when there were few noncustodial parents, the courts might have been the appropriate enforcement agency for child support. But in our current world where court dockets are crowded and there are many more noncustodial fathers, we need a more efficient child support collection system. This means moving child support collection from the courts to the tax collection system. While this makes sense for all child support collections, this discussion focuses on a workable child support system for low-income mothers only.

For low-income mothers, I propose a Child Support Assurance (CSA) system, where the state guarantees child support payments, collecting from fathers when possible but making up the difference from state budget dollars when it cannot collect.[5] Most supporters of CSA systems want to guarantee child support payments to single mothers at all income levels, while I propose such support only to low-income single mothers. If CSA covers all single mothers, its costs will be substantially higher, both because of the cost of administering a much larger child support system as well as the cost of additional supplementary payments to nonpoor mothers that the state might have to make. The absent father of a child whose mother has a good job should surely behave as responsibly as the absent father of a child whose mother has only a low-paying job, but there is less reason for the state to supplement unpaid or underpaid child support payments in the first case. (Of course, some states may want to consider more comprehensive systems.)

What makes the CSA proposal unique is that it establishes a floor for how much support a child should receive from the absent father and holds the state responsible for the difference. It is an antipoverty program in the sense that the state subsidizes those children whose fathers are too poor to pay the minimum. To start this program at a budgetarily feasible level, I propose a minimum guarantee of $1,500 per child, below the $2,000 to $2,500 often proposed. Any child whose father's income is so low that he is unable to provide $1,500 in child support over the year would receive a supplement from the state to make up the difference.[6]

A Child Support Assurance system for low-income women will provide strong incentives for the states to be even more active than they are now in identifying paternity and locating absent fathers. Fathers would pay this income through standard withholding mechanisms, just as state income taxes are regularly withheld. The dollars would go into a child support trust fund maintained by the state. Out of this fund, the state would be responsible for sending a monthly check to the mother for the full amount of her child support. Clearly, the better the state is at collecting child support payments from fathers, the fewer additional state dollars will have to be used to pay monthly child support checks.

The primary advantages of a Child Support Assurance system are threefold. *First, it places first responsibility for support of children on their parents.* If we are going to enforce stricter work requirements for low-income women, insisting that they earn more of their income and receive less in public cash support, then it is only a matter of fairness that the fathers of these children contribute to their children's economic well-being as well. With a CSA system, there are strong financial incentives for states to enforce these responsibilities.

Second, a CSA system makes general cash assistance for working single parents unnecessary. While mothers who cannot work at all will still need cash assistance through the Family Assistance program, I demonstrate below that child support payments of $1,500 per child will mean that virtually all single mothers who work at least thirty hours per week at the minimum wage will be able to come close to escaping poverty. (This assumes the presence of the EITC, Food Stamps, and a refundable Dependent Care Tax Credit.)

A CSA program requires states to change the focus of their public assistance activities. It leaves relatively few women in Tier 3 of the Family Assistance program described above. Virtually all workers would be economically self-sufficient, and even nonworkers would need much less cash assistance than before. Thus, state resources would be shifted away from cash assistance programs and instead invested in expanded child support systems, which establish paternity and enforce parental responsibility.

Third, CSA provides a way to link single men into other short-term services. At present, too many poor single men are outside the mainstream economy—in the underground economy, in the care of the judicial system, or just "hanging around" picking up odd jobs. Innovative new programs have linked men who do not pay child support into job search and job training programs.

For instance, Parents' Fair Share is a pilot program being tested in multiple sites around the country. In this program, absent parents brought to court for nonpayment of child support are required to participate in a mix of employment and training activities, combined with responsible parenting classes and mediation on problem issues between custodial and noncustodial parents. The evaluation results of Parents' Fair Share are not yet available, but preliminary evidence suggests that those required to participate in the program report changes in behavior, and a high percentage of participants have shown strong attendance and participation records in the program.[7]

In short, rather than viewing child support as a solely punitive measure enforced on fathers ("We'll make them pay, or else!"), a Child Support Assurance system will create the incentives for governments to think in new and creative ways about how to bring absent fathers back into the community as well as enforce their responsibilities to their children.

Child Support Assurance failed to get on the public policy agenda as part of the recent welfare reform debate. Why should I propose this again, particularly given the statement at the beginning of this chapter that I want to present only feasible program alternatives? There are at least two reasons why this proposal should be reconsidered.

First, over time, the demands for absent parents to support their children will continue to increase. As AFDC payments and other forms of assistance are cut back under budget pressures in the mid-1990s, the call for better monitoring and enforcement of child support will grow. If we want to demand responsible parenting behavior, asking mothers to work and support their children, we should make similar demands on fathers.

Second, limiting CSA to low-income women makes it a much less expensive program to operate. The support for a targeted CSA program for poor single mothers should be greater than for a universalist program for all single parents, as has been proposed in the past. If costs continue to be a concern, there are a number of other ways to limit the costs of a CSA system and still benefit the women who need it the most. For instance, the guaranteed child support level may be placed below the $1,500 proposed above. Even a $1,000 per year child support guarantee for the children of single mothers would be preferable to the current situation in which too many mothers receive no support at all.

It is also worth remembering that increases in child support guarantees mean less money spent on other forms of cash assistance to single mothers. If CSA is targeted toward low-income women, less money will have to be spent on Family Assistance or on Food Stamps. Thus, the state dollars that supplement child support payments are not entirely new budget money, but the redirection of money away from general income support toward support that enforces parental responsibility.

What Would These Changes Mean for Poor Families?

Table 7.1 indicates how these proposals help working adults support their families without using the Family Assistance program. It shows the result of taking the EITC (at its 1994 level), making the Dependent Care Tax Credit refundable, and enacting a Child Support Enforcement system for poor women, assuming a modest $1,500 child support payment is guaranteed per child.[8] Note that there is no budget line for Family Assistance payments. If states enact further cutbacks in cash assistance, it is possible that many employed women will have no access to Family Assistance dollars. Thus, I want to show that *for employed women*, this system works without reliance on any general cash assistance program.

The first part of table 7.1 shows the effects of these programs for a working single mother with two children, while the second part looks at a married couple with two children. Obviously, the CSA system has no impact on this second family. These are the same two families we observed in table 3.2 of chapter 3, where we showed how the existing mix of programs affected their income. Table 7.1 shows how these new proposals would affect their income.

As table 3.2 showed, under the public assistance system existing in 1995, a single mother with two children did not escape poverty unless she worked full-time at $6.50 per hour, a wage rate above that earned by most less-skilled women. Under the system proposed here, with the refundable child care credit and with CSA income she comes near the poverty line when working only part-time at the minimum wage (column 1), and escapes poverty when she works full-time at the minimum wage. At a wage of $6.50 per hour, she is above the poverty line (for a family of three) even when working part-time. In short, this system makes work pay, without any traditional "welfare" payments. Only when this woman doesn't work at all, or when she works limited hours at a low wage, will she need other forms of income assistance beyond those shown here. Finally, it is also worth noting that for many low-income women, the income supplements shown in table 7.1 are *not* all paid by the government. Her biggest supplement, the $1,500 per child in child support payments, may be paid at least in part by the father of her children.

The bottom of table 7.1 shows a married couple with two children. If the husband works full-time at the minimum wage, the family remains near but still below the poverty line. If the husband earns a higher wage (which is more likely for less-skilled men than for equivalent women) or if the wife goes to work part-time, they will escape poverty. Unlike table 3.2, where there was little gain in family income from the wife's employment, there is a clear gain

TABLE 7.1
Effect of Proposed Programs on Take-Home Income

Example 1: Single Mother with Two Children
Poverty line = $11,940

	Pt-time Work at $4.25	Pt-time Work at $6.50	Full-time Work at $4.25	Full-time Work at $6.50
Earnings	$ 5,313	$ 8,125	$ 8,500	$13,000
EITC	1,598	2,438	2,528	2,178
Food Stamps	2,557	1,882	2,272	1,192
Child support	3,000	3,000	3,000	3,000
Gross income	$12,468	$15,445	$16,300	$19,370
−(Soc. Sec. tax)	(404)	(618)	(646)	(988)
−(Fed. Income tax)	0	0	(54)	(731)
−(Child care costs)	(2,500)	(2,500)	(4,000)	(4,000)
Dependent Care Credit	750	725	1,160	1,080
Take-home income	$10,314	$13,052	$12,760	$14,731
Share of poverty	.86	1.09	1.07	1.23

Example 2: Married Couple with Two Children
Poverty Line = $15,029

Wife: Husband:	No Work Full-time at $4.25	No Work Full-time at $6.50	Pt-time at $4.25 Full-time at $6.50
Earnings	$8,500	$13,000	$18,313
EITC	2,528	2,178	1,232
AFDC	0	0	0
Food Stamps	2,932	1,852	1,297
Child support	0	0	0
Gross income	$13,960	$17,030	$20,842
−(Soc. Sec. tax)	(646)	(988)	(1,392)
−(Fed. Income tax)	0	0	(324)
−(Child care)	0	0	(2,500)
Dependent Care Credit	0	0	625
Take-home income	$13,314	$16,042	$17,251
Share of poverty	.89	1.07	1.15

in table 7.1. Before, their increased child care expenses almost outweighed the earnings gain for the wife. With the refundable dependent care credit, there is now a real increase in family income from the wife's employment.

The dollars proposed here for these programs are only approximate estimates of what might be provided. The primary conclusion from this section is that we *can* make work pay and abolish traditional cash welfare payments.

But it will require other forms of income supplements. Most Americans, however, are far more willing to help a working poor mother pay child care and receive child support assistance than they are willing to pay for general cash support for a nonworking mother.

7.3 MONEY MATTERS

SUMMARY. *The financing of public assistance programs is crucial to their success. The policies proposed in this chapter are not likely to cost any less than we currently spend, but neither are they likely to cost substantially more. In truth, there is no way to both* improve *public assistance programs and to* cut *their costs dramatically. In the face of declining wages for less-skilled workers, moving people from cash income assistance toward greater employment will still require ongoing supplements to their earnings. In addition, the appropriate design of shared federal/state financing is important to assure reliable funds for public assistance programs.*

So far, this chapter has been about the design of publicly run programs, and what they can and cannot be expected to accomplish. We have ignored the question of economics: How can such programs be funded and how much will they cost?

The most irresponsible part of the recent welfare reforms enacted in Congress is their financing, best characterized as "wishful thinking economics." Those who support deep federal funding cuts seem to believe that the problems of poverty will go away if the United States just stops spending money to help the poor. Not only is there no evidence to support this view, but substantial evidence that past funding *has* played an important role in reducing need among America's low-income families, as discussed in chapter 4, which also indicated that there is little evidence of unusual levels of "waste, fraud and abuse" in these programs. While some efficiencies are always possible, there is little reason to believe that the same services can be provided at a much lower cost. Similarly, chapter 5 indicated the impossibility that individual families or nonprofit charities could fill the gap of billions of dollars of lost federal funding. Finally, chapter 5 also discussed the improbability that states will be able to fund substantially larger budgets for antipoverty programs.

The base conclusion should not be surprising to anyone: we can't get something for nothing. Eliminating substantial safety net programs is likely to create greater poverty and need, particularly among those families least able to cope with further economic deprivation. The flip side of this problem is that good programs—programs that encourage people to work and make employment a supportable option—are not necessarily cheap programs.

Even those job search and training programs that produce good effects—

increased hours of work and reduced public assistance—cost a substantial amount up front to operate. For effective programs, evaluations indicate that this money can be recouped through reduced welfare spending and increased tax payments. But as wage and earning opportunities among less-skilled workers continue to decline, the gains associated with employment will continue to shrink. If we want people to escape poverty while working in the available low-wage jobs, we will have to provide the Earned Income Tax Credit and child care subsidies for poor working parents. This shifts government spending away from the simple income supplements that more traditional welfare programs provide and toward more employment-focused assistance. But it does not eliminate the need for public assistance to low-income families.

Some legislative changes have proposed cutting government spending on traditional welfare programs and cutting funding to employment and job-focused programs at the same time. This is foolish and shortsighted. This book suggests that we *can* reconfigure our public assistance system in some useful ways. But anyone who believes that we can do this "on the cheap" has little contact with the real world labor market facing less-skilled workers.

Finally, it is worth emphasizing again that the amount of money we currently spend on public assistance programs is not at outrageous levels. The two programs most closely associated with "welfare"—AFDC and Food Stamps—accounted for only 3 percent of total federal expenditures in 1995. This is in sharp contrast to the 22 percent that went to Social Security assistance, or the 20 percent going to national defense. Public assistance remains a relatively small share of overall spending.

Overall Costs

The proposals that I outlined in the first two sections of this chapter reconfigure the public assistance system so that it provides greater incentives to work. The precise details of funding depend upon the exact nature of the programs that are put together, and there is still a great deal of discretion left to policymakers in these proposals. There is no reason to believe that this reconfigured system will be much more costly than the current system.

On the one hand, this system will spend less in cash support. Some people will be moved out of public assistance more quickly by being eligible only for short-term aid in Tier 1 of the Family Assistance program. The Child Support Assurance for low-income single-parent families will also substantially reduce Family Assistance cash support payments. A growing amount of this money over time will come from absent parents, as states work to more effectively collect child support and offset their own costs. In 1993, for every dollar a state spent on collecting child support payments due to AFDC recipients, it received more than a dollar back in payments, suggesting that states can reduce cash assistance expenditures by spending money on child support collections instead.[9]

On the other hand, there will be increased expenditures necessary for the child care tax credit and that share of the Child Support Assurance system that involves state subsidies rather than payments from absent parents. The higher the Child Support Assurance amount and the more extensive these guarantees are to nonpoor women, the greater the increased expenditures needed to implement this system.

Relative to the cost of the system of public assistance as it existed in the mid-1990s, the cost of the revised system suggested here is probably within a few billion dollars, assuming that Child Support Assurance is primarily focused on women with incomes below 150 percent of the poverty line, and that the guarantee level is around $1,500 per child. That is to say, it will not cost significantly more than we are spending now, but it will not cost significantly less either. We are not in a world where fighting poverty is easy or cheap. If wages were rising and if unemployment were falling among the less skilled, then I would argue that in the long run we can spend less and accomplish more. But in the real world, the amounts we need to spend on public assistance are not likely to change greatly.

State-Federal Issues in Program Finance

Some of the biggest recently enacted changes in antipoverty policy involve the relative roles of the states versus the federal government. Under block grants, states will be given much greater power over the design of cash transfer and employment programs for low-income families. This movement to block grants may create serious financial problems. In particular, there are three aspects of the financing arrangements between the federal and state governments for these block grants that are important for the long-term stability of public assistance programs.

First, the federal dollars to these programs must be pegged so that they can vary with the economic cycle, expanding as need expands (when state budgets are least able to grow) and shrinking as the economy grows (when state budgets are expanding and need is declining). Typically, this means pegging the federal contribution to some cyclical measure, such as unemployment within a state. The TANF block grant allows the federal government to give each state a flat dollar amount equal to some share of the amount they provided during the early 1990s for AFDC and related employment programs. This formula is a recipe for future financial disaster in these programs.

A flat level of funding takes no account of the effect of business cycles on state financing and public assistance need. Almost all states operate under strict balanced budget requirements and have little ability to do deficit financing. Yet, it is when unemployment is high that the need for public assistance is greatest, even though state tax revenues are at their lowest. The current funding arrangements place the risk of economic recession entirely on the shoulders of the states, even though state budgets are less able to deal with this than the federal budget. As was discussed earlier, it was the inability of state and county governments to deal with the needs of low-income families in a time of deep recession in the 1930s that led them to demand federal involvement. The economics have not changed; in the next recession, when state budgets are squeezed by declining tax revenues and balanced budget requirements, states will necessarily be forced to cut back on their assistance programs at exactly the time when need is the highest.

Second, federal funds should require matching state dollars rather than simply providing a flat contribution. A matching formula would key the federal contribution to the level of state spending. States that wanted to spend more would get more federal dollars as well.

In fact, matching funds solve some very sticky problems, allowing increases in the federal contribution when changes occur that result in greater need within a state. If immigration continues at its current rate, some coastal states will have a higher share of poor families ten years from now than they do today. If population shifts from northeast to southwest continue over time, there will be less need for public assistance spending in the northeast and more in the southwest. Federal matching funds would provide greater federal monies if and when states choose to provide more of their own dollars to address a problem. This would mean that states which face long-term demographic trends that increase their share of the low-income population will see an increase in federal funds when they increase their own spending on poverty-related problems. Under the current law, the federal share would decline when state spending went up, since the federal dollars are fixed.

In the absence of such adjustments to the federal funding distribution formula, the new block grant laws are a disaster waiting to happen. In the long run, the funding formula will not be equitable across states. In the short run, a downturn in the economic cycle could result in major cuts in assistance programs exactly at the point when there are few jobs or other sources of assistance available to low-income families.

Third, matching funds for employment programs should not be dealt with in the same way as matching funds for cash assistance, but should be split out and provided separately. Current legislation gives states a lump sum payment from the government, equivalent to a share of what they received for *both* cash assistance and welfare-to-work programs in the early 1990s. This ignores the fact that these programs are not interchangeable and have needs that might grow at different rates.

As of 1995, states were required to enroll 20 percent of their AFDC caseload in welfare-to-work programs. Not all states have met this goal; many of those that have met it did so by running only minimal job-search programs, often lasting just a few days. There are clear exceptions to this. Some states have excellent programs in operation, as we discussed in earlier chapters. But most states are very constrained in their funding and able to place only a limited share of their AFDC caseload into these programs.

Under recent legislation, states will be required to have over 50 percent of their caseload in work-related activities soon after the year 2000. This may be an unreasonable requirement. To date, the *most effective* programs have been able to involve about 40 percent of the caseload in work-welfare programs. (thirty to 40 percent of the caseloads are typically declared ineligible for work mandates. Of the remaining 60 to 70 percent facing work mandates, close to two-thirds participated in some sort of activity.)[10] Most states are far from reaching this level. To push above this level will require substantially *more* resources, *more* staff, and *more* funding to create public sector jobs or to subsidize private sector employers to hire disadvantaged workers for short-term job experience. This will cost much more than states are currently spending; to do this at a time when federal funds for job training are frozen at previous levels is impossible.

The federal matching rate on state funds for job programs should be higher than the federal match on cash assistance programs, particularly if the federal government is going to increase its mandates on the states in this area. If cash assistance funds are cut, employment program funds should, if anything, be increased. In addition, there should be some up-front money available from the federal government for states to implement and make new programs operational (programs always cost more in the earlier years, because of the learning curve that program managers necessarily experience) and to experiment with creative employment programs for low-skilled and long-term unemployed adults.

Medicaid—The Biggest Budget Item of All

The biggest budget item for antipoverty programs is Medicaid. More than any other program, its costs *are* out of control. Between 1985 and 1995, Medicaid expenditures increased from $40 billion to $170 billion. Since almost half of these costs are paid by the states, this has caused an enormous increase in both state and federal expenditures on Medicaid. Of course, the cost increases in Medicaid are not unique to this program, but reflect the cost increases that *all* health care programs have faced in recent decades.

So far, I have said nothing about Medicaid in this chapter. In part, this is because it is difficult to see how substantial cuts in Medicaid spending can be accomplished. As was discussed above, the big ticket items for Medicaid are long-term care for poor elderly and disabled individuals, and these are the costs that have increased the most rapidly. This is not care we are likely to refuse to provide in the near future, nor is it something that is likely to become cheaper to provide. Yet, there are actions that might help slow the cost increases in Medicaid.

For instance, enrolling Medicaid recipients in health maintenance organizations (HMOs) might reduce costs among Medicaid recipients who only need occasional medical services. HMOs would be most effective in lowering costs for mothers and children, who currently account for about one-third of total Medicaid costs. Throughout the United States, more and more insured workers are being covered by HMOs, which charge a flat annual rate to provide care over the year. This is in contrast to traditional fee-for-service insurance policies. HMOs cut costs, although they limit some care choices. It is worth noting, however, that this will do nothing to address the costs associated with the most expensive Medicaid population, the disabled and elderly who need long-term and continuous care.

Alternatively, Medicaid could provide greater emphasis on preventive care. Treating individuals for acute health problems related to diseases such as diabetes or emphysema is far more costly than trying to prevent such problems in the first place. Too many Medicaid patients start to receive services only after their health condition has become acute. One low-income woman from a poor neighborhood whose son has severe asthma attacks described her frequent trips with him to the hospital emergency room for treatment (often involving several days of hospitalization). Not until he was five years old, when she visited a new neighborhood clinic, did any medical professional ask her what she was doing to prevent such attacks. Having always believed these were unavoidable medical problems (the doctors in the hospital had never indicated otherwise), she was astonished to learn that she could change things in her home environment to make her son's asthma far less severe. She was angry that no one had taken the time to talk with her. In her words, "They spent a lot of money on us, but they never told us the simple things that would have made it all easier." Avoiding stories like this, by promoting preventative visits for prenatal care, for childhood illnesses, or for chronic complaints, may help Medicaid contain costs.

Given the price of health care in America, nothing is going to make Medicaid an inexpensive program. But there are some reforms that may help reduce the rate of cost increases that have occurred recently. The only change that is likely to result in substantial reductions in Medicaid expenditures is the implementation of some form of rationed care system, whereby certain technologies would not be available to Medicaid patients, or where certain groups of patients would have only limited access to care. This type of medical care rationing, however, has so far been unacceptable within the United States for any health care system. The inequities involved in implementing such a system for only poor families have so far kept this option off the list of politically viable alternatives.

Ultimately, we get what we pay for in public assistance programs. We can cut the budget for these programs substantially, but not without consequences. As earning opportunities continue to decline among less-skilled workers, the negative consequences of cuts in public assistance may be even greater now than fifteen years ago. Few families will be able to fully replace lost public assistance support with wages.

This chapter has proposed ways to reconfigure the public assistance system away from cash support and toward employment support. Such a system is not likely to be less expensive, however. To provide low-income families who work with the income necessary for them to survive will require ongoing public expenditures. No smoke-and-mirrors budgeting can obscure that fact.

7.4 EFFECTIVE JOB PLACEMENT AND TRAINING PROGRAMS

SUMMARY. *This section discusses eight important lessons for effective job placement and training programs, based on our accumulated experience of the past fifteen years with adult job programs, particularly welfare-to-work programs.*

The first section of this chapter proposed a Family Assistance program, containing a Tier 2 job program for assistance recipients. This was briefly described as a job training system with three components, including a job search/job placement component, an education and training component, and a public employment component. What more can be said about how such a system would work?

There are many ways to run effective job training, and no one way is obviously "right." In fact, in different settings, with different populations, some very different models of job training have been effective. In short, it's not just what you do, but how you do it that makes a job program effective. Thus, rather than giving a detailed outline for employment programs, in this section I make recommendations about the design and operation of effective job programs that state and local program planners need to keep in mind as they revise and reform existing programs.

First, be clear that job search, employment, and training programs are different from cash assistance programs. States that operate employment programs as just another required mandate for their AFDC clients are typically least successful in these programs. Such states run the job program out of the same office, with the same staff, and in much the same way as they run AFDC.

In contrast, programs that have been effective have typically dealt quite differently with their employment programs. They make sure their employment program is about *jobs* and staffed by people who understand that. This may mean hiring new staff or, at a minimum, retraining staff who were working with AFDC. Helping people find jobs is *not* the same as certifying them for cash assistance.

One of the immediately striking aspects of the successful California GAIN program in Riverside County is the professionalism of the office. The male staff wear suits and the women wear business clothes. When clients walk in, it's clear they are in a business office rather than a public assistance office; no one is sitting around waiting for hours. The staff provide role models showing what the workplace is about, and how to dress and act as effective employees.

These people are running a *job* program and not a cash assistance program. The cash assistance staff are located elsewhere.

Second, make sure the staff are enthusiastic about the program and promote the need and the opportunities for work with their clients. There's an element of excitement about good employment programs, communicated from the staff to the clients. It is an excitement about the possibilities of work, as well as about the opportunities *this* program will open to clients. People assigned to work programs are sometimes scared, sometimes reluctant, and almost always uncertain about what this work program will mean in their lives. Those who run job training programs need to worry not just about the details of program design, but also about the encouragement and reassurance they provide to help clients make the transition into the labor market.

Effective state job programs market themselves to their clients. At one particularly memorable job site, I was in a room where women were making phone calls to local employers asking about available jobs. The group was interrupted twice in an hour by an outside staff person who burst in, announcing he had just heard about a particular job that was open. He listed the necessary skills; was anyone interested? If not, he'd be back soon with another job. The message sent was that jobs *were* available and that the program was working with the women to try and locate them.

Third, give clients realistic expectations about the jobs available to them. Many jobs will pay low wages; the boss may make constant and sometimes unreasonable demands; there may be little slack for lateness or misbehavior on the job; workers may be on their feet eight hours a day. Clients need to learn not only about the opportunities, but also about the particular problems they are likely to face on their jobs.

One program in Chicago sets up mock situations and has clients act out their responses to an angry boss, an intimidating co-worker, or a rude customer. Another program explicitly counsels clients about both the advantages and the disadvantages of the jobs for which they are interviewing. When new workers have unrealistic expectations about the job they've located, they are less likely to stay in it. Finding a job and being fired in a few weeks may only make it harder to go out job hunting again.

In today's labor market, relatively few less-skilled clients in job programs are going to find initial jobs with good pay, pleasant working conditions, and interesting work. This is one reason why putting employment programs together with other forms of assistance—EITC supplements, child support payments, health insurance, etc.—is so important. If job programs and job placements leave people worse off than before, with less income and all the demands of a crummy job, news of this will spread fast among clients. It will be all the harder to elicit interest and enthusiasm about finding a job and going to work.

Fourth, make sure job placement programs have a strong "follow-up" component, so that those who lose jobs can quickly return to job search and seek new employment. Many people who have been out of the labor market will not be successful in their first job, or maybe even their second and third. Many current job programs operate on the assumption that once a job placement occurs, the program has been effective and its work is over. Someone who is unemployed and without income three months later often reapplies for AFDC, and it might be months or years before she is again assigned to a work program.

The privately run CET vocational training program, which has been replicated around the country, is successful partly because its graduates are considered clients for life. Those who lose jobs can come back and be quickly reconnected with a network of employers and job options. The good news is that most programs find that clients need to come back only a few times before they connect with a job that works. Without the option to return and reaccess the resources of the employment system, however, some clients will too quickly be back in the same situation they started in.

Fifth, realize that if many more women are required to enter employment programs—particularly long-term AFDC recipients—many of these women will require more than a few weeks of job search assistance before they are ready for employment. There is no cheap way to provide employment services to seriously disadvantaged populations, and to produce significant increases in earnings and employment. As we have discussed elsewhere, many long-term public assistance recipients face multiple problems; some women are in abusive relationships, some are clinically depressed, some face substance abuse and addiction problems. Many of those who are long-term users of public assistance face some of these problems. These are not women who are going to be readily hired by employers. If we want *all* AFDC recipients to work, states must directly confront these problems in their job programs.

It may be cheaper to continue to provide cash assistance to some very disadvantaged women and children than to try and provide them with training and counseling that will help them move into steady employment. This is not to say that we shouldn't try to run job programs for these women, but merely that these programs will be more difficult and more expensive than most programs we are currently running for AFDC clients. Simply telling this group to "go out there and get a job" is unlikely to show many results.

There is little knowledge about what is necessary to operate an effective job program for seriously disadvantaged women. The Chicago Commons is currently running a program aimed at low-skilled women with past histories of domestic abuse. Women are required to attend classes for twenty hours per week, combining GED preparation classes and group counseling sessions. Job counseling starts immediately when women enter the program, as women are asked to plan what they're aiming toward. Most women take a year and a half to two years, however, to get to a point where they are ready for employment. This time is spent building skills, since many women enter the program with very low reading and numeracy skills, as well as helping women address some of their family and personal problems. For instance, the program finds that it typically takes at least a year or longer before women in abusive relationships are ready to confront or leave an abusive husband or boyfriend. In the meantime, many of these men work to undermine the women's progress in the program, not wanting them to achieve the financial and personal independence that employment can provide.

Sixth, do not assume that training or education should precede job search. Particularly among people who have little labor market experience, there is increasing evidence that it is work experience that stimulates people to think about their lack of training and skills. Younger dropouts and women who have been out of the labor market for an extended period of time often lack the motivation to seriously participate in skill-building programs until they've been out working. Only with experience do they become motivated to go back into a classroom or into a vocational education program and improve their literacy or their math or acquire additional skills.

This is one reason why programs that simply provide job search assistance tend to be cost effective. They move people into work quickly, which is often the goal of someone who enters a job program. But ultimately, many less-skilled workers will need more skills before they will advance into higher-wage jobs. In some cases, workers will be able to get extra training with their employers. But in many cases, this is not possible.

If we are serious about trying to get people into better-paying jobs, then access to further training opportunities must be available to those who are motivated to take them. In many cases, this may not mean traditional classroom learning (although that is often a piece of any training program). Apprenticeship programs, vocational education programs, and on-the-job training programs may be far more effective for workers who are wary of returning to a school environment they left at an early age (often with bad memories of how they did in the classroom).

Seventh, plan to create some public sector jobs or subsidize some private sector jobs if your program wants to place a high share of the most disadvantaged population into the workforce. Among female high school dropouts, the unemployment rate was 16 percent in 1994; it was 14 percent among males. This means many less-skilled people who seek work will not immediately find jobs. If a large group of AFDC recipients were pushed into the labor market at once, the unemployment situation would only become worse, since the number of jobs available in the short term is typically not very expandable.

In addition, if states are trying to get the most disadvantaged population into work, some of them may simply not be employable in the private sector until they have work experience. For instance, we know that many employers are suspicious of workers who have not held a recent job or who have a criminal record, or they are very reluctant to hire younger black men from ghetto areas. A public assistance system that demands everyone be employed is closer to a command economy than a market economy; if everyone is to work, someone has to guarantee the "jobs of last resort" to those workers who are not hired by private employers. A six-month-long successful employment stint in a publicly created job can show an employer that this worker will show up on time and do the work assigned.

As discussed earlier, public sector jobs create management problems. It is a major challenge to identify positions in public and nonprofit agencies, to match workers and slots, and to monitor both the worker's behavior and the employer's behavior so that the worker is provided with some attention and training. In short, this is neither a cheap nor an easy program to run, and it is not a program most states will want to run at a very large scale. On the other hand, public sector employment can provide an effective way to enforce work requirements regardless of the local rate of unemployment. I expect a number of states will be experimenting more fully with such programs in the near future. There will be a need to do a serious evaluation of these efforts, to try and identify "best practice" techniques that the more successful states are using.

An alternative to public sector job creation is short-term employer subsidies for hiring disadvantaged workers, similar to the Targeted Job Tax Credit discussed in chapter 3. Such programs create incentives for employers to provide jobs to workers they may not otherwise hire. On the one hand, employer subsidies avoid the management problems of running public sector job programs. On the other hand, they may be less effective at increasing employment, particularly if employers are wary about hiring workers who have been out of the mainstream labor market for long periods of time.

Eighth, expect that anything beyond basic job search assistance will not be cheap. The current debate over welfare reform wants to hold onto two contradictory demands. First, we are demanding that people must find employment and cannot claim unlimited cash assistance. This has led states to run welfare-to-work programs. Second, we want to save money by cutting people off welfare. This will not happen if ending cash assistance means running more extensive work programs. In fact, the more that states focus on trying to move the most disadvantaged populations into employment, the more such work programs will cost and the smaller their short-term benefits will be, as they deal with clients who have very limited job skills.

There is no quick, easy, and cheap way to run a good job training program. Job search assistance—the least expensive type of job program—is often effective at increasing work but largely places people in very low-wage and unstable jobs which do not solve their ongoing economic problems. For these workers, ongoing child care supplements and earnings supplements will be necessary. Job training and education programs are much more expensive to run and provide much less immediate results but may increase long-run earnings opportunities. Clearly, a good state job program will provide both types of programs to different groups of people.

The only cheap alternative is to impose "hard" time limits and kick women off cash assistance without providing any job assistance program. Much of the first part of this book is devoted to a discussion of why this would seriously increase poverty and need among women and children. The current job market will *not* provide many less-skilled women with jobs that allow them to become economically self-sufficient; in some cases there may be no job available at all. The best that most women can expect is that work will replace only part of their current cash assistance.

The evaluations of job assistance programs over the past fifteen years indicate clearly that such programs can achieve their goal and increase employment and work hours. Encouraging greater work effort among low-income families is a valid role for the government. Work plays an important role in people's lives. From an economic point of view, it provides income and contributes to the overall productivity of a society. From a social and psychological point of view, work plays an integrating role in people's lives, giving them connections into a community of co-workers, providing a sense of accomplishment, and linking them with the larger society. But job assistance programs must be linked with other subsidy programs in order to assure that the children of working mothers are cared for, and that working adults can pay the bills to support their families.

7.5 HELPING TEENS PREPARE FOR THE FUTURE

SUMMARY. *The problems faced by today's teenagers will shape tomorrow's poverty problems. Teens who drop out of school or have children often lack a sense of future possibilities and do not see the importance of education and schooling for their lives. It is important that interventions for at-risk teens start before the midteen years, before teens become pregnant and before they drop out. The growth in school-to-work programs for non-college-bound teens is one of the most promising developments in helping disadvantaged teens. These and other effective programs set clear rules and expectations, link learning to real-world situations, and tie training to jobs. There is only so much that government policy can do to influence teens, however; it is clear that the messages teenagers receive from families, peer groups, and media are more important to their behavior than anything that happens in government-run programs. This is particularly true for teen mothers.*

There are only limited ways to affect the behavior of adults who left school years ago and have a long history of unstable employment, family problems, and inadequate income. But teenagers are different. Their lives are still largely before them. Early choices, such as dropping out of school or becoming a teenage parent, may create problems for them for years to come. If we can help only one group, surely our major focus must be on preventative programs aimed at teens and young adults. As the economic opportunities available to less-skilled workers deteriorate, this becomes even more important. We must communicate to teens the importance of acquiring skills and receiving formal educational credentials, and we must assure that our schools provide an environment where such skills are readily learned.

Yet it is important to recognize up front that there are only very limited ways by which government programs can affect teenagers. Our schools are clearly the primary public institution where public policy directly influences children and adolescents. But all of the scholarly research on teenage behavior indicates that it is the *family* and *peer* environment that matters most. In this sense, government policy will always play a more distant and less effective role in influencing teenage behavior than it might for older adults. We return to this point below.

As indicated in chapter 4, in too many cases past programs directed at teens have had little or no effect. Programs that have successfully influenced teenage behavior are often very different in the specifics of how they operate. This suggests that recommending specific programs is less useful than identifying the common attributes of existing programs that have been effective.

Communicating the importance of a good education, and instilling teens with the motivation to take school seriously is the best way to assure that they will avoid early pregnancy, involvement in crime, or drop out of high school. It is perhaps obvious that finishing a high school degree and thinking about some form of post–high school vocational training means greater job preparation, and opens the doors to higher-wage jobs with better long-term earning and promotional opportunities. Chapter 2 described the long-term economic consequences for those who leave school early.

What is often less clear is that a long-term sense of economic opportunity is key to addressing other teen problems as well. The women least likely to become teen mothers are those who believe that education is important and who have a sense of future opportunities—and who believe that their school performance will affect those opportunities. Girls who see little advantage to education are much more likely to become pregnant and/or leave school. Similarly, teenage boys who have a sense of future goals are less likely to engage in crime or join gangs. Thus, getting teens to take education more seriously is key to a whole range of teenage behavioral issues. The only question is, "How can we do this?"

The most important lesson of the past ten years of research and evaluation about teen-related policies is this: *Don't wait until the late teen years to start working with at-risk teens.* Chapter 4 showed the discouraging fact that programs aimed at young adults who have already dropped out of high school tend to have few effects. This group appears caught in a set of peer relations that make them resistant to any efforts at change, at least until they acquire more experience. There is evidence, however, that those still in school can be affected by programs designed to increase their school achievement and reduce their probability of dropping out. Similarly, evaluations of teen pregnancy programs indicate those who participate in such programs prior to becoming sexually active often seem more influenced by them than those who participate in them at a later age.

Other evidence reinforces the message that we need to focus more on the early rather than the late teen years. Studying children's achievement as they progress through school, Harvard researcher Ron Ferguson found that young African American boys from poor neighborhoods appear to become caught up in peer influences during the early junior high school years. Around this age, their school attendance and achievement scores are increasingly influenced by peer effects and less determined by family and school characteristics.[11] Clearly, the preteen and early adolescent years are an important time, when at-risk teens begin to listen less to their parents and more to their peers who say "school is useless."

Probably the most useful recent policy development for teens has been the evolution of school-to-work programs for the non-college-bound students, designed to keep them engaged in school and aware of the rewards of completing high school. As we discussed in chapters 3 and 4, hosts of new experimental programs are restructuring the high school environment for disadvantaged teenagers, from freshman year on through the senior year. Career academies utilize special curriculum and run smaller "school-within-a-school" programs for at-risk youth. Private business/public school partnerships set up summer employment and mentoring opportunities for teens, providing them with a sense of the realities of the workplace. Tech prep programs link students with vocationally oriented community college programs long before they graduate from high school.

We know little about the relative effectiveness of these different approaches, as serious evaluation studies of some of the school-to-work transition programs have just recently begun. The results of these evaluations should be closely followed, and local school districts as well as those in charge of state and federal matching funds should continue to encourage creative ways to provide teenagers with the motivation to remain in school and to take their education seriously.

What are the common attributes of those programs that seem to achieve the best results with teens, regardless of whether they operate for in-school students or for dropouts? *First, they establish a clear set of rules and expectations and enforce them.* Job Corps makes it clear from the beginning what sort of attendance they want, how many "excused absences" are allowed, what level of classroom performance has to be maintained. Students know the rules and they know what will happen if they violate them. This both establishes an atmosphere of fairness (everyone operates under the same rules), and it imitates a typical work environment. Certain levels of performance are expected, or you're fired.

Second, learning is closely linked to real-world situations. Teachers use curriculum that make it apparent how a required skill is directly useful to a particular vocation or to a situation that the student is likely to confront once he or she leaves school. This provides a motivation to learn, very different from the type of learning that many low-achievement students perceive goes on in classrooms, where they are told to learn things of apparently little relevance solely at the authority of the teacher.

Third, successful programs are often closely tied into job networks. At the CET vocational training program, graduating students are put into direct contact with employers who have learned over time that these students have a particular set of skills that they need in their workforce. In apprenticeship programs, there is often a clear promise that students who perform well in the program will be hired by the companies offering the apprenticeships. In this way, students can directly connect the program requirements and the promise of future employment.

Creating an effective learning environment is the responsibility of public schools. Teachers need to be well trained and motivated. Students need to feel safe at school, particularly in neighborhoods where children may not feel safe on the street. Classrooms need to be adequate, with enough desks and books and space for all students. Peeling paint, broken desks, and old equipment all communicate to a student, "This isn't very important."

But the public schools and government-operated programs can do only so much to motivate students and keep them in school. This is a community and family responsibility as well. If the community and the family do not communicate the importance of education to a teenager, then the schools will surely fail to do so. In this sense, government programs can only be a part of the solution to high dropout rates and inadequate skills among teens.

Thus, government policies aimed at disadvantaged teenagers or at school reform are inherently limited. This does not mean we should stop running such programs, but that their success will be modest unless they operate in conjunction with other social changes. Community organizations, churches, family members, TV shows, and popular music—all forces that are important in shaping teen behavior—must also work to communicate the message that "school matters," and to provide a sense of future opportunities for those who are willing to work for them. This is too big and too important a job to be accomplished by government policy alone.[12]

Nowhere is this more apparent than with regard to the problem of teen parenting. As this book has discussed at length in several places, teen parenting is not primarily due to welfare benefit payments; lots of teens who might receive such payments do not consider becoming a parent; lots of teens who won't get payments do become parents. Rising birthrates among unmarried teens are primarily the result of the learned messages these teenagers receive throughout their childhood that says, "having sex is adult behavior," "having a baby is even more adult," and "everybody does it." The government is not the primary institution responsible for stopping these messages and sending other ones to preadolescent children. Like the messages children absorb regarding the importance of education and schooling, the family, the community, and the general media are the places from which children learn most about their world.

Teen parenting will become less prevalent when two things happen. *First, more adolescents need to have a sense of future possibilities that motivate them to avoid early parenthood and concentrate in their adolescent years on learning and preparing for adulthood.* This is not just a matter of communicating the importance of education, but for many teens—especially many girls—it includes communicating a sense of *self-confidence* and self-control, independent from boyfriends, girlfriends, or babies. Too many young women, when asked why they had a child, simply respond, "I wanted something that would *love* me." Not surprisingly, girls who have histories of sexual and physical abuse are at high risk of teen pregnancy.

Second, more adolescents need to receive a message from people around them—from parents, from other adults, from older brothers and sisters, and from peers—that raising a child at age 16 is not smart. As a community, we need to do more to protect our children from explicit sexual messages that push them into premature sexual behavior. We need to communicate better that parenthood is about much more than biological functioning; that it is about enduring relationships and long-term responsibility. We need to talk about the costs of teen pregnancy and the constraints it creates on teenagers' lives. These are not easy messages to get across to many teens, and they are usually communicated better through our actions than through our words.

At core, these changes will require more from Americans as individual citizens than it will require from them as taxpayers. As individuals—as neighbors, teachers, relatives, and parents—we are responsible for communicating this message, in part by demonstrating through our own actions that we believe it. As members of churches, youth groups, mentoring programs, and other organizations in touch with teens, we need to give attention to our adolescent acquaintances. As consumers and participants in a world inundated by messages from TV, from movies, and from popular music, we need to demand responsible behavior from those who hold power in these parts of the economy.

This does not mean that there is no role for government policy in addressing teen pregnancy. Public schools have to function effectively, as safe and attractive learning environments. If schools appear to provide little in the way of useful training or preparation, early parenthood seems a more attractive option. As discussed in chapter 4, there are some pregnancy prevention curriculums that seem to have moderate benefits which should be more widely used. We also need to go beyond thinking of "sex education" as the best way to reduce teen pregnancy. Lack of information is only a small part of the problem of rising teen births. We need to develop programs that bring teens, parents, and peers together to address problems of peer pressure and lack of family control. Finally those teens who do become pregnant need to be encouraged to finish school and prepare to be effective parents. For many teens, this push must come from their families and friends. For teen mothers who need public assistance, such support should be strongly linked to programs that help the mother complete her education and participate in job training programs.

There are government-run programs for teens of proven effectiveness, particularly those that try to keep at-risk disadvantaged youth in school and prepare them for future employment. We should be serious about improving and expanding on these programs. But there remain large areas of teenage behavior that are more influenced by the social and family environment which public policy can affect only tangentially. It is foolish to hold only the government responsible for the problems of high dropout rates and early childbearing, or to expect the government alone to solve these problems. These are problems that must be addressed much more broadly. In the words of the African proverb, "It takes a village to raise a child." We are all part of the village in which our children grow up.

7.6 Addressing the Problems of Urban Ghetto Neighborhoods

Summary. *Public policies aimed at improving urban ghetto neighborhoods have not been notably successful in the past. This section discusses individually focused policies, such as job training or mobility programs, as well as neighborhood-focused policies, such as housing rehabilitation or economic development. Both types of policies are important and will reinforce each other. Individually focused efforts will require more intensive interventions and more resources in order to succeed in the poorest neighborhoods, and should work at linking people in these neighborhoods to programs and opportunities in other parts of the metropolitan area. Efforts at broad-scale community change are best spearheaded by nonprofit and private sector groups, with the government acting as a partner rather than as leader.*

Throughout this book, I have talked about the unique problems of our poorest city neighborhoods and the people who live there. The worst face of poverty today is in those ghetto poverty neighborhoods that are racially segregated, physically deteriorating, with inadequate city services, and whose economy has virtually collapsed, with few jobs, few services or stores, and too many people not working, collecting public assistance, or operating in the underground economy. Although only about 12 percent of the poor live in these areas, this is perhaps the most vicious and most destructive type of poverty in America today. Policies designed to work within these communities are an important component of any set of public policies to address poverty.

Any discussion of urban economic development and poverty must start with a serious caveat: the overlapping set of problems that create extreme neighborhood poverty have typically developed over decades and reflect many long-term economic and social trends. There is no way to change these neighborhoods overnight, and indeed, most of our efforts to revitalize neighborhoods have been (at best) only partially successful or (at worst) they have been complete failures.

In this section I try to draw a few useful lessons from the successes and the failures of the past thirty years of economic development efforts. A short section such as this one, however, can only brush the surface of the many issues involved in effective community development. Economic development policies, more than perhaps any other area of policy, must be uniquely adapted to the neighborhood and the city. Thus, like the last two sections, this section focuses more on process than on specific program recommendations.

There are two policy approaches to alleviate the problems of poor urban neighborhoods. One set of policies focuses on people, trying to help individuals find jobs, get additional schooling, stay out of gangs, and so on. Most of our public assistance programs work at this level and many nonprofit community programs do as well. The other set of policies focuses on broader structural changes, including such efforts as housing rehabilitation, school reform, community policing, or attracting new employers and stores into an area. These policies aim to change community institutions and community structures and are the focus of many more traditional community development activities.

The discussion about individual versus structural policy approaches reflects the ongoing debate about behavior versus environment as the fundamental problem in these neighborhoods. Is the primary issue socially deviant behavior (gang membership, criminal activity, excessive idleness, dysfunctional families), or is the primary issue an impoverished environment (poor police protection, bad schools, lack of employment, deteriorated housing)? Ultimately, this is an unfruitful debate. Over time, behavior and environment are mutually reinforcing. If efforts to attract employers are successful, more people in the neighborhood will find jobs. If good job training programs are operating in the neighborhood, employers may be more willing to locate there. Clearly, policies aimed at ghetto neighborhoods need to address *both* individual behavior and environmental decay.

Policies That Help People in Ghetto Neighborhoods

Most of our public assistance policies focus on individuals and families. We provide cash support or Food Stamps, subsidize compensatory preschool programs, or run job training programs. Few of these programs pay any attention to the neighborhood of the recipient; they are assumed to affect the individual, regardless of where he or she lives.

In high-poverty ghetto neighborhoods such programs face their biggest challenge. Many families in these neighborhoods are poor for long periods of time, and many adults are only sporadically employed. For many residents of these neighborhoods, public cash assistance often becomes a major long-term source of income. It is in these neighborhoods that our traditional antipoverty programs are most often charged with "creating dependency" by conservative critics who see the lack of employment and jobs, and with being too stingy and limited by liberal critics who see the enormous needs that continue to exist. To make these programs more effective, three lessons should be kept in mind.

First, efforts to change individual lives will require more time, more funding, and greater effort in these neighborhoods than elsewhere. While these may be the neighborhoods that consume a disproportionate share of cash and in-kind assistance, it will not cost any less in the near future to move from cash support toward job and training programs. As we discussed earlier, among women facing multiple disadvantages and problems in their lives, a short-term job search program is unlikely to have much effect. Programs that work with disadvantaged women in inner-city neighborhoods typically find that at least two years of services (literacy training, jobs skills assistance, domestic abuse counseling) are needed before women can find and hold a job. Similarly, summer job programs for youth in these neighborhoods have no long-term employment effects. A single summer's job isn't enough to change the attitudes of these teens toward work and school.

Benefit reductions or cold-turkey cut-offs of cash assistance to long-term poor families in ghetto neighborhoods may satisfy the desire to do something quickly about long-term welfare recipients. But this will almost surely create more problems than it will solve. For families who see no way out (partly due to their own inadequate sense of alternatives and partly because they face many difficult barriers to changing their lives), income support programs provide an economic cushion. If such support were withdrawn, it is true that more people would seek to earn income. But in a neighborhood where there are few jobs or connections into outside job networks, substantial withdrawals of public assistance income would further isolate many people, driving them deeper into the underground economy or into abusive or overcrowded living situations.

Second, one of the most important tasks for individually focused programs in poor ghetto neighborhoods is to create linkages between people in ghetto neighborhoods and people and institutions in other parts of the metropolitan area. In these neighborhoods, more than in other places, programs should do more than simply provide services to people. They should provide a sense of the alternatives and opportunities that are available outside the neighborhood. Job training programs, for instance, should encourage participants to visit other neighborhoods in the city and seek jobs outside the immediate familiar area. Teen-focused education and employment programs should give teens experiences outside their immediate neighborhood, introducing them to people and places they may not otherwise visit.

The most promising example of this is the mobility programs, discussed in earlier chapters. Some of these programs explicitly link workers in poor communities into suburban job networks. Other programs actually try to help poor families move elsewhere by locating apartments in other areas of the city which are eligible for Section 8 housing subsidies. In a similar vein, many nonprofit programs in poor neighborhoods try to provide linkages to another world for their members, through such efforts as mentoring programs for youth, or athletic competitions with groups in other areas of the city.

Third, it is important to realize that small individually focused programs in these neighborhoods are unlikely to have major effects on behavior; this is why broader structural development efforts are required. In a situation where neighborhood institutions are not functioning effectively (poor schools, inadequate policing, few local stores or employers) and where many individuals choose socially isolating behavior (drug use, early school departure, sporadic employment), individually focused programs with modest effects cannot be expected to produce much in the way of behavioral change.

While changes in individual behavior must occur if ghetto communities are going to change, it is not clear that this is best accomplished by starting with individually focused programs. People who feel caught—by their own life history, by their lack of economic resources, or by their surrounding friends and neighborhood—may need some sense of hope and possibility coming from outside themselves. They may need to see evidence of other changes before they start thinking that change in their own lives is a possibility. This brings us back to where we started, with the idea that larger structural neighborhood changes are a necessary component to the success of more individually focused efforts in poor neighborhoods.

Policies That Initiate Structural Changes in Ghetto Communities

Programs that focus on larger structural issues rather than on individuals and families include a range of community development, neighborhood organizing, and institutional reform efforts. Some of these have been government initiated, such as enterprise zones, discussed in earlier chapters. Many are initiated by community development corporations and other community groups, which solicit support from a broad range of sources, both public and private.

Those who work to produce physical and structural change in a neighborhood must be willing to take a long-term perspective. There are an uncountable number of examples of failed efforts at neighborhood change. The many economic and social problems in poor neighborhoods, the inertia of existing institutions, the sense of alienation and frustration among many residents of these neighborhoods, and the active hostility of most city governments toward reform efforts work against efforts at structural change. Those efforts that succeed often have the following attributes.

Most neighborhood development efforts that accomplish real change are initiated by local community organizations and institutions, and not by government programs. In most cases, there is important governmental involve-

ment in these efforts—public funds, friends in the mayor's office, or a sympa-
thetic planning board—but the initial push comes locally. This occurs in part
because local organizations are more apt to work on problems that are key
community concerns and around which they can mobilize broad-based local
support. In part, it also occurs because local organizations have more credibil-
ity and trust with local residents. A government staff person who arrives from
city hall to announce "Here's what we're going to do for your neighborhood"
is less likely to receive active support and assistance.

One reason local groups are important in leading community development
efforts is that they look at their own community with a different lens than
outsiders do. *Neighborhood programs that succeed tend to see a neighborhood as a place of potential opportunities to be drawn forth and strengthened,
rather than a set of problems that need to be fixed from outside.* Urban community development specialist John McKnight has long talked about the need
for successful community change efforts to start by identifying the *strengths*
of the community rather than starting with the list of problems.[13] Michael
Porter, a Harvard Business School professor, has recently received a great
deal of attention talking about the economic *advantages* of poor neighborhoods and how these can be used to stimulate economic development in such
areas.[14]

In addition, *most effective neighborhood development efforts bring together many organizations and constituencies.* Increasingly, good development projects are seen as *collaborative* projects.[15] In their planning and their
implementation, they involve a broad group of actors, including parents from
local schools, neighborhood improvement groups, local businesses, churches,
city-based foundations, nonprofit organizations, public officials, and so on.
Why is such a broad cast of characters necessary? Precisely because the factors that produce and maintain blighted neighborhoods are so complex and
overlapping. Working only on changing local schools may be ineffective if
crime and gang problems are not also dealt with. Trying to bring employers
into an area may be ineffective if available workers have low skills and poor
work habits. Trying to run job training programs may be ineffective if workers
who graduate from these programs have few connections into other areas of
the city where jobs may be more abundant.

As a result, one has to work on multiple fronts at once in an effective community development effort. At a minimum this means coordinating the efforts
of a variety of different organizations. Community development efforts need
to choose their issues carefully, starting with more isolated problems that can
be readily dealt with and progressing on to more complex problems where
multiple actors need to be involved in planning and implementing change.

Perhaps the hardest lesson for public policymakers wanting to intervene in
the poorest communities is that economic development in these communities
will require much more attention, interest, and mobilization than the government by itself can possibly provide. The active leadership and involvement of
private sector and nonprofit organizations, particularly community-based

groups, is vital if such efforts are going to be effective.[16] Public programs always work best when they reinforce and work with other economic and social changes that are moving in the same direction. When public programs are asked to resist and even push back the major economic and social forces acting on a neighborhood, they are almost never effective without the support and assistance of many other partners.

This does not imply there is no role for government involvement in neighborhood economic development. Government grants or low-interest loans can be crucial in starting community development efforts that are considered high-risk by traditional private sector financial institutions. Similarly, government assistance through tax breaks or wage subsidies can make it easier to retain or attract new businesses. In addition, local governments often need to be flexible about real estate and building regulations that are sometimes used by absentee landlords to hinder housing rehabilitation or new land-use proposals.

The reason poverty is so high in urban ghetto neighborhoods is because a whole host of destructive forces has evolved over time, with institutional problems in the schools, reinforced by lack of nearby employment, reinforced by poorly maintained public housing structures that become centers for drug and gang activities, and so on. The problems in these neighborhoods are deeply structural and environmental at the same time that they are deeply behavioral. It is difficult to know how to break out of the vicious circle.

The best hope for long-term change in these neighborhoods lies in a combination of large-scale collaborative neighborhood improvement and economic development efforts, combined with the more traditional efforts to work with individuals, providing them with the resources, information, and connections that help them move toward more stable lives. While the public sector has a role in each of these activities, it may not be the leadership role. Large-scale development efforts are probably best initiated by neighborhood and city-based groups, with government agencies as active partners.

CHAPTER 8

Conclusions

THIS BOOK is designed to deepen the reader's understanding of the nature of poverty in the United States, and the interaction between poverty and the public policies designed to alleviate it. In part, this book is a response to the extremely narrow and all-too-often misinformed images and stylized "facts" that have dominated the public conversation about poverty and welfare reform in this country in recent years:

- If poor adults just went to work they wouldn't be poor.
- Today's poor all live in ghetto neighborhoods and rely on public assistance.
- Spending on never-married women and their children is busting the federal budget and needs to be controlled.
- Antipoverty programs have ended up hurting people rather than helping them; if we got rid of welfare, there would be much less poverty.
- If we decreased government assistance to the poor, nonprofit charities would help them instead.

As we have seen, all of these common beliefs—and many others—simply don't stand up to the facts.

A great deal of time, energy, and money has been spent studying the problem of poverty in the United States over the past thirty years. As a result of this, we know much more about the nature of poverty and about the effectiveness of different antipoverty programs than we did thirty years ago. This book relies on that body of evidence to explore the *facts* regarding poverty and policy.

To sum up, there are three general themes in this book. *First, over the past decade Americans have misunderstood the nature of poverty in this country.* We have come to believe that it is more ghetto based, more behavioral, and more unalterable than it actually is. The result is a growing sense of alienation and "otherness" in how middle-income Americans perceive poor families. In reality, the poor are an extremely heterogeneous group. Only a very small percentage live in high-poverty urban ghetto neighborhoods. Many among the poor work regularly, although there are often economic and family constraints that limit their work so that it is not full-time nor full-year. In short, the poor behave far more like the nonpoor than many Americans want to believe.

Second, our ideas about the ability of the poor to escape poverty through work have lagged behind the economic facts. Twenty years ago a book like this would have confidently pointed to economic growth as the most effective way to decrease poverty. Not today. Our understanding of the relationship between work and poverty must change as a deteriorating set of economic opportunities is available to less-skilled adults in this economy, even as the overall economy continues to grow. With hourly wages declining among both less-skilled men and women, the opportunities to escape poverty through employment have declined. The results of this economic change are far too often misinterpreted as evidence that the poor have become lazier. In reality, work is a less reliable source of economic support, for reasons relating to long-term economic shifts which the poor have been powerless to prevent or offset. Not only has this made life harder for many low-income families, but it has also made antipoverty efforts harder, since it has essentially eliminated the effectiveness of general economic growth as a way to reduce poverty.

Third, we have misunderstood the role of public assistance. Unlike the impression held by most Americans, many of our antipoverty efforts have accomplished exactly what they set out to accomplish. Poor families are unambiguously better off today than the poor of thirty years ago, because of the greater availability of medical care through Medicaid, because of improved nutrition through Food Stamps and other programs, and because of income transfers that they receive. The absence of these programs would make the poor worse off along a variety of measures.

The hostility that many Americans feel toward antipoverty programs is partly based on misinformation, and is partly due to a misunderstanding of the purposes of these programs. Few so-called antipoverty programs were actually designed to assist families out of poverty; either they provided resources (food, housing, medical care) that are not included in our current poverty calculations, or they provided such low levels of income support that they could not possibly have raised many families above the official poverty line.

At the same time, it is important to recognize that the current system of public assistance to the poor can and should be improved. Too much help is available to those who are out of the labor market, and too little help is available to low-wage employed workers. The primary cash support program historically available to low-income parents, AFDC, was particularly badly designed and often poorly administered. The unpopularity of this program has led to calls for its abolishment in the mid-1990s, although it is too early to tell whether replacement programs designed by the states would be able to avoid some of the pitfalls that trapped the AFDC program.

I propose a reconfigured system of public assistance that moves us away from large-scale cash support and toward a more work-focused system. In particular, I propose a set of changes that would assure that working adults, even with relatively low wages, will be able to support their children and will not be poor. But this proposal also recognizes that this will not work for *all* among the poor; there are those who will not find employment in the near future, who will need ongoing assistance, and for whom we need to continue to operate safety net programs.

Much of the substance of this book is not about specific program design (although there is some of that), but about the knowledge we have gained regarding how to run effective antipoverty programs that increase work among adults and increase education among teens. The success of a broad range of diverse programs suggests that it is not *what* you do that often matters as much as *how* you do it. Thus, this book is not about a "one-size-fits-all" antipoverty program. Indeed, one of the problems with existing programs is that they often lump together people who should be treated differently, and end up being ineffective. The judgment and accumulated knowledge presented here can guide program design for local, state, and federal policymakers, whether they are designing effective job search and training programs or are putting together a package of policies aimed at reducing inner-city poverty. But policymakers in different cities with different populations will want to design the details in their own way.

Poverty is not a new problem, but like all aspects of our modern society, the nature of poverty has been changing over time. The solutions of the 1960s are no longer appropriate in the 1990s. As we have seen, some of our old policy responses simply do not work in the current economic environment. As the nature of poverty changes, the policies designed to address poverty need to change as well.

The good news is that there is a host of policies that have been tested and shown to be effective. This is particularly true of job search and placement programs for less-skilled women. We should be expanding the use and further improving the design of these efforts.

The bad news is that there is no "silver bullet" against poverty. While many programs produce beneficial results, these results are inevitably modest. They help people stabilize their incomes a bit more than before, they increase employment and hours of work a bit more than before, or they increase high school graduation rates a bit more than before. These are not inconsequential achievements, but none of them will "solve poverty." If we expect too much of any one program, we will inevitably be disappointed. Rather than viewing each new policy proposal (as too often occurs in the political arena) as "the new answer to poverty," we should view individual programs as important components within a larger network of programs.

An appropriate antipoverty system is one that works on many fronts. It should provide nutritional assistance and medical care as an underlying safety net to all low-income citizens. It should support employment and make it possible for those who put a reasonable effort into the labor market to support their families. It should encourage all parents to be responsible for their children, providing both financial and nurturing support. It should encourage teenagers to finish school and to delay parenting until they are better prepared to raise children. None of these tasks is simple; no single program can possibly accomplish any one of them completely, much less all of them together. Our current array of antipoverty programs recognizes that there are a multitude of goals. Inevitably, this means that programs sometimes overlap and conflict with one another.

There are ways to run a better set of public assistance programs. But our expectations must be realistic. "Ending poverty" is not a likely outcome in the foreseeable future. But bringing more of the poor into employment, increasing high school graduation and skills among the non-college-bound, and creating a strong system of support for working low-income families is very possible. These are the things we should be doing.

All levels of government must play a role in assistance to the poor. The federal government has particular advantages in redistributional financing and in program oversight and evaluation. State and local governments are where programs are implemented. Program design may be best located at the federal level for large, uniform programs, but occur at the state and local level for programs that need to adapt to changing local circumstances.

In the end, however, poverty is not just a problem for government bureaucrats to worry about. If we are serious about wanting to help children grow up with a sense of opportunity, if we want to see adults working in the economic mainstream, and if we want to eliminate the blighted urban neighborhoods in the core of our cities, then we all bear responsibility to address the problems that create poverty in this country. We *all* send messages to our teenagers and to our children about their expectations in life. We *all* teach others by how we behave toward those who talk a different language, or whose skin color is different. We *all* have a voice in the debate over budget cuts and welfare reform. We *all* have an opportunity to participate in volunteer service activities, in community development organizations, or in mentoring opportunities for low-income youth.

Our government programs will be much more effective if they are implemented in an environment where poverty is recognized as a national problem that affects us all and to which we are all expected to respond. Just as the government has not created the problem of poverty in America, the government by itself will not solve that problem. Our social and economic institutions need to recognize their role in this effort. Private sector businesses can be involved in school-to-work training programs or can provide employment opportunities to low-income women seeking work. Nonprofit organizations can run a wide variety of service and community programs, working in partnership with the public sector. Individuals can reach out to other individuals one-on-one and through church and community organizations. Only when these efforts occur, *jointly* with well-run and effective government public assistance programs, will this nation truly be a land of opportunity for all its people.

$$\bullet \quad N \quad O \quad T \quad E \quad S \quad \bullet$$

INTRODUCTION

1. These data are discussed in chapter 2.

2. A thorough discussion of the current U.S. definition of poverty, some of its problems, and recommendations for change are given in National Research Council (1995) and in Ruggles (1990).

3. Official data on poverty is only reported with a lag. When this book was written in late 1995, limited official poverty statistics were available for 1994. See U.S. Bureau of the Census (1995b). The last year with complete published data was 1993. See U.S. Bureau of the Census (1995a). In many cases in the following chapters, I use the original survey data from which official poverty statistics are calculated, the March Current Population Survey, to tabulate numbers not available in the published statistics. The most recent release of these data is for the year 1994, which provides data on poverty numbers for 1993.

4. National Research Council (1995). The author was one of the panel members who produced this report.

5. Mayer and Jencks (1994).

6. Data on negative incomes and student poverty calculated by the author from the 1994 March Current Population Survey.

CHAPTER 1
THE CHANGING FACE OF POVERTY

1. Unless otherwise referenced, all 1994 data on poverty (the most recent year available) come from the U.S. Bureau of the Census (1995b). Unfortunately, when this book went to press, only limited 1994 data were available. Data for 1993 and earlier, unless otherwise referenced, come from the U.S. Bureau of the Census (1995a).

2. Data in figures 1.1a through 1.1d are tabulated by the author from the 1994 March Current Population Survey.

3. Data on never-married poor single mothers for 1983 and 1994 are tabulated from the 1983 and 1994 March Current Population Surveys. 1983 is the earliest year in which such tabulations can be made because earlier years contain coding errors in the ways subfamilies are defined (see Ellwood and Bane 1985).

4. Author's tabulations from the 1994 March Current Population Survey.

5. Kollman (1995).

6. Reno (1993), table 2.

7. Author's tabulations from the 1994 March Current Population Survey. We define as a family any group of related people who live together, including single individuals (living alone or with other unrelated persons) as one-person families.

8. These data come from the Panel Survey of Income Dynamics (PSID) and are based on the interviews from 1980 through 1992 asking about economic resources in the previous year. The individuals are weighted with the 1989 sample weights, the last set of weights available at the time these calculations were made. For each of these thirteen years, I can calculate which individuals live in families whose income was below the poverty line during that year. Cumulating the data over time, I can count the number of

years each person is poor. The sample is big enough so that I can look at the extent of poverty among whites and blacks, and among children and adults, but it is not big enough to look at smaller groups such as Hispanics. Calculation of annual poverty is based on the NEEDS variable (based on the U.S. poverty line) available in the PSID data for 1979 to 1988, and calculated by the author in a consistent manner for 1989 to 1991. For other studies of poverty spells (that produce results quite consistent with these), see Bane and Ellwood (1986) and Stevens (1994, 1995). These data define poverty based on annual income, in the same way as official government statistics do. I am unable to observe shorter spells of poverty, i.e., people whose incomes were very low for only three or six months over the year. These data therefore undercount short spells of poverty.

9. The reasons for spell beginnings and endings are calculated based on all observed spells of poverty that start and end during the thirteen years of the data, excluding one-year spells. (Including one-year spells has only minor effects on the numbers.) Spell beginnings are classified in the following hierarchical manner: (1) All individuals who become poor by being born into poverty are placed in the category "Child Born into Poverty"; (2) among those who remain, all those in a family where a previous wife becomes a head are placed in the category "Married Couple Breaks Up"; (3) among those who remain, all those in a family whose new head was the child of the head in the previous year are placed in the category "Child Forms Own Family"; (4) among those who remain, all those where the number of adults in the family falls or where the number of children increases are placed in the category "Other Changes in Family Composition"; (5) among those who remain, all those where the (continuing) head's income falls more than $1,000 in 1980 dollars are placed in the category "Earnings of Head Fell"; (6) among those who remain, all those whose wife's income falls more than $1,000 in 1980 dollars are placed in the category "Earnings of Wife Fell"; (7) among those who remain, all those whose unearned income falls more than $1,000 are placed in the category "Other Income Fell." This is similar to the methodology followed by Bane and Ellwood (1986) in classifying movements into poverty.

10. Spell endings are classified in the following hierarchical manner: (1) All individuals in a family where a previous head becomes a wife are placed in the category "Married Couple Forms"; (2) among those who remain, all those in a family whose new head was the child of the head in the previous year are placed in the category "Child Moves Out of Poor Family"; (3) among those who remain, all those where the number of adults in the family increases or where the number of children decreases are placed in the category "Other Changes in Family Composition"; (4) among those who remain, all those where the (continuing) head's income rises more than $1,000 in 1980 dollars are placed in the category "Earnings of Head Rose"; (5) among those who remain, all those whose wife's income rises more than $1,000 in 1980 dollars are placed in the category "Earnings of Wife Rose"; (6) among those who remain, all those whose unearned income rises more than $1,000 are placed in the category "Other Income Rose." This is similar to the methodology followed by Bane and Ellwood (1986) in classifying movements out of poverty.

11. Harrington (1962).

12. Data on 1990 ghetto poverty from Jargowsky (forthcoming.) A discussion of equivalent 1980 data is in Jargowsky and Bane (1991).

13. 1970 data from U.S. Bureau of the Census (1971), tables 3 and 4. 1993 data are from supplemental tables provided by the U.S. Bureau of the Census (1995a, labeled table 20).

14. Data from Blank and London (forthcoming). Unless otherwise referenced, all data cited in this section are from the same source, primarily tables 2 and 3 and figure 3, or from the sources cited in those tables.

15. One definitional comment is necessary here. I use the term "family" to refer to all related people who live together, including single persons living without other relatives as a one-person family. (The Census Bureau never includes single individuals when it uses the term "family.") Thus, a married couple with their two children are a single family. Two adult sisters who live together are a single family. But two unrelated young adults who share an apartment are two families. Lying behind this language is the assumption that related people who live together share income, but unrelated people who live together do not, and their economic status should be calculated separately.

16. Alter (1994).

17. Population data for 1960–1970 from U.S. Bureau of the Census (1961 to 1971); 1971–1989 from U.S. Bureau of the Census (1972 to 1990). Birthrate data for 1960–1989 from U.S. National Center for Health Statistics (1993d); 1990 data from U.S. National Center for Health Statistics (1993b); 1991 data from U.S. National Center for Health Statistics (1993c); 1992 data from U.S. National Center for Health Statistics (1994); 1993 data from U.S. National Center for Health Statistics (1995a).

18. Bachu (1993).

19. Eurostat (1990).

20. For a more extensive discussion of the data briefly reviewed here, and for a longer review of the causal factors behind rising rates of nonmarital births, see U.S. Department of Health and Human Services, Public Health Service (1995).

21. See Geronimus and Korenman (1992 and 1993) and Hoffman et al. (1993).

22. Hotz et al. (1995).

23. Author's tabulation from the 1994 March Current Population Survey.

24. Divorce data through 1988 available from U.S. National Center for Health Statistics (1991b). More recent data from the U.S. National Center for Health Statistics, *Monthly Vital Statistics Report*, various issues.

25. See footnote 3, this chapter.

26. Washington State Institute for Public Policy (1993). Raphael (forthcoming) summarizes some of the domestic abuse data for women on welfare. Musick (1993) summarizes evidence on abuse among teen mothers. Evidence on the age of unmarried teens' partners is in Landry and Forrest (1995).

27. Blank (1993), table 2-9.

28. Evidence on children in single-parent families is summarized in McLanahan and Sandefur (1994). Evidence on children in poverty is from Miller and Korenman (1994) and Korenman et al. (1995). Of course, it is difficult to infer causality about the extent to which child outcomes are due to poverty versus single parenting versus a host of other factors in children's lives. Mayer (forthcoming) tries separately to identify the effect of poverty on children's outcomes.

29. These numbers are from Freeman (1995). Similar data are in Mauer and Huling (1995).

30. For a review of the problem relating criminal involvement to labor market earnings and participation, see Freeman (1992, 1995). Wilson and Petersilia (1995) provide a range of evidence on recent changes in criminal behavior, its causes and implications.

31. For instance, see Mincy (1994).

32. U.S. House of Representatives (1994), page 470.

33. Data in table 1.2 and the textual discussion from U.S. Bureau of the Census (1991).

34. See Pirog-Good and Good (1995).

35. Edin and Lein (forthcoming).

36. For a discussion of the estimated impact of child support enforcement on poverty status, see Robins (1986) or U.S. House of Representatives (1994), pp. 500–502. More extensive child support assurance systems would do more to reduce poverty, as Meyer et al. (1992) indicate.

37. McLanahan and Sandefur (1994), fig. 12.

38. Crime statistics in Maguire et al. (1993). These statistics are the result of regularly asking a representative sample of people if they have been the victim of these crimes. They differ from official police records of crime reported and are believed to be both more consistent over time and more accurate. In particular, the police have become more sophisticated at crime reporting, leading police reports to show increasing crime rates because of an improved sophistication in reporting rather than because of an increase in overall crimes. Over the past decade, the police-reported crime rates show stability rather than a decline in many crime categories. See Jencks (1991) or Freeman (1995) for a discussion of these two data sources.

39. Maguire and Pastore (1994).

40. U.S. Department of Justice (various years).

41. For a review of the evidence on the relationship between media violence and aggressive behavior, see Donnerstein and Linz (1995).

42. U.S. National Center for Health Statistics (1993a), table 43.

43. U.S. National Center for Health Statistics (1993a), table 47.

44. U.S. Department of Health and Human Services, National Institute on Drug Abuse (1991, tables 2.6, 2.7 and 2.8); U.S. Department of Health and Human Services, Public Health Service (1994, tables 5B, 6B, and 7B).

45. U.S. Department of Health and Human Services, National Institute on Drug Abuse (1991), table 2.14; U.S. Department of Health and Human Services, Public Health Service (1994), Table 9B.

46. Besharov (1989); Dicker and Leighton (1991); U.S. Department of Health and Human Services, National Institute on Drug Abuse (1994).

CHAPTER 2
A CHANGING ECONOMY

1. Blank and Blinder (1986).

2. Data on per capita Gross Domestic Product from the *Economic Report of the President* (1995), various tables. All 1993 and earlier poverty data used in this chapter (unless otherwise referenced) are from U.S. Bureau of the Census (1995a). 1994 poverty data are from U.S. Bureau of the Census (1995b).

3. The discussion and results in the remainder of this section follow Blank (1993). For related discussion, see Blank and Blinder (1986) and Blank and Card (1993).

4. Blank and London (forthcoming).

5. For more detail on the topics discussed in this section, see Blank (1994a, 1995).

6. Male and female unemployment rates from the *Economic Report of the President* (1995).

7. Data on unemployment rates by skill level, gender, and race are calculated from

the 1994 March Current Population Survey. Data refer to reported unemployment in the week prior to the survey.

8. Data on weekly wages by education level among full-time, full-year workers from 1967 through 1993 are tabulated from the annual March Current Population Surveys, 1968–1994.

9. As more of the least skilled men have dropped out of the labor market entirely, the composition of those who remain has changed. Most evidence suggests that the "worst" workers along a range of dimensions have dropped out. The result is that these wage trends probably *understate* the actual wage changes among the least skilled, since the increasing selectivity of those left behind would tend to push their average wages upward.

10. There are two primary ways through which these wage declines have occurred. First, when workers change jobs or when young workers enter the labor market, they receive lower wages than earlier workers did in the same job. Second, wages for low-skilled jobs have not kept up with price changes, so even workers who continue in their same job have seen an erosion in their postinflation wages even though their nominal wages have not fallen.

11. Data on pension and health insurance availability tabulated from the 1994 March Current Population Survey. For further discussion of changes in fringe benefits, see Blank (1995).

12. Data from the National Assessment of Educational Progress, as described in U.S. Department of Education (1994), tables 105, 106, 115. These data are based on regular national achievement tests given to a random group of students in selected grades. This is in contrast with scores from the SAT exams, taken only by high school seniors who plan to attend college, which show a long-term decline in scores. Much of the decline in SAT scores is due to the changing mix of students who take these exams.

13. U.S. Department of Education (1993).

14. U.S. Bureau of the Census (1973, 1993b).

15. Altonji and Card (1991).

16. A growing research literature investigates causes of the widening wage distribution. Among the articles used as background for this section are Levy and Murnane (1992), Bound and Johnson (1992), Katz and Murphy (1992), Danziger and Gottschalk (1993, 1995), and Juhn, Murphy and Pierce (1993).

17. Data on employment by gender, race, and skill level in 1970 and 1993 tabulated from the 1970 and 1994 March Current Population Surveys. Further discussion of these issues is in Blank and London (forthcoming).

18. Juhn (1992).

19. Data on part-time work from Blank (1995), updated with data from U.S. Department of Labor (1994). Figure 1.10 does not include 1994 data since definitional changes in part-time work by the Bureau of Labor Statistics make the data for more recent years noncomparable with the earlier years.

20. Data from the U.S. Bureau of the Census (1960, 1990).

21. For a discussion of the causes and impacts of housing segregation on the African American community, see Massey and Denton (1993).

22. Data from the Chicago Department of Planning and Development (1973, 1992), based on U.S. Census data.

23. This phrase came into widespread use following its use by Wilson (1987).

24. Newman and Lennon (1995).

25. For two quite different discussions of the role of job networks in job finding among urban residents, see Holzer (1996, chap. 3) and Sullivan (1989).

26. For information on commuting times within major cities, see Kasarda (1995), tables 6 and 14.

27. The data in figure 2.11 are derived from the methodology of Peter Gutmann, using data from the *Economic Report of the President* (1995). We calculate the size of the underground economy in each year, t, as

$$\text{Underground Economy}_t = (\text{GNP}_t{}^*(M_t - DD_t{}^*1.217))/(DD_t{}^*1.217),$$

as described in Molefsky (1982). M_t represents the money supply in year t, while DD_t represents demand deposits. This is a midrange estimate. For a comprehensive set of estimates see Molefsky (1982), Porter and Bayer (1989), and Fichtenbaum (1989).

28. Advisory Commission on Intergovernmental Relations (1994), table 58.

29. U.S. Department of Justice statistics indicate low-income persons are more likely to be victims of all types of crime. See Maguire et al. (1993), table 3.25.

30. Molefsky (1982), table 3.4, reports on data from a 1979 IRS study of the underground economy.

31. See Freeman (1992).

32. This is the share of single men ages 16 to 30 among all poor persons. Tabulated by the author from the 1994 March Current Population Survey.

33. Edin and Lein (forthcoming).

34. Data on percent of less skilled workers below a given earnings level (column 2 in table 1.1) are tabulated from the 1994 March Current Population Survey, based on earnings in 1993. For this reason, the table uses the 1993 poverty line as a comparison.

CHAPTER 3
CHANGING POLICY

1. Roper Center for Public Opinion Research (1995). A Kaiser Foundation poll done about the same time found similar results, with 40 percent of respondents believing that welfare spending on the poor was one of the two largest areas of federal spending (both Social Security and Defense spending are far larger). See Kaiser Family Foundation (1995).

2. Note that the data in table 3.1 are for 1993 (the last year for which all of the participation and expenditure information was available), which is *before* recent EITC expansions, so it shows an EITC program that is smaller than 1995 or 1996 data would show.

3. Budget data from U.S. Office of Management and Budget (1995). Interpretation of these data is clear in U.S. Office of Management and Budget (1994).

4. Omitted from figure 3.1 are job training programs for low-income families, whose budget is not separately reported in the federal budget. The job training programs are minuscule in their federal cost.

5. State expenditures exclude dollars received from intergovernmental transfers from the federal government. There are several sources of state expenditure data which are not entirely consistent with each other. Figure 3.2 uses data from U.S. Bureau of the Census (1993c). Data from the National Association of State Budget Officers (1993) shows a breakdown of expenditures that is very similar to that shown in the federal data.

6. Nixon's negative income tax proposal was probably the high-water mark of efforts to provide large-scale cash assistance rather than behaviorally tied assistance to the poor. The earlier history of public aid shows an ongoing focus on behavioral regulations as a precondition for assistance. See Doolittle (1982) for a discussion of the related legal battles.

7. For a discussion of this, see Peterson (1995).

8. Table 3.2 is based on calculations derived from 1994 program rules and 1994 federal tax rules, using the 1994 poverty line. I do not include Medicaid assistance in the calculations in table 3.2. (The entire single-mother family would be eligible for Medicaid only when they received AFDC. The children in both the single-parent and married-couple families would be eligible as long as their families were below 125 percent of the poverty line.) Table 3.2 assumes these families face no ongoing health problems. Medicaid provides no income to help families pay their regular monthly bills and should not be counted against the poverty line, which measures cash resources. Only if the family becomes worse off along a noneconomic dimension—a family member becomes ill—will Medicaid help the family buy medical assistance.

9. This price is close to the average reported cost of child care purchased by low-income women with more than one child. See U.S. Bureau of the Census (1992).

10. Her AFDC check reflects the fact that child care expenses up to $175 per month per child are deducted from earnings before her AFDC benefits are calculated.

11. For more detailed information on both the AFDC and SSI programs, see U.S. House of Representatives (1994). All information in this chapter not otherwise noted is from this source.

12. In fact, most widows and their children are now covered by Social Security payments, which are far more generous than the assistance available through AFDC.

13. These data were presented in Blank (1994a) and updated with information from U.S. House of Representatives (1994).

14. Blank and Ruggles (1996).

15. For a summary of the programs in place in the mid-1990s, see Winkler (1995).

16. Unless otherwise noted, all information about Food Stamps, Medicaid, and housing subsidies come from the U.S. House of Representatives (1994). For more information specifically on Food Stamps, see Ohls and Beebout (1993).

17. Figure 3.3 uses data first presented in Blank (1994a), with updates from the U.S. House of Representatives (1994). Original data are from a variety of government sources showing Food Stamps and AFDC benefit levels each year since 1970.

18. This calculation adjusts annual Medicaid spending by the Consumer Price Index for medical care between 1980 and 1994.

19. For a discussion of housing assistance programs, see Newman and Schnare (1992).

20. Tabulated from the 1994 March Current Population Survey.

21. U.S. Department of Housing and Urban Development (1992), table 2.

22. For more extensive information on the EITC, see Hoffman and Seidman (1990) or Scholz (1993–94).

23. A discussion of the EITC expansion is in U.S. House of Representatives (1994).

24. For a particularly interesting study of EITC recipients and their views of this program, see Olson and Davis (1994).

25. See Eissa and Lehman (1995) and Dickert et al. (1995).

26. Historic data on minimum wage levels are from Ehrenberg and Smith (1994), table 3.3, adjusted by the GNP price deflator.

27. For a review of these studies, see Card and Krueger (1995). Further discussion of recent evidence on the minimum wage and employment is in the *Industrial and Labor Relations Review* (1995).

28. See Mincy (1990) for a discussion of the effects of minimum wage changes on the poor. See also chapter 9 in Card and Krueger (1995).

29. Much of the information in this section is from Katz (forthcoming). See that article for a more extended discussion of employer-based tax credits.

30. See Burtless (1985).

31. Information in this section is from the U.S. House of Representatives (1994), unless otherwise referenced.

32. Bloom et al. (1993), table 3.6.

33. JTPA provides an example of how wage subsidy programs and employment assistance programs overlap. While most adult JTPA recipients are in formal training programs in settings like community colleges, others are placed with firms for training, and these firms are provided with wage subsidies. Hence, JTPA operates not just as a job search and skill training program, but it also provides wage subsidies to employers for some workers.

34. Data provided by the Office of Employment and Training Programs, U.S. Department of Labor.

35. For a review of the economic effects of the CETA program, see Barnow (1987).

36. For an extensive discussion of the evolution of child support legislation, see U.S. House of Representatives (1994). Unless otherwise referenced, data in this section are from this source. See also Garfinkel (1992) for a discussion of the current child support system.

37. U.S. Department of Education (1994).

38. A description of the Head Start program is provided in U.S. House of Representatives (1994). All information in this section is from that source unless otherwise noted.

39. For further discussion of these different programs, see Rosenbaum (forthcoming) or Pauly et al. (1995). Career academies are extensively described in Stern et al. (1992).

40. A more thorough discussion of federal housing and urban renewal programs is in Mitchell (1985). See also Newman and Schnare (1992).

41. See Weiss (1985) and Mollenkopf (1983).

42. For a description of these efforts, see Green (1991) or Papke (1993).

43. Gugliotta (1994).

44. For a further discussion of mobility programs, see Hughes and Sternberg (1993).

45. Rosenbaum and Popkin (1991) describe this program more thoroughly.

CHAPTER 4
WHAT DO ANTIPOVERTY PROGRAMS DO?

1. U.S. Office of Management and Budget (1995).

2. Murray (1984), p. 9.

3. In Murray's own words, "The proposed program [to reform public welfare], our final and most ambitious thought experiment, consists of scrapping the entire federal welfare and income-support structure for working-aged persons, including AFDC,

Medicaid, Food Stamps, Unemployment Insurance, Worker's Compensation, subsidized housing, disability insurance, and the rest" (p. 228).

4. U.S. General Accounting Office (1985), p. 18, estimates the caseload reduction due to the provisions of the Omnibus Budget Reconciliation Act of 1991 (OBRA) at 442,000. This is 12 percent of the 1983 caseload (U.S. House of Representatives, 1994, table 10-24.)

5. U.S. General Accounting Office (1985), p. iv. Other studies (all of which reach similar conclusions) include Danziger (1983), Hutchens (1986), Moffitt and Wolf (1987), and Research Triangle Institute (1983).

6. See Sandra Danziger and Kossoudji (1995).

7. Tabulations from the 1994 March Current Population Survey. Cash transfer income that is set to zero in columns 2 and 4 is AFDC and General Assistance income and SSI income.

8. These are calculations made by Smeeding (1992).

9. See Palmer et al. (1988), Smeeding et al. (1993), or Smeeding et al. (1995).

10. For a full discussion of the U.S./Canadian comparisons, see Blank and Hanratty (1993) or Hanratty and Blank (1992).

11. For instance, see Rector (1993).

12. SSI data in figure 4.2 are from U.S. House of Representatives (1994, table 6-25) and start in 1973 when that program is initiated. AFDC data are from U.S. House of Representatives (1994, table 10-21) for 1970–93. For 1965–69, U.S. Office of Management and Budget (1994, table 11-3) provides data on federal spending on AFDC. This is scaled up to reflect both federal and state spending, using the fact that federal spending is approximately 90 percent of all AFDC expenditures in the early 1970s (U.S. House of Representatives 1994, table 10-21). Poverty rates in figure 4.1 are from the historical poverty data, U.S. Bureau of the Census (1995a).

13. Typically, money paid for child care expenses or required work expenses are deducted from income before AFDC benefits are reduced. Otherwise most working mothers would end up *losing* money through work.

14. The recent literature is summarized in Moffitt (1992); earlier literature is summarized in Danziger et al. (1981). Robins (1985) summarizes the results from the negative income tax experiments.

15. This estimate is on the higher end of elasticity estimates. See Moffitt (1992), table 5, or Robins (1985), table 7. It includes the net effect of changes in labor force participation and changes in hours of work.

16. Table 4.2 is based on author's tabulations from the 1994 March Current Population Survey. Row 1 includes all cash income, while row 2 excludes AFDC dollars. Row 3 excludes AFDC income and adjusts women's work behavior using the higher-end elasticity estimates described in the two previous paragraphs and documented in the previous footnote.

17. Edin and Lein (forthcoming).

18. Robins and Fronstin (forthcoming) summarize much of this research, which includes Acs (1994), An et al. (1993), Duncan and Hoffman (1990), Lundberg and Plotnick (1990, 1995), Murray (1993), Plotnick (1990), Rank (1989), and Winegarden (1988).

19. Moffitt (1992), p. 31.

20. U.S. data from U.S. National Center for Health Statistics (1991a); Canadian data from Statistics Canada (1988); European data from Eurostat (1990).

21. See Ellwood and Bane (1985), Hutchens et al. (1987), Winkler (1992), or Moffitt et al. (1995).

22. Cited in Pear (1995).

23. These are data based on extensions to Pavetti (1993), who has extensively studied time patterns in AFDC use and provided this updated data. Bane and Ellwood (1994, pp. 32, 39) provide comparable data based on annual income calculations (Panel Survey of Income Dynamics), while Pavetti uses monthly data (Survey of Income and Program Participation), combined with long-term data from the National Longitudinal Survey of Youth. The two sources are very similar for lifetime AFDC use (which is reassuring.) Pavetti's monthly data are a better source for single spells on AFDC, since many women move on and off within a year.

24. Blank and Ruggles (1994) and Bane and Ellwood (1994).

25. Studies investigating the determinants of welfare spells include Ellwood (1986), Blank (1989a), Fitzgerald (1991), and Gritz and MaCurdy (1992).

26. Blank (1989a) or Fitzgerald (1991).

27. For instance, see Riccio et al. (1994), table 2.13.

28. Blank and Ruggles (1996).

29. Riccio et al. (1994), table 5.6.

30. Herr and Halpern (1991).

31. For instance, see Altonji and Dunn (1994), Solon (1992), or Featherman and Hauser (1978).

32. Economic mobility among fathers and sons has been much more studied than among mothers and daughters.

33. These data taken from Gottschalk (1992), table 2.

34. See Gottschalk (1992 and forthcoming) or Zimmerman and Levine (1993).

35. For a further discussion of management problems with the AFDC system, see Bane and Ellwood (1994), chapter 4.

36. For evidence on state exclusions, see Piven and Cloward (1971).

37. U.S. Senate (1979), p. 44.

38. These studies include Basiotis et al. (1987), Ranney and Kushman (1987), or Senauer and Young (1986). For a summary of these results, see Ohls and Beebout (1993), tables V.3 and V.4, or Fraker (1990).

39. Fraker et al. (1995a). As this paper notes, one of these studies showed zero effects, but the experiment in this case was quite different from other experiments and designed in a manner that would have greatly minimized the effects of cashing out Food Stamps. These studies show results for all Food Stamp participants. Results of cash-out experiments for elderly and disabled Food Stamps recipients show few effects on consumption. Fraker et al. (1995b) also note that cashing out Food Stamps does result in lower administrative costs.

40. Ohls and Beebout (1993), table V.5, provides evidence showing a link between food consumption and nutrition. If Food Stamps users consume more, this implies their nutrition is higher. Direct studies of the impact of Food Stamps on nutrition are reviewed more skeptically in Fraker (1990). Basiotis et al. (1987) and Devaney et al. (1989), which are among the best recent studies, show positive effects of Food Stamps on nutrition.

41. Food Research and Action Center (1991a), table 2.2.

42. Mathematica Policy Research, Inc. (1990).

43. U.S. General Accounting Office (1992) summarizes seventeen of these studies. Food Research and Action Center (1991b) provides an annotated bibliography of

thirty-eight such studies. One of the most recent and best-done studies is Devaney et al. (1992).

44. Evidence on the value of eating breakfast is in Meyers et al. (1991) and Nicklas et al. (1993). Evidence on the school breakfast program is from Devaney and Fraker (1989) and Gleason (1995). The first study is based on data from 1980–81, and the second on data from 1992. It is possible that there might have been bigger effects of the School Breakfast Program in the earlier years of its operation.

45. Devaney and Fraker (1989) and Gordon et al. (1995).

46. Gordon et al. (1995). For evidence on food content in school lunches, see Chapman et al. (1995).

47. For more information on these programs, see the articles in Burghardt and Devaney (1995). For information on the effects of school programs on family expenditures, see Long (1991).

48. U.S. Bureau of the Census (1993b). For more detailed information, see Employee Benefit Research Institute (1995).

49. See Blank (1989b).

50. This literature is reviewed and cited in Blank (1989b). See also Freeman et al. (1990).

51. Hanratty (forthcoming).

52. Currie and Gruber (1995).

53. Both Currie and Gruber (1995) and Shore-Sheppard (1995) underscore the ongoing problems in access to medical care providers among poor children.

54. Table 4.3 comes from a variety of tables in U.S. House of Representatives (1992, 1993b, 1994).

55. Hamilton et al. (1989).

56. These data are published in Sarver (1994). Because these charities have to pay for fund-raising, I subtract fund-raising costs. Shown in table 4.4 is the calculation

$$\frac{\text{Administrative Expenses}}{(\text{Administrative Expenses} + \text{Program Expenses})}.$$

57. For a discussion of the existing quality control systems in these four programs, see Affholter and Kramer (1987).

58. U.S. Department of Agriculture (1994), table 21.

59. Figure 4.5 is from U.S. House of Representatives (1994), tables 10-36 (AFDC) and 18-7 (Food Stamps); U.S. House of Representatives (1993a), appendix O, table 2 (SSI and Medicaid).

60. For a discussion of caseload characteristics, administrative procedures, and quality control error rates in AFDC and Food Stamps, see Kingson and Levin (1984) or Puma and Hoaglin (1987).

61. Wrafter (1984) and U.S. House of Representatives (1994).

62. See the discussion in Brodkin (1986) or Brodkin and Lipsky (1983).

63. Viadero (1995) estimates Food Stamp fraud at $414 million, excluding Food Stamp trafficking problems. Leahy (1994) cites the $1 billion figure, and it reappears in various public discussions. No one appears to know where this number originated, which suggests that it has little empirical validity.

64. U.S. General Accounting Office (1994), p. 25.

65. *Economic Report of the President* (1964), p. 77.

66. For a general summary of U.S. job programs and their results, see U.S. Department of Labor (1995).

67. For more details on JOBS requirements, see U.S. House of Representatives (1994). See Nathan (1993) for a discussion of the implementation of welfare-to-work programs, based on state experience prior to the enactment of JOBS legislation.

68. Gueron and Pauly (1991) review the literature on state welfare-to-work programs prior to the implementation of JOBS. LaLonde (1995) provides a more recent summary. Two major evaluations of JOBS programs have been completed for California and Florida and support these earlier results. See Kemple and Haimson (1994), and Riccio et al. (1994). Other JOBS-related evaluations include Freedman and Friedlander (1995) and Knox et al. (1995). Long-term effects are discussed in Friedlander and Burtless (1995). Other recent evidence consistent with that cited here is in Couch (1992) and Bell and Orr (1994). A good review of the issues involved in evaluating welfare-to-work training programs is provided in Manski and Garfinkel (1992).

69. Gueron and Pauly (1991), table 1.1, and their Appendix, table B.1.

70. Riccio et al. (1994), table 1.

71. Bloom et al. (1993).

72. Gueron and Pauly (1991). In a few cases in the California GAIN evaluations, the men did as well as the women. See Riccio et al. (1994).

73. See the results summarized in Hollister et al. (1984).

74. Kirschenman and Neckerman (1991) or Holzer (1996).

75. For instance, Heckman (1993) shows the impossibility of expecting job training programs to offset the declining wage levels of less-skilled workers. The improvements they produce in employment and earnings levels are extremely small relative to the magnitude of recent labor market changes.

76. For a review of evidence on the range of effects of public assistance programs on children, see Currie (1995).

77. See Casto and Mastropieri (1986) and McKey et al. (1985).

78. This literature is well summarized in Barnett (1992).

79. The most recent update of the Perry Preschool Study evaluation is Schweinhart et al. (1993).

80. Currie and Thomas (1995).

81. For broader discussion of some of the programs cited here that compares and contrasts their results, see Doolittle (1995), Ivry (1995), and the discussion in chapter 1 of Quint et al. (1994). A review of the results of adolescent employment and training programs is in U.S. Department of Labor (1995).

82. For a summary of this research, see Ivry (1995). One recent program with particularly strong effects for in-school youth and few effects for dropouts is the Teen Parent Demonstration project, summarized in Maynard (1993).

83. Polit et al. (1988).

84. Long et al. (1994), table 1.1.

85. Hollister et al. (1984).

86. Cave et al. (1993).

87. Bloom et al. (1993).

88. Mallar et al. (1982).

89. See Mallar et al. (1982).

90. See Cave et al. (1993), tables 5.12 and 5.13.

91. Cameron and Heckman (1993).

92. For instance, JOBSTART had little overall effect on employment and earnings during four years of followup analysis, but did increase GED completion among its participants.

93. For instance, see the results for JOBSTART (Cave et al. 1993), for the Teenage Parent Demonstration (Maynard 1993), from Project Redirection (Polit et al. 1988), or from New Chance (Quint et al. 1994).

94. For a brief review of this literature, see Webster and Weeks (1995). A slightly dated review is in chapter 6 of Hayes (1987); a less comprehensive review of the research but a good summary of the findings is in Grossman and Halpern-Felsher (1995). The most comprehensive recent review is by Moore et al. (1995).

95. For example, see Kirby et al. (1991).

96. Moore et al. (1995), p. x, Executive Summary.

97. Gittell (1992). For a general review of a wide set of economic development policies, aimed at both poor and nonpoor areas, see Bartik (1991).

98. For a discussion of problems with existing evaluations of economic development policies, see Courant (1994).

99. *Journal of Housing* (1970).

100. See the discussion of this in Mollenkopf (1983).

101. For a discussion of these issues, see Newman and Schnare (1992).

102. For a review of the literature on the impact of public housing programs in inner city neighborhoods, see Schill and Wachter (1995).

103. Gordon (1995).

104. Newman and Schnare (1992).

105. For a review and discussion of many of these efforts, see Green (1991) or Gunn (1993).

106. Papke (1993). There is some evidence that enterprise zones do better when only a few are designated within a state and when their implementation is adequately staffed.

107. U.S. General Accounting Office (1988).

108. Papke (1994).

109. Rubin and Armstrong (1989) did the initial study. For a critical response, see Boarnet and Bogart (forthcoming).

110. Bartik (1992).

111. See Rosenbaum and Popkin (1991) and Rosenbaum et al. (1993).

112. Dreier and Moberg (1996) discuss some of these issues at more length.

CHAPTER 5
WHO SHOULD HELP THE POOR?

1. Rawls (1971).

2. For discussion of the "citizenship" and shared social aspects of public welfare programs, see Marshall (1964) or Goodin (1985).

3. National (U.S.) Conference of Catholic Bishops (1986), paragraph 13.

4. See Altonji et al. (1996) or Cox and Rank (1992).

5. This number is very approximate. Cox and Jakubson (1995) provide no breakdown for low-income families only, but some simple assumptions would indicate that family transfers constitute 20.7 percent of government transfers. Rosenzweig and Wolpin (1994) provide data in the text to suggest this number is between 18.2 and 23.2 percent. Schoeni (1994) provides data suggesting this is 21.3 percent. Unfortunately, each of these papers use somewhat different samples, and are looking at a different mix of transfer programs. Schoeni investigates only AFDC income; Rosenzweig and Wolpin look at AFDC income and Food Stamps; Cox and Jakubson look at all cash transfers plus

Food Stamps. It is a sign of the potential problems with this estimate that those who use more inclusive public transfer definitions do not find a smaller share of family transfers relative to public transfers.

6. This is 20 percent of the total expenditures on AFDC plus Food Stamps plus SSI ($77 billion) in 1995. (None of these studies considers medical care as part of public assistance; the twenty cents to a dollar trade-off occurs on regular monthly income assistance.) As discussed in the previous footnote, this is at best a very rough guess.

7. American Association of Fund-Raising Counsel (1994). In addition to individual donations and bequests, gifts also came from corporations and foundations, so total giving was $125 billion.

8. Independent Sector (1992), table 4.25. The $2 billion in total expenditures counts direct assistance to individuals and donations to other organizations by congregations. The $6.6 billion also includes donations within the denomination. This last figure, however, includes a substantial amount of support paid for denominational staff and administration that should not be counted as "donations." Clearly, the accurate number lies somewhere in between.

9. American Association of Fund-Raising Counsel (1994).

10. Salamon (1995) indicates that 40 percent of the expenditures of these agencies go for services to the poor.

11. This estimate includes the 10 percent of $126 billion total budget of private philanthropic organizations ($12.6 billion) that goes to human service organizations, and takes about 40 percent of that as representing the share going to low-income families (see note 10). To this is added the maximum estimate of 14 percent of religious expenditures going to the needy ($6.6 billion), which adds up to $11.6 billion.

12. Clotfelter (1985), pp. 96–99. While these numbers are based on total charitable giving, most observers expect that all categories of giving—including charitable giving to the needy—are larger in the United States than elsewhere.

13. Weisbrod (1975).

14. For further discussion and data, see Sarver (1994) and Mehegan (1994).

15. Cited in Salamon (1995).

16. Lampman and Smeeding (1983).

17. Schoeni (1994). Consistent with this, Rosenzweig and Wolpin (1994) estimate the effect of AFDC on the likelihood that parents will provide economic support to low-income daughters, and find very small effects of changes in AFDC benefits on the likelihood of parental support. They do not look at level of support.

18. Cox and Jakubson (1995), p. 150.

19. Rose-Ackerman (1986).

20. Schiff (1990).

21. Schiff (1990) calculates whether the cuts in federal spending in the early Reagan years led nonprofit social service organizations to expand their programs for those who lost public assistance. The government cuts in the early 1980s reduced both publicly provided assistance and government revenues to nonprofit social service organizations. Increases in charitable giving that occurred at the same time allowed these nonprofit agencies to maintain their preexisting level of services. But they were unable to expand services, and thus were not able to offset any of the cuts in publicly provided assistance.

22. The number of religious congregations is from Independent Sector (1992). This publication also indicates that the average level of contributions per congregation is at

$150,000. These data are from a random survey of all congregations that have a telephone listing.

23. Ironically, one of the effects of the 1986 tax reforms was to reduce private charitable donations. By lowering the tax rates on higher income families, the reform reduced the incentives for these families to make tax-deductible charitable contributions.

24. Of course, by counting family assistance less than dollar-for-dollar against public transfers, this means that families can receive more income before they lose their eligibility for public assistance. Thus, treating family assistance differently from other income sources will not help reduce public spending.

25. Quoted in Trattner (1989), p. 63.

26. For a recent discussion of the changing role of the states versus the federal government, see Derthick (1994).

27. For further discussion of these breakdowns of responsibility, see DiIulio and Kettl (1995).

28. This is sometimes referred to as the "principle of subsidiarity."

29. Nathan (1990) argues that there are cycles in this phenomenon. States are more innovative in times of federal retrenchment and conservatism, while the national government is more innovative in periods of federal budget expansion.

30. The strong support for Food Stamps from the agricultural lobbies was also important in this debate.

31. See Peterson (1995).

32. For instance, see Brown and Oates (1987).

CHAPTER 6
THE MOVEMENT TOWARD TARGETED PROGRAMS

1. For instance, see the writings of Katz (1983), Skocpol (1992), or Gordon (1994).
2. See Garfinkel (1992).
3. Ellwood (1988).
4. For instance, see Skocpol (1991) or Haveman (1988).
5. Tabulations by author from the 1994 March Current Population Survey.
6. Derthick (1994) and Blank (1994b).
7. Riccio et al. (1994), table 3.4.
8. Cave et al. (1993), table 7.2.
9. Riccio et al. (1994), table 7.6.

CHAPTER 7
WHERE SHOULD WE GO FROM HERE?

1. One way to view Tier 1 is as a substantial expansion of the emergency assistance component of AFDC that some states already utilize.
2. Bloom and Butler (1995).
3. Clark and Long (1995).
4. The Bush administration proposed making the Dependent Care Credit refundable, but this did not pass Congress.
5. Irwin Garfinkel has been particularly influential in writing about the design and implementation of a CSA system for all single parents. See Garfinkel (1992).

6. If we assume that fathers are required to pay 17 percent of their income into child support for one child (as proposed in Garfinkel 1992), then any father of one child earning less then $8,824 would have his child support payments supplemented by the state (17 percent of $8,824 is $1,500.)

7. Bloom and Sherwood (1994).

8. Table 7.1 is calculated using the program and tax rules in effect in 1994 and the 1994 poverty line.

9. U.S. House of Representatives (1994), table 11-23.

10. These statistics on caseload percentages were provided by Gayle Hamilton at Manpower Demonstration Research Corporation (MDRC), which evaluated the California GAIN program and which is currently running a national evaluation of the welfare-to-work programs initiated by the Family Support Act of 1988. For evidence on participation rates among those classified as eligible for work-welfare programs, see Hamilton (1995).

11. Ferguson (1991).

12. For instance, recent rigorous evaluation of the Big Brother/Big Sister mentoring program has indicated that teens in this program engage in fewer problem behaviors (Tierney et al. 1995).

13. Kretzmann and McKnight (1993).

14. Porter (1995).

15. For a review of collaborative initiatives aimed at producing development in high-poverty neighborhoods, see Fishman and Phillips (1993).

16. For instance, Sviridoff (1994) discusses the growing importance of Community Development Corporations as key actors in urban renewal.

• R E F E R E N C E S •

Acs, Gregory. 1994. "The Impact of AFDC on Young Women's Childbearing Decisions." Urban Institute Discussion Paper. Washington, D.C.: The Urban Institute.

Advisory Commission on Intergovernmental Relations. 1994. *Significant Features of Fiscal Federalism*, vol. 1. Washington, D.C.: ACIR.

Affholter, Dennis P., and Fredrica D. Kramer, eds. 1987. *Rethinking Quality Control: A New System for the Food Stamp Program*. Washington, D.C.: National Academy Press.

Alter, Jonathan. 1994. "The Name of the Game Is Shame." *Newsweek*, December 12, p. 41.

Altonji, Joseph G., and David Card. 1991. "The Effects of Immigration on the Labor Market Outcomes of Less-Skilled Natives." In *Immigration, Trade, and the Labor Market*, John M. Abowd and Richard B. Freeman, editors. Chicago: University of Chicago Press.

Altonji, Joseph G., and Thomas A. Dunn. 1994. "An Intergenerational Model of Wages, Hours and Earnings." National Bureau of Economic Research Working Paper No. 4950. Cambridge, Mass.: NBER.

Altonji, Joseph G., Fumio Hayashi, and Laurence Kotlikoff. 1996. "The Effects of Income and Wealth on Time and Money Transfers between Parents and Children." National Bureau of Economic Research Working Paper No. 5522. Cambridge, Mass.: NBER.

American Association of Fund-Raising Counsel. 1994. *Giving USA: The Annual Report on Philanthropy for the Year 1993*. New York: AAFRC Trust for Philanthropy.

An, Chong-Bum, Robert Haveman, and Barbara Wolfe. 1993. "Teen Out-of-Wedlock Births and Welfare Receipt: The Role of Childhood Events and Economic Circumstances." *Review of Economics and Statistics* 75(2): 195–208.

Bachu, Amara. 1993. *Fertility of American Women: June 1992*. U.S. Bureau of the Census, Current Population Report P20–470. Washington, D.C.: U.S. Government Printing Office.

Bane, Mary Jo, and David T. Ellwood. 1986. "Slipping Into and Out of Poverty: The Dynamics of Spells." *Journal of Human Resources* 21(1, Winter): 1–23.

Bane, Mary Jo, and David T. Ellwood. 1994. *Welfare Realities: From Rhetoric to Reform*. Cambridge, Mass.: Harvard University Press.

Barnett, W. Steven. 1992. "Benefits of Compensatory Preschool Education." *Journal of Human Resources* 27(2, Spring): 279–312.

Barnow, Burt S. 1987. "The Impact of CETA Programs on Earnings: A Review of the Literature." *Journal of Human Resources* 22(2, Spring): 157–93.

Bartik, Timothy J. 1991. *Who Benefits from State and Local Economic Development Policies?* Kalamazoo, Mich.: W. E. Upjohn Institute for Employment Research.

Bartik, Timothy J. 1992. "The Effects of State and Local Taxes on Economic Development: A Review of Recent Research." *Economic Development Quarterly* 6(1, February): 102–10.

Basiotis, P. Peter, S. R. Johnson, Karen J. Morgan, and Jain-Shing A. Chen. 1987. "Food Stamps, Food Costs, Nutrient Availability, and Nutrient Intake." *Journal of Policy Modeling* 9(3, Fall): 383–404.

Bell, Stephen H., and Larry L. Orr. 1994. "Is Subsidized Employment Cost Effective for Welfare Recipients?" *Journal of Human Resources* 29(1, Winter): 42–61.

Besharov, Douglas J. 1989. "The Children of Crack: Will We Protect Them?" *Public Welfare* 47(4, Fall): 7–11.

Blank, Rebecca M. 1989a. "Analyzing the Length of Welfare Spells." *Journal of Public Economics* 39(3, August): 245–73.

Blank, Rebecca M. 1989b. "The Effect of Medical Need and Medicaid on AFDC Participation." *Journal of Human Resources* 24(1, Winter): 54–87.

Blank, Rebecca M. 1993. "Why Were Poverty Rates So High in the 1980s?" In *Poverty and Prosperity in the USA in the Late Twentieth Century*, Dimitri B. Papadimitriou and Edward N. Wolff, editors. London: Macmillan Press Ltd.

Blank, Rebecca M. 1994a. "The Employment Strategy: Public Policies to Increase Work and Earnings." In *Confronting Poverty*, Sheldon H. Danziger, Gary D. Sandefur, and Daniel H. Weinberg, editors. Cambridge, Mass.: Harvard University Press.

Blank, Rebecca M. 1994b. "Public Sector Growth and Labor Market Flexibility: The United States versus the United Kingdom." In *Social Protection versus Economic Flexibility: Is There a Tradeoff?* Rebecca M. Blank, editor. Chicago: University of Chicago Press.

Blank, Rebecca M. 1995. "Outlook for the U.S. Labor Market and Prospects for Low-Wage Entry Jobs." In *The Work Alternative*, Demetra Smith Nightingale and Robert H. Haveman, editors. Washington, D.C.: The Urban Institute Press.

Blank, Rebecca M., and Alan S. Blinder. 1986. "Macroeconomics, Income Distribution, and Poverty." In *Fighting Poverty*, Sheldon H. Danziger and Daniel H. Weinberg, editors. Cambridge, Mass.: Harvard University Press.

Blank, Rebecca M., and David Card. 1993. "Poverty, Income Distribution, and Growth: Are They Still Connected?" *Brookings Papers on Economic Activity* 1993(2): 285–339.

Blank, Rebecca M., and Maria J. Hanratty. 1993. "Responding to Need: A Comparison of Social Safety Nets in Canada and the United States." In *Small Differences That Matter*, David Card and Richard E. Freeman, editors. Chicago: University of Chicago Press.

Blank, Rebecca M., and Rebecca A. London. Forthcoming. "Trends in the Working Poor: The Impact of Economy, Family and Public Policy." In *Working and Poor in Urban America*, Thomas R. Swartz, editor. Notre Dame, Ind.: Notre Dame Press.

Blank, Rebecca M., and Patricia Ruggles. 1994. "Short-Term Recidivism among Public Assistance Recipients." *American Economic Review* 84(2, May): 49–53.

Blank, Rebecca M., and Patricia Ruggles. 1996. "When Do Women Use AFDC and Food Stamps? The Dynamics of Eligibility vs. Participation." *Journal of Human Resources* 31 (1, Winter): 57–89.

Bloom, Dan, and David Butler. 1995. *Implementing Time-Limited Welfare: Early Experiences in Three States*. New York: Manpower Development Research Corporation.

Bloom, Dan, and Kay Sherwood. 1994. *Matching Opportunities to Obligations: Lessons for Child Support Reform from the Parents' Fair Share Pilot Phase*. New York: Manpower Demonstration Research Corporation. April.

Bloom, Howard S., Larry L. Orr, George Cave, Stephen H. Bell, and Fred Doolittle. 1993. *The National JTPA Study: Title II-A Impacts on Earnings and Employment at*

18 Months. Report Submitted to the U.S. Department of Labor. Bethesda, Md.: Abt Associates, Inc.

Boarnet, Marlon G., and William T. Bogart. Forthcoming. "Enterprise Zones and Employment: Evidence from New Jersey." *Journal of Urban Economics.*

Bound, John, and George Johnson. 1992. "Changes in the Structure of Wages in the 1980s: An Evaluation of Alternative Explanations." *American Economic Review* 82(3, June): 371–92.

Brodkin, Evelyn Z. 1986. *The False Promise of Administrative Reform: Implementing Quality Control in Welfare*. Philadelphia: Temple University Press.

Brodkin, Evelyn, and Michael Lipsky. 1983. "Quality Control in AFDC as an Administrative Strategy." *Social Service Review* 57(1, March): 1–34.

Brown, Charles C., and Wallace E. Oates. 1987. "Assistance to the Poor in a Federal System." *Journal of Public Economics* 32(3, April): 307–30.

Burghardt, John A., and Barbara L. Devaney, eds. 1995. *The American Journal of Clinical Nutrition* (Suppl.) 61 (1S, January).

Burtless, Gary. 1985. "Are Targeted Wage Subsidies Harmful? Evidence from a Wage Voucher Experiment." *Industrial and Labor Relations Review* 39(1, Winter): 105–14.

Cameron, Stephen V., and James J. Heckman. 1993. "The Nonequivalence of High School Equivalents." *Journal of Labor Economics* 11(1, part 1, January): 1–47.

Card, David, and Alan B. Krueger. 1995. *Myth and Measurement: The New Economics of the Minimum Wage*. Princeton, N.J.: Princeton University Press.

Casto, G., and M. Mastropieri. 1986. "The Efficacy of Early Intervention Programs: A Meta-Analysis." *Exceptional Children* 52(5, January): 417–24.

Cave, George, Hans Bos, Fred Doolittle, and Cyril Toussaint. 1993. *JOBSTART: Final Report on a Program for School Dropouts*. New York: Manpower Demonstration Research Corporation.

Chapman, Nancy, Anne R. Gordon, and John A. Burghardt. 1995. "Factors Affecting the Fat Content of National School Lunch Program Lunches." *American Journal of Clinical Nutrition* 61(1S, January): 199S–204S.

Chicago Department of Development and Planning. 1973. *Chicago Statistical Abstract: 1970 Census*. Report Prepared for the U.S. Bureau of the Census, Chicago.

Chicago Department of Planning and Development. 1992. *Social and Economic Characteristics of Chicago's Population: Community Area Profiles 1990*. Report Prepared for the U.S. Bureau of the Census, Chicago.

Clark, Sandra, and Sharon Long. 1995. "Child Care Block Grants and Welfare Reform." *Welfare Reform Briefs*, no. 15. Washington, D.C.: The Urban Institute.

Clotfelter, Charles T. 1985. *Federal Tax Policy and Charitable Giving*. Chicago: University of Chicago Press.

Couch, Kenneth A. 1992. "New Evidence on the Long-Term Effects of Employment Training Programs." *Journal of Labor Economics* 10(4, October): 380–88.

Courant, Paul N. 1994. "How Would You Know a Good Economic Development Policy If You Tripped Over One? Hint: Don't Just Count Jobs." *National Tax Journal* 7(4, December): 863–81.

Cox, Donald, and George Jakubson. 1995. "The Connection between Public Transfers and Private Interfamily Transfers." *Journal of Public Economics* 57(1, May): 129–67.

Cox, Donald, and Mark R. Rank. 1992. "Inter-Vivos Transfers and Intergenerational Exchange." *The Review of Economics and Statistics* 74(2, May): 305–14.

Currie, Janet. 1995. *Welfare and the Well-Being of Children*. Series on Fundamentals of Pure and Applied Economics 59. Chur, Switzerland: Harwood Academic Publishers.

Currie, Janet, and Jonathan Gruber. 1995. "Health Insurance Eligibility, Utilization of Medical Care, and Child Health." National Bureau of Economic Research Working Paper No. 5052. Cambridge, Mass.: NBER.

Currie, Janet, and Duncan Thomas. 1995. "Does Head Start Make a Difference?" *American Economic Review* 85(3, June): 341–64.

Danziger, Sandra K., and Sherrie A. Kossoudji. 1995. "When Welfare Ends: Subsistence Strategies of Former GA Recipients." Final Report of the General Assistance Project. Ann Arbor: University of Michigan, School of Social Work.

Danziger, Sheldon. 1983. "Budget Cuts as Welfare Reform." *American Economic Review* 73(2, May): 65–70.

Danziger, Sheldon, and Peter Gottschalk, eds. 1993. *Uneven Tides: Rising Inequality in America*. New York: Russell Sage Foundation.

Danziger, Sheldon, and Peter Gottschalk. 1995. *America Unequal*. Cambridge, Mass.: Harvard University Press.

Danziger, Sheldon, Robert Haveman, and Robert Plotnick. 1981. "How Income Transfers Affect Work, Savings, and the Income Distribution: A Critical Review." *Journal of Economic Literature* 97(3, September): 975–1028.

Derthick, Martha. 1994. "The States in American Federalism: The Paradox of the Middle Tier." In *National Health Reform: What Should the State Role Be?* Forrest P. Chisman, Lawrence D. Brown, and Pamela J. Larson, editors. Washington, D.C.: National Academy of Social Insurance.

Devaney, Barbara, and Thomas Fraker. 1989. "The Dietary Impacts of the School Breakfast Program." *American Journal of Agricultural Economics* 71(4, November): 932–48.

Devaney, Barbara, Pamela Haines, and Robert Moffitt. 1989. *Assessing the Dietary Effects of the Food Stamp Program*, vol. 2, Empirical Results. Princeton, N.J.: Mathematica Policy Research.

Devaney, Barbara, Linda Bilheimer, and Jennifer Schore. 1992. "Medicaid Costs and Birth Outcomes: The Effects of Prenatal WIC Participation and the Use of Prenatal Care." *Journal of Policy Analysis and Management* 11(4, Fall): 573–92.

Dicker, Marvin, and Eldin A. Leighton. 1991. "Trends in Diagnosing Drug Problems, among Newborns: United States, 1979–1987." Paper Prepared for the National Institute on Drug Abuse, Bethesda, Md.

Dickert, Stacy, Scott Houser, and John Karl Scholz. 1995. "The Earned Income Tax Credit and Transfer Programs: A Study of Labor Market and Program Participation." In *Tax Policy and the Economy 9*, James M. Poterba, editor. Cambridge, Mass.: MIT Press.

DiIulio, John J., Jr., and Donald F. Kettl. 1995. *The Contract with America, Devolution, and the Administrative Realities of American Federalism*. Brookings Institution Center for Public Management Report CPM 95–1. Washington, D.C.: The Brookings Institution.

Donnerstein, Edward, and Daniel Linz. 1995. "The Media." In *Crime*, James Q. Wilson and Joan Petersilia, editors. San Francisco: ICS Press.

Doolittle, Fred. 1982. "State-Imposed Nonfinancial Eligibility Conditions in AFDC: Confusion in Supreme Court Decisions and a Need for Congressional Clarification." *Harvard Journal on Legislation* 19(1, Winter): 1–48.

Doolittle, Fred. 1995. "Second Chance Programs for Youth." In *Changing Populations/Changing Schools*, Irwin Flazman and A. Harry Passow, editors. 94th Yearbook of the National Society for the Study of Education. Chicago: University of Chicago Press.

Dreier, Peter, and David Moberg. 1996. "Moving from the Hood: The Mixed Success of Integrating Suburbia." *The American Prospect* 24 (Winter): 75–79.

Duncan, Greg J., and Saul D. Hoffman. 1990. "Welfare Benefits, Economic Opportunities, and Out-of-Wedlock Births among Black Teenage Girls." *Demography* 27(4, November): 519–35.

Economic Report of the President. 1964. Washington, D.C.: U.S. Government Printing Office.

Economic Report of the President. 1995. Washington, D.C.: U.S. Government Printing Office.

Edin, Kathryn, and Laura Lein. Forthcoming. *Making Ends Meet: How Single Mothers Survive Welfare and Low-Wage Work*. New York: Russell Sage Foundation.

Ehrenberg, Ronald G., and Robert S. Smith. 1994. *Modern Labor Economics: Theory and Public Policy*. 5th ed. New York: HarperCollins College Publishers.

Eissa, Nada, and Jeffrey B. Lehman. 1995. "Labor Supply Response to the Earned Income Tax Credit." Burch Center for Tax Policy and Public Finance Working Paper B95–10. Berkeley, Calif.

Ellwood, David T. 1986. "Targeting 'Would-Be' Long-Term Recipients of AFDC." Report Prepared for U.S. Department of Health and Human Services by Mathematica Policy Research. Princeton, N.J.: Mathematica Policy Research.

Ellwood, David T. 1988. *Poor Support: Poverty in the American Family*. New York: Basic Books.

Ellwood, David T., and Mary Jo Bane. 1985. "The Impact of AFDC on Family Structure and Living Arrangements." *Research in Labor Economics* 7: 137–207.

Employee Benefit Research Institute. 1995. *Sources of Health Insurance and Characteristics of the Uninsured: Analysis of the March 1994 Current Population Survey*. Special Report SR-28, Issue Brief Number 158. Washington, D.C.: EBRI.

Eurostat. 1990. *Demographic Statistics 1990*. Luxembourg: Statistical Office of the European Community.

Featherman, David L., and Robert M. Hauser. 1978. *Opportunity and Change*. New York: Academic Press.

Ferguson, Ronald F. 1991. "Racial Patterns in How School and Teacher Quality Affect Achievement and Earnings." *Challenge: A Journal of Research on Black Men* 2(1, May): 1–35.

Fichtenbaum, Rudy. 1989. "The Productivity Slowdown and the Underground Economy." *Quarterly Journal of Business and Economics* 28(3, Summer): 78–91.

Fishman, Nancy, and Meredith Phillips. 1993. *A Review of Comprehensive, Collaborative Persistent Poverty Initiatives*. Working Paper of the Center for Urban Affairs and Policy Research. Evanston, Ill.: Northwestern University.

Fitzgerald, John. 1991. "Welfare Durations and the Marriage Market." *Journal of Human Resources* 26(3, Summer): 545–61.

Food Research and Action Center. 1991a. *Community Childhood Hunger Identification Project: A Survey of Childhood Hunger in the United States*. Washington, D.C.: Food Research and Action Center.

Food Research and Action Center. 1991b. *WIC: A Success Story*. Washington, D.C.: Food Research and Action Center.

Fraker, Thomas M. 1990. *The Effects of Food Stamps on Food Consumption: A Review of the Literature*. A Report for Food and Nutrition Service, United States Department of Agriculture. Washington, D.C.: Mathematica Policy Research.

Fraker, Thomas M., Alberto P. Martini, and James C. Ohls. 1995a. "The Effects of Food Stamp Cashout on Food Expenditures: An Assessment of the Findings from Four Demonstrations." *Journal of Human Resources* 30(3, Fall): 633–49.

Fraker, Thomas M., Alberto P. Martini, James C. Ohls, and Michael Ponza. 1995b. "The Effects of Cashing Out Food Stamps on Household Food Use and the Cost of Issuing Benefits." *Journal of Policy Analysis and Management* 14(3, Summer): 372–92.

Freedman, Stephen, and Daniel Friedlander. 1995. "The JOBS Evaluation: Early Findings on Program Impacts in Three Sites." Report from Manpower Demonstration Research Corporation to the U.S. Department of Health and Human Services/U.S. Department of Education. New York: MDRC. Draft, September.

Freeman, Howard E., Linda H. Aiken, Robert J. Blendon, and Christopher R. Corey. 1990. "Uninsured Working-Age Adults: Characteristics and Consequences." *Health Services Research* 24(6, February): 811–23.

Freeman, Richard B. 1992. "Crime and the Employment of Disadvantaged Youths." In *Urban Labor Markets and Job Opportunity*, George E. Peterson and Wayne Vroman, editors. Washington, D.C.: The Urban Institute Press.

Freeman, Richard B. 1995. "The Labor Market." In *Crime*, James Q. Wilson and Joan Petersilia, editors. San Francisco: ICS Press.

Friedlander, Daniel, and Gary Burtless. 1995. *Five Years After: The Long-Term Effects of Welfare-to-Work Programs*. New York: Russell Sage Foundation.

Garfinkel, Irwin. 1992. *Assuring Child Support: An Extension of Social Security*. New York: Russell Sage Foundation.

Geronimus, Arline T., and Sanders Korenman. 1992. "The Socioeconomic Consequences of Teen Childbearing Reconsidered." *Quarterly Journal of Economics* 107(4, November): 1187–214.

Geronimus, Arline T., and Sanders Korenman. 1993. "The Socioeconomic Costs of Teenage Childbearing: Evidence and Interpretation." *Demography* 30(2, May): 281–96.

Gittell, Ross J. 1992. *Renewing Cities*. Princeton, N.J.: Princeton University Press.

Gleason, Philip M. 1995. "Participation in the National School Lunch Program and the School Breakfast Program." *American Journal of Clinical Nutrition* 61(1S, January): 213S–20S.

Goodin, Robert E. 1985. *Protecting the Vulnerable*. Chicago: University of Chicago Press.

Gordon, Anne R., Barbara L. Devaney, and John A. Burghardt. 1995. "Dietary Effects of the National School Lunch Program and the School Breakfast Program." *American Journal of Clinical Nutrition* 61(1S, January): 221S–31S.

Gordon, Linda. 1994. *Pitied but Not Entitled: Single Mothers and the History of Welfare*. New York: The Free Press.

Gordon, Nancy M. 1995. Testimony for the Congressional Budget Office before the Subcommittee on VA, HUD, and Independent Agencies, Committee on Appropriations, United States Senate. January 26.

Gottschalk, Peter. 1992. "The International Transmission of Welfare Participation: Facts and Possible Causes." *Journal of Policy Analysis and Management* 11(2, Spring): 254–72.

Gottschalk, Peter. Forthcoming. "Is the Correlation in Welfare Participation across Generations Spurious?" *Journal of Public Economics.*

Green, Roy E., ed. 1991. *Enterprise Zones: New Directions in Economic Development.* Newbury Park, Calif.: Sage Publications.

Gritz, R. Mark, and Thomas MaCurdy. 1992. "Patterns of Welfare Utilization and Multiple Program Participation among Young Women." Stanford University Working Papers in Economics. January.

Grossman, Jean B., and Bonnie L. Halpern-Felsher. 1995. *Research Findings on the Effectiveness of Youth Programming: Support for a Developmental Approach.* Philadelphia: Public/Private Ventures.

Gueron, Judith M., and Edward Pauly. 1991. *From Welfare to Work.* New York: Russell Sage Foundation.

Gugliotta, Guy. 1994. "HUD Chooses Baltimore for $100 Million in Aid; D.C. Loses Bid to Be an 'Enterprise Zone.'" *Washington Post*, December 22, p. A1.

Gunn, Elizabeth M. 1993. "The Growth of Enterprise Zones: A Policy Transformation." *Policy Studies Journal* 21(3, Spring): 432–49.

Hamilton, Gayle. 1995. *The Jobs Evaluation: Monthly Participation Rates in Three Sites and Factors Affecting Participation Levels in Welfare-to-Work Programs.* Report from Manpower Demonstration Research Corporation to the U.S. Department of Health and Human Services/U.S. Department of Education. New York: MDRC. Draft, September.

Hamilton, William L., Nancy R. Burstein, Margaret M. Hart, Susan H. Bartlett, Mary Beth Sullivan, and Ruy A. Teixeira. 1989. *Factors Affecting Food Stamp Certification Cost*, vol. 1. Report Prepared by Abt Associates Inc. for the U.S. Department of Agriculture Food and Nutrition Service. Cambridge, Mass.: Abt Associates.

Hanratty, Maria J. Forthcoming. "Canadian National Health Insurance and Infant Health." *American Economic Review.*

Hanratty, Maria J., and Rebecca M. Blank. 1992. "Down and Out in North America: Recent Trends in Poverty Rates in the United States and Canada." *Quarterly Journal of Economics* 107(1, February): 233–54.

Harrington, Michael. 1962. *The Other America: Poverty in the United States.* Baltimore: Penguin Books.

Haveman, Robert. 1988. *Starting Even.* New York: The Twentieth Century Fund.

Hayes, Cheryl D. 1987. *Risking the Future*, vol. 1. Washington, D.C.: National Academy Press.

Heckman, James. 1993. "Assessing Clinton's Program on Job Training, Workfare, and Education in the Workplace." National Bureau of Economic Research Working Paper No. 4428. Cambridge, Mass.: NBER. August.

Heiser, Nancy, and Suzanne Smolkin. 1993. *Characteristics of Food Stamp Households 1991.* Report Prepared by Mathematica Policy Research Inc. for the U.S. Department of Agriculture Food and Nutrition Service. Washington, D.C.: Mathematica Policy Research.

Herr, Toby, and Robert Halpern. 1991. *Changing What Counts: Rethinking the Journey Out of Welfare.* Project Match, Center for Urban Affairs and Policy Research. Evanston, Ill.: Northwestern University.

Hoffman, Saul D., E. Michael Foster, and Frank F. Furstenberg, Jr. 1993. "Reevaluating the Costs of Teenage Childbearing." *Demography* 30(1, February): 1–13.

Hoffman, Saul D., and Laurence S. Seidman. 1990. *The Earned Income Tax Credit.* Kalamazoo, Mich.: W. E. Upjohn Institute for Employment Research.

Hollister, Robinson G., Jr., Peter Kemper, and Rebecca A. Maynard. 1984. *The National Supported Work Demonstration*. Madison: University of Wisconsin Press.

Holzer, Harry J. 1996. *What Employers Want: Job Prospects for Less-Educated Workers*. New York: Russell Sage Foundation.

Hotz, V. Joseph, Susan Williams McElroy, and Seth G. Sanders. 1995. "The Costs and Consequences of Teenage Childbearing for Mothers." Irving B. Harris Graduate School of Public Policy Working Paper Series 95–1. University of Chicago.

Hughes, Mark Alan, and Julie E. Sternberg. 1993. *The New Metropolitan Reality: Where the Rubber Meets the Road in Antipoverty Policy*. Washington, D.C.: The Urban Institute.

Hutchens, Robert M. 1986. "The Effects of the Omnibus Budget Reconciliation Act of 1981 on AFDC Recipients." *Research In Labor Economics* 8: 351–87.

Hutchens, Robert M., George Jakubson, and Saul Schwartz. 1987. "AFDC and the Formation of Subfamilies." *Journal of Human Resources* 24(4, Fall): 599–628.

Independent Sector. 1992. *From Belief to Commitment: The Community Service Activities and Finances of Religious Congregations in the United States*. Washington, D.C.: Independent Sector.

Industrial and Labor Relations Review. 1995. Review Symposium, "Myth and Measurement: The New Economics of the Minimum Wage." 48(4, July): 827–49.

Ivry, Robert J. 1995. Testimony before the Subcommittee on Postsecondary Education, Training, and Life-Long Learning of the House Committee on Economic and Educational Opportunity, March 7, 1995. New York: Manpower Demonstration Research Corporation.

Jargowsky, Paul A. Forthcoming. *Ghetto Poverty in the United States, 1970–1990*. New York: Russell Sage Foundation.

Jargowsky, Paul A., and Mary Jo Bane. 1991. "Ghetto Poverty in the United States, 1970–1980." In *The Urban Underclass*, Christopher Jencks and Paul E. Peterson, editors. Washington, D.C.: The Brookings Institution.

Jencks, Christopher. 1991. "Is Violent Crime Rising?" *The American Prospect* 1991(4, Winter): 98–109.

Journal of Housing. 1970. "Urban Renewal: In Review, In Prospect" 27(9, October 20): 467–68.

Juhn, Chinhui. 1992. "Decline of Male Labor Market Participation: The Role of Declining Market Opportunities." *Quarterly Journal of Economics* 107(1, February): 79–122.

Juhn, Chinhui, Kevin M. Murphy, and Brooks Pierce. 1993. "Wage Inequality and the Rise in Returns to Skill." *Journal of Political Economy* 101(3, June): 410–42.

Kaiser Family Foundation. 1995. "Survey Shows 'Two Faces' of Public Opinion on Welfare Reform." New Release, January 12. Washington, D.C.

Kasarda, John D. 1995. "Industrial Restructuring and the Changing Location of Jobs." In *State of the Union*, vol. 1, *Economic Trends*, Reynolds Farley, editor. New York: Russell Sage Foundation.

Katz, Lawrence F. Forthcoming. "Wage Subsidies for the Disadvantaged." In *Demand Side Economics*, Richard B. Freeman and Peter Gottschalk, editors. New York: Russell Sage Foundation.

Katz, Lawrence F., and Kevin M. Murphy. 1992. "Changes in Relative Wages, 1963–87: Supply and Demand Factors." *Quarterly Journal of Economics* 107(1, February): 35–78.

Katz, Michael B. 1983. *Poverty and Policy in American History*. New York: Academic Press.

Kemple, James J., and Joshua Haimson. 1994. *Florida's Project Independence: Program Implementation, Participation Patterns, and First-Year Impacts*. New York: Manpower Development Research Corporation.

Kingson, Eric R., and Marianne Levin. 1984. "Local Administrative Practice and AFDC Error in Maryland." *Journal of Social Service Research* 7(3, Spring): 41–57.

Kirby, Douglas, Richard P. Barth, Nancy Leland, and Joyce V. Fetro. 1991. "Reducing the Risk: Impact of a New Curriculum on Sexual Risk-Taking." *Family Planning Perspectives* 23(6, November): 253–63.

Kirschenman, Joleen, and Kathryn M. Neckerman. 1991. " 'We'd Love to Hire Them, But . . .': The Meaning of Race for Employers." In *The Urban Underclass*, Christopher Jencks and Paul E. Peterson, editors. Washington, D.C.: The Brookings Institution.

Knox, Virginia W., Amy Brown, and Winston Lin. 1995. *MFIP: An Early Report on Minnesota's Approach to Welfare Reform*. New York: Manpower Demonstration Research Corporation.

Kollman, Geoffrey. 1995. "Social Security: The Relationship of Taxes and Benefits for Past, Present and Future Retirees." *CRS Report for Congress*. Washington, D.C.: Library of Congress, Congressional Research Service. January 9.

Korenman, Sanders, Jane E. Miller, and John E. Sjaastad. 1995. "Long-Term Poverty and Child Development in the United States: Results from the NLSY. *Child and Youth Services Review* 17(1/2, January/February): 127–55.

Kretzmann, John P., and John L. McKnight. 1993. *Building Communities from the Inside Out*. Chicago: ACTA Publications.

LaLonde, Robert J. 1995. "The Promise of Public Sector-Sponsored Training Programs." *Journal of Economic Perspectives* 9(2, Spring): 149–68.

Lampman, Robert J., and Timothy M. Smeeding. 1983. "Interfamily Transfers as Alternatives to Government Transfers to Persons." *The Review of Income and Wealth* 29(1, March): 45–66.

Landry, David J., and Jacqueline Darroch Forrest. 1995. "How Old Are U.S. Fathers?" *Family Planning Perspectives* 27(4, July/August): 159–65.

Leahy, Patrick G. 1994. Testimony before the Senate Committee on Agriculture, Nutrition, and Forestry, February 2, 1994. Washington, D.C.: U.S. Senate.

Levy, Frank, and Richard J. Murnane. 1992. "U.S. Earnings Levels and Earnings Inequality: A Review of Recent Trends and Proposed Explanations." *Journal of Economic Literature* 30(3, September): 1333–81.

Long, David, Robert G. Wood, and Hilary Kopp. 1994. *LEAP: The Educational Effects of LEAP and Enhanced Services in Cleveland*. New York: Manpower Demonstration Research Corporation.

Long, Sharon K. 1991. "Do School Nutrition Programs Supplement Household Food Expenditures?" *Journal of Human Resources* 26(4, Fall): 654–78.

Lundberg, Shelly, and Robert D. Plotnick. 1990. "Effects of State Welfare, Abortion, and Family Planning Policies on Premarital Childbearing among White Adolescents." *Family Planning Perspectives* 22(6, November): 246–51, 275.

Lundberg, Shelly, and Robert D. Plotnick. 1995. "Adolescent Premarital Childbearing: Do Economic Incentives Matter?" *Journal of Labor Economics* 13(2, April): 177–200.

Maguire, Kathleen, and Ann L. Pastore, eds. 1994. *Sourcebook of Criminal Justice Statistics, 1993.* Washington, D.C.: U.S. Government Printing Office.

Maguire, Kathleen, Ann L. Pastore, and Timothy J. Flanagan, eds. 1993. *Sourcebook of Criminal Justice Statistics, 1992.* Washington, D.C.: U.S. Government Printing Office.

Mallar, Charles, Stuart Kerachsky, Craig Thornton, and David Long. 1982. *Evaluation of the Economic Impact of the Job Corps Program, Third Follow-Up Report.* Princeton, N.J.: Mathematica Policy Research.

Manski, Charles F., and Irwin Garfinkel, eds. 1992. *Evaluating Welfare and Training Programs.* Cambridge, Mass.: Harvard University Press.

Marshall, T. H. 1964. *Class, Citizenship, and Social Development.* Garden City, N.J.: Doubleday.

Massey, Douglas S., and Nancy A. Denton. 1993. *American Apartheid.* Cambridge, Mass.: Harvard University Press.

Mathematica Policy Research, Inc. 1990. *The Savings in Medicaid Costs for Newborns and Their Mothers from Prenatal Participation in the WIC Program.* Report Prepared for U.S. Department of Agriculture. Princeton, N.J.

Mayer, Susan. Forthcoming. *Does More Money Buy Better Children?* Cambridge, Mass.: Harvard University Press.

Mayer, Susan, and Christopher Jencks. 1994. "Has Poverty Really Increased among Children Since 1970?" Center for Urban Affairs and Policy Research Working Paper no. 94–14. Evanston, Ill.: Northwestern University.

Maynard, Rebecca, ed. 1993. *Building Self-Sufficiency among Welfare-Dependent Teenage Parents: Lessons from the Teenage Parent Demonstration.* Princeton, N.J.: Mathematica Policy Research.

Mauer, Marc, and Tracy Huling. 1995. *Young Black Americans and the Criminal Justice System: Five Years Later.* Washington, D.C.: The Sentencing Project.

McKey, R. H., L. Condelli, H. Ganson, B. Barrett, C. McConkey, and M. Plantz. 1985. *The Impact of Head Start on Children, Families, and Communities.* Final Report of the Head Start Evaluation, Synthesis, and Utilization Project. Washington, D.C.: Department of Health and Human Services.

McLanahan, Sara, and Gary Sandefur. 1994. *Growing Up with a Single Parent: What Hurts, What Helps.* Cambridge, Mass.: Harvard University Press.

Mehegan, Sean. 1994. "The Federal Connection." *The NonProfit Times.* November, p. 43.

Meyer, Daniel R., Irwin Garfinkel, Donald T. Oellerich, and Philip K. Robins. 1992. "Who Should Be Eligible for an Assured Child Support Benefit?" In *Child Support Assurance: Design Issues, Expected Impacts, and Political Barriers as Seen from Wisconsin*, Irwin Garfinkel, Sara McLanahan, and Philip K. Robins, editors. Washington, D.C.: The Urban Institute Press.

Meyers, Alan F., Amy E. Sampson, and Michael Weitzman. 1991. "Nutrition and Academic Performance in School Children." *Clinics in Applied Nutrition* 1(2, April): 13–25.

Miller, Jane E., and Sanders Korenman. 1994. "Poverty and Children's Nutritional Status in the United States." *American Journal of Epidemiology* 140(3, August): 233–43.

Mincy, Ronald B. 1990. "Raising the Minimum Wage: Effects on Family Poverty." *Monthly Labor Review* 113(July): 18–25.

Mincy, Ronald B. 1994. *Nurturing Young Black Males.* Washington, D.C.: The Urban Institute Press.

Mitchell, J. Paul, ed. 1985. *Federal Housing Policy and Programs: Past and Present.* New Brunswick, N.J.: Rutgers University, Center for Urban Policy Research.

Moffitt, Robert. 1992. "Incentive Effects of the U.S. Welfare System: A Review." *Journal of Economic Literature* 30(1, March): 1–61.

Moffitt, Robert A., Robert Reville, and Anne E. Winkler. 1995. "Beyond Single Mothers: Cohabitation, Marriage, and the U.S. Welfare System." Brown University Department of Economics, Working Paper Series. Providence, R.I.

Moffitt, Robert, and Douglas A. Wolf. 1987. "The Effect of the 1981 Omnibus Budget Reconciliation on Welfare Recipients and Work Incentives." *Social Service Review* 62(2, June): 247–60.

Molefsky, Barry. 1982. "America's Underground Economy." In *The Underground Economy in the U.S. and Abroad*, Vito Tanzi, editor. Lexington, Mass.: Lexington Books.

Mollenkopf, John F. 1983. *The Contested City.* Princeton, N.J.: Princeton University Press.

Moore, Kristin A., Barbara W. Sugland, Connie Blumenthal, Dana Glei, and Nancy Snyder. 1995. *Adolescent Pregnancy Prevention Programs; Interventions and Evaluations.* Report Prepared for the U.S. Department of Health and Human Services. Washington, D.C.: Child Trends, Inc.

Murray, Charles. 1984. *Losing Ground.* New York: Basic Books.

Murray, Charles. 1993. "Welfare and the Family: The U.S. Experience." *Journal of Labor Economics* 11(1, part 2, January): S224–62.

Musick, Judith S. 1993. *Young, Poor, and Pregnant: The Psychology of Teenage Motherhood.* New Haven: Yale University Press.

Nathan, Richard P. 1990. "Federalism—The Great 'Composition'." In *The New American Political System*, Anthony King, editor. Washington, D.C.: AEI Press.

Nathan, Richard P. 1993. *Turning Promises into Performance: The Management Challenge of Implementing Workfare.* New York: Columbia University Press.

National Association of State Budget Officers. 1993. *1992 State Expenditure Report.* Washington, D.C.: NASBO.

National Research Council. 1995. *Measuring Poverty: A New Approach.* Constance F. Citro and Robert T. Michael, editors. Washington, D.C.: National Academy Press.

National (U.S.) Conference of Catholic Bishops. 1986. "Economic Justice for All: Catholic Social Teaching and the U.S. Economy." *Origins* 16(24, November 27): 409–55.

Newman, Katherine, and Chauncy Lennon. 1995. "Finding Work in the Inner City: How Hard Is It Now?" Russell Sage Foundation Working Paper No. 76. New York: Russell Sage Foundation. October.

Newman, Sandra J., and Anne B. Schnare. 1992. *Beyond Bricks and Mortar: Reexamining the Purpose and Effects of Housing Assistance.* Report 92–3. Washington, D.C.: The Urban Institute.

Nicklas, Theresa A, Weihang Bao, Larry S. Webber, and Gerald S. Berenson. 1993. "Breakfast Consumption Affects Adequacy of Total Daily Intake in Children." *Journal of the American Dietetic Association* 93(8, August): 886–91.

Ohls, James C., and Harold Beebout. 1993. *The Food Stamp Program: Design Tradeoffs, Policy, and Impacts.* Washington, D.C.: The Urban Institute Press.

Olson, Lynn M., and Audrey Davis. 1994. "The Earned Income Tax Credit: Views from the Street Level." Center for Urban Affairs and Policy Research Working Paper 94–1. Evanston, Ill.: Northwestern University.

Palmer, John L., Timothy Smeeding, and Barbara Boyle Torrey. 1988. *The Vulnerable*. Washington, D.C.: Urban Institute Press.

Papke, Leslie E. 1993. "What Do We Know about Enterprise Zones?" In *Tax Policy and the Economy*, James J. Poterba, editor. Cambridge, Mass.: MIT Press.

Papke, Leslie E. 1994. "Tax Policy and Urban Development: Evidence from the Indiana Enterprise Zone Program." *Journal of Public Economics* 54(1, May): 37–49.

Pauly, Edward, Hilary Kopp, and Joshua Haimson. 1995. *Home-Grown Lessons: Innovative Programs Linking School and Work*. San Francisco: Jossey-Bass Publishers.

Pavetti, LaDonna Ann. 1993. "The Dynamics of Welfare and Work: Exploring the Process by Which Women Work their Way off Welfare." Ph.D. Dissertation, Harvard University, Cambridge, Mass.

Pear, Robert. 1995. "House Backs Bill Undoing Decades of Welfare Policy." *New York Times*, 144: 50,011, March 25, p. 1.

Peterson, Paul E. 1995. *The Price of Federalism*. Washington, D.C.: The Brookings Institution.

Pirog-Good, Maureen A., and David H. Good. 1995. "Child Support Enforcement for Teenage Fathers: Problems and Prospects." *Journal of Policy Analysis and Management* 14(1, Winter): 25–42.

Piven, Frances Fox, and Richard A. Cloward. 1971. *Regulating the Poor: The Functions of Public Welfare*. New York: Vintage Books.

Plotnick, Robert D. 1990. "Welfare and Out-of-Wedlock Childbearing: Evidence from the 1980s." *Journal of Marriage and the Family* 52(3, August): 735–46.

Polit, Denise F., Janet C. Quint, and James A. Riccio. 1988. *The Challenge of Serving Teenage Mothers: Lessons from Project Redirection*. New York: Manpower Demonstration Research Corporation.

Porter, Michael E. 1995. "The Competitive Advantage of the Inner City." *Harvard Business Review* 73(1, January/February): 55–71.

Porter, Richard D., and Amanda S. Bayer. 1989. "Monetary Perspectives on Underground Activity in the United States." In *The Underground Economy*, Edgar L. Feige, editor. Cambridge, England: Cambridge University Press.

Puma, Michael J., and David C. Hoaglin. 1987. *The Effect of Caseload Characteristics and Socioeconomic Conditions on Food Stamp Payment Error Rates*. Report Prepared by Abt Associates Inc. for the U.S. Department of Agriculture Food and Nutrition Service. Cambridge, Mass.

Quint, Janet C., Denise F. Polit, Hans Bos, and George Cave. 1994. *New Chance: Interim Findings on a Comprehensive Program for Disadvantaged Young Mothers and Their Children*. New York: Manpower Demonstration Research Corporation.

Rank, Mark R. 1989. "Fertility among Women on Welfare: Incidence and Determinants." *American Sociological Review* 54(April): 296–304.

Ranney, Christine K., and John E. Kushman. 1987. "Cash Equivalence, Welfare Stigma, and Food Stamps." *Southern Economic Journal* 53(4, January): 1011–27.

Raphael, Jo Ann. Forthcoming. "Domestic Violence and Welfare Receipt." *Harvard Women's Law Journal*.

Rawls, John. 1971. *A Theory of Justice*. Cambridge, Mass.: Harvard University Press.

Rector, Robert. 1993. "Why Expanding Welfare Will Not Help the Poor." The Heritage Lectures, no. 450. Washington, D.C.: The Heritage Foundation.

Reno, Virginia P. 1993. "The Role of Pensions in Retirement Income: Trends and Questions." *Social Security Bulletin* 56(1, Spring): 29–43.

Research Triangle Institute. 1983. *Final Report: Evaluation of the 1981 AFDC Amendments*. Report Submitted to the U.S. Department of Health and Human Services. Research Triangle Park, N.C.: RTI.

Riccio, James, Daniel Friedlander, and Stephan Freedman. 1994. *GAIN: Benefits, Costs, and Three-Year Impacts of a Welfare-to-Work Program*. New York: Manpower Demonstration Research Corporation.

Robins, Philip K. 1985. "A Comparison of the Labor Supply Findings from the Four Negative Income Tax Experiments." *Journal of Human Resources* 20(4, Fall): 567–82.

Robins, Philip K. 1986. "Child Support, Welfare Dependency, and Poverty." *American Economic Review* 76(4, September): 768–88.

Robins, Philip K., and Paul Fronstin. Forthcoming. "Welfare Benefits and Family-Size Decisions of Never-Married Women." *Population Research and Policy Review*.

Roper Center for Public Opinion Research. 1995. CBS News/New York Times Poll conducted April 1–4, 1995. Accessed via Dialogue, file 468, Public Opinion on Line.

Rose-Ackerman, Susan. 1986. "Do Government Grants to Charity Reduce Private Donations?" In *The Economics of Nonprofit Institutions*, Susan Rose-Ackerman, editor. New York: Oxford University Press.

Rosenbaum, James E. Forthcoming. "Schools and the World of Work." In *The Urban Crisis: Linking Research to Action*, Burton A. Weisbrod and James C. Worth, editors. Evanston, Ill.: Northwestern University Press.

Rosenbaum, James E., Nancy Fishman, Alison Brett, and Patricia Meaden. 1993. "Can the Kerner Commission's Housing Strategy Improve Employment, Education, and Social Integration for Low-Income Blacks?" *North Carolina Law Review* 71(5, June): 1519–56.

Rosenbaum, James E., and Susan J. Popkin. 1991. "Employment and Earnings of Low-Income Blacks Who Move to Middle-Class Suburbs." In *The Urban Underclass*, Christopher Jencks and Paul E. Peterson, editors. Washington, D.C.: The Brookings Institution.

Rosenzweig, Mark R., and Kenneth I. Wolpin. 1994. "Parent and Public Transfers to Young Women and Their Children." *American Economic Review* 84(5, December): 1195–212.

Rubin, M., and R. B. Armstrong. 1989. "The New Jersey Urban Enterprise Zone Program: An Evaluation." Report Prepared for the New Jersey Department of Commerce, Trenton.

Ruggles, Patricia. 1990. *Drawing the Line: Alternative Poverty Measures and Their Implications for Public Policy*. Washington, D.C.: The Urban Institute Press.

Salamon, Lester M. 1995. *Partners in Public Service: Government-Nonprofit Relations in the Modern Welfare State*. Baltimore: Johns Hopkins University Press.

Sarver, Patrick. 1994. "Some Surprising Facts Emerge from a Year of Gains among Nonprofits." *The NonProfit Times*, November, pp. 25–31.

Schiff, Jerald. 1990. *Charitable Giving and Government Policy: An Economic Analysis*. Westport, Conn.: Greenwood Press.

Schill, Michael H., and Susan M. Wachter. 1995. "The Federal Bias of Federal Housing Law and Policy." *University of Pennsylvania Law Review* 143(5, May): 1285–342.

Schoeni, Robert F. 1994. "Does Aid to Families with Dependent Children Displace Familial Assistance?" Unpublished manuscript. Santa Monica, Calif.: RAND.

Scholz, John Karl. 1993–94. "Tax Policy and the Working Poor: The Earned Income Tax Credit." *Focus* (Institute for Research on Poverty, University of Wisconsin) 15(3, Winter): 1–12.

Schweinhart, Lawrence J., Helen V. Barnes, and David P. Weikart. 1993. "Significant Benefits: The High/Scope Perry Preschool Study Through Age 27." *Monographs of the High/Scope Educational Research Foundation*, no. 10. Ypsilanti, Mich.: High/Scope Press.

Senauer, Ben, and Nathan Young. 1986. "The Impact of Food Stamps on Food Expenditures: Rejection of the Traditional Model." *American Journal of Agricultural Economics* 68(1, February): 37–43.

Shore-Sheppard, Lara D. 1993. "An Evaluation of the Effect of Recent Legislation on the Enrollment of Children in the Medicaid Program." Unpublished manuscript. Princeton, N.J.: Princeton University.

Skocpol, Theda. 1991. "Targeting within Universalism: Politically Viable Policies to Combat Poverty in the United States." In *The Urban Underclass*, Christopher Jencks and Paul E. Peterson, editors. Washington, D.C.: The Brookings Institution.

Skocpol, Theda. 1992. *Protecting Mothers and Soldiers: The Political Origins of Social Policy in the United States*. Cambridge, Mass.: Harvard University Press.

Smeeding, Timothy M. 1992. "Why the U.S. Antipoverty System Doesn't Work Very Well." *Challenge* 35(1, January): 30–35.

Smeeding, Timothy M., Sheldon Danziger, and Lee Rainwater. 1995. "The Western Welfare State in the 1990s: Toward a New Model of Antipoverty Policy for Families with Children." Luxembourg Income Study, CEPS Working Paper No. 128. August.

Smeeding, Timothy M., Peter Saunders, John Coder, Stephen Jenkins, Johan Fritzell, Aldi J. M. Hagenaars, Richard Hauser, and Michael Wolfson. 1993. "Poverty, Inequality, and Family Living Standards Impacts across Seven Nations: The Effect of Noncash Subsidies for Health, Education and Housing." *Review of Income and Wealth* 39(3, September): 229–56.

Solon, Gary R. 1992. "Intergenerational Income Mobility in the United States." *American Economic Review* 82(3, June): 393–408.

Statistics Canada. 1988. *Vital Statistics of Canada*, vol. 1, *1986*. Ottawa: Statistics Canada, Health Division, Statistics and Disease Registries.

Stern, David, Marilyn Raby, and Charles Dayton. 1992. *Career Academies: Partnerships for Reconstructing American High Schools*. San Francisco: Jossey-Bass Publishers.

Stevens, Ann Huff. 1994. "The Dynamics of Poverty Spells: Updating Bane and Ellwood." *American Economic Review* 84(2, May): 34–37.

Stevens, Ann Huff. 1995. "Climbing Out of Poverty, Falling Back In: Measuring the Persistence of Poverty over Multiple Spells." National Bureau of Economic Research Working Paper 5390. Cambridge, Mass.: NBER.

Sullivan, Mercer L. 1989. *Getting Paid: Youth, Crime, and Work in the Inner City*. Ithaca, N.Y.: Cornell University Press.

Sviridoff, Mitchell. 1994. "The Seeds of Urban Revival." *The Public Interest* 114 (Winter): 82–103.

Tierney, Joseph P., Jean Baldwin Grossman, and Nancy L. Resch. 1995. *Making a*

Difference: An Impact Study of Big Brothers/Big Sisters. Philadelphia: Public/ Private Ventures.

Trattner, Walter I. 1989. *From Poor Law to Welfare State: A History of Social Welfare in America*, 4th ed. New York: The Free Press.

U.S. Bureau of the Census. 1960. *1960 Census of Population and Housing*, vol. 1, *Census Tracts, Chicago, IL, SMSA*. Report PHC(1)-26. Washington, D.C.: U.S. Government Printing Office.

U.S. Bureau of the Census. Years 1961 to 1971. *Marital Status and Family Status*. Current Population Reports, Series P20. Washington, D.C.: U.S. Government Printing Office.

U.S. Bureau of the Census. 1971. *Characteristics of the Low-Income Population, 1970*. Current Population Reports, Series P60–81. Washington, D.C.: U.S. Government Printing Office.

U.S. Bureau of the Census. 1973. *National Origin and Language*. Census of Population Subject Reports Final Report PC(2)-1A. Washington, D.C.: U.S. Government Printing Office.

U.S. Bureau of the Census. Years 1972 to 1990. *Marital Status and Living Arrangements*. Current Population Reports, Series P20. Washington, D.C.: U.S. Government Printing Office.

U.S. Bureau of the Census. 1990. *1990 Census of Population and Housing, Census Tracts, Chicago, IL, PMSA*. Report CPH-3–113B. Washington, D.C.: U.S. Government Printing Office.

U.S. Bureau of the Census. 1991. *Child Support and Alimony, 1989*. Current Population Reports, Series P60–173. Washington, D.C.: U.S. Government Printing Office.

U.S. Bureau of the Census. 1992. *Who's Minding the Kids? Child Care Arrangements: Fall 1988*. Current Population Reports, Series P70–30. Washington, D.C.: U.S. Government Printing Office.

U.S. Bureau of the Census. 1993a. *Poverty in the United States, 1992*. Current Population Reports, Series P60–185. Washington, D.C.: U.S. Government Printing Office.

U.S. Bureau of the Census. 1993b. *Social and Economic Characteristics*. Census of Population Report 1990-CP-2–1. Washington, D.C.: U.S. Government Printing Office.

U.S. Bureau of the Census. 1993c. *State Government Finances, 1992*. GF/92–3. Washington, D.C.: U.S. Government Printing Office.

U.S. Bureau of the Census. 1995a. *Income, Poverty, and Valuation of Noncash Benefits: 1993*. Current Population Reports, Series P60–188. Washington, D.C.: U.S. Government Printing Office. February. Supplemental unpublished tables to this publication also provided by the U.S. Bureau of the Census.

U.S. Bureau of the Census. 1995b. "Press Briefing on 1994 Income and Poverty Estimates." Washington, D.C.: U.S. Bureau of the Census. October 5. Supplemental unpublished tables also provided by the U.S. Bureau of the Census.

U.S. Department of Agriculture. 1994. *Food Stamp Quality Control Annual Report, Fiscal Year 1993*. Washington, D.C.: U.S. Department of Agriculture, Food and Nutrition Service. November.

U.S. Department of Education. 1993. *Adult Literacy in America: A First Look at the Results of the National Adult Literacy Survey*. National Center for Educational Statistics, Office of Educational Research and Improvement. Washington, D.C.: U.S. Government Printing Office.

U.S. Department of Education. 1994. *Digest of Educational Statistics, 1994*. U.S. National Center for Education Statistics, Office of Educational Research and Improvement. Washington, D.C.: U.S. Government Printing Office.

U.S. Department of Health and Human Services, National Institute on Drug Abuse. 1991. *National Household Survey on Drug Abuse, Main Findings, 1990*. Washington, D.C.: U.S. Government Printing Office.

U.S. Department of Health and Human Services, National Institute on Drug Abuse. 1994. "Summary Tables: Annualized Estimates from the National Pregnancy and Health Survey." National Institute on Drug Abuse Press Briefing. Washington, D.C.

U.S. Department of Health and Human Services, Public Health Service. 1994. *Preliminary Estimates from the 1993 National Household Survey on Drug Abuse*. Washington, D.C.: U.S. Government Printing Office.

U.S. Department of Health and Human Services, Public Health Service. 1995. *Report to Congress on Out-of-Wedlock Childbearing*. Washington, D.C.: U.S. Government Printing Office.

U.S. Department of Housing and Urban Development. 1992. *Characteristics of HUD-Assisted Renters and Their Units in 1989*. Washington, D.C.: U.S. Government Printing Office.

U.S. Department of Justice. Various years. *Crime in the United States: Uniform Crime Reports*. Washington, D.C.: U.S. Government Printing Office.

U.S. Department of Labor. 1989. *Handbook of Labor Statistics*. Bulletin 2340. Washington, D.C.: U.S. Government Printing Office.

U.S. Department of Labor. Years 1990–93. *Employment and Earnings*. Washington, D.C.: U.S. Government Printing Office.

U.S. Department of Labor. 1994. *Employment and Earnings*. Washington, D.C.: U.S. Government Printing Office.

U.S. Department of Labor. 1995. *What's Working (and What's Not): A Summary of Research on the Economic Impacts of Employment and Training Programs*. Washington, D.C.: U.S. Department of Labor, Office of the Chief Economist.

U.S. General Accounting Office. 1985. *An Evaluation of the 1981 AFDC Changes: Final Report*. Washington, D.C.: U.S. Government Printing Office.

U.S. General Accounting Office. 1988. *Enterprise Zones: Lessons from the Maryland Experience*. Washington, D.C.: U.S. Government Printing Office.

U.S. General Accounting Office. 1992. *Early Intervention: Federal Investments Like WIC Can Produce Savings*. Washington, D.C.: U.S. Government Printing Office.

U.S. General Accounting Office. 1994. *Food Assistance: Potential Impacts of Alternative Systems for Delivering Food Stamp Program Benefits*. Washington, D.C.: U.S. Government Printing Office.

U.S. House of Representatives. 1992. *1992 Green Book: Overview of Entitlement Programs*. Washington, D.C.: U.S. Government Printing Office.

U.S. House of Representatives. 1993a. *1993 Green Book: Overview of Entitlement Programs*. Washington, D.C.: U.S. Government Printing Office.

U.S. House of Representatives. 1993b. *Medicaid Source Book: Background Data and Analysis 1993*. Washington, D.C.: U.S. Government Printing Office.

U.S. House of Representatives. 1994. *1994 Green Book: Overview of Entitlement Programs*. Washington, D.C.: U.S. Government Printing Office.

U.S. National Center for Health Statistics. 1991a. *Vital Statistics of the U.S., 1987*, vol. 1. Washington, D.C.: U.S. Government Printing Office.

U.S. National Center for Health Statistics. 1991b. *Vital Statistics of the U.S., 1987*, vol. 3. Washington, D.C.: U.S. Government Printing Office.

U.S. National Center for Health Statistics. 1993a. *Health, United States, 1992*. Washington, D.C.: U.S. Government Printing Office.

U.S. National Center for Health Statistics. 1993b. *Monthly Vital Statistics Report* 41(9, Supplement, February 25): 33. Washington, D.C.: Centers for Disease Control and Prevention.

U.S. National Center for Health Statistics. 1993c. *Monthly Vital Statistics Report* 42(3, Supplement, September 9): 30–31. Washington, D.C.: Centers for Disease Control and Prevention.

U.S. National Center for Health Statistics. 1993d. *Vital Statistics of the U.S., 1989*, vol. 1. Washington, D.C.: U.S. Government Printing Office.

U.S. National Center for Health Statistics. 1994. *Monthly Vital Statistics Report* 43(5, suppl., October 25): 32, 47. Washington, D.C.: Centers for Disease Control and Prevention.

U.S. National Center for Health Statistics. 1995a. *Monthly Vital Statistics Report* 44(3, suppl., September 21): 33, 48. Washington, D.C.: Centers for Disease Control and Prevention.

U.S. National Center for Health Statistics. 1995b. *Vital Statistics of the U.S., 1991*, vol. 1. Washington, D.C.: U.S. Government Printing Office.

U.S. Office of Management and Budget. 1994. *Budget of the United States Government, Analytic Perspectives*. Washington, D.C.: U.S. Government Printing Office.

U.S. Office of Management and Budget. 1995. *Budget of the United States Government, Historical Tables, 1996*. Washington, D.C.: U.S. Government Printing Office.

U.S. Senate. 1979. *Hunger in America: Ten Years Later*. Hearings before the Subcommittee on Nutrition, Committee on Agriculture, Nutrition, and Forestry. Washington, D.C.

Viadero, Roger C. 1995. Testimony on the Enforcement of the Food Stamp Act before the Committee on Agriculture, U.S. House of Representatives, February 1, 1995.

Washington State Institute for Public Policy. 1993. "Women in Transition: A Family Income Study Newsletter." Olympia, Wash.: Evergreen State College.

Webster, Carol, and Greg Weeks. 1995. "Teenage Pregnancy: A Summary of Prevention Program Evaluation Results." Olympia, Wash.: Washington State Institute for Public Policy.

Weisbrod, Burton A. 1975. "Toward a Theory of the Voluntary Nonprofit Sector in a Three-Sector Economy." In *Altruism, Morality, and Economic Theory*, Edmund S. Phelps, editor. New York: Russell Sage Foundation.

Weiss, Marc A. 1985. "The Origins and Legacy of Urban Renewal." In *Federal Housing Policy and Programs: Past and Present*, J. Paul Mitchell, editor. New Brunswick, N.J.: Rutgers University, Center for Urban Policy Research.

Wilson, James Q., and Joan Petersilia, editors. 1995. *Crime*. San Francisco: ICS Press.

Wilson, William Julius. 1987. *The Truly Disadvantaged: The Inner City, the Underclass, and Public Policy*. Chicago: University of Chicago Press.

Winegarden, C. R. 1988. "AFDC and Illegitimacy Ratios: A Vector-Autoregressive Model." *Applied Economics* 20(12, December): 1589–601.

Winkler, Anne E. 1992. "The Impact of Housing Costs on the Living Arrangements of Single Mothers." *Journal of Urban Economics* 32(3, November): 388–402.

Winkler, Anne E. 1995. "What Lies behind States' Rush to Reform Welfare?" Unpublished manuscript, University of Missouri at St. Louis.

Wrafter, John. 1984. "QC: Abbreviation for Failure." *Public Welfare* 42(4, Fall): 14–21.

Zimmerman, David J., and Phillip B. Levine. 1993. "The Intergenerational Correlation in AFDC Participation: Welfare Trap or Poverty Trap?" Wellesley College, Department of Economics Working Paper No. 93–07. Wellesley, Mass.

Ghetto. *See* Urban ghetto

Giving U.S.A., 202

Goodwill Industries, administrative costs of, 169

Government. *See also* Federal government
assistance to single mothers, 149–150
in displacing private charity, 203–204
role of, in public assistance programs, 7, 9
spending on public assistance programs, 133
trends against interference by, 90

Grand Rapids, Parents Fair Share program in, 248–249

Great Depression
comparative advantage of federal government in, 215
direct family transfers during, 204

Habitat for Humanity, administrative costs of, 169

Head Start, 85, 123, 124, 179–180
and administrative capacity argument, 197
cost/benefit analysis of, 236
goals of, 124
natural constituency of support for, 234
need for coordination between elementary schools and, 250–251
role of charitable organizations in, 203

Health care. *See also* Medicaid
and capacity to respond argument, 197
effect of subsidized health insurance programs on, 165–166
explosion in costs, 93
impact of in-kind programs on, 161–166

Health maintenance organizations in providing Medicaid coverage, 108, 272–273

High-rise public housing projects, failure of, 186–187

High school dropouts
decline in jobs availability for, 65
ineffectiveness of programs focusing on, 181–183
participation of, in labor market, 68–69
wage levels for, 60, 61

Hispanics
behavioral problems of men, 43–44
in urban areas, 73

Hispanic women, AFDC use by, 154

Hispanic workers
poverty level of, 21
unemployment rates for, 59
in urban ghettos, 29

Homeless shelters, 207
as targeted program, 233

Housing assistance, 105, 109–110. *See also* In-kind assistance programs; Public housing
availability of, 109
division of responsibility within, 208–209
expected legislative changes in, 110
fraud in, 172
and job search mandates, 239
in project-based housing, 109–110
Section 8 vouchers for, 110, 129, 160, 187, 189, 232

Housing discrimination for Black Americans, 21, 28–29

Human dignity argument, for operating public social safety net, 196

Hunger, impact of Food Stamps on, 162–164

"Hunger in America," 162

Illegal activities
and poverty, 47–51
young male involvement in, 75–76, 78

Illegal income, in underground economy, 77–78

Immigrant aid societies, 207

Immigrants
cultural and language barriers of, 21
inflows of, and declining wages, 65–66
poverty level of, 21

Immunization programs
and capacity to respond argument, 197
as targeted program, 233

Income supplementation in welfare reform, 260–262

Income tax. *See also* Earned Income Tax Credit (EITC)
negative, 89–90, 228
and underground economy, 78–79

Infant mortality rates, 165

In-kind assistance programs, 105–110, 226, 232. *See also specific program*
eligibility for, 105
federal spending in, 105
impact of, on health and nutrition, 161–166
for low-income children and families, 110
social stigma attached to, 105–106

Inner-city African American churches, aid from, 207

Intergenerational use of AFDC, 151–152, 154, 156–157

Internationalization, of U.S. economy, 66–67

Investment/positive externalities argument for operating public social safety net, 194–195

IQ scores, impact of Head Start on, 179

Students, poverty of, 20
Suburban areas
job availability in, 72, 73, 75
labor shortages in, 75
mobility programs for, 127, 131–132, 189–190, 286–287
poverty in, 30
programs to identify jobs in, 189
Summer youth jobs programs, 118, 123, 286
Supplemental Security Income (SSI), 98, 103–104. *See also* Cash assistance programs
administrative costs of, 167–169
calculation of benefit amounts, 104
comparison to Aid to Families with Dependent Children (AFDC), 104
division of responsibility within, 208–209
for elderly, 20
expected legislative changes in, 104–105
government expenditures on, 93
lack of social stigma for, 104
magnitude of, 85–88
overpayment error rates in, 170–171
Supported Work program, 182

Targeted Jobs Tax Credit (TJTC), 116
Targeted programs, 221–222
advantages of, 233–235
budget limitations of, 233–234
cost-effectiveness of, 236
disadvantages of, 235–237
effectiveness criteria for, 238, 246–251
long-term effects of, 237
multiple, 249–250
as primary antipoverty device, 226–227
problems and promises of, 232–237
types of, 226, 232–233
Tax. *See* Earned Income Tax Credit (EITC); Income tax
Tax avoidance, incentives for, 78–79
Tax incentives, 127
Tech prep, 127
Teenage mothers
assistance programs aimed at, 125
education programs aimed at, 119, 183
Teenage parenting, 282–283
Teenage pregnancy. *See also* Out-of-wedlock births
and absent fathers, 44–45
long-term effects of, 38
modern concerns over, 33–39
programs designed to prevent, 183–184, 280–281
statistics on, 150

Teenage programs, 180–184
natural constituency of support for, 234
proposed changes for, 279–284
Transportation
mobility programs for, 127, 131–132, 189–190, 286–287
problems in, for less-skilled workers, 74–75
Trickle down economics, death of, 53–56
Two-parent families. *See* Married-couple families

Uncompensated care, 165
Underclass neighborhoods, 28. *See also* Urban ghettos
media coverage of, 11
urban ghettos as, 74
Underground economy, 53
identifying money makers in, 76–77
illegal income in, 77–78
poor in, 75–79
tracking growth rate of, 76–77
unreported income in, 78–79
Unemployment
correlation of, with need for assistance, 218
frictional, 58
by gender, 58
for less-skilled workers, 31, 52–53, 120
trends in, 57–60
for women, 59
Unemployment Compensation benefits, 201
Unemployment Insurance, 85
Unfunded mandates, proliferation of, 211
Union jobs, disappearance of, 67
Universalist public transfer programs, 228–229
Unmarried women, growth in numbers of, 36
Unreported income, for AFDC recipients, 148
Unskilled workers. *See* Less-skilled workers
Unwed motherhood. *See* Out-of-wedlock births
Upper-income families, contribution level from, 206
Urban areas. *See also* Urban ghettos
decline in living conditions in, 73
demographic and racial mix in, 73
Empowerment Zones in, 131–132
homicides in, 49–50
job availability in, 72–75
public housing in, 73
Urban Development Action Grant (UDAG) program, 130